M000302295

ARAB NATIONALISM

IN THE TWENTIETH CENTURY

ARAB NATIONALISM

IN THE TWENTIETH CENTURY

From Triumph to Despair

ADEED DAWISHA

PRINCETON UNIVERSITY PRESS
PRINCETON AND OXFORD

Copyright © 2003 by Princeton University Press

Published by Princeton University Press, 41 William Street,
Princeton, New Jersey 08540

In the United Kingdom: Princeton University Press,
3 Market Place, Woodstock, Oxfordshire OX20 1SY

All Rights Reserved

Library of Congress Cataloging-in-Publication Data

Dawisha, A. I.

Arab nationalism in the twentieth century : from triumph to
despair / Adeed Dawisha.

p. cm.

Includes bibliographical references and index.

ISBN 0-691-10273-2 (alk. paper)

1. Arab nationalism—History—20th century. I. Title.

DS63.6 .D38 2003

320.54′089′927—dc21   2002070389

This book has been composed in Sabon and Futura Book

Printed on acid-free paper. ∞

www.pupress.princeton.edu

Printed in the United States of America

10 9 8 7 6 5 4 3 2 1

Contents

ARAB NATIONALISM
IN THE TWENTIETH CENTURY

CHAPTER ONE

DEFINING ARAB NATIONALISM

The men and women of the nationalist generation who had sought the political unity of the Arab people must have cast weary eyes at one another when they heard their acknowledged leader call a truce with those they considered to be anti-unionists; they must have dropped their heads and thrown their hands in the air when he announced the onset of a new era where "solidarity" among Arab states would replace the quest for a comprehensive political unity. Had Gamal 'Abd al-Nasir, the President of Egypt and the hero of Arab nationalism, reneged on the principles of the Arab nationalist creed when in 1963 he declared that it was Arab solidarity "which constituted the firm basis upon which Arab nationalism could be built,"[1] and that Arab solidarity would make "the Arab states stronger through their cooperation in the economic, military and cultural fields, and in the sphere of foreign policy"?[2] The nationalist generation must have hoped and prayed that Nasir would reconsider, come to his senses, and retread the

---

[1] Al-Jumhuriya al-'Arabiya al-Muttahida, *Majmou'at Khutab wa Tasrihat wa Bayant al-Rai's 'Gamal Abd al-Nasir* (The collection of the speeches, statements and communiques of President Gamal 'Abd al-Nasir), vol. 4 (Cairo: Maslahat al-Isti'lamat, n.d.). (Hereafter cited as *Khutab*), p. 175.

[2] *Khutab*, p. 455.

path of revolutionary Arab nationalism with its unequivocal commitment to organic Arab unity.

But their hero's intent was different, more complex, and more subtle. Nasir, after all, was both an ideologue and a politician. To him the path to Arab unity was fraught with both opportunities and constraints, and an organic unity of all the Arabs in one unified state would be the ultimate aim of a long and dialectical process consisting of "several stages."[3] Arab solidarity constituted one of these stages; it was "a step toward unity."[4] Solidarity was a pragmatic course of action when political constraints made impractical the aggressive pursuit of comprehensive Arab unity. But even when bending to political realities, the Egyptian president would reiterate the belief, shared by all Arab nationalists, that without the goal (or at a minimum, the aspiration) of Arab political unity, Arab nationalism would be a creed without a purpose, indeed without a meaning.[5]

To this, Sati' al-Husri, who, as we shall see later, was the foremost theoretician of Arab nationalism, would say, "Amen." Throughout his numerous writings on Arab nationalism, Husri never lost sight of the ultimate goal of the ideology he so vigorously propagated, namely the political unity of the Arabic-speaking people. "People who spoke a unitary language," Husri maintained, "have one heart and a common soul. As such, they constitute one nation, and so they have to have a unified state."[6] In another instance, he wrote that the happiest of nations were the ones in which political and national boundaries were fused into one another.[7]

---

[3] E.S. Farag, *Nasser Speaks: Basic Documents* (London: Morssett Press, 1972), p. 142. This notion that political unity is achieved in stages can also be found in the writings of Michel Aflaq, the philosopher of the Ba'th Party. See for example his *Fi Sabil al-Ba'th* (For the sake of resurrection) (Beirut: Dar al-Tali'ah, 1963), p. 230.

[4] *Egyptian Gazette* (Cairo), January 29, 1958.

[5] United Arab Republic, *The Charter* (Cairo: Information Department, 1962), p. 79; *Al-Ahram* (Cairo), October 19, 1962; *al-Muharir* (Beirut), April 2, 1963; *Khutab*, p. 447.

[6] Abu Khaldun Sati' al-Husri, *Ma Hiya al-Qawmiya?: Abhath wa Dirasat 'ala Dhaw'i al-Ahdath wa al-Nadhariyat* (What is nationalism?: enquiries and studies in light of events and theories) (Beirut: Dar al-'Ilm li al-Malayeen, 1963), p. 57.

[7] Abu Khaldun Sati' al-Husri, *Ara' wa Ahadith fi al-Qawmiya al-'Arabiya* (Views and discussions on Arab nationalism) (Beirut: Dar al-'Ilm li al-Malayeen, 1964), p. 23. Husri

Husri considered the Arab states to be artificial creations of the imperialist powers. Driven by their imperial interests, these powers proceeded to carve up what essentially was a natural cultural entity with an inalienable right to political sovereignty. An intended consequence of this perfidious parceling of the "Arab nation" was to keep the Arabs politically ineffectual and militarily feeble. In one of his writings, Husri says that he is constantly asked how was it that the Arabs lost the 1948–1949 war over Palestine when they were seven states and Israel was only one? His answer is unequivocal: The Arabs lost the war *precisely because* they were seven states.[8] The conclusion is unambiguous: To avoid losing future wars, the Arabs had to unite into one Arab state.

The founders of the Ba'th Party, the prominent Arab nationalist organization, felt the same about the connection between nationalism and organic political unity. The opening article of the party constitution promulgated in 1947 unequivocally declares: "The Arabs form one nation. This nation has the natural right to live in a single state. [As such] the Arab Fatherland constitutes an indivisible political and economic unity. No Arab country can live apart from the others."[9] The party's founder and philosopher, Michel Aflaq, in his most important canonical document, posited the party's Arab nationalist creed as a mission to resurrect the Arab people, to revive their intrinsic humanity and creativity, which lay dormant because of the political divisions in the Arab world. And how was this to be accomplished? Aflaq's remedy was clear: by uniting these "artificial and counterfeit countries and statelets" into one Arab nation-state. Only then could the Arabs return to their true selves "their upstanding spirit, clear ideas and upright morality,"

---

once told Iraqi historian, Majid Khadduri, that "public attention should focus on the problem of unity: it is the national duty of every Arab to support the leader who is capable of achieving Arab unity." Majid Khadduri, *Political Trends in the Arab World: The Role of Ideas and Ideals in Politics* (Baltimore: Johns Hopkins Press, 1970), p. 201.

[8] Abu Khaldun Sati' al-Husri, *al-'Uruba Awalan* (Arabism first) (Beirut: Dar al-'Ilm li al-Malayeen, 1965), p. 149.

[9] An English translation of the Ba'th Party Constitution can be found in Sylvia Haim, ed., *Arab Nationalism: An Anthology* (Berkeley: University of California Press, 1962), pp. 233–241. This particular quote is on p. 233.

and only then would "their minds be able to create."[10] To Aflaq, therefore, Arab unity is not only an intrinsic element of Arab nationalism; it is also a necessary precondition for the revival of the Arab spirit and Arab intellect.

As the membership of the party grew in the years to follow, and as its ideas spread throughout the Arab world, members would squabble over the meaning and role of such fundamental Ba'thist principles as freedom, socialism, and religion. Yet not until the eclipse of the Arab nationalist idea itself was there ever any questioning of "unity" as an absolutely essential component of the party's Arab nationalist doctrine.[11] Thus, whether Arab nationalism was expressed through Nasirist or Ba'thist discourse,[12] or through the writings of Sati' al-Husri, it was inexorably linked to Arab political unity. In short, to the thinkers and activists who made up the nationalist generation, Arab nationalism would be a hollow and meaningless concept if it did not strive to gather its children under one roof in one unified and sovereign Arab state. And it is this definition of Arab nationalism, with its necessary goal of Arab political unity, that will be used in this study.

But why this detailed and deliberate emphasis on the seemingly abiding link between Arab nationalism and Arab political unity? Can this link be anything other than self-evident? Well, not necessarily. In fact, an ongoing debate among specialists on Arab and Middle Eastern politics over the nature of nationalism has centered on whether achieving or desiring statehood was by necessity a core element of nationalism. Hence, the argument has predicated on whether the concept of nationalism is one of culture or one of poli-

---

[10] Aflaq, *Fi Sabil al-Ba'th*, p. 181; see also Haim, *Arab Nationalism*, p. 248.

[11] See John F. Devlin's excellent discussion of Ba'thist ideology in his *The Ba'th Party: A History from its Origins to 1966* (Stanford, California: Hoover Institution Press, 1976), pp. 23–45.

[12] There were, of course, other Arab nationalist groups and organizations, most notably, *Harakat al-Qawmiyeen al-'Arab* (the Arab nationalists movement), but none was as consequential or as resilient as 'Nasirism' or 'Ba'thism', and in any case, all shared in the belief that Arab unity could not be intellectually separated from Arab nationalism. See, for example, 'Abdallah Saloom al-Samarai', "Harakat al-Qawmiyeen al-'Arab wa Dawruha fi al-Wa'i al-Qawmi" (The Arab Nationalists Movement and its role in the national consciousness), *al-Mustaqbal al-'Arabi* (Beirut), no. 84 (February 1986): 75–99.

tics. A spirited and instructive dialogue on the subject occurred on the pages of the *International Journal of Middle East Studies*. In their book, *Redefining the Egyptian Nation, 1930–1945*,[13] Israel Gershoni and James Jankowski argue that the Egyptians' sentiments of affiliation and loyalty which had centered on Egypt alone were gradually shifted in the 1930s and 1940s to Arab and Islamic referents,[14] a claim that was vigorously contested by Charles D. Smith.[15] The relevant debate for our purposes was a difference in the interpretation of one of the central theses of Benedict Anderson's influential book, *Imagined Communities: Reflections on the Origins and Spread of nationalism*.[16] Anderson defines the nation as an imagined community:

> It is imagined because the members of even the smallest nation will never know most of their fellow members, meet them, or even hear of them, yet in the minds of each lives the image of their communion. . . . [It] is imagined as a community, because regardless of the actual inequality and exploitation that may prevail in each, the nation is always conceived as a deep, horizontal comradeship.[17]

Using this definition and relying on another assertion by Anderson that "nationness" and nationalism are "cultural artifacts of a particular kind,"[18] Gershoni and Jankowski conceive of the nation as a cultural construct, existing without the necessary addendum of the state. Indeed, to them, "Anderson's great insight and chief contribution to the study of nationalism is precisely his emphasis on its cultural-semiotic nature, its 'imagined' character."[19] Smith, on

[13] (London: Cambridge University Press, 1995).

[14] Israel Gershoni and James Jankowski, "Print Culture, Social Change and the Process of Redefining Imagined Communities in Egypt; Response to the Review by Charles D. Smith of *Redefining the Egyptian Nation*," *International Journal of Middle East Studies*, vol. 31, no. 1 (February 1999): 82.

[15] Charles D. Smith, "Imagined Identities, Imagined Nationalisms: Print Culture and Egyptian Nationalism in Light of Recent Scholarship," *International Journal of Middle East Studies*, vol. 29, no. 4 (November 1997): 607–622.

[16] (London: Verso, 1991).

[17] Ibid., pp. 6–7.

[18] Ibid., p. 4.

[19] Gershoni and Jankowski, "Print Culture, Social Change and the Process of Redefining Imagined Communities in Egypt," p. 89.

the other hand, insists that Anderson posited his "imagined communities" as linked to political boundaries. After all, he argues, Anderson does specify that the imagined community (the nation) "inhabits territorial and social space," and that it "is inherently limited and sovereign." It is limited, Anderson explains, because it "has finite if elastic boundaries beyond which lie other nations," and it is sovereign because "the gage and emblem of [a free nation] is the sovereign state."[20] Smith concludes that Anderson cannot be more adamant in postulating a statal referent to nationalism.

Gershoni and Jankowski are undoubtedly right in arguing that historically the absence of a state has not been a barrier to nationalist imaginings. They point to the many groups, Palestinians, Basques, Kurds, etc., that have existed and continue to exist that claim to be a nation even though they lack a state, and they further argue that to insist on positing the state as the essential criterion for nationalism would deny these groups their claims for nationhood.[21] The crucial point here, however, is that while lacking a state, all these groups are in fact adamantly and vociferously *desirous* of a state.[22] And it is perhaps in this context, in the need for a sovereign state whether it exists or not, that Anderson's imagined community could best be understood.

These criteria are evident in the way Bernard Lewis, the notable historian of the Middle East, defines the nation. To Lewis, a nation denotes "a group of people held together by a common language, belief in a common descent and in a shared history and destiny. They usually but do not necessarily inhabit a contiguous territory; they often enjoy, and if they do not enjoy they commonly seek,

[20] Charles D. Smith, " 'Cultural Constructs' and other Fantasies: Imagined Narratives in *Imagined Communities*; Surrejoinder to Gershoni and Jankowski's 'Print Culture, Social Change, and the Process of Redefining Imagined Communities in Egypt,' " *International Journal of Middle East Studies*, vol. 31, no.1 (February 1999): 97.

[21] Gershoni and Jankowski, "Print Culture, Social Change, and the Process of Redefining Imagined Communities in Egypt," p. 89.

[22] Transplanted on to the Arab situation, Ghassan Salame contends that the desire for Arab unity denotes a kind of legitimacy which compels Arab officials to refer to it constantly. See Salame's *al-Siyasa al-Sa'udia al-Kharijia Mundhu 'Am 1930* (Saudi foreign policy since 1940) (Beirut: Ma'had al-Inma'i al-'Arabi, 1980), p. 214.

sovereign independence in their own name."[23] Lewis acknowledges the importance of the cultural elements, but goes beyond cultural proximity by incorporating the notion of "sovereign independence" into the definition.

It is in this sense, in the explicit distinction between the cultural and the political that an ethnic group could most profitably be distinguished from a nation. Adrian Hastings identifies the crucial elements that transform a culturally bonded ethnic group into a nation as its claim *"to political identity and autonomy, together with the control of specific territory"*[24] [italics added]. In this definition Hastings echoes the emphasis on a nation's desire for political separateness voiced a century earlier by John Stuart Mill: "Where the sentiment of a nationality exists in any force, there is a *prima facie* case for uniting all members of the nationality under the same government, and a government to themselves apart."[25] He then tellingly adds that the "the strongest of all identity is that of political antecedents."[26] Max Weber concurs: "If one believes that it is at all expedient to distinguish national sentiment as something homogeneous and specifically set apart, one can do so only by referring to a tendency toward an autonomous state. [Hence] a nation is a community of sentiment which would adequately manifest itself in a state of its own."[27] In other words, what distinguishes a nation from an ethnic group or any other collectivity has to be the nation's self-derived desire to achieve political sovereignty within a recog-

---

[23] Bernard Lewis, *The Multiple Identities of the Middle East* (New York: Schocken Books, 1998), p. 81.

[24] Adrian Hastings, *The Construction of Nationhood: Ethnicity, Religion, and Nationalism.* (Cambridge, England: Cambridge University Press, 1997), p. 3.

[25] Alan Ryan, *J. S. Mill* (London: Routledge and Kegan Paul, 1974), p. 214; see also Lynn Williams, "National Identity and the Nation State: Construction, Reconstruction and Contradiction," in *National Identity,* ed. Keith Cameron. (Exeter, England: Intellect, 1999), p. 7.

[26] John Stuart Mill, "Considerations on Representative Government," in *The Nationalism Reader. eds.* Omar Dahbour and Micheline R. Ishay. (Atlantic Heights, New Jersey: Humanities Press, 1995), p. 98. Quoted also in Ilya Prizel, *National Identity and Foreign Policy: Nationalism and Leadership in Poland, Russia, and Ukraine* (Cambridge, England: Cambridge University Press, 1998), p. 12.

[27] H. H. Gerth and C. Wright Mills, eds., *From Max Weber: Essays in Sociology* (London: Routledge and Kegan Paul, 1948), p. 179.

nized territory. Lacking such a desire, a group can be a number of things but not a nation. That is precisely why Canada is, and the old Yugoslavia was, a multinational society, since significant ethnic groups within these two countries agitated for political independence, hence constituting nations. The United States, on the other hand, with its profusion of culturally based ethnicities, is not a multinational society, but rather a multiethnic society, since none of its ethnic groups desires political separation and sovereignty.

It is the recognition of the political element, centered on the ultimate goal of Arab political unity and the desire for a unitary Arab state, that anchors the definition of Arab nationalism to be used in this study. This would also help us avoid the conceptual overlap, at times harboring on confusion, in the use of the term Arab nationalism. As a concept, "Arab nationalism" has tended to be used in the literature of Middle Eastern politics and history interchangeably with other terms such as Arabism, Pan-Arabism, and even sometimes Arab radicalism, thus blending the sentiment of cultural proximity with the desire for political action. To say one is an Arab should denote a different connotation from saying one is an Arab nationalist. The former concedes one's cultural heritage, expressed best in the term "Arabism, " whereas the latter, as we have seen, imbues this cultural oneness with the added ingredient of political recognition.

If this seems a reasonable distinction, it certainly has not been reflected in the literature. The present author himself, in a book published in 1976, follows the practice of other analysts of the Middle East by ascribing to "Arabism" properties best affixed to "Arab nationalism" then declaring the two terms interchangeable.[28] Shibley Telhami concludes an excellent study, subtitled "The New Arabism", by trying to differentiate this new phenomenon from Nasir's "Arabism of the 1950s and 1960s."[29] Telhami tells us

---

[28] A. I. Dawisha, *Egypt in the Arab World: The Elements of Foreign Policy* (London: Macmillan, 1976), p. 129.

[29] Shibley Telhami, "Power, Legitimacy, and Peace-Making in Arab Countries: The New Arabism," in *Ethnic Conflicts and International Politics in the Middle East,* ed. Leonard Binder. (Gainesville: University Press of Florida, 1999), p. 56.

that this "new Arabism," which emerged toward the latter part of the twentieth century, was centered on intellectual elites and driven by a small sector of the media that was relatively free of governmental control. It facilitated expressions of political concern that were "Arabist," in the sense that they transcended state boundaries, and were independent of state governments. This was especially true in the effort to maintain a political focus on the issue of Palestine and Arab relations with Israel.[30] Illuminating as Telhami's analysis undoubtedly is, nevertheless, to affix the same term, that of "Arabism," to the Nasir-led movement of the 1950s and 1960s is to so stretch the term as to attenuate its definitional clarity. Nasir, after all, led an army of vocal and activist Arab nationalists throughout the length and breadth of the Arab world who believed fervently that the overriding purpose of their political struggle was to return the Arab people to their "natural" condition, united into one sovereign Arab state. One wonders how many of the "new Arabists" would take seriously even the remote possibility of such an outcome?

R. Stephen Humphreys, in an erudite and meticulous study of Middle Eastern history,[31] treads a similar path of conceptual trespassing. In a chapter entitled "The Strange Career of Pan-Arabism," he traces, in an admirably concise analysis, the growth and the decline of the Arab nationalist movement. Here again though, Humphreys sees little need for a conceptual distinction among the terms "Arab nationalism," "Arabism," and "Pan-Arabism," and as such uses the three terms interchangeably.[32] In one section, he concludes an analysis of the withering fortunes of the Arab nationalist movement in the last three decades of the twentieth century by asking the question: "Where is Pan-Arabism or Arab Nationalism in any form?"[33] Similarly, in a study of the changes that occurred in the Arab world during the 1970s, the dean of Egyptian

---

[30] Ibid., pp. 56–57.

[31] R. Stephen Humphreys, *Between Memory and Desire: The Middle East in a Troubled Age* (Berkeley: University of California Press, 1999).

[32] Ibid., pp. 60–65.

[33] Ibid., pp. 63–64.

political science, Ali Hillal Dessouki, employed "pan-Arabism" and "Arabism" essentially to describe sentiments of political allegiance that transcended the Arab state "to a larger human and social body."[34] Dessouki did not endeavor to conceptually separate one term from the other, because, one presumes, they meant more or less the same thing to him.

In all this definitional overlap, there indeed was unanimity over the meaning of "pan-Arabism," which was generally understood to be the drive, or at a minimum the desire, for Arab political unity. Here is how the distinguished scholar, Walid Khalidi, expounded on the doctrine of pan-Arabism in the late 1970s:

> The Arab states' system is first and foremost a "Pan" system. It postulates the existence of a single Arab Nation behind the facade of a multiplicity of sovereign states. . . . From this perspective, the individual Arab states are deviant and transient entities: their frontiers illusory and permeable; their rulers interim caretakers, or obstacles to be removed. . . . Before such super-legitimacy, the legitimacy of the individual state shrinks into irrelevance.[35]

Of interest, in a later issue of the same journal, another distinguished scholar and commentator, Fouad Ajami, took issue with Khalidi's depiction of the potency of pan-Arabism. Ajami argued that pan-Arabism "which had dominated the political consciousness of modern Arabs [was by the end of the 1970s] nearing its end, if it [was] not already a thing of the past." Ajami agreed that in an earlier era Arab states that "resisted the claims of pan-Arabism were at a disadvantage—their populations a fair target for pan-Arabist appeals, their leaders to be overthrown and replaced by others more committed to the transcendent goal." In contrast to Khalidi, however, Ajami argued that by the end of the 1970s *raison d'etat* was gaining ground, and "a normal state system [in the Arab

---

[34] Ali E. Hillal Dessouki, "The New Arab Political Order: Implications for the 1980s," in *Rich and Poor States in the Middle East: Egypt and the New Arab Order*, eds. Malcolm H. Kerr and El-Sayed Yassin (Boulder, Colorado: Westview Press, 1982), pp. 326–327.

[35] Walid Khalidi, "Thinking the Unthinkable: A Sovereign Palestinian State," *Foreign Affairs*, vol. 56, no. 4 (July 1978): 695.

world was] becoming a fact of life."[36] Writing twenty years later, Bernard Lewis agreed with Ajami's conclusions:

> Pan-Arabism . . . for long was a sacrosanct ideological principle in all the Arab countries, some of which even incorporated it in their constitution. But as the various Arab states established themselves more firmly and defined and pursued their various national interests with growing clarity, their commitment to pan-Arabism became more and more perfunctory. At the present time, after a series of bitter inter-Arab conflicts, even the customary lip service is often lacking.[37]

Notice, however, that while Ajami and Lewis disagree with Khalidi on the relative potency of pan-Arabism, they accept the basic definition of pan-Arabism as a movement and a doctrine of Arab political unity. So do a score of other historians, political scientists, and commentators of the Middle East.

What is rather baffling about all this is the glaring paucity in the use of the term pan-Arabism in Arabic texts. There are authentic Arabic equivalents for a number of terms that are of significance for our subject: al-qawmiya al-'Arabiya (Arab nationalism), al-'Uruba (Arabism), al-Wuhda al-'Arabiya (Arab unity), al-Ittihad al-'Arabi (Arab union), al-Iqlimiya (regionalism), and al-Wataniya (state patriotism). These terms appear constantly in Arabic texts as speeches of leaders, radio and newspaper editorials, and political books and pamphlets. But one is hard put to find the literal Arabic translation of pan-Arabism (presumably, al-'Uruba al-Shamila) in any of these texts.

The reason is self-evident: the desire for, as well as the pursuit of, political unity for the Arabs, which is how Western literature has defined and portrayed pan-Arabism, is incorporated, in the minds and discourse of the Arab nationalists themselves, in the very definition of Arab nationalism itself. To those who thought of themselves as Arab nationalists—the men and women who were

[36] Fouad Ajami, "The End of Pan-Arabism," *Foreign Affairs*, vol. 57, no.2 (Winter 1978 / 1979): 355.

[37] Lewis, *The Multiple Identities of the Middle East*, p. 140.

consumed by the idea, who were prepared to endure hardships on its behalf, who drew courage from its promise, who celebrated its triumphs and mourned its setbacks—to all those people, Arab nationalism was meaningless *without* its ultimate goal of Arab unity. After all, what would be so distinctive about an Arab world that was nothing more than a region with a multiplicity of states, the vast majority of whose population were Muslim and happened to speak Arabic and share in Arabic culture? How would that be any different from, for example, Catholic and (Brazil-less) Spanish-speaking Latin America? At some point, the cultural bond that presumably tied citizens of the various Arab countries together under the banner of Arabism would have to acquire geographic and political rationalization. We have already seen that in contrast to an ethnic group, a nation desires and seeks a sovereign political identity, and those who identified themselves as Arab nationalists fervently believed that the Arab nation could not continue to allow its children to be scattered among different Arab states.

In his introduction to an edited volume on the origins of Arab nationalism, the noted historian Rashid Khalidi, in setting out the arguments of the various chapters, contends that "there was a clear difference before 1914 between the majority of Arabists, whose emphasis on Arab identity was linked to continued loyalty to the Ottoman Empire, and the tiny minority of extreme Arab nationalists who called for secession from the empire."[38] In this account, those who Khalidi calls "Arabists" are aware of their cultural separateness from the Ottoman Turks, but have no aspirations for political sovereignty, yet Khalidi's "Arab nationalists" go beyond the cultural domain to demand political separation. And this trait need not be reserved only to the extreme elements, but, as has been argued here, it should constitute the characteristic of *all* true nationalists.

The desire for political separateness, therefore, will be a constituent element in the definition of nation and nationalism used in

[38] Rashid Khalidi, Lisa Anderson, Muhammad Muslih, and Reeva S. Simon, *The Origins of Arab Nationalism*. (New York: Columbia University Press, 1991), p. ix.

this book. The nation thus defined is: *a human solidarity, whose members believe that they form a coherent cultural whole, and who manifest a strong desire for political separateness and sovereignty.*

Applied to the Arab world, this definition goes beyond the linguistic, religious, historical, and emotional bonds that tie the Arabic-speaking people to each other. For the purpose of conceptual precision, this cultural uniformity would be termed *Arabism*. But Arabism with the added element of a strong desire (and preferably articulated demands) for political unity in a specified demarcated territory—that is what will be termed *Arab nationalism*.

CHAPTER TWO

EARLY STIRRINGS: THE NINETEENTH AND EARLY TWENTIETH CENTURIES

The area that stretches from the Atlantic Coast in North Africa all the way east to the Persian Gulf in Asia, terminating at the frontiers of Farsi Iran to the east and Turkey to the north, and excluding Jewish Israel, is usually referred to by its inhabitants, as well as by outsiders, as the "Arab world." This concept is of course a cultural rather than a political construct, and consequently, there has been considerable shift over time in the conceptual delineation of the land mass inhabited by "Arabs." By the middle of the twentieth century, most of these inhabitants had accepted a definition of "Arabness" which emphasized their historical bonds under early Islamic rule, the proximity of their manners and traditions, and above all their ability to claim "Arabic" as their mother tongue. The nationalist narrators might have disagreed over the relative merits of the other elements, but they all agreed on the centrality of the Arabic language as a unifying force.

To be sure the "Arabness" of the people of this area does not exclude other forms of national and subnational identities. An "Arab" living along the banks of the Tigris River may identify himself also as an Iraqi (his state), a Sunni (his religious sect), and / or a Dulaimi (his tribe). Multiple identities need not necessarily be mutually exclusive. For instance, in his study of Palestinian identity, Rashid Khalidi maintains that intellectuals and politicians in late nineteenth and early twentieth centuries "identified with the Ottoman Empire, their religion, Arabism, their homeland Palestine, their city or region, and their family, without feeling any contradiction, or sense of conflicting loyalties."[1] However, the narrators of the various identities have tended to project their own as the most deserving of paramount loyalty. The power of the narrative is aided or impeded by purposeful environmental changes, events, and accidents of history—the packaging of a nationalist school curriculum, a war won or lost, the emergence of a charismatic leader. Over time, and depending on the circumstances, a specific identify can become the focus of peoples' loyalties, while other identities are marginalized, even excluded. As we shall see, during the 1950s and 1960s Arab nationalism became the people's focus of loyalty to such an extent that other identities were not only marginalized, but indeed were turned into negative, even derogatory, notions.[2] This was no longer the case by the end of the twentieth century, when Arab nationalism seemed to have been eclipsed not only by strong Islamic sentiment, but also by state and substate identities; still, throughout the second half of the century, people continued to cling to their "Arabness," albeit with varying degrees of intensity.

To call the area the "Arab" world, therefore, need not raise any eyebrows. To say someone is an Arab should not be a point of controversy. And on the whole it was not. What was vigorously debated was the question pertaining to the origins and political manifestations of this identity: when was it that the inhabitants of the area began to feel that they constituted (or should constitute) a "nation"; when was it, to use the terminology of Ernest Renan and Benedict Anderson, that they *imagined* themselves to consti-

[1] Rashid Khalidi, *Palestinian Identity: The Construction of Modern National Consciousness* (New York: Columbia University Press, 1997), p. 19.

[2] See, for example, Selim Mattar, *al-Dhat al-Jariha: Ishkalat al-Hawiya fi al-'Iraq wa al-'Alam al-'Aabi "al-Shirqani,"* (Wounded essence: problems of identity in Iraq and the "Eastern" Arab world) (Beirut: al-Mu'asasa al-'Arabiya li al-Dirasat wa al-Nashr, 1997).

tute a *deep, horizontal* solidarity deserving of political recognition?[3] This is not an esoteric debate conducted within the annals of historiography, with no relevance to our understanding of contemporary Arab politics. If national identity emerges as a result of purposeful narrative, then it is essential to comprehend accurately when the narrative began, for its later development and contemporary impact has to have something to do with the intellectual, ideological, and political influence under which it emerged.

Of course, some form of Arab consciousness has existed throughout the history of the Arabs. Albert Hourani sees in the life of Ibn Khaldun, the great fourteenth century Arab philosopher, an allegory for the cultural space that was the domain of the Arabs. Ibn Khaldun's life, Hourani tells us, says something about the world to which he belonged:

> A world where a family from southern Arabia could move to Spain, and after six centuries return nearer to its place of origin and still find itself in familiar surroundings, had a unity which transcended divisions of time and space; the Arabic language could open the door to office and influence throughout that world; a body of knowledge, transmitted over the centuries by a known chain of teachers, preserved a moral community even when rules changed; places of pilgrimage, Mecca and Jerusalem, were unchanging poles of the human world even if power shifted from one city to another; and belief in a God who created and sustained the world could give meaning to the blows of fate.[4]

So it was Islam and the Arabic language that preserved this sense of belonging through the ages, a process that gained vast impetus with the magnificent flowering of culture in the Arab Islamic empires that grew out of the Muslim conquests. It was then that Baghdad of the Abbasids, Cairo of the Fatimids, Qairawan of the North

---

[3] Ernest Renan, "What is a Nation?" in *Nation and Narration*, ed. Homi K. Bhabha. (London: Routledge, 1990); Benedict Anderson, *Imagined Communities: Reflections on the Origin and Spread of Nationalism* (New York: Verso, 1990).

[4] Albert Hourani, *A History of the Arab Peoples* (New York: Warner Books, 1991), p. 4.

African Aghlabids, and Cordoba of the Spanish Ummayads were the centers of dazzling civilizations at a time when Europe was mired in illiteracy, poverty, and disease.

But by the dawn of the sixteenth century, the Arabs were no longer the primary bearers of power and culture. Their empires and civilizations had disintegrated and they lay ready to be devoured by new and aggressive social solidarities eager to expand their power and domain. It was one such group, the Turkish Ottomans, that was destined to rule over the Arabs for the next five centuries. Very soon, Constantinople, not the famed Arab cities, would become Islam's center of gravity, and in the Friday prayers, the voice of *Mu'azzins* in Arab cities and towns would invoke the blessings of Allah not for Arab rulers, but for the Turkish sultan. At times, the political and military reach of the Ottoman Turks seemed limitless. The great sixteenth century Ottoman sultan, Sulayman, known as "the Magnificent," would address a letter to the King of France which began, "I who am Sultan of Sultans, Sovereign of Sovereigns . . . the shadow of God on earth, the Sultan and Sovereign Lord of the White Sea and the Black Sea, of Rumelia, Azerbaijan, Persia, Damascus, Aleppo, Cairo, Mecca, Medina, Jerusalem, Arabia, Yemen and many other lands . . . which my August Majesty has made subject to my flaming sword and my victorious blade. I, Sultan [Sulayman] Khan . . . to thee, who art Francis, King of the land of France."[5]

What is interesting, however, is that this pervasive power of the Turks over Arab lands and populations in no way diminished the place of the Arabic language. In fact, the Ottomans, Muslims themselves, regarded Arabic as the sacred language, according it due respect and deference,[6] and so while Turkish became the language of government and bureaucracy, Arabic retained its elevated status as the medium for law and religious studies and more often than

[5] Anthony Nutting, *The Arabs: A Narrative History from Muhammed to the Present* (New York: New American Library, 1964), p. 212.

[6] H.A.R. Gibb, *Islamic Society and the West: A Study of the Impact of Western Civilization on Moslem Culture* (London: Oxford University Press, 1950), p. 160.

not for history and biography.[7] So it was the Arabic language, and its unrivaled status as the language of the Qur'an, which nourished and sustained a sense of cultural proximity in the Arab lands of the empire throughout the centuries of Ottoman rule.

Instrumental in this process, paradoxically enough, was the West. As early as the sixteenth century, the Rome papacy began to establish colleges for training priests of the eastern churches, a number of which incorporated the study of Arabic into their theological and historical explorations and commentaries. This process was accelerated in the nineteenth century in the Levant under the enlightened rule of Ibrahim Pasha who encouraged Western missionaries and educationists to open schools and other educational institutions. To remedy the shortage of Arabic texts these institutions imported their own printing presses. All this led to an Arabic literary revival, which was to become the basis for the early nationalist stirrings in the Arabic-speaking provinces of the Ottoman Empire.

It is thus hardly surprising that the intellectual seeds of twentieth century Arab nationalism should be traced to the ideas and endeavors of a number of nineteenth century thinkers and activists. Muslims and Christians, their central focus was the contemporary condition and future aspirations of the Arabic-speaking citizens of the Ottoman Empire. Their eyes opened by the expansion of education to the growing nationalist movements in the Balkan lands of the Empire, these early Arab writers and political agitators tended to focus on the ethnic and linguistic differences that separated the Arabs from their Turkish rulers. As we shall see, this ethnic separateness was much stronger among the Christians than the Muslims; the latter being tied to Istanbul by the bond of religious belief, and therefore just as much, perhaps more, concerned with the creeping cultural and political domination of Christian Europe.

Perhaps the earliest of these thinkers and political agitators, whose writings and activities were held in great reverence by the

---

[7] Albert Hourani, *Arabic Thought in the Liberal Age. 1798–1939* (London: Oxford University Press, 1970), p. 239.

Arab nationalists of the twentieth century, were Jamal al-Din al-Afghani (1839–1897) and his pupil Muhamed 'Abdu (1849–1905). Admittedly, neither spoke directly to Arabism, for Afghani and 'Abdu were essentially Islamic reformers who recognized and feared the cultural threat of the Christian West, and sought to confront this threat through advocating Islamic reform, resurgence, and unity. Their purpose was to regenerate the stagnant Muslim society, and to educate it into adapting to the ideas and institutions of the modern world. They argued that the arsenal of the West's undoubted contemporary superiority—philosophy, reason, and science—were not only compatible with Islam, they in fact were imbedded in the very essence of the Muslim faith. To Afghani, "Islam was in harmony with the principles discovered by scientific reason, was indeed the religion demanded by reason."[8] Thus, it was not Islam *per se*, but the Muslims' intellectual backwardness, brought about by centuries of subjugation and neglect, as well as the disunity of the Islamic *Umma*, that was responsible for the inferior status of the Muslim world.[9] Time and again the two reformers would enjoin Muslims not to blindly imitate the West, but to delve into the real meaning of their religion, study it well, and model their lives on its teachings. If that were to happen, the world of Islam would be strong again.[10] It was this determined declaration of authenticity, this unambiguous reiteration of cultural independence, even superiority, that later would spur twentieth century nationalists to consider Afghani and 'Abdu as having contributed to the Arab nationalist cause.[11]

[8] Ibid., p. 123.

[9] For analyses of the ideas of Afghani and Abdu, see Hourani, *Arabic Thought in the Liberal Age*, pp. 103–160; Majid Khadduri, *Political Trends in the Arab World: The Role of Ideas and Ideals in Politics* (Baltimore,: Johns Hopkins Press, 1970), pp. 56–65; Nadav Safran, *Egypt in Search of Political Community: An Analysis of the Intellectual and Political Evolution of Egypt, 1804–1952* (Cambridge, Massachusetts: Harvard University Press, 1961), pp. 43–46, 62–75; Sylvia Haim, *ed. Arab Nationalism: An Anthology* (Berkeley: California University Press, 1962), pp. 6–20.

[10] Hourani, *Arabic Thought in the Liberal Age*, p. 113.

[11] See the thorough summary of such opinions by Elie Chalala, "Arab Nationalism: A Bibliographical Essay," in *Pan Arabism and Arab Nationalism: The Continuing Debate. ed.* Tawfic E. Farah. (Boulder, Colorado: Westview Press, 1987), pp. 24–25.

If this is to be the case, however, the most that could be said about Afghani and 'Abdu is that they were Arab nationalists by implication, and even that is tenuous at best. According to the eminent Arab historian, Nicola Ziadeh, Afgahni single-mindedly advocated the concept of the *Islamic Umma* (Islamic community) at the expense of the national state. The *Umma*, according to Afghani, constituted all Muslims, regardless of their countries, nationalities, and languages.[12] 'Abdu, too, "always spoke of and to the *Ummah* in the traditional sense of the community of all Muslims."[13] As for Arab national and linguistic bonds, these were dismissed by Afghani, who insisted that Muslims had but one nationality: their religion.[14] To Afghani and 'Abdu, the "religion of Islam is the one bond which unites Muslims of all countries and obliterates all traces of race or nationality."[15] Indeed, they were adamant that it was the "foreigners" who touted secular nationalism in order to divide the Muslim *Umma*. Nationalism thus was "conceived as a divisive rather than a unifying spirit—a cover, in fact, for tyranny and injustice."[16] Moreover, neither Afghani nor 'Abdu was particularly hostile to Ottoman rule over Arab lands.[17] Indeed, Afghani was Persian by birth, and if any nationalism, beyond Muslim unity, is to be implied from 'Abdu's writings, it would be Egyptian rather than Arab.

More perceptible "Arabist" proclivities are found in the writings of another leading Islamist, Rashid Rida (1865–1935). Rida's writings on the structure and reform of the Islamic world tended to

---

[12] Nicola Ziadeh, *Shamiyat: Dirasat fi al-Hadhara wa al-Tarikh* (Shamiyat: studies in culture and history) (London: Riad El-Rayyes Books, 1989), pp. 287–288.

[13] Safran, *Egypt in Search of Political Community*, p. 75.

[14] See Abu Khaldun Sati' al-Husri, *Ma Hiya al-Qawmiya?: Abhath wa Dirasat 'ala Dhaw'i al-Ahdath wa al-Nadhariyat* (What is nationalism?: enquiries and studies in light of events and theories) (Beirut: Dar al-'Ilm li al-Malayeen, 1959), p. 221.

[15] Quoted in Charles C. Adams, *Islam and Modernism in Egypt: A Study of the Modern Reform Movement Inaugurated by Muhammad 'Abduh* (London: Oxford University Press, 1933), p. 59.

[16] Malcolm H. Kerr, *Islamic Reform: The Political and Legal Theories of Muhammad 'Abduh and Rashid Rida* (Berkeley: University of California Press, 1966), pp. 138–139.

[17] Jacob M. Landau, *The Politics of Pan-Islam: Ideology and Organization* (Oxford: Clarendon Press, 1990), pp. 18–26; Martin Kramer, *Islam Assembled: The Advent of the Muslim Congresses* (New York: Columbia University Press, 1986), pp. 7–21.

give Arabs pride of place. To Rida, the Arabic language was the only language "in which the doctrines and laws of Islam could be thought about."[18] Accordingly, to invest the office of the Khalifa with the Ottoman rulers in Istanbul was a travesty. Indeed, Rida goes even further by insisting that Islam, in fact, "had been undermined by the Ottoman rulers."[19] After all, was it not the Turks who tyrannized the community, killing even the Khalifas? Worst of all, in Rida's eyes, the Turks "usurped the [office of the Khalifa] from the 'Abbasids and so took it out from the hands of the Quraysh clan which had been chosen by God to spread the Qur'an over the world, after it had given Islam its prophet, its language, and its adherents."[20] And while the Ottomans had certainly built a great empire, it is dwarfed by the early Arab conquests. In an article Rida wrote in 1900, in which he evaluates Arab and Ottoman conquests, he is adamant in preferring the former: "I want to say that the greatest glory in the Muslim conquests goes to the Arabs, and that religion grew, and became great through them; their foundation is the strongest, their light is the brightest, and they are indeed the best *Umma*."[21] In these and other writings, there is no mistaking the conscious ethnic distinction between the Arabs and the Ottoman Turks, in which the pride of place goes to the Arabs. Indeed, later on, in the wake of the 1916 Arab revolt, Rida advocated political separation and statehood for the Arabs, which, he argued, would be of benefit to all Muslims.[22]

Yet here again, as in the case of Afghani and 'Abdu, Rida's primary concern was with the realm of Islam. Whatever arguments and recommendations he proposed were primarily aimed to serve the interests and glorification of Islam. If "Arabism" appeared as an element of Rida's writings, it was at best a corollary force to be used solely for the rejuvenation of Islam and the Muslim *Umma*. The cause of Arabism was in no way meant to supercede that of

[18] Hourani, *Arabic Thought in the Liberal Age*, p. 240.
[19] Khadduri, *Political Trends in the Arab World*, p. 181.
[20] Safran, *Egypt in Search of Political Community*, p. 80.
[21] Haim, *Arab Nationalism*, pp. 22–23.
[22] Anis al-Abyadh, *Rashid Rida: Tarikh wa Sira* (Rashid Rida: history and biography) (Tripoli: Jarrus Press, 1993), p. 53.

the wider Islamic solidarity, and so his antagonism toward the "Turkish usurpers" was not meant to undermine the Ottoman Empire, for he saw the continued health of the Empire as a strength for Islam.[23] Consequently, Rida remained committed to his Ottoman nationality until the last years of World War I when Ottoman defeat loomed in the horizon. Indeed, Rida was proud that in a nationalist age, the Arabs were the last ethnic group to feel its stirrings "because the vast majority of them are Muslims feeling almost nothing but their religious identity."[24] Rida, in fact, was very much against doctrinal nationalism, seeing it as a Western-inspired assault against the solidarity of the Islamic *Umma*. To Rida, nationalism was "not only a new source of dissension among Muslims, but something close to apostasy."[25] In 1911, he submitted a memorandum to the Ottoman authorities recommending the establishment of a *Madrasat al-Da'wa wa al-Irshad* (School of Religious Persuasion and Instruction), in which "students would be selected from promising candidates in the Muslim countries, especially those in need of Islamic knowledge, such as Java, China and North Africa. The [school] would emphasize morals, manners and a spirit of unity, eschewing both racial nationalism and politics."[26] An attachment to a "homeland" was permissible only if it served the interest of the broader Muslim community. "A Muslim," Rida told his coreligionists, "is a member of a body bigger than his people, his own personal homeland is only a part of his religious homeland, and he must therefore seek to make the progress of the part a means toward the progress of the whole."[27] In Rida's scheme of things, ethnic nationalism, including Arab nationalism, in no way would be advocated as an autonomous ideological formulation; it would be

[23] Ibid., p. 33.

[24] Quoted in Zeine Nur al-Din Zeine, *Nushu' al-Qawmiya al-'Arabiya ma'a Dirasa Tarikhiya fi al-'Ilaqat al-'Arabiya al-Turkiya* (The emergence of Arab nationalism with a historical study of Arab-Turkish relations) (Beirut: Dar al-Nahar li al-Nashr, 1979), p. 43.

[25] Safran, *Egypt in Search of Political Community*, p. 82; see also Adams, *Islam and Modernism in Egypt*, p. 183.

[26] Landau, *The Politics of Pan-Islam*, p. 126.

[27] Rashid Rida, "Islam and the National Idea," in *al-Manar*, vol. 23 (1933): 192, to be found in Haim, *Arab Nationalism*, p. 76.

tolerated only when it was put at the service of a higher purpose, namely, the bringing together of global Islamic solidarity.

A more forthright and politically conscious ethnic separation of Arab from Turk can be discerned from the writing of the Syrian 'Abd al-Rahman al-Kawakibi (1849–1903). In his book, *Umm al-Qura* (Mother of the Cities), a traditional name for Mecca, Kawakibi berates the Turks for introducing practices into the *Umma* which led to the decadence of Islam, adding that the abode of Islam would have been better off had the Turks not embraced the faith.[28] He then goes so far as to advocate a shift in the balance of power from the Turks to the Arabs by bringing back the caliphate to al-Hejaz, where an Arab from the line of Quraish would be elected by representatives of the Islamic community. Kawakibi rationalizes what amounts to an incendiary proposal by reference to the central position of the Arabs, and especially their language, in Islam.[29] He adds that, unlike other Muslims, the Arabs of the Arabian Peninsula, not having been weakened by racial and sectarian divisions, continued to constitute a true solidarity, and were the most zealous in preserving their religion. The Arabs, Kawakibi maintained, are "of all nations the most suitable to be an authority in religion and an example to the Muslims; the other nations have followed their guidance at the start and will not refuse to follow them now."[30] In advocating placing religious authority in the hands of the Arabs, Kawakibi, more so than Rida, infuses a quasi-political dimension to his anti-Turkish sentiment, which is crystallized by his insistence on the transfer of the caliphate to al-Hejaz.

Yet this is hardly a clearly enunciated nationalist doctrine, rather it is more an articulated sentiment against Turkish political domination, fueled possibly by a political grudge against Istanbul for furthering the political ambitions of the head of a rival family in Kawakibi's own town of Aleppo.[31] More generally, Hanna Batatu

---

[28] William L. Cleveland, *A History of the Modern Middle East*, 2nd ed. (Boulder, Colorado: Westview Press, 2000), p. 126.

[29] Hourani, *Arabic Thought in the Liberal Age*, pp. 272–273.

[30] Haim, *Arab Nationalism*, p. 27.

[31] Hourani, *Arabic Thought in the Liberal Age*, p. 271.

argues that the centralizing efforts of the reformist Ottoman sultans of the nineteenth century increasingly encroached upon "all the elements of power hitherto diffused among a crowd of landed families, tribal shaykhs, and privileged corporate orders. . . . The *ashraf* (the class to which Kawakibi belonged) found themselves being slowly and gradually edged out of their former power."[32] In terms of doctrine, Kawakibi's overriding intellectual concern, not unlike Afghani, 'Abdu, and Rida, related first and foremost to the condition of Islam and the Islamic community.[33] After all, the bulk of *Umm al-Qura*'s discourse centers on the decay of the Muslim world, brought about by despotic rulers supporting false religion.[34] Thus, the shift in religious authority from the Turks to the Arabs was proposed for the sole purpose of Islamic regeneration, and the Arabian khalifa was projected to be not a revolutionary nationalist, but a symbol of Islamic unity. Note that the proposed khalifa would have only *religious* authority over the *Umma*[35], and the only temporal authority he was granted by Kawakibi was over al-Hejaz. Indeed, Kawakibi made sure not to call "for a break in Ottoman unity."[36] Nor did the notion of Arab political separation figure much in Kawakibi's second book, *Tabai' al-Istibdad* (Characteristics of Tyranny),[37] which focused on the evils of repressive authoritarian rule and the many virtues of representative government. The book, by implication, was an attack on the tyranny of the Ottoman sultan, 'Abd al-Hamid, but did not advocate Arab sovereignty.

[32] Quoted in George Kirk, "The Arab Awakening Reconsidered," *Middle Eastern Affairs*, vol.13, no.6 (June-July 1962): 164–165.

[33] See Ziadeh, *Shamiyat*, p. 293; Landau, *The Politics of Pan-Islam*, p. 34. See also the considered introduction to Kawakibi's work written by the noted Syrian writer Adonis ('Ali Ahmad Sa'id) in Adonis and Khalida Sa'id, *al-Kawakibi* (Beirut: Dar al-'Ilm li al-Malayeen, 1982), pp. 7–19.

[34] Only the last few pages, which are in the form of an appendix and an epilogue, are devoted to the centrality of the Arabs in Islam and the necessity for an Arab khalifa from Quraysh. The full text of *Umm al-Qura* can be found in Muhamed Jamal Tahan, *al-A'mal al-Kamila li al-Kawakibi* (The complete works of al-Kawakibi) (Beirut: Markaz Dirasat al-Wuhda al-'Arabiya, 1995), pp. 265–411.

[35] Ibid., pp. 397–398.

[36] Khadduri, *Political Trends in the Arab World*, p. 16.

[37] Tahan, *al-A'mal al-Kamila li al-Kawkibi* (The complete works of al-Kawakibi), pp. 430–535.

The reluctance of Afghani, 'Abdu, Rida, and Kawakibi to champion political independence for the Arabs reflected the general intellectual disposition of Muslim thinkers of the time. Their overriding concern was for the "close cooperation between the two national communities: the Turks and the Arabs."[38] That, however, was not good enough for Christian thinkers and writers. These individuals had no qualms about breaking Ottoman unity, promoting a separate Arab identity, and advocating an independent political realm for those whose mother language was Arabic. Perhaps the earliest to advocate the break-up of the Ottoman empire and the creation of an independent Arab state was the Syrian Christian, Negib 'Azoury (d.1916). 'Azoury echoed Rida's and Kawakibi's contempt for the Turks, but whereas the hostility of Rida and Kawakibi lay in what the Turks allegedly did to Islam and the Muslim world, 'Azoury blamed the Turks for having "ruined the Arabs. Without them, the Arabs would have been among the most civilized nations in the world."[39] To 'Azouri, the Arabs are not just Muslims, but also Arabic-speaking Christians, and together they constitute the same "nation" that had to be politically independent of the Ottoman Turks.[40] The frontiers of this nation-state would stretch from the Tigris and the Euphrates to the Suez Isthmus, and from the Mediterranean to the Arabian Sea. Obvious from this designation is the exclusion of Egypt, because "Egyptians do not belong to the Arab race; they are of African Berber family and the language which they spoke before Islam bears no similarity to Arabic."[41] This Arab state was to be a secular, liberal, and constitutional sultanate, following in the path of England and France.

Another Christian from Syria, Ibrahim al-Yaziji (1847–1906) went even further in his advocacy of an Arab nation, for not only did the Arabs constitute a nation, they were "the most remarkable

---

[38] Youssef M. Choueiri, *Arab Nationalism: A History* (Oxford: Blackwell Publishers, 2000), p. 79.

[39] Hourani, *Arabic Thought in the Liberal Age*, p. 278.

[40] Ziadeh, *Shamiyat*, p. 293.

[41] Negib Azoury, "Program of the League of the Arab Fatherland," in Haim, *Arab Nationalism: An Anthology*, p. 81.

of nations."[42] Their achievements spoke for themselves, and only when foreigners, particularly the Turks, came to dominate them, did Arab civilization begin to decline. Thus in order for the Arabs to reclaim their past glories, they needed to expel the Turks from their midst. Then, "the old vigor of the Arab nation would return and the Arabs would resume their former progress in civilization."[43] Of course, in Yaziji's words, there is an unambiguous appeal to the Muslim majority to join with the Christians in their "Arab nationalism" and rise against the admittedly Muslim, yet ethnically distinct, Ottoman Turks.

While slight variations in points of emphases, nuances, and ideological direction could be found in the writings of other Christian intellectuals of the period,[44] the primary focus of these writers invariably was on the national distinctiveness of the Arabs, Muslims, and Christians alike, and their membership of one indivisible Arab nation that would find its true expression and would fulfill its promise only through a secular and liberal nation-state.

But theirs were isolated and lonely voices. The problem for the Christian propagators of Arab nationalism was that, on the whole, their message fell on deaf ears among the intellectual elite of Arab Muslims. Many Muslims resented the secularist orientation of the Christians, believing it to be a spurious effort at dividing the Islamic *Umma*. They further were angered by the "spectacle of Christians assuming the air of masters of Arab learning, [thus adopting] the battle cry, 'Arabic shall not be Christianized'."[45] The truth is that, as we have seen, the concept of an Arab nation striving for political sovereignty and independence was truly marginal to the concerns of the nineteenth century Arab Muslim intelligentsia, who undoubtedly put greater store in the rejuvenation of the Islamic

---

[42] C. Ernest Dawn, *From Ottomanism to Arabism: Essays on the Origins of Arab Nationalism* (Urbana: University of Illinois Press, 1973), p. 132.

[43] Ibid.

[44] Succinct analyses of the ideas of such intellectuals as Jurji Zaidan, Francis Marash, Shibli Shumayyil, Farah Antun, Salama Musa, and others can be found in Hourani, *Arabic Thought in the Liberal Age*, pp. 245–259 and in Khadduri, *Political Trends in the Arab World*, pp. 89–94.

[45] Dawn, *From Ottomanism to Arabism*, pp. 132–133.

Umma than in fashioning a secular Arab nation-state. Indeed, doubts over the advisability of an Arab nation seemed even to have crossed Christian minds, for as Albert Hourani tells us, "they could not be certain that Arab nationalism would not turn out to be a new form of Islamic self-assertion."[46] Squeezed, therefore, between Muslim obsession with the abode of Islam and Christian advocacy that had no resonance among the majority, Arab nationalism as an intellectual construct could hardly be said to have jelled, let alone flowered, in the nineteenth century.

Yet, the argument that the roots of the Arab nationalist movement were to be found in the nineteenth century does not rest solely on the intellectual output of the few Christian and Muslim thinkers of the time. Later nationalists also would point to the anti-Ottoman activities of a number of public and clandestine Arab political organizations, seeing these as manifestations of Arab nationalist fervor that was sweeping the Arabic-speaking parts of the Ottoman empire in the late nineteenth and early twentieth centuries, culminating in the "Great Arab Revolt" in 1916.

Until recent historiography rendered a number of its central conclusions questionable, George Antonius's book, *The Arab Awakening,* was the standard work that traced the inception and development of these nationalist manifestations and activities.[47] The thrust of Antonius's thesis is that on the eve of the First World War, "the masses as well as the thinkers" had been moved by "the Arab will to freedom."[48] According to Antonius, the genesis of the Arab nationalist movement could be traced back to the early nineteenth century to the political ambition of Muhamed Ali, the Albanian-born governor of Egypt, to establish an Arab kingdom independent of the Ottoman Empire. Ali and his son Ibrahim Pasha, who conquered Syria and became its governor in 1833, appealed to the Arabs' sense of separateness and to their ethnic and national differences from the Turkish Ottomans. Ibrahim Pasha, during his years

---

[46] Hourani, *Arabic Thought in the Liberal Age,* p. 277.

[47] George Antonius, *The Arab Awakening: The Story of the Arab National Movement* (Beirut: Khayat's, 1938).

[48] Ibid., p. 121; see also Kirk, "The Arab Awakening Reconsidered," p. 162.

in Syria tried hard to stimulate an Arab national consciousness. After more than three centuries of being part of an all-inclusive Ottoman empire, the Arabs for the first time could ponder their separateness from those who ruled over them. Antonius relates that these initial national stirrings came to nothing primarily because of British opposition. In 1833, the British prime minister, Lord Palmerston, explained his antipathy to an Arab kingdom under Muhamed Ali: "There might be no harm in such a thing in itself; but as it would imply the dismemberment of Turkey, we could not agree to it. Besides, Turkey is as good an occupier of the road to India as an active Arabian sovereign would be."[49]

But the "Perfidious Albion" was not the only reason for the project's failure. The Arabs themselves, as Antonius readily admits, were not yet ready for it. To say that at the time there was nothing approaching an awareness of a national identity among the "Arabs" is perhaps to understate the obstacles faced by Muhamed Ali and his son. Peoples' loyalties were particularistic, primarily "regional and sectarian, according to the district, clan or creed to which they belonged. . . . Patriotism in the national sense was unknown."[50] The very term "Arab" was bereft of national symbolism; in general it was used to describe the desert bedouin.[51] Given the opposition of Great Britain and the formidable cultural obstacles it encountered, it was no wonder that the first real efforts to construct an Arab nation and give it a political manifestation came to very little.

Antonius insists, however, that the failure was not total. The seeds had been sown. The new ideas encouraged by Ibrahim Pasha in Syria, in addition to his relatively tolerant rule which opened the country to Western education through missionary schools, contributed to the growth of nationalist sentiment in the generations that followed. During the second half of the nineteenth century, and

---

[49] Quoted in Antonius, *The Arab Awakening*, p. 31.

[50] Ibid., pp. 32–33.

[51] Zeine, *Nushu' al-Qawmiya al-'Arabiya ma'a Dirasa Tarikhiya fi al-'Ilaqat al-'Arabiya al-Turkiya* (The emergence of Arab nationalism with a historical study of Arab-Turkish relations), p. 43.

especially in its later years, Antonius would characterize the stirrings of nationalism among the Arabic-speaking populations of the
Ottoman Empire as an "infant" national movement. To Antonius,
this was clearly discernible from the growth of overt and covert
Arab societies and organizations. The earliest of these was the initially clandestine *al-Jim'iya al-'Ilmiya al-Suriya* (the Syrian Scientific Society), formed in 1857,[52] to be followed in 1875 by another
secret association headquartered in Beirut,[53] and then later on in
the early twentieth century by two public societies, *al-Muntada al-
Adabi* (the Literary Club) and the Ottoman Decentralization Party,
as well as three clandestine organizations, *al-Qahtaniya, al-Fatat,*
and *al-'Ahd.*[54] It was these organizations and their activities, Antonius tells us emphatically, that carried the Arab nationalist torch,
spreading its sparks among the Arab masses.

The effect of Antonius's analysis and conclusions was to create
a historiographic tradition that projected an almost idealized historical period, stretching from about the middle of the nineteenth
century to the First World War, as the era in which a national
identity took roots among the Arabic-speaking populations of
the Ottoman Empire. For some time into the twentieth century,
the Antonius thesis was not seriously challenged, and not until the
post-World War II period did new scholarship begin to question
the methods and conclusions of Antonius's work.

In a seminal work, C. Ernest Dawn asserts that prior to October
1914, only 126 men were known to have been "public advocates
of Arab nationalism, or members of Arab nationalist societies. . . .
Using the only available population estimates for 1915, there were
3.5 Arab nationalist leaders per 100,000 of total population in
Syria . . . 3.1 in Palestine and 2.4 in Lebanon."[55] In a later study,
Eliezer Tauber identifies 180 activists[56]—an infinitesimally tiny

---

[52] Antonius, *The Arab Awakening*, pp. 53–55.
[53] Ibid., pp. 79–89.
[54] Ibid., pp. 108–121.
[55] Dawn, *From Ottomanism to Arabism*, pp. 152–153.
[56] Eliezer Tauber, *The Emergence of the Arab Movements* (London: Frank Cass, 1993),
p. 289.

number, hardly indicative of a widespread swell of nationalist emotions among the Arab populations of the Ottoman Empire. Indeed, Tauber further shows that those who agitated against Ottoman control prior to World War I were more likely to form societies promoting regional interests, such as independence for Syria, Lebanon, or Iraq, than demanding political separation under an all-inclusive Arab identity.[57] In the case of Syria, for instance, Hassan Kayali, using extensive Ottoman archives, as well as Arabic and European sources, argues that "it would be more appropriate to refer to 'Syrianism' rather than Arab nationalism in the period before the world war. Both the decentralists in the major towns of Syria and the Arab voices calling (mostly from Europe or Egypt) for a political existence independent of Istanbul thought in terms of Syria when espousing Arab group consciousness as a political idiom."[58] And in this, these societies simply reflected the general proclivities of the masses, the vast majority of whom were indifferent to Arab nationalist concerns.

Indeed, even those supposedly Arab nationalist societies intermittently felt the strains of regional loyalties. After World War I *al-'Ahd* disintegrated into a Syrian faction, *al-'Ahd al-Suri,* and an Iraqi faction, *al-'Ahd al-'Iraqi.*[59] And in any case, those Arabist societies seemed more concerned with promoting the growth of the political and cultural standing of the Arab citizens of the Ottoman Empire vis-à-vis their Turkish compatriots, than with advocating outright Arab political independence and sovereignty. Their political demands generally were for some form of autonomy within the Ottoman Empire. For instance, the first article of *al-'Ahd*'s program, enunciated in 1913, stated that the society's goal was "to work for internal independence for the Arab countries, so that they will remain united with the Istanbul government," and the second

---

[57] Ibid., Tauber identifies 207 such regionalist activists. See also Efraim and Inari Karsh, "Reflections on Arab Nationalism," in *Middle Eastern Studies*, vol. 32, no. 4 (October 1996): 373.

[58] Hasan Kayali, *Arabs and Young Turks: Ottomanism, Arabism and Islamism in the Ottoman Empire, 1908–1918* (Berkeley: University of California Press, 1997), p. 212.

[59] Tauber, *The Emergence of the Arab Movements*, p. 333.

article pledged the society "to the Islamic caliphate remaining as a consecrated trust in the hands of the Ottoman dynasty."[60]

As a general rule, it was, as has already been shown, the Arab Christians who tended to favor complete independence. This was to be expected since the Christians had the inferior standing of a religious minority in an Islamic state, and independence leading to a secular Arab state would grant them equal footing with the Muslims. Antonius asserts that "the Arab national movement may be said to have uttered its first cry"[61] with the poem by the Lebanese Christian, Ibrahim Yaziji, whose first line exhorts the Arabs to arise and awaken. In Antonius's view, "the poem did much to foster the national movement in its infancy . . . with its utterance, the movement for political emancipation sang its first song."[62] Be that as it may, it is interesting that the dramatic nationalist exhortation of the poem's first line is followed by appeals to "the Muslims to forget religious divisions and abjure fanaticism [and to] remember that among the Arabs there are both Christians and Muslims."[63] Indeed, the Beirut secret society which was organized in 1875 by Yaziji and four other Christians, and to which Antonius attaches great importance for its impact on the Arab national movement,[64] floundered in 1882–1883 for lack of Muslim support.[65] Moreover, Antonius's claim that the society was formed to liberate Arab lands from Istanbul, is disputed by Zeine N. Zeine, who tapped the same source used by Antonius. Zeine states that the society's objective was focused on the liberation of Lebanon, *not* other Arab countries, from Turkish domination.[66] And even here, the primary impulse would more accurately be described as subnational: it was

[60] Ibid., pp. 221–222.
[61] Antonius, *The Arab Awakening*, p. 54.
[62] Ibid., p. 55.
[63] Haim, *Arab Nationalism*, p. 5.
[64] Antonius, *The Arab Awakening*, p. 79.
[65] Haim, *Arab Nationalism*, pp. 4–5.
[66] Zeine N. Zeine, *The Emergence of Arab Nationalism: With a Background Study of Arab-Turkish Relations in the Near East*, 3rd ed. (Delmar, New York: Caravan Books, 1973), pp. 51–54. See also Haim, *Arab Nationalism*, pp. 4–5; also Kirk, "The Arab Awakening Reconsidered," p. 163.

only the Lebanese Christians, not the other groups within Lebanon, who felt their interests would be served by independence from the Empire.

As for the general public, subnational identification with religion or sect, town and village, family and tribe remained the most relevant focus of an individual's loyalty. Gertrude Bell, who spent almost all of her adult life in the Arab world, and who, as the British Colonial Office representative in Baghdad in the 1920s, became the "uncrowned queen of Iraq" after the latter's independence, captures this lack of national bond well: "There is little or no territorial nationality. . . . If you ask a (Syrian) to what nationality he belongs he will reply . . . that he is a native of Damascus or Aleppo—I have already indicated that Syria is merely a geographic term corresponding to no national sentiment in the breasts of the inhabitants."[67] In another instance, Bell used stronger language in describing the same phenomenon:

> Of what value are the pan-Arabic associations and inflammatory leaflets that they issue from foreign printing presses? The answer is easy: they are worth nothing at all. There is no nation of Arabs; the Syrian merchant is separated by a wider gulf from the bedouin than he is from the Osmanli (Ottoman), the Syrian country is inhabited by Arabic-speaking races all eager to be at each other's throats, and only prevented from fulfilling their natural desires by the ragged half fed soldier who draws at rare intervals the Sultan's pay.[68]

The only identity that seemed able to bind this human and communal mosaic was Islam. Talib Mushtaq, an Iraqi bureaucrat-politician, reminiscing on the Arab situation in the Ottoman period, was

---

[67] Janet Wallach, *Desert Queen: The Extraordinary Life of Gertrude Bell* (New York: Doubleday, 1996), pp. 77–78.

[68] Quoted in Martin Kramer, *Arab Awakening and Islamic Revival: The Politics of Ideas in the Middle East* (New Brunswick, New Jersey: Transaction Publishers, 1996), p. 24. Echoing Gertrude Bell's observation, the wife of the British Council in Syria commented in late nineteenth century that the Syrians "hate one another. The Sunnis excommunicate the Shias and both hate the Druze; all detest the Alawis. . ." Quoted in Martha Neff Kessler, *Syria: Fragile Mosaic of Power* (Washington, D.C.: National Defense University Press, 1987), p. 22.

categorical on where his loyalty lay: "Were we really subjects of imperialism when Iraq was under Ottoman rule? Never! We were one nation, living under one flag. The bond of religion bound us in the firmest of ties. Islam united our hearts and our feelings, and made us one bloc, supporting each other, like a solid building."[69] And indeed, with the gradual loss of the "Christian" Balkans, the Ottoman Empire acquired an increasingly more coherent religious identity that bound Arab and Turk in one Islamic brotherhood.

Prior to World War I, therefore, the majority of the Arab population were not ready for a break with Istanbul, and the small minority who formed themselves into oppositional groups demanded little more than an improvement in their social and political conditions *within* the Empire. This is to be clearly discerned from the proposals formulated by Arab activists who met in Paris in June 1913. The most relevant of these proposals, which were communicated to the Ottoman authorities are summed up as follows:[70] that political reforms were necessary for all citizens; that Arabs would participate more actively in the Empire's government; that a decentralized administrative regime would be established in every Arab province; and that Arabic would be the official language in the Arab provinces, and furthermore would be recognized as the second official language in the Empire.

These proposals are an accurate depiction of the political orientations of the activist few.[71] They might have considered themselves culturally distinct from their fellow Turkish citizens, and if so they would be called "Arabists"; but they were hardly "Arab nationalists," for "they sought neither the separation of the Arab territories from the empire, nor the creation of a distinct Arab nation with

[69] C. Ernest Dawn, "The Origins of Arab Nationalism," in *The Origins of Arab Nationalism*, eds. Rashid Khalidi, Lisa Anderson, Muhamed Muslih, and Reeva S. Simon (New York: Columbia University Press, 1991), p. 23.

[70] Only proposals relevant to our discussion are taken from the full list of proposals as summarized in Majid Khadduri, *Political Trends in the Arab World*, pp. 17–18.

[71] Walid Kazziha argues that the A'yan (socioeconomic elites) in their efforts to protect their economic and administrative interests against the increasingly intrusive Ottoman state were central to the propagation of decentralization and Arab unity. See his "al-Qawmiya al-'Arabiya fi Marhalat ma bayn al-Harbayn al-'Alamiyatayn" (Arab nationalism in the period between the two world wars) *al-Mustaqbal al-'Arabi*, no. 5 (January 1979): 61.

defined territorial boundaries."[72] And even these modest demands
never elicited widespread support. As late as the early twentieth
century, a Syrian Christian judge, who was later to become a Minister in the post-World War I Arab administration in Damascus under
the Hashemite Faysal, remarked that if there were any national sentiment, it was felt only by a few members of the upper class.[73] And
there certainly was no serious move to extract the Arab lands of the
Empire from Istanbul until the "Great Arab Revolt" proclaimed by
Husayn ibn 'Ali, the sharif of Mecca, in the spring of 1916.

The Great Arab Revolt came to be enshrined in nationalist memory and historiography as the patriotic spark that would ignite the
Arab nationalist movement, gain Arab independence, and launch
the Arabs on their quest for political unity in one state under one
government. In reality, however, the terms on which the revolt was
originally launched had little to do with Arab nationalism. William
Cleveland asserts that the revolt "was proclaimed in the name of
preserving Islam, not in the name of Arabism or the Arab nation."[74]
'Aziz al-'Azmeh is more categorical: "The Arab Revolt . . . does
not belong to the register of . . . Arab nationalism, and it really
ought to be excised from the chronicles of Arab nationalism. It was
Arab only in the narrow ethnological, pre-nationalist sense. It was
an Islamist rebellion, undertaken in the name not of the Arabs, but
of a Meccan Caliphate under the Sharif Husayn bin Ali."[75] Indeed,
Husayn himself felt that the Arabs would unite only under the banner of Islam.[76] It was hardly surprising, therefore, that Sharif Hu-

---

[72] Philip S. Khoury, *Urban Notables and Arab Nationalism: The Politics of Damascus,
1860–1920* (London: Cambridge University Press, 1983), p. 67. On the same theme, see,
among others, Albert Hourani, "The Arab Awakening Forty Years After," in Albert Hou-
rani, *The Emergence of the Modern Middle East* (London: Macmillan, 1981); Moshe Ma'oz,
"Attempts to Create a Political Community in Modern Syria," in *Middle Eastern Politics and
Ideas: A History from Within*, eds. Ilan Pappe and Moshe Ma'oz (London: Tauris Academic
Studies, 1997); Karsh and Karsh, "Reflections on Arab Nationalism;" Kayali, *Arabs and
Young Turks*, p. 212; Khadduri, *Political Trends in the Arab World*, p. 19.

[73] See Ma'oz, "Attempts to Create a Political Community in Modern Syria," p. 213.

[74] Quoted in Chalala, "Arab Nationalism: A Bibliographic Essay," p. 28.

[75] Aziz al-Azmeh, "Nationalism and the Arabs," in *Arab Nation, Arab Nationalism*, ed.
Derek Hopwood. (New York: St. Martin's Press, Inc., 2000), p. 69.

[76] That was what Husyan had told Jamal al-Din al-Afghani as recorded by Wilfrid Blunt.
See Martin Kramer, *Islam Assembled*, p. 20.

sayn would characterize the Young Turks as impious innovators who had put Islam in danger, thus justifying his call to arms against the Turks as a defense of the faith.[77] The sharif and his sons were indeed cognizant of the hostility of the Arab Muslims to their revolt, which explains, if not wholly, at least partially, why the revolt was couched in Islamic rather than Arab symbolism. The sharif's third son, Prince Faysal, who was to become King of Syria for a short period, and then King of Iraq, confided that "the position of the Sharifian family had become difficult after Muslims accused it of destroying the Islamic (Ottoman) Empire."[78] And in any case, the "Arab nationalist" credentials of Sharif Husayn himself are rather questionable. C. Ernest Dawn has persuasively shown that up to 1914 Husayn was a loyal supporter of the Ottoman Empire, who was not averse to using his Arab forces in support of Turkish troops against the Arabs in the Arabian Peninsula.[79] He rebelled against Istanbul only after the Ottomans rejected his demands for a hereditary monarchy in al-Hejaz.

Not only had the motives of the sharif little to do with Arabism, the support his call for rebellion received from the Arabic-speaking populations of the Ottoman Empire was nowhere near as spontaneous and enthusiastic as originally portrayed, putting into question whether the sharif's rebellion was, or should in any way be called, the "Great Arab Revolt." The most strident attack, akin to a frontal assault, on the old thesis of widespread Arab support was provided by Efraim and Inari Karsh in two articles published in *Middle Eastern Studies* in 1996 and 1997.[80] Relying mainly on Brit-

[77] Haim, *Arab Nationalism*, p. 34. In his initial contact with the British, Husayn's son, 'Abdallah welcomed cooperation with the British against the Ottomans because of the "neglect by Constantinople of religion and its rights." See Mary C. Wilson, "The Hashemites, the Arab Revolt, and Arab Nationalism," in Khalidi, et al., *The Origins of Arab Nationalism*, p. 212.

[78] Khayriya Qasmiyya, *Al-Hukuma al-'Arabiya fi Dimashq, 1918–1920* (The Arab government in Damascus, 1918–1920) (Cairo: Dar al-Ma'arif bi Misr, 1971), p. 107.

[79] C. Ernest Dawn, "The Amir of Mecca al-Husayn ibn 'Ali and the Origins of the Arab Revolt," in Dawn, *From Ottomanism to Arabism*, pp. 1–53.

[80] Karsh and Karsh, "Reflections on Arab Nationalism," and Efraim and Inari Karsh, "Myth in the Desert, Or Not the Great Arab Revolt," *Middle Eastern Studies*, vol. 33, no. 3 (July 1997). The main arguments of these articles later appeared in the authors' book,

ish documents of the period, especially Foreign Office dispatches and intelligence reports, the Karshes paint a picture of, if anything, a prevailing mood of apathy directed against the person of the sharif as well as against the general notion of a revolt spurred by a commitment to the extrication of the "Arab nation" from under the hegemony of the Turks.

The Karshes argue that not even in his own backyard, al-Hejaz, did the sharif receive universal or overwhelming support. Medina, and perhaps less so Taif, seem to have been more inclined to the Turks than to the man who crowned himself "King of the Arab Countries," and later accepted the British and French designation, King of al-Hejaz. Even in his own seat of power, his hometown of Mecca, things were not that rosy. A British intelligence report, dated December 1916, a full six months after the sharif proclaimed the revolt, found the people of Mecca "almost pro-Turk."[81]

The tribes, individualistic and divided, had posed a special challenge for the sharif. Here again, the Karshes energetically question the account by George Antonius. According to Antonius, the sharif's savviest son, Faysal, tried to convert the tribes to the sharifian cause through the "three levers—gold, influence, and a message."[82] But Antonius holds that while money and influence were important levers, it was the message, "the gospel of Arab emancipation" that would "fire the minds of the tribes." He continues:

> ... the gospel which Faysal preached found ears attuned to its music. By his own faith sustained, he worked indefatigably, month after month, until the barriers were removed, the reconciliations effected, and the inveterate enemies of several generations, inflicted with his faith, had taken an oath to serve as brothers in arms under him for the liberation of all Arabs, and to hold independence dearer than family, property or life itself.[83]

Empires of the Sand: The Struggle for Mastery in the Middle East, 1789–1923 (Cambridge, Massachusetts: Harvard University Press, 1999), especially pp. 171–243.

[81] Quoted in Karsh and Karsh, "Reflections on Arab Nationalism," p. 376.

[82] Antonius, *The Arab Awakening*, p. 219.

[83] Ibid., p. 220.

And indeed, it is this view that most Arabs held for most of the twentieth century. The Karshes hold it to be a romanticized fantasy of a reality that was vastly different. To them, it was "the glitter of British gold and the promise of ample bounty that rallied the Hejaz bedouins behind the Sharif."[84] Tribal chiefs would negotiate endlessly over remunerations until military operations were delayed, and once paid, many would withdraw from the sharif's war. If they felt any duty or commitment, it was to the British monetary coinage. "In this part of the world," observed a British military advisor to the sharifian army, "gold is now so plentiful that the British sovereign may almost be said to be the unit of coinage."[85] And according to T. E. Lawrence, himself a great sympathizer with the sharifian cause, it was the availability of British gold that allowed Faysal to buy off the tribes, for "nothing else would have maintained a nomad force for five months in the field."[86] Contrary to the idealized account of Antonius, British money seems to have been a far more potent weapon in bringing the tribes to the sharifian cause than Faysal's "message" of Arab emancipation from Turkish rule.

Other parts of the Arabic-speaking lands of the Ottoman Empire exhibited a similar lack of enthusiasm for the revolt. After all, no fewer than 300,000 Arabs fought in the Ottoman army during the war.[87] Egypt's response to the sharif's revolt was avowedly hostile. The Egyptian newspaper, al-Ahram, rhetorically asked whether the revolt was really a nationalist appeal, and its answer was an emphatic no, for "the Turkish people as a whole have not tried to deprive other races from their birthright."[88] Antonius, himself, concedes this antipathy within Egypt, describing it as "real and scarcely veiled [deriving] its strength from anti-British as much as from pro-Turkish sentiment."[89] But Antonius is more charitable to the Syrians and Iraqis who, he claims, responded to the sharifian

[84] Karsh and Karsh, "Reflections on Arab Nationalism," p. 376.
[85] Karsh and Karsh, Empires of the Sand, p. 191.
[86] Karsh and Karsh, "Reflections on Arab Nationalism," p. 376.
[87] Ibid., p. 374.
[88] Karsh and Karsh, Empires of the Sand, p. 187.
[89] Antonius, The Arab Awakening, p. 207.

revolt with "universal enthusiasm."[90] Later historical studies, however, do not support such a sweeping contention. Hasan Kayali,
for instance, maintains that the preponderance of localist and Otto-
manist attitudes resulted in Syrian "ambivalence about Sharif Husayn's revolt."[91] Philip Khoury goes even further. He argues that
Syria's urban notables, constituting the political leadership, not
only did not embrace the revolt, but actually saw it as a treasonous
act.[92] As we have seen, Faysal, the sharif's son, conceded that Muslims generally blamed his family "for destroying the Islamic (Ottoman) empire."[93] No wonder then that as late as 1918, when the
tide of war was clearly turning against the Ottomans, Lawrence in
a secret dispatch to London would write that a spontaneous anti-
Ottoman rebellion in Syria was "an impossibility."[94]

Nor was the sentiment any different in Palestine. Two full years
after the beginning of the sharifian revolt, a British report stated
that the Muslims of Palestine took little interest in the Arab national movement, and in fact were as hostile to it as the Egyptians
in Cairo and Alexandria.[95] Colonel Richard Meinertzhagen, director of intelligence in the Egyptian Expeditionary Force, relates an
incident that speaks volumes about prevailing attitudes in Palestine
at the time. In December 1917, a full eighteen months after the
sharif's declaration of his revolt, British forces entered the Palestinian town of Ramleh, a few miles south of Jaffa.

> A large batch of Turkish prisoners were being marched through the
> village but they were not preceded by their British guard. The Arabs,
> thinking that it was the return of the Turkish army, turned out in
> force, yelling with delight and waving Turkish flags; it was not till
> the end of the column appeared and they saw the British soldiers
> with fixed bayonets that they realized their mistake, and great was

[90] Ibid.

[91] Kayali, *Arabs and Young Turks*, p. 212.

[92] Khoury, *Urban Notables and Arab Nationalism*, p. 78.

[93] Qasmiyya, *Al-Hukuma al-'Arabiya fi Dimashq bayn 1918–1920* (The Arab government in Damascus, 1918–1920), p. 107.

[94] Kirk, "The Arab Awakening Reconsidered," p. 170.

[95] Karsh and Karsh, "Reflections on Arab Nationalism," p. 379.

their confusion. Their faces fell with a bump and they slunk discon-
solate to their hovels.[96]

As for the Iraqis of Mesopotamia, it certainly would be a gross
exaggeration to describe their reaction to the revolt, as Antonius
did, as universally enthusiastic. The majority of the population was
Shiite with little affinity for the Sunni sharif. Indeed, the Shiite
clergy were generally hostile to the sharif's alliance with the "English infidels against the Muslim Ottoman state."[97] Moreover, both
the tribal and urban political leaders, such as Seyyid Taleb, the
leading member of Basrah's notables, showed little inclination to
give way to the sharif. Indeed, Taleb had his own extensive contacts
with the British. He wanted to be the ruler, preferably, of Iraq, but
at a minimum of Basrah.[98] Nor did the thriving Christian and Jewish communities of Iraq find palatable their incorporation into a
Muslim-dominated kingdom ruled from Mecca. Indeed, the Iraqis
generally were so lukewarm to the sharif that the British "had great
difficulties in persuading Mesopotamian prisoners of war, detained
in India, to join the Sharif's revolt."[99] Notwithstanding Antonius's
claims, the people of Mesopotamia seem to have been no more
enthusiastic about the sharif than their counterparts in Egypt,
Syria, and Palestine.

The intellectual and scholarly debate regarding Antonius and his
claims about the genesis of the Arab nationalist movement did not
abate by the end of the twentieth century. But by then its focus had
shifted. It centered not on whether Antonius was right or wrong,
but on whether at least some of his judgments and conclusions
were valid.[100] On the whole, if a judgment on early Arab national-

[96] Quoted in Karsh and Karsh, *Empires of the Sand*, p. 189.

[97] 'Ali al-Wardi, *Lamahat Ijtima'iya min Tarikh al-'Iraq al-Hadith, al Jusi' al-Sadis, min'Am 1920 ila 'Am 1924* (Sociological aspects of modern Iraqi history, part six, 1920–1924) (London: Dar Kofan li al-Nashr, 1992), pp. 128–129.

[98] Wallach, *Desert Queen*, p. 236; also Karsh and Karsh, *Empires of the Sand*, pp. 174–177.

[99] Karsh and Karsh, "Reflections on Arab Nationalism," p. 378.

[100] See, for example, Hourani, "The Arab Awakening Forty Years Later"; Rashid Khalidi, "Arab Nationalism: Historical Problems in the Literature," *American Historical Review*, vol. 96, no. 5, (December 1991); Karsh and Karsh, "Reflections on Arab Nationalism";

ism is to be made, cumulative historical evidence seems to strongly
endorse Majid Khadduri's view:

> Before World War I . . . Arab nationalism scarcely aimed beyond
> the rehabilitation of the Arab race in a multinational empire. Some
> thinkers called for a restoration of the Arab empire, presumably
> implying that Arab political leadership should be separated from
> that of the Turks, but most Arabs were content to remain within
> the frame of the Ottoman unity, as long as their proper place was
> recognized by the Turkish rulers.[101]

As we have seen, the few thinkers who extolled the uniqueness
and many virtues of the "Arab nation," and most significantly its
racial and cultural separateness, were mainly Christians with
whom very few, if any, of the Muslim majority concurred. To the
Muslim thinkers, the concept of the "Arab nation," if they thought
about it at all, was completely subsumed within, and subservient
to, the vision of the Islamic *Umma*. And as with the secret and
public "Arab nationalist" societies, and even with the sharifian revolt, the vast majority of the Arab populations seemed detached
from, or at best lukewarm about, any activity that spelled separation from Istanbul.

The debate among the early nationalists as to whether the ethnically different Arabs should strive for political independence, or
whether they should eschew the ethnic and linguistic divide in favor
of Islamic solidarity and remain within the Ottoman framework
became irrelevant in the wake of the Ottoman defeat in World War
I and the consequent collapse of the Ottoman Empire. The Arabs
were now treading new and unfamiliar grounds that, in the words
of Albert Hourani, "faced everyone, and in particular the members
of the ruling elite, with an inescapable choice."[102] It was thus only
after the end of World War I that the "Arab nation" emerged as a

---

Liona Lukitz, "The Antonius Papers and *The Arab Awakening* Fifty Years On," *Middle
Eastern Studies*, vol. 30, no. 4 (October 1994).

[101] Khadduri, *Political Trends in the Arab World*, p. 19.

[102] Hourani, "The Arab Awakening Forty Years After," p. 203.

pertinent concept,[103] and Arab nationalism gradually took form as a political movement.

Beyond the collapse of the Ottoman Empire, Arab participation in World War I on the side of the British yielded a number of benefits for the Arab national movement. At a minimum, it allowed Arab leaders to take part in the post-World War I political debates over the future of the Middle East. Less tangible, but just as crucial, was its psychological impact. Later generations of determined nationalists would magnify, even mythologize, the Arab military contribution in their efforts to gain and inspire adherents. Most important, the Arab involvement in the war led to the creation, with British help, of an Arab government in Syria.

The Ottomans had suffered major military setbacks in 1917, opening the way for British forces under the command of General Allenby to move into Palestine from Egypt, capturing Jerusalem in December of that year. Arab forces led by Emir Faysal, Sharif Husayn's son, paralleled Allenby's effort. Encouraged by British Liaison officers, particularly Captain T. E. Lawrence, Faysal's tribal forces moved from al-Hejaz to capture Aqaba, then continued northward along Allenby's right flank. Focusing primarily on disrupting Ottoman communications and supply lines, Faysal was able to lead his troops into Damascus on October 1, 1918. He set out immediately to form an Arab administration.

Herein was a real opportunity for the idea of Arab nationalism to be institutionalized, for it found a compelling and emphatic spokesman in the person of Faysal. Needing to bestow legitimacy on his rule, which he thought could be tarnished by his Hejazi origins,[104] he vigorously extolled the virtues of the larger Arab identity. He reminded the citizens of Syria that he and they belonged to the same people, the Arabs, who lived in "the region which is bounded by the sea in the east, the south, and the west,

---

[103] Ghassan Salame, *Al-Siyasa al-Kharijiya al-Sa'udia mundhu 'Am 1930* (Saudi foreign policy since 1930) (Beirut: Ma'had al-Inma'i al-, p. 207.

[104] 'See Qasmiyya, *Al-Hukuma al-'Arabiya fi Dimashq Bein 1918–1920* (The Arab government in Damascus, 1918–1920), p. 107.

and by the Taurus mountains to the south."[105] Time and time again
he would extol the Arabs' social unity, belittling the notion that
the Arabs of the desert were somehow distinct from the Arabs of
the cities. He would place loyalty to the "Arab nation" above all
loyalties, even above allegiance to religious beliefs. "The Arabs,"
he declared in a speech in Aleppo, "were Arabs before Moses,
Christ and Muhamed."[106] Indeed, Muhamed was an "Arab before
being a prophet."[107]

These ideas were put into operation by the national government.[108] The government's policies were consciously and purposely
nationalist and secularist. A number of Christians joined Faysal's
administration, participating actively in the country's politics.
Along with their Muslim colleagues, they generally were nationalists who believed in cementing Syria's Arab nationalist identity.
Echoing the European nationalists' emphasis on education, they
set out to reform the educational system with the purpose of infus-
ing future generations with the nationalist spirit. The man who
spearheaded this effort was Sati' al-Husri, an ex-Ottoman official
of Syrian descent, who had been appointed by Faysal to be his
minister of education. Husri embarked on a wholesale Arabization
of the Syrian school system. Textbooks were translated into Arabic,
historical and social studies were expected to reflect Arab nationalist concerns, and an Arab academy was established to find Arabic
terms for scientific and technological use.

The tenure of Faysal's Arab government was, however, too
short-lived for these reforms to make themselves felt throughout
the country. The 1916 Sykes-Picot agreement had parceled off the
Arab Middle East into British and French zones of influence, an
arrangement confirmed and given legal status at the San Remo
Conference of April 1920, which granted France mandatory powers over Syria. A month earlier, however, a Syrian congress had

[105] Haim, *Arab Nationalism: An Anthology*, p. 35.
[106] Suleiman al-Madani, *Ha'ula'. . .Hakamu Suriya, 1918–1970* (Those who ruled Syria,
1918–1970) (Damascus: Dar al Anwar, 1996), p. 26.
[107] Haim, *Arab Nationalism: An Anthology*, p. 35.
[108] This paragraph draws its information from Tabitha Petran, *Syria* (New York: Praeger
Publishers, 1972), pp. 57–60.

proclaimed the independence of Greater Syria (including Lebanon and Palestine) with Faysal as its king. France, considering this action to be a usurpation of its rights, issued an ultimatum demanding that Faysal accept the French mandate and recognize French control over the country. Faysal had little alternative but to succumb. His acceptance of French conditions however did not reach the French High Command by the specified time. (Some suspect that it was deliberately disregarded by the French). General Henri Gouraud, commander of the French forces in the Levant, immediately marched his forces toward Damascus. A small Arab force, disorganized and poorly equipped, under the command of Faysal's Minister of Defense Yousif al-'Azma, blocked the path of the advancing French at the Maisalun Pass. The Arab units were utterly outnumbered and outgunned by the advancing French. They were soon summarily defeated, and in the process, 'Azma was killed. Damascus was duly occupied on July 24, 1920, and Faysal was forced into exile. The French then proceeded to divide the country into four separate districts, Greater Lebanon, Aleppo, Latakia, and Damascus, a politico-administrative arrangement that persisted until World War II.

Short-lived and at times chaotic and inefficient, the Arab national government, nevertheless, was the first actual realization of the ideals of Arab nationalism. The purposeful efforts of the government to publicly carry the Arab nationalist torch and consciously endeavor to instill its sparks in the hearts and minds of the Syrian population would become the blueprint for later nationalist thinkers and activists. And 'Azma's "martyrdom" for the nationalist cause would remain imprinted on the collective consciousness of successive nationalist generations. Told and retold, the tale gained in myth and heroic proportions to become the nationalist staple for Syrian youth.

Yet here again, as with the circumstances relating to the 1916 "Great Arab Revolt," the Arab nationalist character of the Syrian state had been exaggerated in nationalist discourse. It is thus important not to overstate the inroads that Arab nationalism had made into the political consciousness of the Syrian people under

Faysal's government. While the Syrian population on the whole welcomed the use of Arabic as opposed to Turkish or French, and while many seemed to accept the notion of linguistic and religious proximity with other Arabic-speaking peoples, they were still intellectually very distant from Faysal and his nationalist cadres in their understanding of, and susceptibility to, the Arab nationalist project. The political and social structures of post-World War I Syria created immense cultural and political obstacles to the realization of Arab nationalist aspirations.

There were to begin with a host of other identities that competed with, and in many instances proved to be stronger than, the Arab nationalist identity. There were strong regional sensitivities that separated Damascus from other parts of Syria. Indeed the rivalry, even mistrust, that existed between Damascus and Aleppo was legendary. There were deeply ingrained clannish and tribal loyalties that did not necessarily coincide with the wider national interests of Faysal's government. Many in the influential Christian community in Lebanon worked in tandem with the French to frustrate Arab nationalist goals that they considered to be merely a camouflage for Muslim domination. Indeed, the vast majority of the Christian Maronites of Lebanon were vehemently opposed even to an independent Syrian state.[109] Even in Damascus, the politically and economically influential al-A'yan (the class of urban notables made up of wealthy landowners and merchants) eyed their own privileged interests far more zealously than any notion of Arabism.[110] Indeed, even though the battle of Maisalun was bravely fought by the Arab army, the Arab defeat at the hands of the French had been attributed not only to French superiority, but also to Syrian divisions and dissensions that were the hallmark of an inade-

---

[109] Zeine Nur al-Din Zeine, *Al-Sira' al-Duwaly fi al-Sharq al-Awsat wa Wiladat Dawlatai Suriya wa Lubnan* (The international struggle in the Middle East and the birth of the two states of Syria and Lebanon) (Beirut: Dar al-Nahar li al-Nashr, 1977), pp. 153–155.

[110] On the general connection between the political orientations of the A'ayan and their socioeconomic situation, see Walid Kazziha, "Al-Qawmiya al-'Arabiya fi Marhalat ma bien al-Harbayn al-'Alamiyatayn,"(Arab nationalism in the period between the two world wars), *al-Mustaqbal al-'Arabi*, no. 5 (January 1979).

quate sense of national identity.[111] A promise to Faysal of 10,000 fully armed men by a tribal leader never materialized. Bands of men from various Syrian clans fought with the French, attacking the right and left flanks of the Arab army, as well as its rear, which allowed the French army to concentrate on the middle core. A number of *al-A'yan* from Damascus cut the telegraph lines between Maisalun and the capital, leaving the nationalist circles in Damascus without news of the battle. And when the victorious French army arrived in Damascus, the same *al-A'yan*, accompanied by prominent religious leaders, received the French as conquerors.[112]

Moreover, even among the nationalist circles, the concept of nationalism was perhaps more likely to refer to "Syrian" rather than "Arab" nationalism. Faysal seems to have quickly grasped this, since in a memorandum submitted to the Paris Peace Conference in January 1919, he advocated different solutions for the various parts of the Arab world, including some form of sovereignty for Syria.[113] And, when later in the year he negotiated on behalf of his father with the Europeans for a more encompassing Arab kingdom, some of Syria's political elites decided to open their own independent channel to the British asking only for Syrian administrative rule.[114] The British must have leaked these Syrian unofficial contacts to Faysal, since on his return to Damascus, he quickly and publicly proclaimed that he had told the European powers that the Syrians desired independence for their own country, and that Syria should be considered autonomous from the rest of the Arab world.

The most visible manifestation of the primacy of Syrian over Arab identity among the Syrians was in the way Faysal's trusted Iraqi commanders and confidants were perceived and treated in

---

[111] See, for example, Naji Abd al-Nabi Bazzi, *Suriya: Sira' al-Istiqtab; Dirasa wa Tahlil li Ahdath al-Sharq al-Awsat wa al-tadakhulat al-Duwaliya fi al-Ahdath al-Suriya, 1917–1973* (Syria: the struggle of polarization; a study and analysis of Middle Eastern affairs and international affairs, 1917–1973) (Damascus: Dar Ibn al-'Arabi, 1996), pp. 78–84; see also Malcolm B. Russell, *The First Modern Arab State: Syria under Faysal, 1918–1920* (Minneapolis: Bibliotheca Islamica, 1985), p. 174.

[112] Bazzi, *Suriya: Sira' al-Istiqtab* (Syria: the struggle of polarization), pp. 82–83.

[113] Karsh and Karsh, *Empires of the Sand*, p. 275.

[114] Muhamed Ismat Sheikho, *Suriya wa Qadhiyat Falasteen, 1920–1949* (Syria and the issue of Palestine, 1920–1949) (Damascus: Dar Qutayba, 1982), pp. 67–69.

Syria. Iraqi ex-Ottoman officers had formed the backbone of the officer corps of Faysal's northern army that marched into Damascus in October 1918, and consequently ended up claiming high-ranking positions in the new Syrian government and army, hence the first commander of the newly formed Syrian army was the Iraqi, Yassin al-Hashimi. Syrian officers, who had served in the Ottoman army returned to Syria after the Ottoman defeat to discover that many senior positions were occupied by Iraqis. There was little sense of "Arab nationalism," even of "Arabism," in the Syrian response. They complained bitterly that they "had become strangers in their own country."[115] Indeed by 1919, such headlines as "Syria for the Syrians" began to appear in the Syrian press. Anti-Iraqi organizations, such as al-Shabiba al-Suriya (the Syrian Youth) and Hizb al-Watani al-Suri (the Syrian National Party), were founded, the main purpose of which was to "protect Syrian rights against the non-Syrian 'strangers.' "[116] Anti-Iraqi propaganda spread throughout the Syrian cities to such an extent that a number of prominent Iraqis were compelled to go to Faysal and complain that they felt like "unwanted foreigners."[117] A British officer relates a conversation in August 1919 which he had with Nuri al-Sai'd, one of the high-ranking Iraqi officers, who later was to follow Faysal into Iraq and become that country's most powerful politician:

> Over drinks that evening, Nuri al Said startled me by going off into a long tirade damning the Syrians and all their works. Things were undoubtedly going awry. The trouble arose, in part, from a sort of parochialism. Having supported, in principle, the ideal of a revival of the Arabs as a single nation, it was not long after their liberation that the Syrians resented being ordered about by Hejazis and Iraqis.[118]

[115] Eliezer Tauber, *The Formation of Modern Syria and Iraq* (London: Frank Cass, 1995), p. 174.

[116] Muhammad Muslih, "The Rise of Local Nationalisms in the Arab East," in Khalidi, et al., *The Origins of Arab Nationalism*, p. 174.

[117] Tauber, *The Formation of Modern Syria and Iraq*, p. 176. See also Karsh and Karsh, *Empires of the Sand*, p. 282.

[118] Quoted in Tauber, *The Formation of Modern Syria and Iraq*, p. 175.

It was not that the Syrians had no sense of an Arab identity; it was just that local and regional attachments were more potent, and were likely to be the citizen's first point of reference. Nevertheless, the short-lived Faysal government in Damascus was able to undertake the first institutionally organized program to promote Arabist values and sentiment. These early small steps would lay the foundation for the giant strides that Arab nationalism would take a few decades later.

Faysal's loss of office was as brief as his reign in Syria. Eleven months after his expulsion from Syria, Faysal arrived in Iraq to be crowned, two months later, in August 1921, the King of Iraq under British mandate. The British had assembled the country from three provinces of the defunct Ottoman Empire: Baghdad, Mosul, and Basrah. The assembled state had little ethnic or religious rationale.[119] Basrah and the south were overwhelmingly Shiite; Baghdad and the central part were primarily Sunni; and Mosul and the north contained substantial non-Arab populations, the most important of which were the Kurds. Exacerbating these ethnic and sectarian divisions was a vast cultural divide between city and tribe. These schisms made it impossible for a local leader to emerge and be accepted by the population as a whole. The British, therefore, were delighted at the unexpected availability of Faysal.[120] They believed that Faysal's Arab stature would make him acceptable to the Iraqis, or at the very least minimize opposition to him. More to the point perhaps, the British believed that Faysal's experience with the French in Syria, and his malleable, even pliable, character, would make him adopt a pragmatic and nonconfrontational posture to British interests and position in Iraq.

It was in the infant state of Iraq that a coherent theory of Arab nationalism was first launched, then promoted and developed through an extensive national education program. The man re-

---

[119] Adeed Dawisha, "The Assembled State: Communal Conflicts and Governmental Control in Iraq," in *Ethnic Conflict and International Politics in the Middle East,* ed. Leonard Binder (Gainesville: University Press of Florida, 1999), p. 61.

[120] Phebe Marr, *The Modern History of Iraq* (Boulder, Colorado: Westview Press, 1985), p. 36.

sponsible for the effort was Faysal's minister of education in Syria, Sati' al-Husri, who had followed his patron to Iraq. It was Husri who, through numerous lectures in Iraq and in other Arab cities, gave the concept of "Arab nationalism" intellectual coherence and sophistication.[121] He was also responsible for creating an educational infrastructure, the main purpose of which was to disseminate Arab nationalist ideas and sentiment into the consciousness of future Arab generations.

[121] The best English-language accounts of the life and thoughts of Sati' al-Husri can be found in William L. Cleveland, *The Making of an Arab Nationalist: Ottomanism and Arabism in the Life and Thought of Sati' al-Husri* (Princeton, New Jersey: Princeton University Press, 1971) and in Bassam Tibi, *Arab Nationalism: A Critical Enquiry* (New York: St. Martin's Press, 1981), Parts III and IV.

CHAPTER THREE

SATI' AL-HUSRI'S THEORY OF
ARAB NATIONALISM

Sati' al-Husri was born in Yemen in 1882 into a Syrian Muslim family, but spent his formative years in Constantinople. He learned Turkish and French before he studied Arabic, and until the end of his life this intellectual prophet of Arab nationalism would speak Arabic with a slight Turkish accent. He went on to study in Europe where he was exposed to the competing intellectual strands of European nationalism. On his return, he joined the Ottoman bureaucracy, where he eventually held senior posts in the Balkan provinces of the empire at a time when the national, anti-Ottoman movements in these provinces were gathering momentum. The Balkan experience provided him with much food for thought, and later in his enunciations on Arab nationalism, he would refer time and again to the experiences of various Balkan countries as they strove for national independence. During World War I, Istanbul sent him to Syria as the director general of education. He held high-ranking and influential portfolios in the sector of education during Faysal's reign in Syria and in Iraq. Due partly to his voluminous writings and extensive teaching and lecturing, and partly to the immense influence he wielded on the educational system in Iraq's first two decades, Husri was able to make nationalist ideas the central thrust of the country's educational and cultural policies. Echoing Fichte's belief that only through education could a nation be reborn, Husri sought to inculcate into the people, especially the young, a clear and durable sense of Arab national identity that would supercede other prevalent identities, such as tribalism, regionalism, and sectarianism. He saw his mission as promoting national consciousness through the creation of national educational systems.

In the development of the concept of Arab nationalism, there is little doubt that Sati' al-Husri, both as thinker and educator, takes pride of place.[1] Albert Hourani finds in Husri's writings "a pure theory of nationalism with all its assumptions clearly understood and accepted, all its problems faced."[2] To Majid Khadduri, Husri developed "more clearly and consistently than any other writer a systematic and coherent theory of Arab nationalism,"[3] Sylvia Haim describes him as "the man who did most to popularize the idea of nationalism among the literate classes of the Arab Middle East . . ."[4], and to Aziz al-Azmeh, Husri was the Arab thinker who formulated "the most important statements of Arab nationalism."[5] Writing in the mid-1980s, the Iraqi political scientist, Wamidh Jamal 'Umar Nadhmi quotes approvingly a statement contending that Husri's nationalist ideas continue to dominate the thinking of contemporary generations.[6] These sentiments are echoed enthusi-

---

[1] Israel Gershoni, "Rethinking the Formation of Arab Nationalism in the Middle East, 1920–1945: Old and New Narratives," in *Rethinking Nationalism in the Middle East*, eds. James Jankowski and Israel Gershoni (New York: Columbia University Press, 1997), pp. 6–7.

[2] Albert Hourani, *Arabic Thought in the Liberal Age, 1798–1939* (London: Oxford University Press, 1970), p. 312.

[3] Majid Khadduri, *Political Trends in the Arab World: The Role of Ideas and Ideals in Politics* (Baltimore: Johns Hopkins Press, 1970), p. 199.

[4] Sylvia Haim, ed., *Arab Nationalism: An Anthology* (Berkeley: University of California Press, 1962), pp. 42–43.

[5] Aziz al-Azmeh, "Nationalism and the Arabs," in *Arab Nation, Arab Nationalism*, ed. Derek Hopwood. (New York: St. Martin's Press, 2000), p. 69.

[6] Wamidh Jamal 'Umar Nadhmi, "Fikr Sati' al-Husri al-Qawmi (The nationalist thought of Sati' al-Husri), *al-Mustaqbal al-'Arabi*, no. 81 (November 1985): 148.

astically by the Syrian political scientist, Walid Kazziha.[7] It is not that Husri was the only Arab nationalist thinker, but in the clarity of his vision, in the single-mindedness of his advocacy of this vision, and in the immense influence that his ideas exerted on the thinking of successive Arab generations, Husri has no equal.

Like other twentieth century nationalisms, Arab nationalism, as formulated by Husri (and by other nationalist thinkers such as Qustantin Zurayq, Edmond Rabath, Zaki al-Arsuzi, Michel Aflaq, etc.), was based on the intellectual tenets of European ideas on the subject. This statement, admittedly, would have been assailed mercilessly by Arab nationalists during the peak of the Arab nationalist movement in the 1950s and 1960s. These nationalists held jealously to the notion that their nationalism was intellectually "authentic." By the end of the century, however, few would contest the statement's historical validity. Indeed, with the decline of Arab nationalism and the resurgence of Islamic fundamentalism, nationalism was being increasingly depicted unkindly as one of the failed imported Western solutions (*al-hulul al-mustawrada*), or more vehemently as Western perfidy designed to divide the Muslims and turn them against one another.[8] Even those Arab writers who argue that the Arabs had in fact constituted a nation over a long period of time now accept that as concepts, *nation* and *nationalism* originated in the West.[9]

From its Latin origin, *natio*, which the Romans pejoratively used to depict foreigners of lesser social status than Roman citizens, to

[7] Walid Kazziha, "Al-Qawmiya al-'Arabiya fi Marhalat ma bein al-Harbayn al-'Alamiyatayn," (Arab nationalism in the period between the two world wars), *al-Mustaqbal al-'Arabi*, no. 5 (January 1979): 60.

[8] Yusuf al-Qardawi, *al-Hulul al-Mustawrada wa Kaifa Janat 'ala Ummatina* (The imported solutions and how they harmed our nation) (Cairo: Maktabat Wahbeh, 1977); see also Shukri B. Abed, "Islam and Democracy," in *Democracy, War and Peace in the Middle East*, eds. David Grantham and Mark Tessler. (Bloomington: Indiana University Press, 1995), pp. 124–126; Bassam Tibi, *Arab Nationalism: A Critical Enquiry* (New York: St. Martin's Press, 1990), p. 10; and Bernard Lewis, *The Multiple Identities of the Middle East* (New York: Scribner, 1998), p. 24.

[9] See, for example, Nadhmi, "Fikr Sati' al-Husri al-Qawmi" (The nationalist thought of Sati' al-Husri), pp. 148–166.

its grandiose use in Europe after the sixteenth century as the ultimate object of peoples' loyalty, the intellectual development of the
concept of the nation mirrored the political contours of European
history.[10] By the middle of the nineteenth century, these nationalist
ideas were clustered into two main intellectual strands.[11] On the
one hand, English and French philosophers could not conceive of
the *nation* without its political corollary, the *state*. Indeed, they
tended to see the nation almost as a creation of the state—that
nations do not develop arbitrarily, but emerge over time molded
and shaped, even though sometimes scarred, by political factors
that are the domain of the state.

The other concept of the nation, essentially German, was completely different. In this thinking, nations were not political
constructs, but *cultural* creations. As such, they predate the state,
their beginnings implanted in a remote, even immemorial, past in
the form of an original tribe or an original linguistic community.
The spirit of the nation is thus maintained over time even in the
face of harsh political realities, and even if its members at times
are not conscious of it. A German is what he is regardless of the
political authority under which he conducts his social and commercial affairs. Indeed, he is a German even if he professes to be
something else.

It is important to explore these two conceptions of the *nation*
in somewhat greater detail[12] since, as we shall see later on, they
represented the two alternative models to the emergent generations of Arab intellectuals, among whom Sati' al-Husri was at the
helm, who found themselves faced with the rapid decline of the
Ottoman Empire and the consequent prospect of independence
and sovereignty.

[10] Liah Greenfeld, *Nationalism: Five Roads to Modernity* (Cambridge, Massachusetts:
Harvard University Press, 1992), pp. 4–9.

[11] See Rogers Brubaker, *Citizenship and Nationhood in France and Germany* (Cambridge, Massachusetts: Harvard University Press, 1992); Hans Kohn, *Prelude to Nation-
States: The French and German Experience, 1789–1815* (London: D. Van Nostrand Company, Inc., 1967).

[12] The following analysis detailing the historical development and philosophical arguments of the two schools draws heavily on parts of Adeed Dawisha, "Nation and National-

It should not come as much of a surprise to learn that to English and French thinkers the concept of a *nation* was tied first and foremost to the notion of *state* and *government*. To begin with, neither the English nor the French could claim to historically have been ethnic and/or linguistic homogeneities. Prior to the Roman conquest, England had been invaded by Celts and Danes and later by a variety of Germanic peoples until the French Normans literally colonized the country. Not only is the English "race" patently mixed, but English as a language emerged from the linguistic influences of the various peoples who had invaded and settled the country.

Similarly, contemporary France, with its French-speaking population, historically had comprised a number of separate languages, such as Basque, Breton, and Provençal.[13] The multiplicity of languages represents an ethnic mix that also includes Vikings, Belgians, Germans, Gauls, and Catalans. The Hundred Years' War (1337–1453) added English, Scot, and Irish to the mix.

While England and France could not claim to have been homogeneous ethnic and linguistic entities, they certainly had existed for a long time as functioning political units. By the time of the accession to the English throne in 1485 of Henry VII, the first Tudor king, the allegiance of the entire country to the crown had been institutionalized.[14] Under the Tudors in the sixteenth century, England was ruled through an expanded bureaucratic structure that administered a uniform common law that ran through "the length and breadth of the realm."[15] Liah Greenfeld is categorical in locating the first nation: "The birth of the English nation was not the birth of a nation; it was the birth of the nations, the birth of nationalism. England is where the process originated; its analysis is essen-

---

ism: Historical Antecedents to Contemporary Debates," *International Studies Review*, vol. 4, no. 1 (Spring 2002).

[13] K. R. Minogue, *Nationalism* (New York: Basic Books, 1967), p. 43.

[14] M. L. Bush, *Renaissance, Reformation and the Outer World* (New York: Humanities Press, 1967), p. 74.

[15] Ibid., p. 79. For a detailed discussion of the growth and development of England's common law under Henry VII and the succeeding Tudors, consult G. R. Elton, *England Under the Tudors*, 2nd ed. (London: Methuen, 1974).

tial for the understanding of the nature of the original idea of the nation, the conditions for its development, and its social uses."[16] It is thus difficult to delve into English history and not see the pivotal role of the English state in molding the English nation.

In France, the process of unifying the country was begun in the fifteenth century under Louis XI with the progressive weakening of the great aristocratic and princely houses. By the time of his death in 1483, the houses of Burgundy and Anjou had reverted to the crown, and before the end of the century, the fiefs of Orleans and Brittany had followed suit. This process culminated almost a century later with the accession to the throne of Henry IV, the Bourbon prince. Henry was assassinated in 1610, but not before he had created a strong and unified French state, accepting of monarchical authority, and well on the way to healing the deep national wounds of the French religious wars. The strength of the French state was further cemented throughout the seventeenth century by Louis XIII and Louis XIV,[17] two strong kings, supported by able ministers committed to the predominance of the central authority, as it was symbolized by monarchical absolutism, over the centrifugal interests of nobles and princes.

Given this historical legacy, it is hardly surprising that the congruence of *state* and *nation* was particularly manifest in the ideas of the English and French philosophers and historians of the eighteenth and nineteenth centuries. Ernest Renan, France's eminent nineteenth century historian saw the role of the French monarch as indispensable to the creation of the French nation. In his celebrated essay, "What is a Nation?", Renan asserts that the French nation was created by "the King of France, partly through his tyranny, partly through his justice."[18] This merging of *state* and *nation* is

[16] Greenfeld, *Nationalism*, p. 23.

[17] For the national development of France under the Bourbons, consult A. Lloyd Moote, *Louis XIII, The Just* (Berkeley: California University Press, 1989); W. E. Brown, *The First Bourbon Century in France* (London: University of London Press, 1971); Vincent Buranelli, *Louis XIV* (New York: Twayne Publishers, Inc., 1966); Maurice Ashley, *The Golden Century: Europe 1598–1715* (New York: Frederick A. Praeger, 1969).

[18] Ernest Renan, "What is a Nation?", in *Nation and Narration*, ed. Homi K. Bhabha (London: Routledge, 1990), p. 11.

evident in Rousseau's writings, in which he uses *nation* and *patrie* interchangeably.[19] To Rousseau, people did indeed come to speak different languages and to have different customs as a result of their varying developments, but they lacked any self-consciousness about their unity. It is government and the system of laws that creates this necessary sense of national unity, this notion of *citizenry*.

The English philosophers were no less adamant in connecting the nation to the state. Edmund Burke, in his *Reflections on the Revolution in France*, for instance, enjoins people to "approach to the faults of the state as to the wounds of a father, with pious awe and trembling solicitude." And why such an intimate relationship? Because a state is "a partnership [among] those who are living, those who are dead, and those who are to be born. Each contract of each particular state is but a clause in the great primeval contract of eternal society."[20] What more vigorous and unequivocal way to subsume the concept of the nation into that of the state.

Other English philosophers, such as Lock, Bentham, and Mill thought of the nation and state as almost symbiotically tied through the knot of liberty, which is unquestionably a concept of politics. Indeed, John Stuart Mill, was to identify "the principle of nationality as a clause of liberalism itself."[21] The liberty of the individual and their absolute right to choose a government is indicative of the English proclivity to think of the nation less in cultural terms and more in political terms, and to tie the nation firmly into the political sphere.

In this construct, the notions of "the consent of the people," and their "free will" are essential in the definition of a nation. Two conclusions emerge. First, affiliation to the nation cannot be forced

[19] Minogue, *Nationalism*, p. 41.

[20] Edmund Burke, *Reflections on the Revolution in France*, edited with an introduction and notes by J.G.A. Pocock (Indianapolis: Hackett Publishing Co., 1987), pp. 84–85. Burke was not strictly "English," as he was born in Dublin, Ireland. However, he moved to England at the age of twenty-one, and spent the rest of his life there. A Protestant (even though his mother was Catholic), he later entered parliament and became one of the institution's most avid defenders. So while "Irish" by virtue of his birth Burke's national attachment, as well as his political ideas, were singularly "English."

[21] Minogue, *Nationalism*, p. 134.

on any individual or group, and second, there is nothing that is predetermined or preordained about the concept; nothing that is necessarily permanent. Based on the "will of the people," a nation is a malleable thing that exists so long as the people want it to. A nation "is a large-scale solidarity," Renan writes in his "What is a Nation?" He continues: "It presupposes a past; it is summarized, however, in the present by a tangible fact, namely, consent, the clearly expressed desire to continue a common life."[22] In an often quoted metaphor, Renan characterizes the nation as a "daily plebiscite." Accordingly, the nation can grow through the absorption of new groups, or it can shrink because of secession. Indeed, Renan entertains the visionary idea that the various European nations might at some point in the future join into a single entity.[23] In the Anglo-French intellectual tradition, the nation is conceived as almost dependent on the state, on its values and its institutions.

Measured against the Anglo-French structural and institutional argument was the conception of the nation as a cultural creation. In this view, nations are "not just political units but *organic* beings, living personalities, whose individuality must be cherished by their members in all their manifestations. The nation [is founded] not on "mere" consent or law but on passions implanted by nature and history."[24] This school of thought was proposed essentially by German writers and thinkers of the romantic school. Romanticism, a movement begun in the second half of the eighteenth century was primarily an intellectual rebellion against the "age of reason," against the principles and ideas of the French Enlightenment. To the romantics, it was not reason, or rational thought, but inner feelings, the exploits of the free spirit, that carved a path to the truth. Emotion was the prime motivator of humans, and should not be stifled by reason.

It was German thinkers who first incorporated the ideas of the romantic school into their formulation of cultural nationalism,

[22] Renan, *What is a Nation?*, p. 19.

[23] Tibi, *Arab Nationalism*, p. 150.

[24] John Hutchinson, *Dynamics of Cultural Nationalism: The Gaelic Revival and the Creation of the Irish Nation-State* (London: Allen and Unwin, 1989), p. 13.

whose central focus was the concept of the *volk*. Originally developed by Johann Gottfried Herder in late eighteenth century, the *volk* was "not simply the people of a country, but a metaphysical entity defined relationally as *that which* produces a particular language, art, culture, set of great men, religion and collection of customs. All of these things are taken, not as products of individual men but as *manifestations* of the spirit of the people, or *volksgeist*."[25] To the rationalist philosophers of the Enlightenment, *volksgeist* was of little value since humanity was invariable, transcending cultural differences, and therefore the ideas and principles derived from it were universally applicable, regardless of the variations in peoples' customs from one locality to another. Here lies the point of departure for Herder and the German romantic nationalists. To them, "people are always found in divided groups which have evolved a language and culture in response to their environment and which express their own national character. In the succession of generations, a people elaborates and develops that culture, and each individual man is what he is because *one or another culture has stamped itself upon him*."[26] (italics added) It is this formulation that shapes the intellectual underpinning for the notion of cultural nationalism. A nation is not a sociopolitical construct; it cannot be, since it resides through an immemorial past in the very being of its people, imposing on them a homogeneity and uniformity that separates them from other human groups. The nation is not created by the state; it creates the state.

It is not a coincidence of history that the great prophets of cultural nationalism turned out to be Germans. For unlike the English and French who, having experienced many centuries of statehood, could not but see the nation as symbiotically tied to the state, the Germans did not have a unified state until 1871. When Herder (1744–1803), the father of German nationalism, was expounding the central ideas of cultural nationalism, Germany was fragmented into almost two thousand separate territories. Some of

---

[25] Minogue, *Nationalism*, p. 57.
[26] Ibid., p. 58.

these were independent states, and, as in the case of Prussia, European powers. Most, however, were tiny and inconsequential domains. Indeed, it was not until 1871, in the wake of the French defeat at the hand of Prussia's Bismarck, that the Prussian-led North German Confederation, itself made up of many states, absorbed the other German states; the kingdoms of Bavaria, Saxony, and Württenberg; five grand duchies, thirteen duchies and principalities; and the free cities of Hamburg, Bremen, and Lubeck, to form the German state.

The absence of German statehood until nearly the last quarter of the nineteenth century is probably the best explanation for the German emphasis on the *volk* and *volksgeist*. With no unified state, what would the German writers, thinkers, and political agitators extol but the people, their ethnic and linguistic originality, and their excellence. While the English and French could readily point to their nations as defined by the unified state, the system of laws, and the long tradition of governance, the Germans' only available definition of their nation was the existence, as they saw it and vigorously preached it, of an original people, untouched by classical antiquity, representing the purest race, and speaking the purest language.[27]

The intellectual ferment reached its zenith in the aftermath of the Prussian defeat at the hands of Napoleon at Jenna in 1806. Whatever German institutions there were, these were dismantled by the victorious French. King Frederick William hastily left Berlin to live in exile in Königsberg, and a new system of administration, French in its conception, direction, and application, was introduced. The Prussian army had been emasculated. Resistance to the occupying French, therefore, could not come from the ruling and political elite, but from the people. The Prussians were especially aggrieved, because while Napoleon treated the South German states cordially, he saved his harshest treatment for the Prussians.[28]

[27] Kohn, *Prelude to Nation-States*, p. 255.

[28] Agatha Ramm, *Germany 1789–1919: A Political History* (London: Methuen, 1967), p. 69.

Johann Gottlieb Fichte (1762–1814), the nationalist thinker and activist, whose ideas proved instrumental in shaping the concept of the German nation, embarked on his nationalist odyssey in the wake of the war of 1806. Prior to that Fichte was a determined cosmopolitan, even a French sympathizer.[29] But the war with France changed all that. Faced with the postwar debris that was the Prussian state, Fichte would lay emphasis on the "eternal" nation. The nation, he wrote, "arises together out of the divine under a certain, special law of divine development." It is this law that, according to Fichte, "determines entirely . . . the national character of a people."[30] Fichte's nation is immemorial and sacred; of course it covets a territorial state as an expression of its political will, but it exists independently of the state.

Central to this endeavor is the spoken and written word. Language is at the very heart of national formation, since it is the medium through which national consciousness spreads. The European languages are a case in point. In medieval times, the predominance of the universal concept of Christendom was sustained by the status and prestige of Latin. But regional vernaculars were already beginning to compete with the "truth language." Through a fusion of Saxon dialects and Norman French, early English became the language of the courts in the fourteenth century, which paved the way for the magnificent sixteenth century flowering of English literature. The "English" Bible played a pivotal role in this process. Its mass impact in "strengthening a common language, installing in all its hearers and readers the idea of nationhood and actually shaping the English of all classes into an awareness of their own nationhood cannot be overstated."[31] Similarly, French became the official language when King François I issued the Ordinance of Villers-Cotteretts in 1539, and by the end of that century the majority of the written works were in French. The ref-

[29] Greenfeld, *Nationalism*, p. 362.

[30] Johann Gottlieb Fichte, "Addresses to the German Nation," in *The Nationalism Reader*, eds. Omar Dahour and Micheline R. Ishay (New York: Humanity Books, 1999), p. 64.

[31] Adrian Hastings, *The Construction of Nationhood: Ethnicity, Religion and Nationalism* (Cambridge, England: Cambridge University Press, 1997), p. 24.

ormation had a similar impact on German. "In the two decades 1520–1540, three times as many books were published in German as in the period 1500–1520, an astonishing transformation to which Luther was absolutely central."[32] These "regional" (as opposed to the "universal" Latin) languages became the most visible manifestations of separate identities,[33] making their "own contribution to the decline of the imagined community of Christendom."[34] Thus, the territorialization of Europe predicated not just on physical boundaries, but also on linguistic frontiers.

It should come as no surprise, therefore, that the German nationalist thinkers and writers would make language the knot that binds the nation together, and the thread that runs through their concept of cultural nationalism. Without a language, Herder argues, a nation cannot exist. This is because the "most brilliant idea remains a dark sensation until the soul finds a distinctive label, and embodies it through the word into memory, into recollection, into the mind, yes finally into the mind of man, into tradition."[35] Fichte goes even further: "Those who speak the same language are linked together, before human intervention takes a hand, by mere nature with a host of invisible ties; they understand each other and are capable of communicating more and more closely with one another, they belong together, they are by nature one indivisible whole."[36] Fichte's argument is steeped in social anthropology and its conclusion is self-evident: Since people disperse geographically over time, and divide into families, tribes, and nations, their languages become a reflection of their unique identities and of the circumstances that are peculiar to them. To the cultural nationalist, therefore, language was the expression of a nation's spirit, of its conscience.

[32] Benedict Anderson, *Imagined Communities: Reflections on the Origins and Spread of Nationalism* (New York: Verso, 1990), p. 39.

[33] See Anthony D. Smith, "The Nation: Invented, Imagined, Reconstructed," in *Reimagining the Nation*, eds. Marjorie Ringrose and Adam J. Lerner. (Buckingham, England: Open University Press, 1993), p. 18.

[34] Anderson, *Imagined Communities*, p. 42.

[35] Quoted in Tibi, *Arab Nationalism*, p. 129.

[36] Quoted in Minogue, *Nationalism*, p. 64.

The development of national consciousness is aided by another language-based medium: the writing of history. On this there is unanimous agreement among all nationalist thinkers be they of the Anglo-French school or of the German cultural tradition. It is history that constitutes the primary laboratory for the ardent nationalist. It is from the annals of history that tales of the heroism, great achievements, and unity of purpose of ancestors are resurrected and told and retold as evidence of the excellence of the nation's "immemorial past." "Ancestors have made us what we are," writes Ernest Renan. "A heroic past, great men, glory (I mean real glory): here is the social capital upon which to build a national ideology."[37] But in fact, it is not just the heroic interludes and the past glories that are the stuff of legend. Even simple stories of everyday life extracted from the history of a people—of hard work, of commitments fulfilled and hardships overcome, can become powerful psychological tools depicting the inner strength of a virtuous society.

The crucial point here is that this is not the history that is to be found in works of scholarship: the facts and figures recorded in an objective and detached manner for the purpose of serving some exalted scholarly purpose. It is rather "an appeal to gifted myth makers who could construct from the debris of the past a grand and glittering edifice to serve as a source of confidence and inspiration for the entire nation."[38] The history that the nationalist seeks is not an academic discipline; it is a political tool to be exploited and manipulated for national aims. This was particularly relevant to peoples (such as the Arabs of the twentieth century) whose achievements in the present or in the recent past had been less than laudatory. The need of Arab nationalists to re-create the real and mythical glories that resided in a distant period in their history would become all the more urgent.[39] In short, and in the telling

[37] Quoted in Lahouari Addi, "The Failure of Third World Nationalism," *Journal of Democracy*, vol. 8 (October 1997): 119.

[38] Paul Salem, *Bitter Legacy: Ideology and Politics in the Arab World* (New York: Syracuse University Press, 1994), p. 53.

[39] Hazem Zaki Nuseibeh, *The Ideas of Arab Nationalism* (London: Kennikat Press, 1972), p. 79; for this general phenomenon, see also Dankwart A. Rustow, *A World of Nations* (Washington D.C.: The Brookings Institution, 1967), pp. 41–47.

words of Elie Keddourie, "nationalists make use of the past in order to subvert the present."[40] This may sound somewhat ferocious, but in fact it is not at all far from the truth. In the Arab case, the way history was written and taught was a major concern of those who saw themselves as the guardians of the Arab nation and the custodians of its heritage.[41]

No wonder then that nationalists of all persuasions have emphasized, first and foremost, education. Jean Jacques Rousseau, himself a patriot who felt that while the French state was strong the sense of community among Frenchmen was weak, would focus on education as the primary means by which a sense of nationhood is instilled in the hearts and minds of the state's citizens. To Rousseau, it was the "test of education to give to each human being a national form, and so direct his opinions and tastes, that he should be a patriot by inclination, by passion, by necessity. On first opening his eyes, a child must see his country, and until he dies must see nothing else."[42] While Rousseau's ideas were the source of lively intellectual debate during his lifetime, it was the French revolution, less than two decades after Rousseau's death, that vigorously put his ideas into practice. The leaders of the French Revolution recognized from the very beginning the pivotal role education would play in uniting the people and the "fatherland." A comprehensive system of education, the first of its kind in Europe, was instituted for the purpose of creating patriotic citizenry, of turning "peasants into citizens."[43] The teaching of patriotic history replaced the classics, and the arts, especially music, were geared to arousing national pride and passion. Schools adopted an aggressive language curriculum where French was taught as the only national language

[40] Elie Keddouri, *Nationalism* (London: Hutchinson University Library, 1961), p. 75.

[41] See Kazziha, "al-Qawmiya al-'Arabiya fi Marhalat ma bein al-Harbayn al-'Alamiyatayn" (Arab nationalism in the period between the two world wars), p. 64.

[42] Quoted in Michael Howard, *The Lessons of History* (New Haven, Connecticut: Yale University Press, 1991), p. 145; see also Minogue, *Nationalism*, p. 41; also Ilya Prizel, *National Identity and Foreign Policy: Nationalism and Leadership in Poland, Russia, and Ukraine* (Cambridge, England: Cambridge University Press, 1998), p. 404.

[43] Eugene Weber, *Peasants into Frenchmen: The Modernization of Rural France, 1870–1914* (London: Chatto and Windus, 1979).

at the expense of the native idioms formerly taught among Basques, Bretons, Alsatians, Catalans, Flemish, and Provençeaux. Higher education received the same treatment,[44] where Latin and classical authors gave way to French and French writers.

Education was also the central focus of Fichte, whose "Addresses to the German Nation," delivered in Berlin in 1807–1808, placed him as the ped゛ゝ ogical prophet of German nationalism. To Fichte, the state had to become *Kulturstaat*,[45] a state representing the national culture. Schools, and of course curriculum, would come under the exclusive direction of the state. Again, the purpose here is not so much to transmit knowledge, but to mold the individual's identity into that of the state;[46] not to make people more knowledgeable or better informed, but to make them better and more determined nationalists. No wonder, therefore, that Ernest Gellner is moved to proclaim that for the state "the monopoly of legitimate education is . . . more important, more central than is the monopoly of legitimate violence."[47]

Nations, therefore, are nourished and sustained through the telling and retelling of their past—the myths, the heroism, the unsurpassed achievements; the many obstacles that are confronted and overcome; the flowering of language and literature; the philosophical and artistic genius that has no peer, while conveniently passing over the less than seemly episodes—the self inflicted wounds; the civil wars, massacres, and human atrocities; the ethnic, linguistic, and religious cleavages and dislocations. It is such grand narratives, embodied in purposeful historical and literary representation, passed on to successive generations through directed education, that mold and preserve nations.

And the Arab nation is no exception. Through the determined advocacy of Sati' al-Husri and his disciples, and the institution of

[44] Hans Kohn, *Nationalism: Its Meaning and History* (Princeton, New Jersey: D. Van Nostrand Company, Inc., 1955), p. 26.

[45] Hajo Holborn, *A History of Modern Germany, 1648–1840* (New York: Alfred A. Knopf, 1966), p. 342.

[46] Keddourie, *Nationalism*, pp. 83–84.

[47] Ernest Gellner, *Nations and Nationalism* (Ithaca, New York: Cornell University Press, 1983), p. 34.

directed educational programs that told a history molded by the
Arab nationalist idea, the concept of the Arab nation was to acquire an ever-increasing recognition and acceptance in the post-
World I period. These were men who were kindled by the incendiary ideas of European nationalism. And from the philosophical
battles fought by European nationalist thinkers a century or so before, a nationalist path most suited to the Arab condition was carefully charted.

In his definition of the nation, Husri opted categorically for the
German idea of cultural nationalism promoted by Herder, Fichte,
and Ernest Moritz Arendt. In this formulation, as we have seen, a
nation cannot depend on such ephemeral bases as the "will of the
people"; rather, a nation is objectively based through the unity of
its linguistic community and the coherence of its history. It is the
individual's language and history, regardless of his own preferences, that determine his national identity. Echoing the German
romantics' definition of what constitutes a "German," Husri
would contend that people who speak Arabic as their mother
tongue are Arabs, the very people who recognize the common
thread of their long and distinguished history. The Arab nation is
therefore predetermined and eternal.

The reasons for opting for the German, rather than the French,
conception are not difficult to discern. The Arab political and geostrategic situation in the 1920s had very little in common with nineteenth century France. Conversely, there was a strong resemblance
to the pre-1871 German condition. Husri would comment that the
French had lived for so long in a unified national state that they
had forgotten the distinction between the concepts of state and
nation, using the term *nationalite* to depict membership in either
or both. However, the Germans, without a unified state until 1871,
were very much aware of the difference, naming membership in a
state *nationalitat* and in a nation *volkstrum*.[48] Lacking a unified

[48] Abu Khaldun Sati' al-Husri, *Abhath Mukhtara fi al-Qawmiya al-'Arabiya* (Selected
studies on Arab nationalism) (Beirut: Markaz Dirasat al-Wuhda al-'Arabiya, 1985), p. 66;
the same argument also appears in Abu Khaldun Sati' al-Husri, *Ara' wa Ahadith fi al-Qawmiya al-'Arabiya* (Views and discussions on Arab nationalism) (Beirut: Dar al-'Ilm li al-

state, the Arabs could assert their national identity only through a German-like emphasis on cultural authenticity,[49] and indeed on several occasions, Husri compares the Arab "nation" in the post-World War I period with the pre-1871 German lands and domains.

In his intellectual commitment to the German cultural conception, Husri launched a vigorous attack on the French model as articulated by Ernest Renan. As we have seen, Renan argued that national attachment is not predetermined, but is based on the free will of the people. It was incumbent on the people to decide whether they wished to live together, a decision that could be reversed at any point in the future. Indeed, Renan went so far as to call the nation a "daily plebiscite." Consequently, a nation cannot be a constant objective entity. Depending on who might want to join or secede, the nation can grow larger or be reduced in size. In terms that are almost sacrilegious to the cultural nationalists, Renan contends that the nation is not eternal; it has a beginning and an end.

Husri not only dismisses Renan's theory of the nation, but attaches malicious motivations to the French thinker. He argues that Renan formulated his voluntarist theory of *nationalite elective* to endow intellectual legitimation to the French annexation of German-speaking Alsace and to France's ambitions across the Rhine. To Husri, Renan did not follow "the path of a neutral researcher, rather he resembled a lawyer who, in preparing his defense, would eschew clear yet damaging evidence, while clinging to the flimsiest of indications that might help his defense."[50] Of Renan's idea that the nation is a "daily plebiscite," an object of the will of the people, Husri is derisively dismissive. Does Renan imply, Husri asks, that

---

Malayeen, 1964), pp. 41–42; see also Paul Salem, *Bitter Legacy: Ideology and Politics in the Arab World* (Syracuse, New York: Syracuse University Press, 1994), p. 57.

[49] But not on racial exclusivity. Husri advocated pride in Arab culture, but was careful not to equate that with notions of racial superiority. See Ilyas Sahab, "Sati' al-Husri: al-Mufakir wa al-Da'iya wa al-Numudhaj," (Sati' al-Husri: the thinker, the advocate and the role model), *al-Mustaqbal al-'Arabi*, no. 1 (May 1978): 83; also Tibi, *Arab Nationalism*, p. 121.

[50] Abu Khaldun Sati' al-Husri, *Ma Hiya al-Qawmiya?: Abhath wa Dirasat 'ala Dhaw'i al-Ahdath wa al-Nadhariyat* (What is nationalism?: enquiries and studies in light of events and theories) (Beirut: Markaz Dirasat al-Wuhda al-'Arabiya, 1985), p. 117.

nations can be equated with political parties which, depending on shifting public opinion, are constantly oscillating between being in and out of vogue? Husri concludes that in defining the nation merely as a group of people who wish to live together, Renan should have realized that this happens only because of the unity of language and history. The wish to live together does not in and by itself form a nation; it occurs as a result of nation formation.[51] That is why, Husri argues, the only correct definition of the nation has to be the German cultural conception.

As we have seen, to the German cultural nationalists language sits at the heart of any definition of the nation. To Herder and Fichte, it is language that creates the inner cultural frontiers of a nation, regardless of whether or not the nation had yet succeeded in establishing its external geographic boundaries.

The emphasis of the German Culturalists on language finds its way into Husri's own formulation. To Husri, "language is the most important spiritual tie which binds an individual to the rest of mankind because it is the medium of communication amongst individuals, in addition to being the means for thinking. . . . Since languages differ between races, it is natural that we find groups of individuals who share the same language drawing nearer to each other than to other groups, thereby forming a nation which is distinct from other nations."[52] As examples, Husri points to the Germans and Italians who, through the preservation of their language, were able eventually to turn chronic political fragmentation into unified states. Husri cites too the example of Bulgaria before World War I, which, Husri relates, suffered from two kinds of oppression. There was the intrusion of the Greek Orthodox Church, which sought to spread the Greek language at the expense of Bulgarian, and there was the Ottoman imperial subjugation of Bulgaria, which was political in nature, and thus not particularly opposed to the Bulgarian

---

[51] Tibi, *Arab Nationalism*, p. 127.

[52] al-Husri, *Abhath Mukhtara fi al-Qawmiya al-'Arabiya*, pp. 35–36. In another passage, al-Husri writes: "The life of a nation is in its language. If [the nation] were to lose its language. . .then it would no longer exist." al-Husri, *Ara' wa Ahadith fi al-Qawmiya al-'Arabiya*, pp. 69–70.

language. Husri's argument was that the Bulgarians could not struggle for political independence from the Ottomans without first achieving linguistic and cultural freedom from the Greeks. Indeed, he points out, that only after a revival of the Bulgarian language had taken place, which was due in great measure to the establishment of a Bulgarian patriarchate which replaced Greek with Bulgarian as the language of worship and education, could the Bulgarians begin their quest for independence from the Ottomans.[53] Indeed, Husri discerns similar conclusions from the case of Poland, where he argues that the Polish language played a pivotal role not only in keeping the Polish nation alive after the partitioning of Poland, but also in later uniting the country again. In the Arab case, Husri's lifelong advocacy for the adoption of "standard" Arabic throughout the Arab world was occasioned by a recognition that Arab dialects were so varied as to make nonsense of the notion of linguistic unity.

Along with language, Husri cites history as the other crucial factor in nationhood. To Husri,

> nationalist feeling depends on historical memories more than anything else. . . . History-related ideas and data play an important role in the life of nations and have a great impact on the direction of historical events. . . . We do not exaggerate when we say that generally the movements for resurrection and the struggle for independence and unity begin only by recalling the past and searching for revelation from history. . . . Love for independence is nourished by memories of the lost independence; the longing for power and glory begins with a lament for the lost power and diminished glory; faith in the future of the nation derives its strength from a belief in the brilliance of the past; and the longing for unification is increased by the renewal of memories of the past unity.[54]

[53] Abu Khaldun Sati' al-Husri, *Muhadharat fi Nushu' al-Fikra al-Qawmiya* (Lectures on the emergence of the national idea) (Beirut: Markaz Dirasat al-Wuhda Al-'Arabiya, 1985), pp. 69–74. See also, Sahab, "Sati' al-Husri: al-Mufakir, wa al-Da'iya wa al-Numudhaj" (Sati' al-Husri: the thinker, the advocate and the role model), p. 84.

[54] Abu Khaldun Sati' al-Husri, *Ara' wa Ahadith fi al-Wataniya wa al-Qawmiya* (Views and discussions on patriotism and nationalism) (Beirut: Markaz Dirasat al-Wuhda al-'Ara-

Much of Husri's work in Iraq as its director general of education concerned the teaching of history in Iraqi schools. He emphasized particularly the teaching of "nationalist history"; the kind of history that would engender among the pupils a sense of primordial attachment to the Arab nation. In this, he echoed Fichte's endorsement of history as perhaps only slightly less important than language in rekindling the nationalist spirit.[55] And in any case, these two factors are inexorably linked to, and interwoven with, each other. In Husri's scheme of things, a common language and a shared history

> form the fundamental bases of nation formation. The union of these two spheres leads to fusion of emotions and aspirations, of sufferings and hopes, and of culture. And in this, people see themselves as members of a unitary nation distinct from other nations. . . . If we want to specify the roles of language and history in the formation of a nation, we can say: language is the soul and the life of the nation; history is its memory and its cognizance.[56]

The originality of the Arabic language, stemming from the early inhabitants of the Arabian Peninsula, who had been protected from external cultural influences by the inhospitable Arabian desert, and the long, continuous stretch of Arab history, predating the advent of Islam and the life and times of the Prophet, make up, in Husri's formulation, the two essential constitutive elements of the Arab's national identity.

Not so with religion. Husri's nationalism is emphatically secular and intellectually extricated from Islamic political thought, even

---

biya, 1984), pp. 95–96; see also William L. Cleveland, *The Making of an Arab Nationalist: Ottomanism and Arabism in the Life and Thought of Sati' al-Husri* (Princeton, New Jersey: Princeton University Press, 1971), p. 143.

[55] This generally accepted contention is questioned by Walid Kazziha, who argues that, unlike Fichte, Husri gives history an equal importance to language in national formation. See Kazziha, "al-Qawmiya al-'Arabiya fi Marhalat ma bein al-Harbayn al-'Alamitayn" (Arab nationalism in the period between the two world wars), pp. 62–63.

[56] al-Husri, *Ma Hiya al-Qawmiya: Abhath wa Dirasat 'ala Dhaw'i al-Ahdath wa al-Nadhariyat* (What is nationalism?: enquiries and studies in light of events and theories), p. 210. See also Tibi, *Arab Nationalism*, p. 122.

though Islam is the religion of the overwhelming majority of the Arab people. In his national formulation, Husri contends that, unlike language and history, religion does not constitute a fundamental element of national formation.[57] While he concedes that at times religion has played an important role in fostering national feelings, he says that this is true only of "national religions," such as Judaism, that serve a particular people. On the other hand, universal religions, such as Islam and Christianity, which are embraced by people of different languages, cultures, and locale, must by definition be opposed to nationalism. And in such a competition, Husri is confident that human solidarity built around religious affiliation would not stand up to the force of secular cultural nationalism. In this, Husri took on not just the Muslim modernist thinkers of the past, but also (as we shall see in later chapters) influential contemporaries who insisted on the primacy of Muslim solidarity.

In support of his secular views, Husri would cite historical instances. After all, did not the various Balkan groups continue to fight with each other even though they were all united by their Greek Orthodox faith? Did the unity of religion and sect stop the separation of Hungary from Austria, or Norway from Sweden? Did the eventual unity of Italy not necessitate long and bloody wars with Austria, even though both were Catholic? On the other hand, religious differences were no obstacle for the national unification of Protestant Prussia and Catholic Bavaria, or the fusion of Christians and Muslims in Albania after the latter's secession from the Ottoman Empire.[58]

To emphasize what to Husri is the indisputable primacy of nationalist ties over religious attachments, he commits the almost sacrilegious intellectual infraction of employing the term *al-Umma* in

[57] Sahab, "Sati' al-Husri: al-Mufakir wa al-Dai'ya wa al-Numudhaj" (Sati' al-Husri: the thinker, the advocate and the role model), p. 84; also Kazziha, "al-Qawmiya al-'Arabiya fi Marhalat ma bein al-Harbayn al-'Alamitayn," (Arab nationalism in the period between the two world wars), p. 62.

[58] al-Husri, *Ma Hiya al-Qawmiya?: Abhath wa Dirasat 'ala Dhaw'i al-Ahdath wa al-Nadhariyat* (What is nationalism?: enquiries and studies in light of events and theories), p. 161; see also Sahab, "Sati' al-Husri: al-Mufakir wa al-Dai'ya wa al-Numudhaj" (Sati' al-Husri: the thinker, the advocate and the role model), p. 84.

a secular, nationalist mode.[59] As we have seen, *al-Umma* is a concept used by Islamic scholars to denote the community of the faithful—those who shared the Islamic faith regardless of the cultural and linguistic distance that separated them. Until then the term usually had been used in its religious context, that of *al-Umma al-Islamiya*. Husri introduced the concept of *al-Umma al-'Arabiya*, united by language and history, which in his narrative was an infinitely more precise designation than the culturally diffuse and atomized Muslim community.

To this end, he is at pains to show that Arab and Islamic history are not co-terminus; that Arabs had existed long before the advent of Islam, that indeed the glorious achievements of Islamic history are but a testament to Arab genius, and that if Arabs cease to be Muslims, they would still be Arabs. This formulation is meant to emphasize the secularism of Husri's Arab nationalism. It thus allows him to incorporate the Arab Christians under the unifying roof of Arab nationalism. Husri pointedly argues that Christians are as proud of their Arab heritage as their Muslim brothers. This pride is evidenced by the struggle of the Arab Christian Orthodox against Greek control in the patriarchate of Antioch and that of the Eastern Uniates against the encroachment of Latin rites and customs.[60] The message is purposely and purposefully stated: a Christian is as Arab as any Muslim.

This "liberalism" toward the minority Christian population in the Arab world is not reflected in the rest of Husri's Arab nationalist doctrine. The concept of liberal democracy is absent from Husri's ideological formulations, and the notion of individual liberty is so tangential to his main concerns as to be irrelevant. In this he was merely mirroring the German romantics upon whose ideas his concept of nationalism was based, and to them the word "liberty" did not refer to the rights of the individual, but to the inde-

---

[59] Kawakibi at one time used *al-Umma* in this sense, but in no way in the same consistent and conscious way that Husri used it. Indeed, overall, Kawakibi followed the accepted norm of defining *al-Umma* in its religious context. See Muhamed 'Ammara, *al-A'mal al-Kamila li 'Abd al-Rahman al-Kawakibi* (The complete works of 'Abd al-Rahman al-Kawakibi) (Beirut: al-Mu'asasa al-'Arabiya li al-Dirasat wa al Nashr, 1975), p. 198.

[60] Hourani, *Arabic Thought in the Liberal Age*, p. 315.

pendence of the nation from foreign rule, through "the unity and power of the group."[61] Fichte, for instance, has no qualms about restricting the freedom of the individual for the higher good of the love of the fatherland.[62] Husri echoes these sentiments.[63] In one of his lectures, he enjoins his audience to understand that

> Freedom is not an end in itself but a means toward a higher life. . . . The national interests which could sometime require a man to sacrifice his life, must by definition require him, in some case, to sacrifice his freedom. . . . He who does not sacrifice his personal freedom for the sake of his nation's freedom, when the situation requires, may forfeit his own freedom along with the freedom of his people and his country. . . . And he who refuses to sublimate (*yufni*) his individual self into that of the nation, may in some cases, be compelled to expire (*yadhtar ila al-fina'*) in a foreign nation which may one day conquer his fatherland. Because of this, *I say unhesitatingly and continuously: patriotism and nationalism above all and before all . . . even above and before freedom.*[64] (italics added)

This illiberal streak translates itself into an attitudinal rigidity toward not just non-Arabs, but also toward those whom Husri considered to be Arabs. As we shall see, a variety of Arabic-speaking people in the period between the two world wars were not necessarily eager to join the ranks of Arab nationalism. Indeed, there were many who insisted that they were not Arabs at all, professing an attachment to an altogether different identity, perhaps Syrian, Pharaohnic, even European. The fact that they spoke Arabic was to them no more than an accident of history, of little consequence, hardly warranting an association with the despised and uncouth bedouin who to many urbanites constituted the true defi-

[61] Kohn, *Prelude to Nation-States*, p. 254.

[62] Tibi, *Arab Nationalism: A Critical Enquiry*, p. 136.

[63] Walid Khadduri, "Al-Qawmiya al-'Arabiya wa al-Dimuqratiya: Muraja'a Naqdiya" (Arab nationalism and democracy: a critical review), *Al-Mustaqbal al-'Arabi*, no.228 (February 1998).

[64] Abu Khaldun Sati' al-Husri, *Safahat min al-Madhi al-Qarib* (Pages from recent history) (Beirut: Markaz Dirasat al-Wuhda al-'Arabiya, 1984), p. 42. See also Haim, *Arab Nationalism*, p. 44; and Cleveland, *The Making of an Arab Nationalist*, pp. 169–170.

nition of an Arab. Husri's response to such attitudes was predictably unbending, even ominous: national identity is predetermined,
and has nothing to do with free will. If these people did not understand this, then they had to be persuaded, and if necessary, forced
into accepting it. In Husri's own words:

> Every Arabic-speaking people is an Arab people. Every individual
> belonging to one of these Arabic-speaking peoples is an Arab. And
> if he does not recognize this, and if he is not proud of his Arabism,
> then we must look for the reasons that have made him take this
> stand. It may be an expression of ignorance; in that case we must
> teach him the truth. It may spring from an indifference or false con-
> sciousness; in that case we must enlighten him and lead him to the
> right path. It may result from extreme egoism; in that case we must
> limit his egoism. But under no circumstances, should we say: "As
> long as he does not wish to be an Arab, and as long as he is dis-
> dainful of his Arabness, then he is not an Arab." He is an Arab
> regardless of his own wishes. Whether ignorant, indifferent, unduti-
> ful, or disloyal, he is an Arab, but an Arab without consciousness
> or feeling, and perhaps even without conscience.[65]

In this instance Husri is not just a formulator of ideas; he is an
unbending, almost autocratic, missionary, an enforcer of the "only
correct ideology," a propagator of the truth as he conceived of it.
At times he would take this to absurd limits. In his capacity as
Iraq's director general of education, he once fired the Iraqi Shiite
poet Muhamed Mahdi al-Jawahiri from his teaching job for sing-
ing the praises of an Iranian summer resort, an endeavor which
Husri considered to be *shu'ubi* (anti-Arab). Jawahiri, one of the
most celebrated twentieth century Arab poets, writes caustically in
his memoirs that he also had written poems praising the resorts of

---

[65] Abu Khaldun Sati' al-Husri, *Abhath Mukhtara fi al-Qawmiya al-'Arabiya* (Selected
studies on Arab nationalism), p. 80. Slightly different versions of Dawisha's own translation
appear in Tibi, *Arab Nationalism*, p. 163; in Cleveland, *The Making of an Arab Nationalist*,
p. 127; and in Martin Kramer, *Arab Awakening and Islamic Revival: The Politics of Ideas
in the Middle East* (London: Transaction Press, 1996), p. 28.

Lebanon, Syria, and Palestine. Would that qualify as *shu'ubi* too?[66] The point, however, was that Husri would not tolerate even the slightest possible deviation from the path he had drawn for Iraqi education. He saw himself as the custodian of a sacred mission to implant the seeds of Arab nationalism into the minds and hearts of the people, and to make Arab nationalism supercede other identities and loyalties. He was determined, even at the risk of denying someone his livelihood, to make the people into "true" Arabs.

This is precisely why, throughout his career, his only official positions were in the field of education. He would later write that from these positions of authority, he was able to employ "every means to strengthen the feelings of nationalism among the sons of Iraq and to spread the belief in the unity of the Arab nation."[67] And how is this most profitably and propitiously done? The answer for Husri as we have seen is through a directed, carefully engineered, presentation of the past.[68] In 1922, he issued the following directive to teachers of history in Iraqi elementary schools:

> The basic goal of historic studies in elementary schools is to teach the history of the fatherland and the past of the nation. The ultimate objective to be derived from this is the strengthening of patriotic and nationalistic feelings in the hearts of the students. Therefore, the history of Iraq and of the Arab nation should be the core of historical studies. As for the history of other countries, it should not be studied in the first courses except as it relates to the history of Iraq and of the Arabs. . . . *The ideas of the unity of the Arab nation*

[66] Muhamed Mahdi al-Jawahiri, *Dhikrayati* (My memoirs) (Damascus: Dar al-Rafidayn, 1988), p. 163. The Iraqi writer, Selim Mattar implies that Husri fired Jawahiri because the poet happened to be born in the Shiite holy city of Najaf and had praised the Shiite 'Ulama (clergy). See, Selim Mattar, *Al-Dhat al-Jariha: Ishkalat al-Hawiya fi al-'Iraq wa al-'Alam al-'Arabi "al-Shirqani"* (Wounded essence: problems of identity in Iraq and the "Eastern" Arab world) (Beirut: al-Mu'asasa al-'Arabiya li al-Dirasat wa al-Nashr, 1997), p. 121.

[67] Cleveland, *The Making of an Arab Nationalist*, p. 62.

[68] See Kazziha, "Al-Qawmiya al-'Arabiya fi Marhalat ma bein al-Harbayn al-'Alami-tayn" (Arab nationalism in the period between the two world wars), p. 64. On the choice for Arab historians between history as an objective intellectual exercise and as an ideological tool, see Hazem Zaki Nuseibeh, *The Ideas of Arab Nationalism* (London: Kennikat Press, 1972), pp. 70–82. A more general treatment can be found in Rustow, *A World of Nations*, pp. 41–47.

and the Arabism of Iraq should be brought out clearly from the beginning.[69] (italics added)

Herein, fused into each other, lie the nation's two pedagogical pillars, history and education: the "right kind" of history, taught for the specific purpose of nourishing and legitimizing (some would argue even creating) the nation. And as long as this history is re-membered and constantly reinforced through directed and pur-poseful education, the nation will live and thrive.

Husri's determined and single-minded pursuit of nationalist edu-cational policy undoubtedly smacks of an overbearing and authori-tarian political attitude. He was a man driven by an obsession with a particular belief system, and his various positions of authority afforded him the opportunity to try and infuse the tenets of this belief system into the hearts and minds of successive generations.

On the other hand, it is not that difficult to understand why Husri and the other custodians of the nationalist narrative would go out of their way to manipulate history, to exaggerate, obfuscate, and even invent historical fact, and then use their official power to im-pose their version of this "doctored" history on successive genera-tions of people. The reason lies in the many hurdles they had to overcome in propagating the very idea of an Arab national iden-tity—hurdles relating to the existence of a host of other identities among the Arabic-speaking peoples, some of which were intrinsi-cally hostile to Arab nationalism. In this critical ideational struggle, Husri and his disciples would argue that their authoritarian and manipulative methods were justified. These efforts would eventu-ally bear fruit. But as we shall see it would not be a smooth journey.

---

[69] Quoted in Cleveland, *The Making of an Arab Nationalist*, p. 147.

CHAPTER FOUR

ARAB NATIONALISM AND COMPETING LOYALTIES: FROM THE 1920s TO THE ARAB REVOLT IN PALESTINE

In the two decades that followed World War I, the custodians of Arab nationalism gave much of themselves to propagate the idea among the Arabic-speaking people of the area. Their efforts did indeed bear fruit, for the message was slowly, yet determinedly, reaching a growing audience. To be sure, as we shall see later on in this chapter, other identities continued to have a greater hold on peoples' psyche. Yet a growing number of voices in the three most important Arab domains of the time, Iraq, Greater Syria, and Egypt, were declaring themselves to be Arabs, sometimes in conjunction with, at other times to the exclusion of, other identities.

To many Arab nationalists in the 1920s and 1930s, Iraq seemed best equipped to fill the heroic role played by Prussia in uniting the German-speaking people into one unified German nation-state. Sami Shawkat, a disciple of Sati' al-Husri, who was Iraq's director general of education in the 1930s wrote: "Prussia sixty years ago used to dream about uniting the German people. What is to prevent Iraq from dreaming about uniting the Arab lands now that it has achieved its dream of becoming independent?"[1] Such hopes of Arab unification seemed to be well invested in Iraq. The nationalists would look back to the past and proudly point to the glittering civilization that flourished in Baghdad under the Abbasid Dynasty at a time when the West languished in the darkness of its medieval ages. By the middle of the ninth century, scholars working in the immense library of Baghdad's *Bayt al Hikma* (The House of Wisdom) had translated and commented on the main works of Aristotle, Plato, Euclid, Ptolemy, Hippocrates, and Galen. Who else could match such a sterling pedigree?

Beyond the claims of historical validity, Iraq in the 1920s and 1930s was, as Shawkat reminded his readers, one of only four countries with a measure of independence, at least in matters of domestic policy. The other three were Yemen, Saudi Arabia, and Egypt. The first two, however, were deemed too backward and tribal to lead an Arab renaissance. Egypt, the most "advanced" Arabic-speaking country, was the natural leader, and should have taken the helm of the Arab nationalist march. But it was not willing to assume that role. While the country's Arab identity was growing, it still resided squarely in the shadow of the far more dominant "Egyptian" identity. Furthermore, it was in Iraq that the intellectual headquarters of Arab nationalism resided in the person of Sati' al-Husri, whose ideas were eliciting a receptive echo among the country's political elites.

Husri and other Arab nationalists, many of whom were his disciples, set out to make Iraq the beacon from which Arab nationalist ideas would spread to the rest of the Arab world. Cognizant of Iraq's societal divisions and the existence of many particularistic identities and loyalties, the nationalists set out to resurrect the idea of Arab nationalism, with the express objective of making it the dominant narrative in the country. Naturally, they focused on the schools, which they hoped would become the breeding ground for future Arab nationalist generations. To this end, Husri made sure

[1] Quoted in Malik Mufti, *Sovereign Creations: Pan Arabism and Political Order in Syria and Iraq* (Ithaca, New York: Cornell University Press, 1996), p. 29.

to appoint teachers who shared his own vision. Often, these teachers were non-Iraqis, a number of them Palestinians, who had received their education from the American University of Beirut. They taught in the secondary schools of Iraq's main cities, and as such exercised extensive influence on the political ideas and proclivities of the next generation of Iraqi leaders.[2] As we have seen, the main thrust of this educational effort was in the teaching of the "right kind" of history.

The organizing framework of the history curriculum had two parametric elements: the idea of the unity of the Arab nation and the Arabism of Iraq.[3] The focus would be on the absolute positive—great Arab achievements, stories of heroism and valor, examples of nobility and generosity, the spirit of sacrifice, fortitude in the face of adversity, all of which, the student was told, formed the essence of the "Arab character." One such textbook written in 1931for the preparatory and secondary schools was titled, *Tarikh al-Umma al-'Arabiya* (The History of the Arab Nation). As the title suggests, the "Arab nation" is taken for granted, and there is no effort to question, analyze, or even defend the concept. And in the spirit of Husri's ordinance, the bulk of the book is a panegyric of the Arabs' military and scientific achievements, and their contribution to the progress of the world under the Ummayad and Abbasid dynasties. The five centuries of Ottoman domination are deemed worthy of no more than eleven pages. This is followed by an equally short section on Europe's political and cultural supremacy, emphasizing primarily the perfidy of the colonialists.[4] The message here reflected the mission of the messenger. History was in fact "guided ideology," a vehicle for the inculcation and/or resurrection of the idea of an "Arab nation," whose roots, students were told, extended deep into the annals of history. The students would fur-

[2] Phebe Marr, "The Development of a Nationalist Ideology in Iraq, 1920–1941," *The Muslim World*, vol. 75, no. 2 (April 1985): 95.

[3] Reeva S. Simon, "The Teaching of History in Iraq Before the Rashid Ali Coup of 1941," *Middle Eastern Studies*, vol. 22, no. 1 (January 1986): 43. See also William L. Cleveland, *The Making of an Arab Nationalist: Ottomanism and Arabism in the Life and Thought of Sati' al-Husri* (Princeton, New Jersey: Princeton University Press, 1971), p. 147.

[4] Marr, "The Development of a Nationalist Ideology in Iraq, 1920–1941," pp. 96–97.

ther be taught that the achievements of their nation were legion, dwarfing its failures, which in any case resulted not from its own shortcomings, but from the sedition of others.

The most susceptible to the ideas of Arab nationalism in Iraq was the urban Sunni population, who, while a minority, constituted the country's political elite. In the 1920s and 1930s, the Sunni presence was felt not just throughout Iraq's political establishment, but also throughout the educational system and among the officer corps of the country's armed forces. Because of their minority status in Iraq, it was natural that the Sunnis would gravitate emotionally as well as rationally outward toward the other Arabs, almost all of whom belonged to the Sunni sect of Islam. Even so, while not in similar numbers or with quite the same ease, more of the educated urban non-Sunni Iraqis were also joining the nationalist ranks. In this, there can be little doubt that the educational system instituted by the state was the prime agent in the socialization of Iraqi citizens to Arab nationalist culture.[5] The swelling of the ranks was evident in the widespread demonstrations that occurred in Baghdad in response to the Syrian revolt against the French (1925–1927), to the visit to Iraq in 1928 of the British Zionist Sir Alfred Mond, and to the 1929 Arab riots against the Jews in Palestine over what came to be known as the Wailing Wall incident. The nationalists in Iraq supported any governmental initiative to make the country the center of an organically united Arab entity, or at a minimum an eventual federation of independent Arab states.

This orientation found intellectual expression in the formation in 1935 of *Nadi Muthana*, the Muthana Club, whose goals were "to provide a forum for the discussion of Pan-Arabism and Palestine, to awake nationalist spirit among the youth, and to spread Arab culture, especially knowledge of the history of the Arabs."[6] Those invited to speak at the club were not only Iraqi nationalist

[5] Israel Gershoni, "Rethinking the Formation of Arab Nationalism in the Middle East, 1920–1945: Old and New Narratives," in *Rethinking Nationalism in the Arab Middle East*, eds. James Jankowski and Israel Gershoni (New York: Columbia University Press, 1997), p. 18.

[6] Reeva S. Simon, *Iraq Between the Two World Wars: The Creation and Implementation of a Nationalist Ideology* (New York: Columbia University Press, 1986), pp. 72–73.

leaders and thinkers such as Husri, but also Arab nationalists from Palestine, Syria, and Egypt. Additionally, the club took part in launching fund-raising drives for Arab nationalist causes, and fomenting and supporting popular eruptions, such as the fierce 1939 demonstrations that took place in Baghdad to support Syria's unsuccessful struggle with Turkey over national rights to the Alexandretta (Iskandarun) region.

Nationalism was stirring in Syria too, but not necessarily among the ranks of the traditional political elites. Unlike Iraq and Egypt, both of which had a measure of political independence, Syria during this period was under French mandate. It is hardly surprising then that Syria's energy was focused overwhelmingly on attaining Syrian independence from the French. Syria's political leadership came from urban notables who had risen to positions of political eminence under the Ottoman Empire. During the mandate period, those leaders formed themselves into the National Bloc. The Bloc's nationalism generally was localized, aimed at the mandate power. Concerns with the wider Arab arena were not a priority. And in any case, the notables were moved less by ideological fervor than by their socioeconomic and political interests. "The urban leaders," Philip Khoury tells us, "shaped nationalism into an instrument by which to create a more desirable balance between themselves and the French. And they molded their movement to suit the particular interests of their class. In their hands, nationalism . . . was a means to win French recognition without upsetting the status quo."[7] The notables, thus, were too preoccupied with the French, too protective of their own class interests to seriously extend their brand of nationalism beyond the borders of Syria.

It was a relatively younger, more radical generation of nationalists that intellectually endeavored to integrate Syria's fight for independence into a much wider regional struggle against colonialism and imperialism. These new nationalists came from an emerging middle class, which was the hallmark of the structural changes that

[7] Philip S. Khoury, "Continuity and Change in Syrian Political Life: The Nineteenth and Twentieth Centuries," *The American Historical Review*, vol. 96, no. 5 (December 1991): 1389.

were occurring in Syria. Coming from a different socioeconomic background, their definition of nationalism diverged from that of the urban notables. In the standard work on Syria in this period, Philip Khoury describes these consequential changes:

> During the 1930s, new political movements emerged in Syria in response to the gradual socio-economic and cultural changes occurring beneath the political surface. . . . More radical than the National Bloc, they expressed and harnessed . . . political sentiment in a bid to expand the base of political activity in Syria. . . . These radicalized movements left their mark on the politics of nationalism. They betrayed a strong middle class component. . . . They wanted a redefinition of nationalism [which] placed more emphasis on social and economic justice for the masses, on pan-Arab unity . . . than on the old nationalist idioms of constitutionalism, liberal parliamentary forms, and personal freedoms.[8]

It was members of this nationalist generation that formed *Usabat al-'Amal al-Qawmi* (the League of National Action) in 1933. The League and its ideas became popular among primarily young Syrians, a popularity that lasted until World War II.[9] The League had two interrelated goals: total Arab sovereignty and comprehensive Arab unity. The League vehemently criticized the National Bloc for its "accomodationist" policies toward the mandatory power, and pledged themselves to carry on the struggle "until full independence had been achieved and the 'greater Arab state' had been formed."[10] The League later was to give way to other Arab nationalist parties, most notably the Ba'th Party; it did however play an important role in popularizing and spreading Arab nationalist ideas.

[8] Philip S. Khoury, *Syria and the French Mandate: The Politics of Arab Nationalism, 1920–1945* (Princeton, New Jersey: Princeton University Press, 1987), pp. 626–627.

[9] John F. Devlin, *The Ba'th Party: A History from its Origins to 1966*, (Stanford, California: Hoover Institution Press), p. 7; also Stephen Hemsley Longrigg, *Syria and Lebanon Under French Mandate* (London: Oxford University Press, 1958), p. 228.

[10] Yehoshua Porath, *In Search of Arab Unity. 1930–1945* (London: Frank Cass, 1986), p. 161.

The balance of forces among nationalist groups in Palestine mirrored that of Syria. Members of the emerging urban middle class came to nationalism from a more radical perspective than the one held by the traditional and conservative leadership. In addition to forming a number of Arabist (as well as Islamic) associations, they founded *al-Istiqlal Party* (the Independence Party), which became the leading Arab nationalist institution of the era. It was members of the middle class—teachers, lawyers, doctors, and the like who swelled the ranks of the party.[11] Their propagation of Arab nationalist ideas played a significant role in the political struggle against the mounting threat of Zionism. This was motivated if not wholly, then at least partly, by the enormity of Jewish immigration. The Jewish population numbered 175,000 in 1931; four years later it had doubled, and in 1940 it stood at 467,000.[12] It was very clear to the Palestinians that support from the rest of the Arabs was needed in order to halt this fundamental demographic shift, which naturally was highly deleterious to the Arab Palestinians.

Arab nationalist sentiment in Egypt also grew during this period even though it came against powerful attitudinal currents engendered by singularly Egyptian and Islamic identities. Support for the Arab idea continued to grow so that by the mid-1930s, those who thought of themselves as Egyptian Arabs could feel confident enough to at least question the validity of the other prevalent identities. This was encapsulated in a famous public debate that raged for several weeks. It occurred as a result of a comment in a piece written by Egypt's leading man of letters, Taha Husayn, in which he identified the Arabs simply as one of the many invaders of Egypt. The Arabist and Arab nationalist writers took this opportunity to launch an attack on all those who believed in Egypt's uniqueness and exceptionalism, and who consciously or by implication re-

---

[11] Yehoshua Porath, *The Palestinian Arab National Movement: From Riots to Rebellion* (London: Frank Cass, 1977), p. 125; also, Ann Mosely Lesch, *Arab Politics in Palestine, 1917–1939: The Frustration of a National Movement* (Ithaca, New York: Cornell University Press, 1979), pp. 105–106; also, Gershoni, "Rethinking the Formation of Arab Nationalism in the Middle East," p. 20.

[12] Porath, *The Palestinian Arab National Movement*, p. 129.

jected the Arab character of its people.[13] They vehemently confirmed their country's Arab identity, insisting that Egyptians were Semitic Arabs, and that Egypt was tied to the rest of the Arab world by bonds of blood and spirit. To 'Abd al-Rahman 'Azzam, acknowledged as the leading exponent of Egypt's Arab character, Egyptians "had not only accepted the religion, customs, language, and culture of the Arabs; in addition, most of the blood of [Egypt's] people is traceable to Arab veins."[14]

These sentiments had sufficient support among the Egyptian intelligentsia for Arab nationalist organizations to be formed. In 1930, the Association of Arab Unity came into being, to be followed three years later by the General Arab Federation.[15] As it happened, neither of these organizations lasted beyond the mid-1930s, but their formation and existence suggest, nevertheless, that a nascent Arab nationalism was making headway in the country.

This is confirmed by the way general Egyptian opinion reacted to the Syrian revolt (1925–1927). Newspapers supported the rights of the Syrians to independence, called on Egyptians to render support to the Syrians, and Egyptian poets composed poems praising the Syrian uprising and lambasting the French for their acts of repression. Fund-raising drives were organized and material support extended to the Syrians. Public sympathy was such that Sa'ad Zaghloul, Egypt's most prominent leader (who at the time did not hold public office) was moved to issue a "declaration to the nation,"[16] supporting Syria's rights to rule itself and condemning French shedding of innocent Syrian blood. Public concern for Syria must have been sufficiently widespread, for Zaghloul, known for his indifference to the rest of the Arab world, to make such a declaration.

[13] The stinging criticism did not dissuade Husayn from repeating his assertion that Egypt resisted the Arab invaders as much as they did other earlier invaders in his later, immensely influential, book, *Mustaqbal al-Thaqafa fi Misr* (The future of culture in Egypt) (Cairo: al-Hay'a al- 'Amma li al-Kutab, 1993), p. 19.

[14] Quoted in Israel Gershoni and James P. Jankowski, *Redefining the Egyptian Nation, 1930–1945* (London: Cambridge University Press, 1995), p. 29.

[15] Porath, *In Search for Arab Unity*, p. 154.

[16] Israel Gershoni and James P. Jankowski, *Egypt, Islam and the Arabs: The Search for Egyptian Nationhood, 1900–1930* (New York: Oxford University Press, 1986), p. 246; also

There can be little doubt that during the 1920s and 1930s a growing number of citizens and members of various countries and regions of the Arabic-speaking Middle East supported the notion that beyond their immediate locale, they also belonged to a wider Arab fraternity, an all-encompassing Arab nation, based on a foundation of common language, culture, and "blood ties." Supporters of the idea, the nationalist intellectuals and political activists, agitated not just for the wider acceptance of their beliefs, but also for a political program aimed at Arab unification. Whether the end result was an organic Arab unity or some kind of federation of Arab states was not at this time as important to the advocates of Arab nationalism as the conviction that there was no necessary contradiction between belonging to the Arab nation, as well as aspiring for an Arab nation-state, and being a member of one of the nation's geographically constituent parts.

That the exponents of the Arab nationalist idea existed within the mainstream of political thought and action, and that they voiced their beliefs forcefully during this period is indisputable. But by the same token their influence and effectiveness must not be exaggerated. Arab nationalists still faced many obstacles to the concept of a coherent and unified Arab nation that in fact dwarfed its support. And this is not that surprising. Beyond the particular circumstances of the Arab Middle East, a large national domain in general is intellectually too amorphous to command the kind of loyalty usually given to more immediate traditional and familiar institutions.[17] In the Arabic-speaking world during this period there were too many institutions and entities with which people identified—region, tribe, sect, etc.—to allow the "Arab nation" to emerge as the first and foremost point of peoples' loyalty.

From the very outset, Arab nationalism, which itself is a form of supranationalism, in the sense that its appeal, as well as its political agenda, extends beyond the geographic boundaries of the Arab

Ralph M. Coury, "Who 'Invented' Egyptian Arab Nationalism? Part 1," *International Journal of Middle East Studies*, vol.14, no. 3 (August 1982): 252.

[17] H.G. Koenigsberger, George L. Mosse, and G.Q. Bowler, *Europe in the Sixteenth Century* (London: Longman, 1989), p. 267.

states, had to compete with Islam, the other great supranational ideology. Undoubtedly, during this period, when almost every part of the Arabic-speaking Middle East was under some form of colonial or imperialist domination, Islamists and Arabists tolerated one another, at times even cooperating with each other. But this was purely tactical, since by definition the goals that defined the very essence of their identities had to be mutually exclusive. Hassan al-Banna, the founder of Egypt's Muslim Brotherhood Organization, depicts Islam as not just a religion and a form of worship, but also, and just as crucially, "a creed . . . a homeland, a nationality . . . and a state."[18] This unequivocal depiction of what essentially is an "Islamic nation-state" had to be diametrically opposed to the concept of a secular, and an ethnically and linguistically-based, Arab nation.

It was within the above context that Sheikh Muhamed Mustafa al-Muraghi, rector of *al-Azhar*, the most respected Islamic institution in the Arab world, would declare to an Egyptian newspaper that he had no views on Arab nationalism; that the concept did not interest him one bit. After all, Islam did not differentiate between the Arab and non-Arab; indeed, the Muslim *Umma* was a unity in which ethnicity played no part.[19] Sati' al-Husri was quick to reply: "How could someone say that Muslim clerics should endeavor to establish unity amongst the Arab, Iranian, Indian, and Turk, but should not work to unify the Syrian, Egyptian and Hejazi? How can someone hope to effect the unity of Muslim lands speaking different languages, but not the unity of one land, speaking one language, especially the land which speaks the language of the Qur'an?"[20] The swiftness and vigor with which Husri responded to the sheikh attests to the potency of the concept of a united Muslim

---

[18] Quoted in Gershoni and Jankowski, *Redefining the Egyptian Nation*, p. 81.

[19] The statement engendered a spirited debate between Muraghi and Sati' al-Husri. For Muraghi's declaration, see Abu Khaldun Sati' al-Husri, "Radd 'ala Tasrihat al-Shaykh al-Muraghi" (A response to the declarations of Sheikh al-Muraghi) in his *Ara'a wa Ahadith fi al-Wataniya wa al-Qawmiya* (views and discussions on patriotism and nationalism) (Beirut: Markaz Dirasat al-Wuhda al-'Arabiya, 1984), p. 105.

[20] Ibid., p. 106.

Umma, as a powerful competing alternative to the idea of a secular Arab nation.

Regional particularism was another obstacle in the path of Arab nationalism. Iraqi, Syrian, Egyptian, and other regional identities competed with the larger, all-encompassing Arab identity. As we have seen, it did not take the Syrians long during Faysal's brief reign in Syria after World War I to resent the Iraqi officers calling them "foreigners" and "usurpers," even though those officers were senior figures in the "Arab" military force that took part in "liberating" Syria from Ottoman Turkish rule. Indeed, as history was later to show us time and again, even with those who genuinely believed in the "Arab" ideal, loyalty to the geographic locale in which they lived (*al-Watan*) always lurked just under the surface, often manifesting itself whenever their *Watan* became an object of some larger Arab unity plan.

The third, and in a way the most ironic, obstacle to the concept of a coherent Arab nation was linguistic diversity. It is ironic because, according to Husri and other nationalist theoreticians and activists, it is the Arabic language that ultimately defines the parameters of the Arab nation. Of course, the reference here is to standard classical Arabic. But this Arabic was the domain of the literate, who constituted only a small minority of the population. During this period, no less than four out of five Arabs depended almost exclusively on the spoken word for communication. And spoken Arabic consisted of a vast array of sufficiently differentiated dialects that in many instances it was difficult (sometimes downright impossible) for an "Arab" from one part of the "Arab world" to communicate with other "Arabs" from a different part of the "Arab world." Sati' al-Husri was fully aware of this problem. At one point he wrote that colloquial dialects constituted a grave danger because they created divisions and weakened national unity.[21]

Due to the preponderance of illiteracy in the Arab world in this period, the spatial awareness of the majority of Arabs was limited to their specific locale. Unable to read, most Arabs were blissfully

[21] Cleveland, *The Making of an Arab Nationalist*, p. 119.

unaware of events occurring in the world at large, and whatever they happened to learn they came by mainly through word of mouth; hardly the kind of communicative effectiveness that Karl Deutsch says is an essential element of national formation and cohesion.[22] An amusing illustration of this limited consciousness is provided by Peter Gubser in detailing an incident that occurred in the town of al-Karak in Trans-Jordan in the 1930s. A Palestinian teacher attempted to raise his students' consciousness about mounting Jewish immigration in Palestine. On the anniversary of the Balfour Declaration, the teacher and some of his students took to the streets shouting "Down with Balfour!" Having no idea what the Balfour Declaration was, the town's people joined the demonstration shouting "Down with Karkour!" On hearing this, Karkour, the local shoemaker, was compelled to run into the street and defend his good name.[23] With the probable exception of nonurban Palestinian locales,[24] this incident could well have occurred in any small town or village along the length and breadth of the Arabic-speaking world.

Two further obstacles, sectarianism and tribalism, were rampant in many parts of the Arabic-speaking Middle East. Indeed, they exerted inordinate influence on peoples' fundamental attitudes in Husri's own backyard, the Kingdom of Iraq. As we shall see, the Sunni-Shiite divide undermined efforts at national unity both at the Iraqi and Arab levels. And this was exacerbated by a tribal structure that not only resisted governmental control, but also was a focus of primordial loyalty for the people. Sectarianism was also a problem for Syria with its Sunni-Druze-'Alawite divide, and in some Syrian regions, especially Latakiya, Jabal Druze, and Jezzira,

[22] Karl W. Deutsch, *Nationalism and Social Communication*, 2nd ed. (Cambridge, Massachusetts: MIT Press, 1966).

[23] Peter Gubser, *Politics and Change in al-Karak, Jordan: A Study of a Small Arab Town and Its District* (London: Oxford University Press, 1973), p. 22.

[24] Rashid Khalidi documents a long history of struggle waged by Palestinian *fellahin* against Zionist efforts to purchase the lands on which they worked. See Rashid Khalidi, *Palestinian Identity: The Construction of Modern National Consciousness* (New York: Columbia University Press, 1997), pp. 89–117. This direct encounter with the Zionist movement gave the Palestinian peasant an intimate knowledge of the Zionist movement that other nonurban, nonliterate, Arabs did not possess.

entrenched tribal attitudes further impeded national consolidation. Throughout the 1920s and into the 1930s, tribes constituted the main problem facing the nascent administration of Trans-Jordan. Tribes constantly waged war against each other and raided settled communities at will. They rarely paid taxes, and maintained tribal law in defiance of central authority. It was not until the British commander John Glubb created the Desert Patrol in the early 1930s that tribal conflicts subsided. The genius of the plan resided in Glubb's successful effort to channel the bedouins' warlike energy and co-opt their services in defense of the state. Consequently, the Desert Patrol, and indeed the whole Arab Legion (Jordan's armed forces), continued throughout the years to consciously manifest strong tribal ties and attitudes. The strength of Jordanian tribal ties is echoed in many other parts of the Arab world. Bassam Tibi writes: "Neither in the imperial nor in the territorial state were tribes transformed into a homogenous polity; tribal ties have always been the basic element of group reference, despite the fact that they were suppressed and rhetorically renounced. This happened in the past within the framework of a universal Islamic *Umma* and in the present with reference to the secular idea of the nation."[25] In some cases, tribalism and sectarianism overlapped with one another, thereby reinforcing the anti-national impulse. The Shiite tribal confederations in Iraq are a case in point, so are the 'Alawite and Druze tribal communities of Syria.

In this ideational and political clash between Arab national identity and the other competing identities, the most consequential Arab countries/regions in this period were Iraq, Syria, and Egypt. This is not to suggest a lack of nationalist sentiment in other parts of the Arabic-speaking Middle East. But none of the other domains could match up to Iraq, Syria, and Egypt in demographic weight, or in peoples' perception of their respective geostrategic position in the Arab world. Saudi Arabia was too remote, overtly tribal, and

[25] Bassam Tibi, "The Simultaneity of the Unsimultaneous: Old Tribes and Imposed Nation-States in the Modern Middle East," in Philip S. Khoury and Joseph Kostiner, *Tribes and State Formation in the Middle East* (Berkeley: University of California Press, 1980), p. 127.

demographically unsophisticated. Lebanon was a geographically small area with a politically influential Christian population that was singularly hostile to any notion of Arab unity. Jordan was perceived throughout the Arab world as an artificial and inconsequential creation by the British to pacify Emir 'Abdallah. Palestine was a hotbed of national sentiment, and in Haj Amin al-Husayni, Palestinians had a popular nationalist leader whose influence extended beyond the confines of Palestine. The country, however, was already a contested domain, oscillating precariously between a Jewish and an Arab identity. And in any case, during this period, many Arabs perceived Palestine (as well as Lebanon and Jordan) as an intrinsic part of Greater Syria, *Bilad al-Sham*. Finally, on the level of political institutions, Iraq, Egypt, and increasingly Syria, were forging rapidly ahead of the other parts of the Arab world. Consequently, the actual and perceived centrality of these three countries in the Arab world of the 1920s and 1930s was such that whatever the outcome of the debates over the various identities, and whatever the direction of the political struggle, the consequent impact was sure to be felt not just locally, but throughout the Arab world.

In detailing the many obstacles to Arab nationalism in the three countries, we might begin with Iraq. The country after all was, during this period, the home of Sati' al-Husri. Because they had a considerable measure of authority over domestic matters, Husri and his associates and disciples, as we have seen, actively endeavored through the medium of school, as well as public, education to lay a sure foundation not just for the national idea, but also for the national state. These determined nationalists were convinced that they could turn Iraq into the Prussia of the Arab world.

The problem for the nationalists was that the country they wanted to turn into a nationalist prototype for the rest of the Arab world was itself a severely fragmented society. Iraq was essentially an artificial state, created through an amalgamation of three ex-Ottoman provinces, and bereft of any ethnic or religious rationale. It therefore lacked the essential underpinnings of a national bond. The province of Mosul to the north had substantial Kurdish and

Turkoman populations, and had strong ties with Turkey and Syria; Basrah in the south was predominantly Shiite with long-standing and deep bonds to Persia; and Baghdad in the center of the country was dominated by Sunnis, with economically influential Jewish and Christian minorities.[26] Over half of the population was Shiite, yet the politically dominant group were the Arab Sunnis who constituted barely a third of the population. Nearly one in ten was non-Muslim, and a quarter were non-Arabic speakers—mainly Kurds, but also Turkoman, Assyrians, Armenians, and others.[27] This social fragmentation was exacerbated by a pervasive tribal structure that posed numerous problems for the king and his government in Baghdad. Hanna Batatu tells us:

> through the whole period of 1921–1939 the monarch, centered in Baghdad, had in effect a social meaning diametrically opposed to that of the tribal shaykhs, the then virtual rulers of the countryside. The shaykh represented the principle of the fragmented or multiple community (many tribes), the monarch the ideal of an integrated community (one Iraqi people, one Arab nation). Or to express the relationship differently, the shaykh was the defender of the divisive tribal *urf* (customs law), the monarch the exponent of the unifying national law.[28]

The ethnic and sectarian divisions, laden in many instances with tribal overtones, seriously hampered the government's quest for national unity which would act as the springboard for an Arab

---

[26] Of the 438 Iraqi members of the 1938–1939 Baghdad Chamber of Commerce, 255 (58%) were Jews and Christians. See Hanna Batatu, *The Old Social Classes and the Revolutionary Movements of Iraq: A Study of Iraq's Old Landed and Commercial Classes and of Its Communists, Ba'thists, and Free Officers* (Princeton, New Jersey: Princeton University Press, 1978), Table 9–3, p. 245. The Jews were particularly powerful in the economic and financial sector. A Lebanese Shiite mujtahid, on a visit to Iraq in 1934–1935, discovered to his surprise that Shiite merchants paid homage to their religious shrines on Saturdays rather than the usual Fridays. He was told that since Jewish merchants and financiers did not work on Saturdays, the Shiites were compelled to take their day off on the same day. See Yitzhak Nakash, *The Shi'is of Iraq* (Princeton, New Jersey: Princeton University Press, 1994), p. 233.

[27] Mufti, *Sovereign Creations*, pp. 23–24.

[28] Batatu, *The Old Social Classes and the Revolutionary Movements of Iraq*, pp. 27–28.

identity.[29] As we have seen, the Baghdad government continued its efforts to construct a national identity, but the bulk of its energy was focused on confronting the many communal schisms that periodically erupted in violent rebellions. For instance, a book was published in 1933 in which the Iraqi Shiite population was equated with the Sassanid Persians, and in which the author accused Shiite teachers in Iraq of being more loyal to Iran than to Iraq. This engendered widespread acts of sedition, including attacks on security forces. The disturbances were quelled only after an appeal by the highest Shiite cleric.[30] Such events were commonplace throughout the 1930s. In 1935–1936 alone, the government quelled seven serious tribal uprisings. Even though the government used modern and sophisticated weaponry to brutally put down these and other rebellions, instability, particularly in the south and in the north of the country, persisted throughout this period.[31] The bulk of the rebellions occurred in the Shiite south. The Shiite mistrust of the dominant Sunni class was such that Shiites, on a number of occasions, expressed a wish "to return to the days of absolute British control [rather] than be under the heel of an entirely Sunni administration."[32]

The eminent Iraqi sociologist 'Ali al-Wardi relates an incident in the early days of the Iraqi state during one of the annual re-enactments of the martyrdom of Imam Husayn at the hands of the Ummayad army, in which the new Iraqi flag would only be allowed in the vicinity of those representing the Ummayads, thus becoming a target of the biting denunciations and curses of the Shiite mourn-

[29] See Adeed Dawisha, "The Assembled State: Communal Conflicts and Governmental Control in Iraq," in *Ethnic Conflicts and International Politics in the Middle East*, ed. Leonard Binder (Gainesville: University Press of Florida, 1999), especially pp. 61–66.

[30] Abd al-Razzak al-Hasani, *Tarikh al-Wizarat al-'Iraqiya, al-Jusi' al-Thalith, 1930–1933* (The history of Iraqi cabinets, vol. 3, 1930–1933) (Baghdad: Dar al-Shu'un al-Thaqafiya al-'Amma, 1988), p. 243.

[31] Fadhil al-Barak, *Dawr al-Jaysh al-'Iraqi fi Hukumat al-Difa' al-Watani wa al-Harb ma'a Britania sanat 1941* (The role of the Iraqi army in the national defense government and the war with Britain in 1941) (Baghdad: al-Dar al-'Arabiya li al-Tiba'a, 1979), pp. 54–56.

[32] Quoted in Liona Lukitz, *Iraq: The Search for National Identity* (London: Frank Cass, 1995), p. 65; see also Yitzhak Nakash, *The Shi'is of Iraq*, pp. 116–117.

ers.[33] Such an attitudinal polarity slowed down the state's effort to create and expand national institutions, as instanced by the violent reactions of the Shiite (as well as the Yazidi) tribes to Baghdad's intention to introduce a bill for universal military conscription. The great difficulty of assimilating the Shiites into the "Iraqi state," naturally undermined the efforts of the country's political establishment to propagate the ideas of Arab nationalism. And in any case, the Shiites tended to view Arab nationalism as a Sunni project designed to reduce the Shiites to an insignificant minority in an expanded Sunni Arab domain.

If the Shiites were difficult to assimilate into the Arab nationalist culture, the Kurds in the mountainous north of Iraq were impossible to bring in under the umbrella of "the Arab nation" because they considered themselves ethnically distinct from the Arabs. Being non-Semitic and speaking an Indo-European language, the Kurds had little in common with the Arabs of Iraq apart from their Sunni Muslim faith. Fiercely independent, they had vigorously agitated for political independence. In fact, the 1920 Treaty of Sevres had provided for an autonomous Kurdish state, but the treaty was never implemented. The Kurds, however, never accepted their inclusion into Iraq, waging periodic insurrections against the Baghdad government. Unlike the Shiites, who spoke Arabic and shared the same ethnic characteristics of the Iraqi Sunnis, the Kurds were only too aware of their ethnic uniqueness in an essentially Arab society. Deep down, therefore, the Kurds continued to desire a state of their own.[34] It is in this context that someone such as Bakr Sidqi, a military hero and Iraq's strong man in the mid-1930s, would confide to the German charge d'affaires in Baghdad that, being the son of a Kurdish father, the dream of a Kurdish state would always "reside in his heart."[35]

---

[33] 'Ali al-Wardi, *Lamahat Ijtima'iya min Tarikh al-'Iraq al-Hadith, al Jusi' al-Sadis, min 'Am 1920 ila 'Am 1924* (Sociological aspects of modern Iraqi history, part six, 1920–1924), pp. 128–129.

[34] Dawisha, "The Assembled State," pp. 64–65.

[35] Najdat Fathi Safwat, *Al-'Iraq fi Mudhakarat al-Diblumasiyeen al-Ajanib* (Iraq in the memoirs of foreign diplomats) (Baghdad: Maktabat Dar al-Tarbiya, 1984), p. 117.

The ethnic, sectarian, and tribal impediments to the institution of a unifying national ideology in Iraq seemed at times too great to be surmounted. As late as 1933, King Faysal would lament:

> In Iraq there is still . . . unimaginable masses of human beings, devoid of any patriotic ideal, imbued with religious traditions and absurdities, connected by no common tie, giving ear to evil, prone to anarchy, and perpetually ready to rise against any government whatsoever. Out of these masses we want to fashion a people which we would train, educate and refine. . . . The circumstances being what they are, the immenseness of the efforts needed for this (can only be imagined).[36]

Tribalism, sectarianism, and regionalism were also responsible for slowing down nationalist integration in Syria during this period. Even though 85 percent of the population was Arabic speaking, they nevertheless were divided by a number of sectarian/religious affiliations. While some 60 percent of the population were Sunni Arabs, the rest consisted of Arabic-speaking 'Alawites, Druzes, Ismailis, and Christians, as well as non-Arab Kurds, Armenians, Turkomans, and Circassians. In the case of the Druzes, 'Alawites, and Kurds, the sectarian and/or ethnic divides were crisscrossed with further tribal segmentation.[37] Bassam Tibi, for instance, tells us that while 'Alawites "distinguish themselves from other Arabs by embracing a myth of common descent and a common belief," they themselves are subdivided into four tribes and three subsect loyalties.[38] The French, cognizant of these divisions and no doubt following the imperial dictum of "divide and rule," endeavored to endow the particularistic impulses of the various

---

[36] Quoted in Batatu, *The Old Social Classes and the Revolutionary Movements of Iraq*, p. 28. Faysal's letter in its entirety, which is rich in its detail of the enormous obstacles facing the king and his government in their effort to integrate the people of Iraq, can be found in Naji Shawkat, *Sira wa Dhikrayat thamaneena 'Aman, 1894–1974* (Biography and memoirs of eighty years, 1894–1974) (Baghdad: Maktabat al-Yaqdha al-'Arabiya, 1990), pp. 622–631.

[37] Raymond A. Hinnebusch, *Authoritarian Power and State Formation in Ba'thist Syria: Army, Party, and Peasant* (Boulder, Colorado: Westview Press, 1990), p. 21.

[38] Bassam Tibi, "The Simultaneity of the Unsimultaneous: Old Tribes and Imposed Nation-States in the Modern Middle East," p. 138.

communities with political legitimacy. They created independent states in Aleppo, Damascus, and in the 'Alawite domain, as well as autonomous units in Alexandretta (eventually lost to Turkey), the Jazira, and Jebel Druze.

The indigenous divisions, politically and administratively solidified by the mandate power, and accentuated by primordial ties to family, clan, village, tribe, and/or sect, proved much stronger than the nascent loyalty to nation during this period. Indeed, even though, in Tibi's words, "the center of nationalism was the town and of separatism the tribal countryside,"[39] particularistic tendencies and narrow loyalties showed themselves among the city leaders and notables as well. Most nationalist leaders came from major cities, such as Damascus, Aleppo, and Hama, and they remained attached to their city base psychologically and politically.[40] In this respect, the competition between Damascus and Aleppo was the most intense and most damaging to the national idea. Aleppo had absorbed Turkish culture and language far more readily than Damascus. Indeed, many of Aleppo's elites had Turkish blood, and marriage to Turks was widespread. Moreover, Aleppo's economic well being depended on continued commercial ties with Anatolia as well as with Iraq. As Philip Khoury tells us: "Damascus leaders continued to feel more comfortable in Beirut or Jerusalem than in Aleppo . . . while Aleppo leaders looked to Iraq (and even Turkey) as much as they did to Damascus."[41] Thus a clear attitudinal divide existed between the Damascene and Aleppine notables. Because of such narrow, town-centric loyalties and competitions, the efforts of the city notables to mobilize the mass population in the name of nationalism and national unity remained tenuous at best.

Much greater obstacles were felt outside the main cities. The peasantry, distrustful of central government, alienated from the nationalist urban leaders, who naturally had diametrically opposed class interests, isolated by geographic compartmentalization, and

---

[39] Ibid., p. 148.

[40] Khoury, *Syria and the French Mandate*, p. 622.

[41] Ibid., p. 622. For a more detailed exposition of the rivalry between Damascus and Aleppo, see ibid., pp. 102–104; 440–441.

drawn to powerful primordial ties that took precedence over national and nationalist considerations, were hardly receptive to the
concept of nationalism. It is undoubtedly true that peasants formed
the bulk of the body mass of the major uprisings against French
rule in the 1920s, but on one level, the peasants fought "under a
tribal-like patriarchical leadership," and on another level, the revolts "took on the character of an Islamic Jihad against the infi-
del."[42] Generally speaking, particularistic tendencies and loyalties
had the effect of producing separatist movements, especially in the
rural areas of Jabal Druze, the ʿAlawite territories, and the Jazira,
which threatened the very fabric of Syria's quest for national unity,
to say nothing of the broader idea of one Arab nation. As Shukri
al- Quwatly, the Damascene notable, who was fully attuned to the
ideas of Arab nationalism, would remark: "as long as the French
were still able to convince the Druzes of the benefits of independence from Syria, then it was useless to try to unite Beirut with
Basrah and Baghdad with Damascus."[43]

A young school-age Syrian at the end of the twentieth century
might be utterly mystified by the reference to the Druze quest for
separateness, since it was from Jebel Druze that the idealized and
idolized Syrian uprising against the French emerged in 1925. To
this day, Syrians cling to a memory of the uprising as a great national revolt, fueled by nationalist goals, and universally supported
by all Syrians regardless of sect, creed, or regional affiliation. The
facts tell a different story. To begin with, very few people participated in the uprising—no more than ten thousand, half of whom
were Druze tribesmen. Some support came from workers in the
cities of Damascus and Hama, and from a few Muslim merchants
who saw the revolt as a way of undermining their Christian com-
petitors, but only a small minority of notables joined in. The uprising was by no means the great national movement it was portrayed
as by later narrators of the nationalist idea. It was "at heart a traditional movement fueled by religion, factional rivalries and ambi-

---

[42] Hinnebusch, *Authoritarian Power and State Formation in Baʿthist Syria*, p. 43.
[43] Khoury, *Syria and the French Mandate*, p. 519.

tions, and hopes of plunder."[44] Indeed, had the French been more sensitive to Druze religious practices, the whole tragic episode could have been averted.[45]

The Druze community in the 1920s could hardly be portrayed as a bastion of Syrian, let alone Arab, nationalism. The community was very much divided on the question of integration within Syria. As late as 1939, the high commissioner of France believed that two thirds of the Druzes were against union with Syria; the remaining third supported the union, but with a number of conditions, including a measure of autonomy from Damascus and the demand that only Druze officials be appointed to the Druze areas.[46] Whatever their tactical objectives, it seems clear that the strategic goals of the uprising that was led by the Druze were local and traditional; indeed, the Druze were hardly sold on the notion of being an integral part of Syria.

Nor were the 'Alawites or the inhabitants of the Jazira. As we have seen, the 'Alawites possessed a vision of themselves that cast them apart from the rest of the Syrians and from other Arabs. The separatist impulse was real and intense, made stronger by the fact that under the long Ottoman rule, much of the Latakia province, where the 'Alawites lived, was largely autonomous. But on the whole, these separatist sentiments did not translate into widespread rebellions. The main reason for this was that the community itself was divided tribally, geographically and by religious subsects.[47] Their energy was consumed by internal dissension and bickering. But still "a great majority of 'Alawis opposed union which appeared to mean the political reinforcement of the economic

---

[44] M. E. Yapp, *The Near East since the First World War: A History to 1995*, 2nd ed. (London: Longman, 1996), p. 92. While Philip Khoury agrees that the objectives of the Druze leadership "may have been old and familiar—the retention or restoration of its power in the Jebel—," he contends that at least the tactics they used in actively seeking alliances beyond the Jebel were new. Khoury, *Syria and the French Mandate*, p. 166. Pages 151–204 of Khoury's book provide a detailed history of the revolt.

[45] Nasim Nasr and Sami Mufrij, *Multaqa al-Shu'ub: aw Mujaz Tarikh Syriya wa Lubnan* (The meeting of peoples: an abridged history of Syria and Lebanon) (Damascus: Matba'at al-Jami'a, n.d.), pp. 116–118.

[46] Khoury, *Syria and the French Mandate*, p. 519.

[47] Ibid., p. 523.

power of the absentee Sunni landowners who dominated the region."[48] This in no way meant that the 'Alawites were French collaborators; but neither could they be characterized as Syrian or Arab nationalists. The majority of 'Alawites, Patrick Seale tells us, wanted "only to run their own affairs as they had done for centuries."[49] A similar picture emerges in the Jazira, with its heterogeneous population consisting of Syrian and Armenian Christians who inhabited the urban areas, especially Qamishli, and the rural Arab and Kurdish tribes. The area was socioculturally and politically underdeveloped, in which loyalty to traditional patriarchal symbols were paramount among the mixed population. Thus, the notion of Syrian unity (to say nothing of the larger and more abstract concept of an Arab nation) "was foreign to most of the Jazira inhabitants."[50] The center-periphery divide in Syria during this period, with the periphery's entrenched patriarchal and essentially localized attitudes and tendencies, was too pronounced to allow for the emergence of an imagined national community.

Yet there were problems even at the supposedly "nationalist" center. Among Syria's urban notables, the country's renowned nationalist leaders, nationalism was conveniently cast aside if it happened to collide with their other interests, especially their business concerns. Shukri al-Quwatly, for instance, the ardent Arab nationalist and vigorous defender of Palestinian rights, visited Palestine in October 1935 to win Jewish clients for his Conserves company.[51] And this happened at a time of mounting tensions between the Arab Palestinians and the Jews, which was to erupt into the 1936–1939 Arab revolt in Palestine. Indeed, during the general strike in Palestine, which was the initial phase of the Arab revolt, a number of these Syrian notables who had business interests in Palestine were so alarmed by their lack of access to the lucrative Palestinian market that they demanded Syria's political leadership to pressure the Pal-

---

[48] Yapp, *The Near East Since the First World War*, p. 95.

[49] Patrick Seale, *Asad: The Struggle for the Middle East* (Berkeley: University of California Press, 1988), p. 18.

[50] Khoury, *Syria and the French Mandate*, p. 527; see also Yapp, *The Near East since the First World War*, p. 95.

[51] Khoury, *Syria and the French Mandate*, p. 284.

estinians to end the strike.[52] If the periphery's indifferent attitudes
to nationalism was a function of particularistic, subnational loyalties, the fragility of the center's Arab nationalist credentials was a
manifestation of the primacy of economic interests over all other
concerns and loyalties. This economic nationalism was one indication of the rise of a specifically local Syrian nationalism (*wataniya*)
at the expense of the larger Arab nationalism (*qawmiya*).

The rise in popularity of Syrian nationalism was spearheaded by
the writings and political agitation of Antun Sa'ada. Born in 1904,
in Mount Lebanon into a Greek Orthodox family, Sa'ada emi-
grated with his father to the New World in 1919, settling in Brazil
after a two-year stay in the United States. In 1930, at the age of
twenty-six, he returned to Syria and within two years he founded
the Syrian Social Nationalist Party (SSNP). Although outlawed and
constantly harassed by the French, the party rapidly gained adherents among the urban populations, becoming an important player
among the radical underground opposition. Indeed, by the end of
World War II, it had a broad popular base, a fact that did not
escape the attention of the indigenous leaderships of the newly independent states of Syria and Lebanon. In July 1949, Sa'ada was
arrested, and within twenty-four hours summarily tried and executed. By the time of Sa'ada's death, the SSNP had grown into a
major political force, so much so that Sati' al-Husri, necessarily an
antagonist, was moved to declare in 1948: "There is no party in
the Arab world which can compete with the SSNP for the quality
of its propaganda, which influences reason as well as the emotions,
and for the strength of its organization, which is as efficient on the
surface as it is underground."[53] The party remained a force well
into the 1950s, eventually to be eclipsed by the spectacular ascent
of Arab nationalism during that decade.

A foe of Arab nationalism, Sa'ada maintained that the "Syrians"
constituted a unique nation which was defined by geography as
well as history. The confluence of land and people was indispens-

---

[52] Ibid., p. 544.
[53] Quoted in Bassam Tibi, *Arab Nationalism: A Critical Enquiry* (New York: St. Martin's
Press, 1981), p. 170.

able to Sa'ada's definition of the Syrian nation.[54] The land (which to
Sa'ada included contemporary Syria as well as Lebanon, Palestine,
Jordan, the Sinai, and even Cyprus) had natural frontiers, and had
been inhabited continuously by a mixture of people, Can'anites,
Caldeans, Hittites, and others who over the long history of Syria
fused into one nation.[55] Any identification with Arab nationalism,
argued Sa'ada, was a surrender of Syria's uniqueness, and an acceptance by its gifted people of an inferior status.[56] It is this unequivocal
message of a specifically Syrian nationalism that found an echo
among the educated urban population, particularly the youth,
which accounts for the meteoric rise in the fortunes of the SSNP.

It was primarily in the same such mode of state nationalism (*al-
wataniya*) that Egypt confronted the encroachment of Arab nationalism. And it was not that difficult for Egyptians to intellectually
defend this separatist orientation. After all, to most Egyptians there
always had been an "Egypt" which was as ancient as the Nile,
and whose sociopolitical roots could be traced all the way back to
pharaonic times. This pharaonic orientation (*al-Nuz'a al-fir'aw-
niya*) had gathered support with the extensive excavations that
took place after Napoleon's invasion of Egypt.[57] Moreover, during
the nineteenth century, Egypt had tread a historical path that was
markedly different from the rest of the Arab world. Muhamed 'Ali
and his successors had established an independent dynasty that was
attached to the Ottoman Empire in nothing but name. Later on,
when the Egyptians fell under the political control of the British,
all of Egypt's nationalist energy was harnessed in opposition to
British control, while most of the rest of the Arabic-speaking world
were on the whole still pliant members of the Ottoman Empire.

---

[54] Haytham A. Kader, *The Syrian Social Nationalist Party: Its Ideology and Early History*
(Beirut: n.p., 1990), pp. 24–56.

[55] Selim Mattar, *Al-Dhat al-Jariha: Ishkalat al-Hawiya fi al-'Iraq wa al-'Alam al-'Arabi
"al-Shirqani"* (Wounded essence: problems of identity in Iraq and the "Eastern" Arab
world) (Beirut: Al-Mu'asasa al-'Arabiya li al-Dirasat wa al-Nashr, 1997), pp. 248–249.

[56] Majid Khadduri, *Political Trends in the Arab World: The Role of Ideas and Ideals in
Politics* (Baltimore: Johns Hopkins Press, 1970), p. 189.

[57] Anwar G. Chejne, "Egyptian Attitudes Toward Pan-Arabism," *Middle East Journal*,
vol. 11, no. 3 (Summer 1957): 254.

It is hardly surprising that Egypt was a late convert to the idea of an all-encompassing Arab nation, one of whose parts would be Egypt.[58] Sati' al-Husri himself testifies to the weakness of Arab nationalist sentiment among the Egyptians in this period. After the collapse of nationalist rule in Syria in 1920, Husri and other members of the short-lived Arab government made their way to Egypt expecting widespread support. They were to be bitterly disappointed. "Most [Egyptians] did not care about the events in Syria," recalls Husri. "Even the collapse of the Syrian Arab State itself engendered among them no amount of regret that is worth noting." And why this indifference? Husri's answer is unequivocal: "they did not possess an Arab nationalist sentiment; did not accept that Egypt was a part of the Arab lands, and would not acknowledge that the Egyptian people were part of the Arab nation."[59] And to Husri's chagrin, the Egyptians seemed to keep Arab nationalist concerns at arms length into the 1930s, for he relates in his memoirs that in 1931 a group of Egyptian students and their professors were visibly astonished when their Iraqi hosts broached the subject of Arab nationalism.[60] Indeed, to most Egyptians, who for centuries had been settled cultivators, the word "Arab" conjured up the image of the contemptuous, indolent nomad.[61] Thus, the eminent Arab historian and thinker, Nicola Ziadeh says emphatically, that from the end of the nineteenth century until World War II, nationalism to the Egyptian meant essentially Egyptian nationalism and the nationalist struggle was perceived as exclusively an Egyptian struggle against foreign control.[62] In light of this cultural proclivity, any assault on Arab nationalism could be mounted with an impres-

---

[58] See among others, Patrick Seale, *The Struggle for Syria: A Study of Post-War Arab Politics, 1945–1958* (New Haven, Connecticut: Yale University Press, 1986), p. 16; Cleveland, *The Making of an Arab Nationalist*, p. 132; Coury, "Who Invented Egyptian Arab Nationalism, Part 1," p. 273.

[59] Abu Khaldun Sati' al-Husri, *Ara' wa Ahadith fi al-Qawmiya al-'Arabiya* (Views and discussions on Arab nationalism) (Beirut: Dar al-'Ilm li al-Malayeen, 1964), p. 17.

[60] Porath, *In Search of Arab Unity*, p. 176.

[61] Sylvia Haim, ed., *Arab Nationalism: An Anthology* (Berkeley: California University Press, 1962), p. 52.

[62] Nicola Ziadeh, *Shamiyat: Dirasat fi al-Hadhara wa al-Tarikh* (Shamiyat: studies in culture and history) (London: Riadh al-Rayyas li al-Kutub wa al-Nashr, 1989), p. 287.

sive array of arguments steeped in the symbolism of a well-developed Egyptian identity.

It was the intellectuals who took up the challenge. Some of Egypt's most prominent literary figures assailed the Arabs, their inferior culture, and their archaic customs and traditions. Abbas Muhamed al-'Aqqad, a literary giant of the period who differentiated the "cultured Egyptian nation" from "bedouin" nations,[63] and who saw Egyptian art as superior to Arabic art,[64] wrote of the existence of a wide gulf between the retrogressive mentality of the Arabs and the progressive outlook of twentieth century Egyptians, which was focused on the possibilities of the future rather than on the past. 'Aqqad accordingly counseled Egyptians to blot out the memory of "our past Arab centuries lest we ourselves be asphyxiated by the dust of these centuries."[65] Salame Musa, another eminent Egyptian intellectual of the period, agreed: "We do not owe the Arabs any loyalty. Our youth should not spend too much time on Arab culture. We need to get them accustomed to writing according to modern Egyptian methods than to archaic Arab styles. And they need to know that we are superior to the Arabs."[66] And why this purposeful separation? Because, to Musa, Egypt's fundamental connection is not with the Arabs, but with Europe from which Egypt took its contemporary culture and civilization.[67] Taha Husayn, the dean of modern Egyptian letters, in perhaps his most influential book, *Mustaqbal al-Thaqafa fi Misr* (The Future of Culture in Egypt), likewise distanced Egypt from its Arab past, arguing that Egyptian civilization was older than any other civilization, and

[63] 'Abbas Mahmud al-'Aqqad, "Misr wa al-Misriyun" (Egypt and the Egyptians) in 'Aqqad et al., *Sawt Misr* (The voice of Egypt) (Cairo: al-Hay'a al-Misriya al-'Amma il al-Kutab, 1975), p. 7.

[64] 'Abbas Mahmoud al-'Aqqad, *al-Fusul: Majmou'at Maqallat Adabiya wa Ijtima'iya* (Chapters: a collection of literary and social writings) (Beirut: Dar al-Kitab al-'Arabi, 1967), p. 337.

[65] Quoted in Gershoni and Jankowski, *Egypt, Islam and the Arabs*, p. 109.

[66] Salame Musa, *al-Mu'alafat al-Kamila, al-Mujaled al-Awal: Sanawat al-Takween* (Complete works, volume one: years of formation) (Cairo: Salame Musa li al-Nashr wa al-Tawzi', 1998), p. 658.

[67] Salame Musa, *al-Yawm wa al-Ghad* (Today and tomorrow) (Cairo: Elias Antun Elias, 1928), p. 189.

that the country had retained a distinctive identity through its pharaonic past. In terms of culture and ways of thinking, Husayn maintains that Egypt had always been a part of Europe,[68] and he tellingly minimizes the importance of Arabic as Egypt's national language and Islam as its religion, since neither language nor religion is a primary element of nation building.[69] To the renowned novelist and philosopher, Tawfiq al-Hakim, Egypt and the Arabs were diametrically opposed in spirit and intellect. This is more than evident in his celebrated novel, 'Awdat al-Ruh (The Return of the Soul), in which he contrasts the basic decency of the Egyptian with the militant bellicosity of the Arab bedouin.[70] It is of course true that not all of Egypt's intellectuals shared this "Egyptian *wataniya*" orientation. As we have seen, Arab nationalism had its vigorous supporters. However, during this particular period, the weight of considered intellectual opinion in Egypt was in favor of a uniquely Egyptian identity at the expense of an all encompassing Arab identity, which was depicted as spiritually bankrupt and intellectually backward.

If there was a "supranational" ideology that could challenge the dominance of "Egyptian *wataniya*," it was not Arabism but Islam.[71] A number of Islamic organizations had been founded in the 1920s which had widespread appeal not only among the poorer classes, but also within the ranks of the educated middle class. The Young Men's Muslim Association was created in 1927, and before the end of the decade it was boasting a membership of 15,000. Another grassroot organization, the Muslim Brotherhood, grew rapidly during the 1930s, with its local branches increasing from four in 1929 to some 500 in 1939. These radical Islamists were not

---

[68] Husayn, *Mustaqbal al-Thaqafa fi Misr* (The future of culture in Egypt), pp. 21–33.

[69] Ibid., p. 18.

[70] Tawfiq al-Hakim, *'Awdat al-Ruh* (The return of the soul) (Beirut: Dar al-Kitab al-Lubnani, 1974), pp. 21–28; see also Ghada Telhami, *Palestine and Egyptian National Identity* (New York: Praeger, 1992), pp. 20–21.

[71] See Charles D. Smith, " 'Cultural Constructs' and Other Fantasies: Imagined Narratives in *Imagined Communities*; Surrejoinder to Gershoni and Jankowski's 'Print Culture, Social Change, and the Process of Redefining Imagined Communities in Egypt" *International Journal of Middle East Studies*, vol. 31 (February 1999): 97.

afraid to take on the "heavyweights" of the "Egyptian *wataniya*" orientation. Hasan al-Banna, the charismatic founder and leader of the Muslim Brotherhood, delineated the dividing line between the Islamist and the Egyptian nationalist:

> The point of contention between us and them is that we define the limits of patriotism in terms of creed, while they define it according to territorial borders and geographical boundaries. For every region in which there is a Muslim who says "there is no God but God, and Muhamed is his prophet" is a homeland for us . . . . All Muslims in these geographical regions are one people and one brothers. . . . The advocates of patriotism alone [*al-wataniya faqat*] are not like this, since nothing matters to them except the affairs of that specific, narrowly delimited region of the earth.[72]

The Islamists accepted that the Muslim Egyptian citizen had certain duties to "the place where he lived," but this individual had an even greater duty to the "*fatherland*, the Islamic world, which extends from the farthest east to the farthest west."[73] In such a statement, the Islamic identity challenges not just the notion of an Egyptian, but also an Arab, identity.

It is interesting enough, however, in contrast to official, state-sanctioned Islam, which was hostile to the idea of Arab unity (as discussed earlier in this chapter), these young Islamist activists were not necessarily averse to the tenets of Arab nationalism, including the goal of organic Arab unity. Indeed, they went as far as advocating it. But what separated them from the Arab nationalists was this: To the Arab nationalist, Arab unity was the ultimate goal; to the Islamist, it was simply the means to a higher goal. "The unity of the Arabs," Hasan al-Banna explained, "is an inevitable condition for . . . the establishment of [a Muslim] state, and the strengthening of its power."[74] In this, the Islamists made great use of the concept of *al-Jahilliya*, the age of pre-Islamic "ignorance," where the Arabs were depicted as lacking cohesion, purpose, and disci-

---

[72] Gershoni and Jankowski, *Redefining the Egyptian Nation*, p. 82.
[73] Haim, *Arab Nationalism: An Anthology*, p. 48.
[74] Gershoni and Jankowski, *Redefining the Egyptian Nation*, p. 94.

pline. Only with the advent of Islam, the Islamists argued, did the Arabs become united, moral, and purposeful; traits that allowed them to establish a vast empire and a dazzling civilization. The message here cannot be more clear. Any nationalism, Arab or Egyptian, is subordinated to Islamic unity. And the overriding loyalty of the Muslim Egyptian and/or Arab is to the Islamic *Umma*, the universal community of the faithful which "stretches from the farthest east to the farthest west."

Squeezed between these two identities, the Egyptian and the Islamic, Arab nationalism during this period found in Egypt only limited support. This was reflected in the attitudes and policies of the ruling elites. In 1925, when the possibilities of Arab unity were brought to him, Sa'ad Zaghloul Pasha, the "father" of Egyptian independence, responded: "If you add one zero to another zero, then you add another zero, what will be the sum?"[75] This comment seems to reflect the general attitude of Egypt's political elites. The Syrian uprising in 1925, and France's brutal response galvanized many Egyptians into extending material and verbal support to the "heroic" Syrians. But even on such a dramatic occasion, the government moved slowly and cautiously, almost in spite of itself. There were no official statements regarding the revolt, and there is no record that the government intervened diplomatically in support of the Syrian cause. Moreover, when Zaghloul (who was out of power then) finally addressed the nation on the subject, he referred to Egyptians and Syrians being linked together as "Easterners."[76] The concern of the government and the ruling circle with the revolt was short-lived, quickly and almost thankfully discarded. This hardly suggests a strong attachment to Arab nationalism, even when British influence over Egypt's decision-making process is taken into consideration.

[75] Chejne, "Egyptian Attitudes toward Pan-Arabism," p. 253; Gershoni and Jankowski, *Egypt, Islam and the Arabs*, pp. 245–247; Coury, in "Who invented Egyptian Arab Nationalism?, Part 1," p. 251, argues that Zaghloul's comment did not necessarily mean that the wafdist leader rejected a common Arab identity. However, it is generally accepted that if Zaghloul had any attachment to the idea of Arab nationalism, it was very flimsy indeed.

[76] Gershoni and Jankowski, *Egypt, Islam and the Arabs*, p. 247; Coury, "Who Invented Egyptian Arab Nationalism?, Part 1," p. 252.

To Sati' al-Husri, the indifference to Arab nationalism exhibited by Egypt's political and intellectual elites was especially injurious. To Husri, Egypt's long and distinguished Arab history, which bound Egypt to the other Arabs in language, traditions, culture, and common interests, was a real and tangible thing, dwarfing in contemporary relevance any other ties Egypt might have had in the present or in the past. And those Egyptians who did not see what, to Husri, was a glaring truth had to be suffering from manipulated consciousness.[77] And of all Egyptians suffering from this alleged false consciousness, the most galling to Husri was Taha Husayn, perhaps because Husayn was the most influential literary figure of the time, and/or because of his cavalier dismissal of Egypt's linguistic and historical ties with the Arabs, and his preference to delve deeper into history to search for a pharaonic identity.

Husri therefore takes Husayn to task on this latter point. He asks sarcastically: Is Egypt's dean of letters thinking of restoring the pharaonic language? Which made more sense for the Egyptians, to communicate with a mummy, or with Ibn Khaldun, the great fourteenth century Arab philosopher of history? Husri concludes that all the pyramids and all of the pharaonic past could not extinguish one simple truth—that Egyptians spoke today, and for many centuries, the same language as the rest of the Arab countries.[78] For Husri, the determined advocate of language-based German cultural nationalism, Egypt's Arab character was a given, and Egypt's intellectual elite should not waste precious time and energy trying to deny it.

Husri's assault on those who denied Egypt's Arabism reflected the centrality and importance he accorded the country itself. Indeed, this is a theme that will recur repeatedly in this book. Husri himself admitted, in an article which appeared in the Iraqi newspa-

---

[77] Tibi, *Arab Nationalism: A Critical Enquiry*, p. 154; Cleveland, *The Making of an Arab Nationalist*, pp. 132–133.

[78] Abu Khaldun Sati' al-Husri, *Abhath Mukhtara fi al-Qawmiya al 'Arabiya* (Selected studies in Arab nationalism) (Beirut: Markaz Dirasat al-Wuhda al-'Arabiya, 1985), pp. 168–169; see also Cleveland, *The Making of an Arab Nationalist*, p. 137; also Haim, *Arab Nationalism: An Anthology*, p. 50.

per, *al-Bilad*, in 1936, that he in fact was more interested in Egypt than in Syria or Iraq, since Egypt, through its many attributes, had to be considered the role model that influences the entire Arab world. He continues:

> Nature has endowed Egypt with all the attributes and advantages that makes it imperative for her to assume the leading role in the revival of Arab nationalism. It is situated in the center of the Arab world, between the African and Asian segments. It is also the biggest part [of] the Arab world, [having been exposed] to the civilization of the modern world. So it has become the most important cultural center in the Arab world; it is richer than all the Arab countries combined, and it is the most seasoned in the structures of the modern state.[79]

So powerfully did Egypt loom in Husri's consciousness, that he once was moved to write that his foremost aspiration was for Egypt to lead the crusade for Arab unity just as Prussia and Piedmont did for German and Italian unity, respectively.[80] This, by the way, was being said at a time when a number of his own disciples in Iraq were trying to fashion that country into the same role.

More than two full decades later, Husri was to see Egypt, under a charismatic leader, fully adorn the Arab nationalist identity, and endeavor purposefully to lead the Arabs toward unity. But in the 1920s and most of the 1930s, the Arab nationalist bug had not fully bitten Egypt, or for that matter Syria, Iraq, or the other parts of the Arab world. Powerful competitive identities, such as tribalism, sectarianism, regionalism, and state nationalism (*wataniya*) individually, or in combination with each other, proved to be potent obstacles to the spread of an Arab identity. This is not to suggest that Arab nationalism did not make gains or acquire new ad-

---

[79] Abu Khaldun Sati' al-Husri, "Dawr Misr fi al-Nahdha al-Qawmiya al-'Arabiya," (Egypt's role in Arab nationalist renaissance) in al-Husri, *Abhath Mukhtara fi al-Qawmiya al-'Arabiya*, p. 105. The quote appears in a slightly different form in Tibi, *Arab Nationalism; A Critical Enquiry*, p. 185; see also Cleveland, *The Making of an Arab Nationalist*, pp. 134–135; also Haim, *Arab Nationalism: An Anthology*, pp. 50–51.

[80] Cleveland, *The Making of an Arab Nationalist*, p. 135.

herents. That it certainly did; indeed, this chapter has fully documented the impressive strides that Arab nationalism made during this period. But the growth in the dissemination of the "Arab idea" was slowed considerably by the existence of these other potently competitive identities and loyalties that predominated the Arabic-speaking world at the time.

CHAPTER FIVE

THE PATH TO NATIONALIST ASCENT:
FROM THE PALESTINIAN REVOLT TO
THE EGYPTIAN REVOLUTION

While Arab nationalist concerns did not predominate in the 1930s, neither were they nonexistent. The majority of Syrians, wracked by their own divisions, did not see unity with Iraq or Egypt as a priority. But as we have seen, the Syrians were undoubtedly sensitive to political developments in other Arab countries. The same was true of the other Arabic-speaking regions and countries of the Middle East. We saw how Egypt, the most distant from Arab nationalism, was moved, at least at the popular level, by the Syrian uprising against the French in 1925–1927; indeed there was enough public clamor that the recalcitrant politicians were compelled to make public statements supporting the Syrian revolt. But the one issue that consistently found an echo among the urban, educated Arabic-speaking populations of the Middle East was the increasing danger of Jewish immigration into Palestine. Here was a concern that would unite the Arab nationalist, the Islamist, and the believer in Greater Syria. From their different loyalties and perspectives, they all would agree on the need to resist the demographic changes that were under way in Palestine. The expansion in educational opportunities, the introduction of the radio, and the proliferation of newspapers in the interwar period made the Palestinian issue that more accessible. As early as 1928, the visit to Baghdad by a well-known British Zionist, Alfred Mond, was met with widespread street demonstrations.[1] But on the whole, popular concern was not echoed in official pronouncements and policies. The 1936–1939 Arab revolt in Palestine changed that.

The contours of historical development are shaped by consequential events. Some, such as the American, French, and Russian revolutions, end up having an impact beyond their immediate locale. Others have unintended consequences. Napoleon's defeat of Prussia in 1805 accelerated (one is almost tempted to say, created)[2] German cultural nationalism, which lay the grounds for the unification of Germany in 1871. While not of the same magnitude, the Arab revolt in Palestine, which began as a general strike in 1936, then gathered momentum to become a full-fledged revolt that lasted the best part of three years, and claimed the lives of three thousand Arabs, two thousand Jews, and six hundred British,[3] brought the conflict fully into Arab consciousness, making Palestine a foremost Arab issue. Popular pressure compelled Arab governments and political leaderships to come out publicly in support of the Palestinian Arabs, to intervene with the British on the latter's plans to partition the country, and finally to cooperate so as to speak with one official voice in international conferences.

The 1939 London Conference for Palestinians, Arab governments, and Jews was the first such concerted cooperative effort by Arab governments and leaderships, fostering the belief that Arabs, wherever they were, shared similar interests, concerns, and aspirations. In the words of one contemporary commentator, the Pales-

---

[1] Phebe Marr, "The Development of a Nationalist Ideology in Iraq, 1920–1941," *The Muslim World*, vol. 75, no. 2 (April 1985): 100.

[2] As Hans Kohn puts it, "German nationalism. . .was *born* in the war against France. . ." (italics added), see Hans Kohn, "Arendt and the Character of German Nationalism," *The American Historical Review*, vol. LIV, no. 4 (July 1949): 789.

[3] William L. Cleveland, *A History of the Modern Middle East*, 2nd ed. (Boulder, Colorado: Westview Press, 2000), pp. 252–253.

tinian revolt "joined together and united the hearts of the Arabs in all their regions, and they are now one nation even if their states are many."[4] While undoubtedly overstated, this comment does reflect the popular reception accorded to the involvement of the Arab governments in the Palestinian question, and the heightened awareness by peoples and leaders alike of the possibilities of Arab solidarity. And all this was being continuously fueled by a sustained Palestinian campaign stressing that the Palestine issue should be the concern of every Arab and Muslim. "The defense of the Arab character of Palestine," Yehoshua Porath tells us, "became the first duty of Arab nationalists everywhere."[5] What follows is a description of the popular support for Palestinians in Iraq, Syria, and Egypt, and the consequent policies and pronouncements of the respective governments.

In Iraq, widespread demonstrations erupted in support of the 1936 Palestinian general strike, which became so widespread that the Iraqi government hastened to impose a ban on all demonstrations. But the government could do little else. Public meetings in major Iraqi cities continued to be held in which the British were publicly and vehemently denounced, and donations were collected on a wide scale to the extent that Iraq was deemed to be the main financial source for the Palestinian revolt, which erupted in the wake of the general strike. Sunni and Shiite clerics issued *fetwas* (religious edicts) in support of Palestinian rights.[6] Two organizations were at the center of the turmoil. The Palestine Defense Committee, which under British pressure had been defunct for some time, was reformed and became responsible for coordinating much of the financial assistance. The Muthana Club, an Arab nationalist organization, arranged meetings and lectures in which a number of Palestinian leaders and intellectuals spoke. Most important for Iraq's political future, the Palestinian revolt sharpened Arab na-

---

[4] Quoted in James Jankowski, "The Government of Egypt and the Palestine Question, 1936–1939," *Middle Eastern Studies*, vol. 17, no. 4 (October 1981): 448.

[5] Yehoshua Porath, *In Search of Arab Unity, 1930–1945* (London: Frank Cass, 1986), p. 165.

[6] Ibid., pp. 275–276.

tionalist sentiments among army officers, legitimizing and institutionalizing the entry of the military in Iraqi politics.

Popular support for the Palestinian cause was no less fierce in Syria. Strikes and demonstrations occurred frequently, accompanied by violently anti-Zionist and anti-British pamphlets and petitions. A vast array of contributions, ranging from money to jewelry was made, and Jewish products were successfully boycotted. Most effectively, arms were smuggled from Syria to Palestine, and many Syrians volunteered into the guerrilla campaigns in Palestine.[7] Syrian sentiments of solidarity with Palestinians were augmented by a perception held by many Syrians that in addition to their Arab kinship, Palestine also formed the southern tip of *Bilad al-Sham* (Greater Syria).[8] On both of these levels, Arabism and Syrianism, the Syrians were especially susceptible to Palestinian concerns and aspirations.

The Syrians also had geostrategic and economic reasons for their support of the Palestinians. The prospect of a Jewish state, constituting a physical barrier, was a legitimate concern for Syria, which unlike Iraq, would be the immediate neighbor of such a state. Economically, the dramatic growth of the port of Haifa was already posing a real threat to Beirut, and Syria's nascent industrial base was being quickly outpaced by the developing industrial movement in the Jewish sector of the Palestinian economy.[9]

In its popular reaction to the Palestinian revolt, Egypt was not different from Iraq or Syria. Patrick Seale does not hesitate to characterize the revolt as "the decisive factor which swung Egyptian politicians in favor of a pan-Arab policy."[10] But the politicians were

---

[7] Philip S. Khoury, *Syria and the French Mandate* (Princeton, New Jersey: Princeton University Press, 1987), pp. 542–544.

[8] According to Philip Khoury, this perception seems to have been shared by many Palestinians too. See ibid., p. 542. Rashid Khalidi, however, argues that Palestinian identification with the concept of southern Syria peaked during King Faysal's government in Damascus, then atrophied after the collapse of that government, allowing for the emergence of a Palestinian identity. See Rashid Khalidi, *Palestinian Identity: The Construction of Modern National Consciousness* (New York: Columbia University Press, 1997), pp. 162–175.

[9] Khoury, *Syria and the French Mandate*, pp. 541–542.

[10] Patrick Seale, *The Struggle for Syria: A Study of Post-War Arab Politics, 1945–1958* (New Haven, Connecticut: Yale University Press, 1986), p. 17.

simply responding to popular opinion. Anti-British sentiment reached a crescendo, and a fierce campaign against British policies in Palestine was spearheaded by the Muslim Brotherhood.[11] Highly charged pieces were written about "bleeding Palestine" or "Palestine the martyr," and the events there were depicted as constituting a full-fledged revolution. Popular agitation was such that members of Parliament raised the issue several times, demanding swift and meaningful government action, and a group of them embarked on organizing an international conference on the Palestinian problem, which eventually met in October 1938 under the title, "World Parliamentary Congress of Arab and Muslim Countries for the Defense of Palestine."[12] The convening of the Congress in Cairo, and the anti-British undercurrents which it displayed at a time when the British held an unquestionable position of influence in the country, is a testimony to the strength of the pro-Palestinian sentiments sweeping Egypt in the wake of the Arab revolt.

In addition to the emotional dimension, there were also practical economic and geostrategic dimensions to Egyptian reactions. Businessmen worried that Jewish ascendancy would eventually lead to the establishment of a Jewish state. Such a state could become an economic threat to Egypt by forming a physical barrier that, at a minimum, would hinder the country's commercial relations with the Near East markets. "If Zionism [were to be] established in Palestine," wrote one prominent Egyptian businessman, "its harm [would] not be limited to Palestine alone. Rather, it [would] immediately extend to affect the destiny of all the neighboring countries, to place limits on their economies, industries, trade, wealth and independence."[13] Beyond the economic issue, Egyptians had a

[11] Porath, *In Search of Arab Unity, 1930–1945*, p. 170; Seale, *The Struggle for Syria*, p. 17.

[12] Jankowski, "The Government of Egypt and the Palestine Question, 1936–1939," p. 434.

[13] Ralph M. Coury, "Who Invented Egyptian Arab Nationalism?, Part 2," *International Journal of Middle East Studies*, vol. 14, 1982: 463; see also Israel Gershoni and James P. Jankowski, *Redefining the Egyptian Nation, 1930–1945* (London: Cambridge University Press, 1995), pp. 174–176; also Jankowski, "The Government of Egypt and the Palestine Question, 1936–1939," p. 445.

wider geostrategic concern. It was felt that a Jewish state would be a catalyst for constant tension and crises that would lead to situations of chronic unrest which in turn would invite foreign interventions. Moreover, the pressures of continuous immigration would inevitably push the Jewish state to expand into more Arab lands, depriving more Arab people of their homes and their livelihood. Thus the Palestinian question could not and would not be limited to Palestine; it was, and, in the case of the creation of a Jewish state, would always be a problem for the Arab and Muslim worlds. These fears were expressed succinctly by Muhamed Husayn Haykal, a leading Egyptian intellectual, who was also an influential liberal political figure. To Haykal, the situation in Palestine, particularly if the British partition plan were to be implemented, would have a deleterious impact on Egypt's "future which is firmly linked to the destinies of the lands which neighbor us and are influenced by us as we are influenced by them—in the security of our country, in the sale of our products, in the shaping of our international relations, in the organization of our self-defense, and in the definition of our policy in the Mediterranean."[14]

The British plan to partition Palestine, therefore, engendered such huge fears of the possibility of a Jewish state that immediately after its announcement, and its acceptance by Emir 'Abdallah of Jordan, who saw an opportunity to expand his own domain, plans were set afoot for the convening of a "pan-Arab congress." And indeed, two months later, over four hundred nationalists from Iraq, Egypt, Syria, Saudi Arabia, Palestine, and Trans-Jordan converged on the Syrian city of Bludan to begin a conference that produced vehemently anti-Zionist resolutions and an absolute rejection of any partition of Palestine.[15] The conference, whose attendees were officially sanctioned delegates as well as independent nationalists, was an early instance of the gradual involvement of Arab govern-

---

[14] Gershoni and Jankowski, *Redefining the Egyptian Nation, 1930–1945*, p. 175.

[15] Khoury, *Syria and the French Mandate*, pp. 554–555; also Michael N. Barnett, *Dialogues in Arab Politics: Negotiations in Regional Order* (New York: Columbia University Press, 1998), p. 72. For a lively analysis of the motives and consequences of the conference, see Elie Kedourie, "The Bludan Congress on Palestine, 1937," *Middle Eastern Studies*, vol. 17, no. 1, January 1981: 107–125.

ments in Palestinian and Arab affairs. And this was due largely to popular pressure.

It was the overwhelming pro-Palestinian opinion among the Arab populations that ultimately forced a response from the otherwise recalcitrant Arab governments. After all, the governments had to tread a thin line between two conflicting pressures: the weight of public opinion on the one hand, and on the other, the political demands of the British and the French who, by virtue of their physical presence in these countries, exerted an inordinate amount of influence on the indigenous governments.

The Iraqi government found itself in one such situation in the spring of 1936. Fawzi al-Qawuqchi, a Syrian officer who was serving in the Iraqi army resigned his commission to lead a group of volunteers into Palestine to fight alongside their Palestinian "brethren." Support for Qawuqchi's endeavor was widespread not just among the general population, but also, and more important, within the ranks of Iraq's armed forces. After a meeting with an envoy from the Palestinian Higher Arab Committee (the organization that was leading Palestinian resistance), Iraq's Prime Minister Yasin al-Hashimi agreed to release Qawuqchi and assist in his recruitment of men and acquisition of arms. The British were naturally incensed; they demanded that the prime minister put an end to the whole enterprise immediately. Hashimi had little choice but to summon Qawuqchi and tell him that, due to British pressure, he had no alternative but to call a halt to this whole initiative. Qawuqchi, however, disobeyed the order and took his men to Palestine.[16] To appease the displeased British, Hashimi dispatched his foreign minister to London and Jerusalem to try to mediate the conflict. The novelty about Hashimi's move was "the attempted mediation not only between the Arabs and the mandatory authorities but also between the Arabs and the Zionist leadership."[17]

[16] Michael Eppel, *The Palestine Conflict in the History of Modern Iraq: The Dynamics of Involvement, 1928–1948* (London: Frank Cass, 1994), pp. 41–42.

[17] Abbas Kelidar, "A Quest for Identity," *Middle Eastern Studies*, vol. 33, no. 2 (April 1997): 427.

The government that replaced Hashimi's administration had a distinctly different foreign policy orientation. Led by a Kurd, a Turkoman, and a Shiite, the new government advocated an "Iraq first" policy, which was a veiled attempt to decrease Iraq's involvement in Arab affairs. But the turmoil in Palestine had engendered such intense pro-Palestinian sentiment among the Iraqi population that the government was compelled to follow public opinion.[18] In explaining his government's adamant rejection of the British partition plan in Palestine, the Turkoman prime minister, Hikmat Sulayman, told the British ambassador in July 1937 that "no Iraqi government will be able to remain in power without giving some degree of satisfaction to the public hatred of the proposals for the partition of Palestine."[19] Unfortunately for Sulayman, his statement was a case of too little too late. His government was ousted by Arab nationalist officers a month later, and was replaced by an avowedly nationalist and pro-Palestinian government. Immediately, the new government denounced the partition plan for Palestine, a position vigorously supported by a reportedly fifty thousand-strong mass demonstration.[20]

The entry of Fawzi al-Qawuqchi into Palestine became a catalyst for the involvement of the Syrian authorities under the French mandate in the Palestinian affair. Seven hundred Syrian volunteers, mostly from the poorer classes, but some from notable families in Homs, joined Qawuqchi's force. From then on, bands of Syrian volunteers continued to cross into Palestine, with a number of them assuming leadership positions in the rebellion.[21] Independently, and through the French authorities, the British sought to persuade the Syrian political leadership to curb the activities of these irregular forces. Like their Iraqi counterparts, the Syrian leaders were forced into a delicate balancing act, which was evidenced in the

---

[18] 'Abd al-Razzak 'Abd al-Darraji, *Ja'far Abu al-Timman wa Dawrahu fi al-Haraka al-Wataniya fi al-'Iraq* (Ja'far Abu al-Timman and his role in the Iraqi national movement) (Baghdad: Wizarat al-Thaqafa wa al-Funoon, 1978), pp. 437–438.

[19] Eppel, *The Palestine Conflict in the History of Modern Iraq*, p. 64.

[20] Robert Gale Woolbert, "Pan-Arabism and the Palestine Problem," *Foreign Affairs*, vol. 16, no. 2 (January 1938): 317.

[21] Khoury, *Syria and the French Mandate*, pp. 546–547.

circumspect way in which it supported the Palestinian revolt and the half-heartedness with which it responded to British and French demands.[22] In Syria, however, the leadership's lukewarm support for the revolt also reflected, as we have seen, the concern by members of its socioeconomic class of the revolt's negative impact on the Syrian economy.

A reluctant Egyptian government was also pushed into a proactive stance through increasing popular pressures. Members of the government consistently sought to make pro-Palestinian representations with the British, arguing vehemently against any partition of Palestine, prescribing instead a unitary state with mutual tolerance for all religious communities. The British were reminded, on many occasions, that the position of the Egyptian government as well as their own was being undermined in Egypt by the events in Palestine. Indeed, the government took the occasion of the country's first address to the League of Nations to stress the importance of creating a unitary and independent Palestinian state.[23] And when an effort was made to replace striking Palestinian workers by Egyptians, the government hurriedly intervened to prevent the Egyptians from traveling to Palestine.[24] The British, of course, thought all this was a work of downright hypocrisy on the part of the Egyptian leaders who, the British contended, were trying to divert public attention from rampant domestic ills to an issue about which Egyptian leaders cared little. This British perception was rebutted eloquently by Egypt's foreign minister:

> You may say if you wish (though I think it untrue) that Egyptian politicians do not really care what happens in Palestine, that they raise the question only for demagogic reasons in order to deflect popular attention from the crying need for internal reform—the same charge that is made against the governing clique in Iraq. But does not the very fact that the cabinet feels obliged to defend the

[22] Ibid., pp. 552–562.

[23] Jankowski, "The Government of Egypt and the Palestine Question, 1936–1939," pp. 432–433.

[24] Coury, "Who Invented Egyptian Arab Nationalism? Part 2," p. 255.

Arab case indicate that there must be many Egyptians who do have
a lively interest in Arab nationalism? There is no use dragging a red
herring across the path unless the cat likes herrings. The politicians
may be insecure and their appeal may smack of demagogy, but the
fact that they make it shows the inclinations of the electorate.[25]

Regardless of their true motives, the Arab governments could
not but intervene in one way or another in the Palestinian conflict
because of mounting pressure from the populace (or at least from
important and vocal segments of that populace). Indeed, the events
of 1936–1939 could be seen as the historical instance in which, for
the first time, the Arab leaderships were to embark on a cooperative effort fueled by a realization of common Arab interests. This
was occasioned by the British-sponsored St. James's Conference of
Arab Palestinians, the Jewish Agency and Representatives from
Arab Governments, held in London in 1939. The results of the
conference were inconclusive, but in terms of inter-Arab affairs,
the decision of the Arab leaders to meet in Cairo prior to the conference was perhaps the most important by-product. In Cairo, they
agreed on a common *Arab* position, and in fact, that position was
fully adhered to throughout the duration of the London conference. Nuri al-Sa'id, Iraq's prime minister, later confirmed that inter-
Arab consultation and the agreement on a united front was the
most consequential dimension of the endeavor. He expressed his
hope that "the historic meeting will serve as the foundation stone
for the establishment of an Eastern and Arab League."[26] Prince
Faysal bin 'Abd al-'Aziz, the head of the Sa'udi delegation, echoed
this sentiment: "for the first time in our history, we witness this
clear manifestation of cooperation and solidarity of the Arab countries. For the first time we stand united. Let us hope that this conference may serve as a useful precedent for solving other problems
and strengthening the foundations of our unity."[27]

[25] Woolbert, "Pan-Arabism and the Palestine Problem," p. 319; see also Gershoni and
Jankowski, *Redefining the Egyptian Nation*, p. 179.

[26] Quoted in Y. Porath, *The Palestinian Arab National Movement: From Riots to Rebellion*, vol. 2, 1929–1939 (London: Frank Cass, 1977), p. 284.

[27] Porath, *In Search of Arab Unity, 1930–1945*, p. 172.

This united front held not only during the conference, but also later on when the inconclusiveness of the London meeting prompted the British government to unilaterally publish a white paper promising Palestinian independence within ten years. On the day after its issuance, Egypt's prime minister announced that the Arab governments had decided against recommending the terms of the white paper to the Palestinian Arabs. This concerted and united Arab involvement in the Palestine issue was described by Elie Kedourie, a vigorous critic of British policy and of Arab nationalism as "a fateful and perhaps fatal move," for it introduced the Arab states "into what had been a relatively limited dispute between two groups in a mandated territory."[28] Be that as it may, what is relevant for our purposes is that the Palestinian events of 1936–1939 contributed not only to the growth of Arab nationalist sentiment among the Arab people, but also to a nascent solidarity among the Arab governments.

Increased manifestations of Arabist proclivities and political activity continued during the World War II years. This could be discerned on the popular level by the way the 1941 Rashid 'Ali operation against the British in Iraq was received by other Arabs. Rashid 'Ali al-Gaylani had been Iraq's prime minister since March 1940, but had increasingly favored a neutral position in the European war and had opened negotiations with the Germans. At a time when Syria had come under the control of Vichy France, Britain could not afford to have an Iraqi prime minister who was not a supporter of British interests and policies. Consequently, the British ambassador demanded Rashid 'Ali's resignation, which was finally, and under much duress, given on January 31, 1941. This, however, incensed the Arab nationalist army officers who, since the ouster of the Hikmat Sulayman government in 1937, had become ascendant in the armed forces. Within two months they executed a coup in which Rashid 'Ali was returned to power and all pro-British elements of the ruling elites, including the regent, Prince 'Abd al-

[28] Elie Kedourie, *Arabic Political Memoirs and Other Studies* (London: Frank Cass, 1974), p. 220.

Illah, escaped to British positions or to neighboring countries. War with Britain broke out on May 2. Very soon, however, the British forces in Iraq, aided by units of Jordan's Arab Legion, defeated the Iraqi army, entering Baghdad on June 1, 1941, along with Prince 'Abd al-Illah and the others who had fled the nationalist coup.

A short-lived and unsuccessful affair, the events surrounding the Rashid 'Ali coup and the war with Britain nevertheless fired the imagination of other Arabs, who perceived it as a heroic insurrection by an Arab country against foreign imperial control. There was enthusiastic support for the Iraqis in Syria, where funds were raised and sent to Iraq, and a few officers crossed the border to join their Iraqi brethren. The infant Arab nationalist Ba'th Party took great heart from the events in Iraq and launched a "victory in Iraq" movement.[29] In Egypt, the Rashid 'Ali coup created unrest which added to the problems of the pro-Allied government of Husayn Sirri Pasha.[30] Certainly by now, a broader popular interest in Arab affairs was clearly discernible in Egypt. In 1942, *Nadi al-Itihad al-'Arabi* (the Arab Union Club) was formed, dedicating itself to fostering closer relations and stronger bonds with other Arabs for the purpose of defending the rights of the Arab countries and regions. The club opened branches in Baghdad, Damascus, Beirut, and Jaffa. It became sufficiently influential for the Egyptian Prime Minister Nahas Pasha to endorse the club's platform, confirming that his government took "great interest in the affairs of the sister Arab nations, [was] always ready to defend their interests and rights, [and viewed] with great interest the question of Arab unity."[31] And these were not idle words. Not only Egypt, but also Iraq was beginning to explore various ideas, plans, and proposals for some form of Arab unity.

The process was begun by Iraq's Prime Minister Nuri al-Sa'id, who had been encouraged by a statement made by the British for-

---

[29] Seale, *The Struggle for Syria*, p. 10.

[30] Tom Little, *Modern Egypt* (New York: Frederick A. Praeger, 1967), p. 88.

[31] Porath, *In Search of Arab Unity, 1930–1945*, p. 258; Gershoni and Jankowski, *Redefining the Egyptian Nation, 1930–1945*, p. 198.

eign secretary, Anthony Eden, which affirmed British support for Arab union initiatives.[32] In January 1943, he submitted to the British a plan for a "Fertile Crescent Union."[33] Nuri began his memorandum by emphasizing that Iraq was not just a neighbor to the other Arab countries of the Fertile Crescent; rather it was symbiotically tied to them by fundamental linguistic, national, religious, and economic bonds. Yet, while they all desired some form of Arab unity, Nuri recognized the differences that existed among them.[34] He thus proposed a two-stage process for a comprehensive Arab union. In the first stage, Syria, Lebanon, Palestine, and Trans-Jordan would be united into one state, with some autonomy, guaranteed by the international community, for the Jews in Palestine as well as acceptable safeguards for the Christians of Lebanon. Once this state of "Greater Syria" had been formed, it would join Iraq in an "Arab League" to which other Arab states could later adhere if they so wished. The League would be responsible for defense, foreign affairs, currency, communications, customs, and the protection of minorities.[35] The plan was presented as a first step in a process that would eventually lead to a union of the Arabic-speaking world, the governmental form of which would depend on the preferences and ultimate decisions of the Arab populations.

On one level, the submission of the plan testified to the recognition by Iraq's political elite of their Arab identity. On another level, the plan had as much to do with Hashemite ambition and Iraq's rivalry with Egypt over Arab leadership as with any consuming attachment to the cause of Arab nationalism. But the two motivations need not be mutually exclusive. After all, Iraq's political establishment was made up mostly of Sunnis, and the Sunni community had always been the most susceptible to the ideas of Arab

[32] Eppel, *The Palestine Conflict in the History of Modern Iraq*, p. 128.

[33] The following description of Nuri's plan is taken from Su'ad Rauf Muhamed, *Nuri al-Sa'id wa Dawrahu fi al-Siyasa al-'Iraqiya, 1932–1945* (Nuri al-Sa'id and his role in Iraqi politics, 1932–1945) (Baghdad: Maktabat al-Yaqdha al-'Arabiya, 1988), pp. 250–262.

[34] Ibid., p. 254.

[35] Muhamed, *Nuri al-Sa'id wa Dawrahu fi al-Siyasa al-'Iraqiya, 1932–1945* (Nuri al-Sa'id and his role in Iraqi politics, 1932–1945), pp. 257–258; see also Michael N. Barnett, *Dialogues in Arab Politics: Negotiations in Regional Order*, p. 76.

nationalism. The elder statesmen of the same establishment were also committed Hashemites, almost all of whom had been Faysal's main lieutenants in the Arab revolt against the Ottomans, and then in Faysal's Arab administration in Syria. To them, a fusion of Iraq, Syria, and Trans-Jordan under some kind of eventual Hashemite rule was a compelling political and strategic proposition.[36] And it was not as though the idea had no support in Syria.[37] Nuri had a plan that he believed would serve the Arab nationalist, as well as the Hashemite, cause.

But the plan also had powerful detractors within Iraq. To the non-Arab Kurds, any unity scheme involving Iraq with other Arab countries and domains was not much short of a nightmare. Constituting a significant 20 percent of Iraq's population, the Kurds would become a tiny and thoroughly inconsequential island in an ocean of Arabic-speaking peoples. The Arab Shiites, too, were hardly thrilled by the Fertile Crescent plan. While they were a substantial majority in Iraq, they would constitute a small minority in a predominantly Sunni Arab world. It was not that the Shiites did not think of themselves as Arabs; it was simply politically disadvantageous for them to subsume their Shiite identity into an Arab one. Iraqi Shiites, therefore, perceived such a union as essentially a plan designed to cement Sunni hegemony and further marginalize the Shiites.[38] Shiite and Kurdish response was, on the whole, accordingly negative, constituting an important factor in the plan's ultimate failure.

The other significant factor was Egypt's resistance to the formation of a Hashemite domain in the eastern part of the Arab world that could challenge Egyptian ascendancy in the area. Had Nuri's proposal been made a decade or so earlier, it might not have elicited

---

[36] For the political maneuvering involved in Iraq's unity schemes, see Majid Khadduri, "The Scheme of Fertile Crescent Unity: A Study in Inter-Arab Relations," in *The Near East and the Great Powers*. ed. Richard N. Frye (Cambridge, Massachusetts: Harvard University Press, 1951), pp. 137–177.

[37] Malik Mufti, *Sovereign Creations: Pan Arabism and Political Order in Syria and Iraq* (Ithaca, New York: Cornell University Press, 1996), pp. 46–52.

[38] Yitzhak Nakash, *The Shi'is of Iraq* (Princeton, New Jersey: Princeton University Press, 1994), pp. 133–134.

a response from an Egypt whose Arab nationalist impulse was minimal. But as we have seen, Egypt's involvement in Arab affairs had grown steadily, so that by the 1940s, Egypt's leaders had become well attuned to their Arab milieu, and to the centrality of Egypt in that milieu.[39] This is not to suggest that Arab nationalism had become the dominant ideology in Egypt in the 1940s. Far from it. For most citizens, loyalty to Egypt and Islam was still a more powerful impulse than loyalty to Arab nationalism. But Egypt's response to the Palestinian revolt, even though it might have had a strong Islamic dimension, underscored Egypt's cultural and historic bonds with other Arabs. And the political leaders well understood the political and economic benefits associated with an activist stance in the region. It was hardly surprising then that they would be less than sanguine about an Arab unity scheme that would feature Iraq as its central and most influential member.[40] Political benefits, moreover, need not be always national; often they are personal. To Egypt's Prime Minister Nahas Pasha, who had been imposed on King Farouk by the British, and who as a consequence had developed an antagonistic relationship with the king,[41] asserting Egypt's leadership in the Arab world would allow him to score points at the expense of the king. Indeed, the king himself, who had earlier entertained unfulfilled hopes of recreating the caliphate in Cairo, came to see an Arab leadership role based in Cairo as an acceptable substitute to a caliphate.[42] All of these factors, therefore, necessi-

[39] A position that in fact was more than welcomed by the nationalists in the region, who accepted Egypt's weight and centrality in the Arab world. See, for instance, Abu Khaldun Sati' al-Husri, "Dawr Misr fi al-Nahdha al-Qawmiya al-'Arabiya," (Egypt's role in Arab nationalist renaissance) in his *Abhath Mukhtara fi al-Qawmiya al-'Arabiya* (Selected studies on Arab nationalism) (Beirut: Markaz Dirasat al-Wuhda al-'Arabiya, 1985), p. 105; see also Ilyas Sahab, "Sati' al-Husri: al-Mufakir, wa al-Da'iya wa al-Numudhaj," (Sati' al-Husri: the thinker, the advocate, and the role model), *al-Mustaqbal al-'Arabi*, no.1 (May 1978): 85.

[40] Jamil Mattar and 'Ali al-Din Hillal, *Al-Nidham al-Iqlimi al-'Arabi: Dirasa fi al-'Ilaqat al-Siyasia al-'Arabiya* (The Arab regional system: a study in Arab political relations) (Beirut: Markaz Dirasat al-Wuhda al-'Arabiya, 1980), p. 63.

[41] See P. J. Vatikiotis, *The History of Modern Egypt: From Muhammed Ali to Mubarak*, 4th ed. (Baltimore: Johns Hopkins University Press, 1991), pp. 349–356.

[42] Elie Kedourie, *The Chatham House Version and Other Middle Eastern Studies* (London: Weidenfeld and Nicolson, 1970), p. 206.

tated a response from Egypt. In an address to the Egyptian Senate, Nahas Pasha declared:

> When Mr. Eden made his statement, I thought about it and con-
> cluded that the best way to achieve it is to let the Arab governments
> themselves take care of it. I thought that the Egyptian government
> should take an official initiative by consulting other Arab govern-
> ments, one by one, then Egypt should coordinate these different
> views as much as possible. Egypt will then invite Arab representa-
> tives to discuss the issue collectively. If an agreement is reached,
> Egypt will then convene a meeting in Egypt chaired by the Egyptian
> prime minister.[43]

Accordingly, the Egyptian prime minister embarked on a series of conversations with the leaders of Iraq, Syria, Trans-Jordan, Saudi Arabia, Lebanon, and Yemen about the prospects and feasi-bility of Arab unity. As these bilateral talks progressed throughout 1943 and well into 1944, emphasizing Egypt's determination to etch for itself a leading role, Arab nationalist narrators in Egypt endeavored intellectually to legitimize Egypt's political initiative by emphasizing Egypt's historical Arab roots. Perhaps the most prominent and committed of these narrators, 'Abd al-Rahman 'Azzam, who later became the first secretary general of the Arab League in 1945, would write somewhat expansively that "Egypt was an Arab country before the time of Christ."[44] It is important to note that the effort at legitimation was directed at Egyptians, not at the other Arabs. Regardless of whether they were truly con-vinced that Egypt was genuinely committed to the Arab nationalist cause, nationalists in other Arab countries were nevertheless jubi-lant that Egypt "was beginning to consider itself a part of the Arab world."[45]

---

[43] Quoted in Ghassan Salame, "Inter-Arab Politics: The Return of Geography," in *The Middle East: Ten Years After Camp David*, ed. William B. Quandt. (Washington, D.C.: The Brookings Institution, 1988), p. 338.

[44] Sylvia Haim, ed., *Arab Nationalism: An Anthology* (Berkeley: University of California Press, 1962), p. 51.

[45] Seale, *The Struggle for Syria*, p. 21.

Arab popular approval of Egypt's move was interestingly enough duplicated at the level of political leaderships, many of whom were less than enthusiastic about the "Fertile Crescent Plan" with its intimation of eventual Iraqi leadership. The Saudi king, who had ousted the Hashemites from the Hejaz two decades earlier, could not sanction any scheme that would strengthen Hashemite Iraq. The powerful Damascene faction within the Syrian government insisted on a republican form of government for Syria, and feared that Nuri's plan would become a vehicle for Hashemite irredentism through one of its two branches in Amman or Baghdad. And the Lebanese Christians considered the Egyptians more moderate than the Iraqis, hence they expected a less intrusive proposal than that of the Baghdad government on the independence of Lebanon.

In June 1944, the Egyptian government formally invited the other Arab governments and political leaderships to a conference in Alexandria on the subject of Arab unity and cooperation. The conference lasted from September 25 to October 8, and included representatives of the governments of Egypt, Iraq, Syria, Lebanon, Trans-Jordan, Saudi Arabia, and Yemen, as well as a representative of the Arab Palestinians. At its conclusion, the conference formulated the "Alexandria Protocol" which became the basis for the formal establishment of the Arab League in 1945 to be headquartered in Cairo.

While recognizing the many ties that bind the Arabs together, the Arab League Pact was essentially an agreement among *sovereign Arab states*. The prologue to the agreement characterized the members as "desirous of strengthening the close relations and numerous ties which link the Arab states and anxious to support and strengthen these ties upon a basis of respect for the independence and sovereignty of these states."[46] In a sense, the League represented for the Arab countries a perfect compromise between Arab identity and their more particularistic, local identities. It was a clear

---

[46] For a succinct exposition of the roots and development of the Arab League, see Cecil A. Hourani, "The Arab League in Perspective," *Middle East Journal*, vol. 1, no. 2 (April 1947): 125–136.

affirmation that these countries and domains were members of a larger Arab system in which all the constituent parts were enjoined to seek closer ties, yet the pact also asserted unequivocally the independence and sovereignty of the Arab states. To the Arab leaderships, the creation of the Arab League was a confirmation that the tension between the two competing identities, local (*watani*) versus national (*qawmi*), need not constitute a zero-sum game. That it did not in this particular instance was in fact a function of the goals and interests of the ruling elites. Among the public at large, especially, of course, its urban and educated segments, the League represented a welcome step toward Arab overall cooperation, but also, in stressing political sovereignty, a possible hindrance to future unity endeavors. While perhaps not immediately apparent, the establishment of the Arab League did indeed create a tension between Arab unity and Arab statehood that would be played out in the turbulent decades of the 1950s and 1960s. On another level, the Arab League would institutionalize Egypt's leading role in the Arab world, implanting its presence onto the Arab consciousness, the full force of which would not be felt until a decade later.

Little doubt remains that the establishment of the Arab League generally led to the heightening of Arabist sentiment. Increased interaction among the elites was bound to have a spillover effect on other societal institutions and activities, such as the media, professional associations, and educational and cultural exchanges and interactions. Even critical views of the League from the *qawmi* groups who thought the League's endorsement of state sovereignty hindered organic Arab unity, or from the *watani* crowd who considered the League to be an infringement on state sovereignty and a step toward the eventual demise of the various Arab states, were part of a general debate that was to bring the ideas of Arab nationalism to the forefront of Arab consciousness.

Perhaps it was not coincidental that the Ba'th Party, a vehement, almost fanatical, propagator of Arab nationalism and Arab unity, which later was to become a major player in inter-Arab politics, grew rapidly in the second half of the 1940s. The formal founding congress of the party was convened in April 1947 in Damascus, attracting about 250 attendees from various Arab countries and regions,[47] most of whom were Sunnis and Orthodox Christians who belonged to the urban middle class or were members of the country gentry.[48] The first principle of the party's constitution, which was adopted at the congress affirmed that the Arab world was "an indivisible political and economic unity." Other principles established the Arabs as a cultural unity. Indeed, the Arabs were not just a nation, but a most special nation "with an eternal mission."[49] Even though it had to operate clandestinely, party branches were opened in Lebanon, Iraq, and Jordan, and recruitment was extended to other parts of the Arab world between 1948 and 1951.[50] While not yet a major political force, the Ba'th Party in the second half of the 1940s rapidly gained enough popular support to establish a presence on the Syrian political landscape. The party's growth was a symptom of the gradual acceptability of Arab nationalist ideas among the Arabs, particularly the educated urban classes.

Education played a key role in this process. In the 1920s, no more than 2 percent of the population in the Arabic-speaking world could claim to have had some education,[51] and much of it was at the primary level provided by private institutions, particularly religious establishments. By the 1940s, education had expanded considerably. For example, enrollment in Egyptian secondary schools rose from about 5,000 in 1920 to 120,000 in 1951, and those attending universities increased from 3,000 in 1925 to 32,000 in 1950.[52] More to the point, the expansion in education in Egypt produced a "new effendiya" class (essentially an urban,

[47] John F. Devlin, *The Ba'th Party: A History from Its Origins to 1966* (Stanford, California: Hoover Institution Press, 1976), p. 15.

[48] Robert W. Olson, *The Ba'th and Syria, 1947–1982: The Evolution of Ideology, Party and State* (Princeton, New Jersey: Kingston Press, Inc., 1982), p. 21.

[49] The full text of the constitution of the Ba'th Party can be found in Haim, *Arab Nationalism: An Anthology*, pp. 233–241. For an absorbing critique of Ba'thist ideology, see Kanan Makiya, *Republic of Fear: The Politics of Modern Iraq*, updated ed. (Berkeley: University of California Press, 1998), pp. 201–228.

[50] John F. Devlin, "The Baath Party: Rise and Metamorphosis," *The American Historical Review*, vol. 96, no. 5 (December 1991):1399.

[51] M. E. Yapp, *The Near East Since the First World War: A History to 1945*, 2nd ed. (London: Longman, 1996), p. 19.

[52] Ibid., p. 63.

literate, and professional stratum), which had a less westernized social background. This new class, unlike an earlier generation, was thus oriented less toward Europe and the West and more toward Arabism and Islam.[53] In Iraq, too, the secondary school population grew considerably from 229 in 1921 to 13,969 by 1940, an increase paralleled by the growth of the college student population from 99 to 1,218 during the same period.[54] An important by-product of the spread of secular education in Iraq was the gradual reduction of the sectarian divide between Sunnis and Shiites. This happened as secularist and nationalist values, propagated by the state's school system, reached the Shiites in increasing numbers.[55] Moreover, whereas only fifteen Iraqi students graduated from college in 1921—all lawyers—there were 1,091 graduates from nine different colleges in 1951.[56] In Syria, which did not become independent until 1945, a rapid expansion in education over the next five years doubled the number of primary school students, and quadrupled the number of secondary school students.[57] The bulk of the students in the three countries, especially Egypt and Iraq, were receiving their education from state schools. By the 1950s, private schools were a distinct minority, and religious schools tended to be strictly supervised by the state. Consequently, secular and nationalist values on the whole were inculcated into the growing student populations.

The 1940s were years of rapid expansion of Arab nationalist ideas. By the latter part of the decade, the nationalist ideologues and activists had succeeded in planting Arab nationalism into the consciousness of people hitherto unfamiliar with, or resistant to, the tenets of the idea. No longer an upstart, lagging far behind

---

[53] Gershoni and Jankowski, *Redefining the Egyptian Nation*, pp. 216–217.

[54] Hanna Batatu, *The Old Social Classes and the Revolutionary Movements of Iraq: A Study of Iraq's Old Landed and Commercial Classes and of Its Communists, Ba'thists, and Free Officers* (Princeton, New Jersey: Princeton University Press, 1978), p. 34. Also, Phebe Marr, *The Modern History of Iraq* (Boulder, Colorado: Westview Press, 1985), pp. 137–142.

[55] Marr, "The Development of Nationalist Ideology in Iraq, 1920–1941," p. 100.

[56] Marr, *The Modern History of Iraq*, p. 139.

[57] Raymond A. Hinnebusch, *Authoritarian Power and State Formation in Ba'thist Syria* (Boulder, Colorado: Westview Press, 1990), p. 51.

other loyalties and identities, Arab nationalism now could take its place as a legitimate and serious contender for peoples' political loyalties. And there is little doubt that the 1936–1939 Arab revolt in Palestine contributed significantly to the ascent of the idea.

But this ascent, considerable as it was, should not lull us into thinking that by the 1940s Arab nationalism had become the main focus of peoples' ideological loyalties. The competing identities, which we have already encountered, were equally potent and in some cases far more entrenched, and consequently continued to lay claim to peoples' allegiance. Looking at peoples' enduring iden- tification with their immediate locale, clan, tribe, sect, religion, and country, it can only be surmised that, despite its impressive growth, Arab nationalism was in many ways still a minority sentiment.

In Egypt, Arab nationalism continued to face an uphill struggle in its competition with the Egypt-first orientation, represented by a plethora of political parties and organizations,[58] as well as with a powerfully ingrained Muslim identity, represented by the one million members of the Muslim Brotherhood Organization. In Syria too, Arab nationalist ideas had to compete not only with other equally populist ideologies, such as Communism and Antun Sa'ada's Syrian nationalism, but also with a host of powerful tradi- tional loyalties and a strong attachment to *Bilad al-Sham*, the no- tion of Greater Syria. Indeed, the many overlapping references in the wake of Syrian independence in 1946 to Syria as a nation in its own right and as a part of a larger Arab nation revealed "an ambiguity of identity, not just a carelessness about language."[59]

In Iraq as well, Arab nationalism continued to be confronted by other powerful attachments and political orientations. While the platform of the *Istiqlal* Party and, to a lesser extent during this period, the ideas of the infant Ba'th Party, attracted increasing

[58] The best study on Egyptian parties and organizations in monarchical Egypt, which clearly shows the primacy of "Egyptian" concerns, is 'Ali al-Din Hillal, *Al-Siyasa wa al-Hukum fi Misr: al-'Ahd al Birlimani, 1923–1952* (Politics and rule in Egypt: the parliamen- tary era, 1923–1945) (Cairo: Maktabat Nahdhat al-Sharq, 1977).

[59] Eberhard Kienle, "Arab Unity Schemes Revisited: Interest, Identity, and Policy in Syria and Egypt," *International Journal of Middle East Studies*, vol. 27, no. 1, (February 1997): 59.

numbers of Iraqi youth, other parties and groupings such as the *al-Ahali* group with its manifestly Iraqi orientation and the Communist Party could claim just as committed, and perhaps a greater number of, supporters. In addition, attachment to, and concern about, tribal and sectarian interests, were so embedded in people that they outweighed Arab nationalist considerations. 'Abd al-Karim al-Uzri, one of the few Shiite members of the political elite during this period, implies in his memoirs that during the 1941 war with the British, the tribes around Baghdad, a number of whose members were officers and soldiers in the Iraqi army, were in fact working in tandem with the British against the Rashid 'Ali government and his Arab nationalist officers.[60]

And, in an admittedly somewhat odd and even counterintuitive twist of fate, the first Arab-Israeli war, 1948–1949, which Arab nationalists had hoped would constitute the crowning glory of their creed, in fact ended up, at least in the short-term, reinforcing regional, particularistic, and Islamist orientations at the expense of the Arab "connection." In the eyes of the Arabs, the beginning of the war signified Arab unity of purpose, the foundation upon which Arab unity would be built. By the end of the war, the Arab cooperative effort had given way to a milieu of acrimonious accusations and mutual recriminations, and hopes that had shone so brightly had turned into bitter disillusionment with Arab divisions, jealousies, and incompetence.

The immediate roots of the first Arab-Israeli war could be traced back to February 1947 when British Foreign Minister Ernest Bevin, admitting that Britain, the mandatory power, had lost control over Palestine, referred the matter to the United Nations. On November 29, 1947, the United Nations General Assembly, under heavy pressure from the United States, voted to partition Palestine between the Jews and the Arabs. The Arab League declared that it would not recognize a state for the Jews in Palestine, and that members of the League would be encouraged to intervene in Palestine. Imme-

---

[60] 'Abd al-Karim al-Uzri, *Tarikh fi Dhikrayat al-'Iraq, 1930–1958* (History in memoirs of Iraq, 1930–1958) (Beirut: Markaz al-Abjadiya li al-Saf al-Taswiri, 1982), pp. 148–150.

diately on the final withdrawal of British soldiers from Palestine on May 14, 1948, David Ben-Gurion and other Jewish leaders proclaimed the birth of the state of Israel on the territory under their control on that date. In response to Ben-Gurion's announcement, units from the armies of Egypt, Syria, Trans-Jordan, Lebanon, and Iraq entered Palestine.

The entry of the Arab armies into Palestine affirmed the very tenets of Arab nationalism. Here were the Arab countries, joined in the Arab League a mere three years earlier, united in their commitment to their Arab brethren in Palestine, dispatching their armies to defeat the upstart Israelis. But the ostensible show of Arab unity hid deep divisions that had little to do with ideological commitment and everything to do with personal ambitions and rivalries. King 'Abdallah coveted the incorporation of Palestine into his domain, and preferably the creation of a Hashemite Greater Syria. The Syrians, eyeing 'Abdallah's enormous irredentist appetite "feared Jordan more than Israel."[61] The Iraqis had no objection to a Hashemite takeover so long as *they* became the senior partners; the Egyptians on the other hand were not about to allow the Hashemites to claim the spoils of war; nor would Ibn Sa'ud, whose Saudi Arabia was created only after defeating the Hashemites.

The questionable commitment of the Arab leaders to the cause is clearly shown by the inadequate number of soldiers in the Arab armies and the tactics used in the war. At no time did the combined strength of the Arab armies exceed that of the Jewish regulars. After the war, Israel was to systematically propagate the parable of the Jewish "David" valiantly taking on the Arab "Goliath." The truth, however, was starkly different. "In mid-May 1948," Avi Shlaim tells us, "the total number of Arab troops, both regular and irregular, operating in the Palestine theater was under 25,000, whereas the IDF (Israel's Defense Forces) fielded over 35,000

---

[61] Joshua Landis, "Syria and the Palestine War: Fighting King 'Abdullah's 'Greater Syria Plan'," in Eugene L. Rogan and Avi Shlaim, *The War for Palestine: Rewriting the History of 1948* (Cambridge, England: Cambridge University Press, 2001), p. 185.

troops. By mid-July the IDF mobilized 65,000 men under arms, and by December its numbers had reached a peak of 96,441."[62] In addition to their quantitative inferiority, the Arab armies were "as wary of each other as they were of the Israelis, and their military operations were sometimes tailored to keep an eye on each other's military positions and intentions. The Israelis were a prime beneficiary of such inter-Arab suspicions."[63] The result was a political fiasco and a military debacle. The Arab populations, told to expect swift victory, waited expectantly for the fruits of the Arabs' united action. Instead they were witness to Arab armies and governments competing for their own slice of Palestine, and for the glory that would be accrued by them individually. Their "united" effort lacked any coordination on the field; so much in fact that they went out of their way not to come to the aid of each other, and indeed, in some cases, sabotaged one another.

It was not surprising that in the immediate aftermath of the war, Arab nationalism was dealt a substantial blow. It was not that the idea lost its appeal, rather it was merely the recognition that contemporary political structures in the Arab world were not only incapable, but also, and more dishearteningly, unwilling to realize Arab nationalist aspirations. It was not difficult for Arab populations to see that on the whole it was political ambitions and competition, not fidelity to Arab national interests, that dictated the war effort. And for those who still were willing to give Arab political leaders the benefit of the doubt, Emir 'Abdallah of Trans-Jordan was soon to stifle any lingering optimism. In September 1948, the Egyptians suggested the creation of a Palestinian government on land occupied at the time by the Egyptian and Jordanian armies. Emir 'Abdallah vehemently rejected any such initiative, and instead engineered the convening of a conference in Jericho which advocated the annexation of the West Bank into Trans-Jordan. This produced a howl of protest in the Arab world. Even the gov-

[62] Avi Shlaim, *The Iron Wall: Israel and the Arab World* (New York: W.W. Norton and Company, 2000), p. 35.
[63] Barnett, *Dialogues in Arab Politics*, p. 91.

ernment of Hashemite Iraq, under pressure of public opinion, condemned the idea, extracting a promise from 'Abdallah to freeze the proposal for the time being. 'Abdallah agreed as long as the Arab countries withdrew their support from any notion of a Palestinian government.[64]

In the meantime, 'Abdallah conducted secret negotiations with the Israelis on the possibility of a peace agreement that would institutionalize the absorption of the West Bank into Jordan.[65] When these negotiations were made public, the Arab League, responding to universal popular distaste of the Jordanian-Israeli negotiations, met in the spring of 1950, and in an undisguised reference to 'Abdallah, prohibited any Arab country from concluding a peace treaty with Israel. 'Abdallah responded by announcing the absorption of the West Bank into what now became known as the Hashemite Kingdom of Jordan. Incensed at the Jordanian action, and fearing a diminution in its perceived centrality in the area, Egypt demanded Jordan's expulsion, but Iraq and the Yemen lobbied against Egypt's position, and when Britain and the United States supported 'Abdallah's action, Egypt and the League's opposition fizzled out.[66] It was probably at this point that the Arab public became skeptical of the Arab League and of unity initiatives embarked upon by the Arab governments.

This wariness about governmental intentions was evident in an initiative for Syrian-Iraqi federation in late 1949. In October, members of the hierarchy of Syria's ruling People's Party, which was traditionally close to the Iraqis, opened negotiations with Baghdad for some form of union between the two countries. While the Syrians sought a loose federation that would maintain their republican political order, the Iraqis went for a more organic union. They de-

[64] 'Abd al-Razzak al-Hasani, *Tarikh al-Wizarat al-'Iraqiya, al-Jusi' al-Thamin* (The history of Iraqi cabinets, vol. 8) (Baghdad: Dar al-Shu'un al-Thaqifiya al-'Ama, 1988), pp. 36–38.

[65] The best account of these negotiations and the goals and political maneuvers of King 'Abdullah is Avi Shlaim, *Collusion across the Jordan: King Abdullah, the Zionist Movement, and the Partition of Palestine* (Oxford, England: Clarendon Press, 1988).

[66] Ismail Ahmad Yaghi, *Al-'Ilaqat al-'Iraqiya al-Urdiniya, 1941–1958* (Iraqi-Jordanian relations, 1941–1958) (Cairo: Dar al-Sahwa, 1988), p. 28.

manded a centralized federal leadership, a common diplomatic corps, financial and monetary integration, and the merger of the two armies under a unified command.[67] Perceiving it as essentially a union that would bolster the regional power not only of Hashemite Iraq, but also of its great-power ally, Britain, the initiative was coolly received among the governments and populations of the Arab world. Even in Iraq, opposition was widespread, not just from the usual suspects, in this case the Kurds and Shiites, the traditional opponents of Arab unity initiatives, but also from an appreciable segment of the Sunni population.[68] These individuals felt that it was not so much Arab nationalism, but the personal political ambitions of the universally disliked Iraqi regent, Prince 'Abd al-Illah, that determined Iraq's quest for union and its negotiating position and tactics in the talks. Most consequentially, antagonism to unity with Iraq was prevalent among the ranks of the Syrian army. The Syrian officers were determined not to be hoodwinked into a union with monarchical Iraq, and were adamant about preserving the independence of Syria's institutions.[69] Distrustful of their government's motivations and wary about Hashemite intentions, the Syrian army decided to make its move before the talks came to fruition. On December 19, the army executed a successful coup and immediately severed talks with the Iraqis. While the military coup was not necessarily an anti-*qawmi* move, it nevertheless exhibited an increasing sense of Syrian *wataniya*, a tendency to measure the efficacy of unity initiatives in light of their costs and benefits to Syria.

Of all the Arab countries, the one that shifted inward the most was Egypt. In the wake of the debacle of the Palestinian war, there was a renewed affirmation of Egyptian *wataniya*. Some went so far as to call for Egypt's withdrawal from the Arab League so the coun-

---

[67] Khadduri, "The Scheme of Fertile Crescent Unity," p. 162.

[68] Ahmad 'Abd al-Karim, *Hisad: Sineen Khasba wa Thimar Mura* (Harvest: fertile years and bitter fruit) (Beirut: Bisan li al-Nashr wa al-Tawzi', 1994), p. 154.

[69] Khalid al-'Azm, *Mudhakirat Khalid al-'Azm, al-Mujalad al-Thani* (The memoirs of Khalid al-'Azm, second volume) (Beirut: al-Dar al-Muttahida li al-Nashr, 1972), p. 220; see also Mufti, *Sovereign Creations*, p. 53.

try could focus on its own affairs following the example of Mustafa Kemal Attaturk in Turkey after World War I.[70] And when a half-baked Syrian plan for Arab unification was presented to the Arab League in 1951, a prominent Egyptian journalist, recalling the Arab disaster in Palestine, quipped contemptuously that the Arabs resembled "a man who had failed to cultivate one half *feddan* (0.519 acres), and now they impose on him the cultivation of one thousand *feddans*."[71] The response of the Egyptian army was perhaps the most revealing. Its attention was turned fully toward Egypt. It saw the defeat in Palestine as proof of the corruption and incompetence of the monarchical regime and of the debilitating impact British imperialism had on Egyptian society and politics. The army's mission therefore was to cleanse Egypt from these twin evils. There was little effort to see Egypt as part of a more general imperialist phenomenon that at that time was afflicting the entire Arab world. The army's concern was focused exclusively on Egypt,[72] and ironically the war in Palestine had to bear at least a measure of the blame for turning Egyptian minds away from the Arab nation.

Historical ironies, however, are the staple of human development. Despite its negative impact on Arab nationalism in the short term, the war in Palestine ended up being a major catalyst for the dramatic resurgence of Arab nationalism in the 1950s. Like so many other events in history, it was the unintended consequences of the war that contributed to the surge in Arabist sentiment less than a decade later. And it happened in Egypt, the least hospitable land to the ideas of Arab nationalism and organic Arab unity. Three years after the army's humiliation in Palestine, embittered young officers, blaming the Palestine debacle and the corruption in

[70] Anwar C. Chejne, "Egyptian Attitudes Toward Pan-Arabism," *Middle East Journal*, vol. 11, no. 3, Summer 1957: 259–261.

[71] Ibid., p. 262.

[72] Ahmad Hamroush, "Fikrat al-Qawmiya al-'Arabiya fi Thawrat Yuliyu," (Arab nationalist thought in the July revolution) in *Misr wa al-'Uruba wa Thwrat Yuliyu* (Egypt, Arabism and the July revolution), eds. Sa'ad al-Din Ibrahim, et al. (Beirut: Markaz Dirasat al-Wuhda al-'Arabiya, 1983), pp. 83–84.

their own country on their government, executed a military coup that toppled the monarchical regime. The officers were led by a young and quiet, yet charismatic, colonel by the name of Gamal 'Abd al-Nasir. More than any other political figure or institution, Colonel, and later, President Nasir and his policies would be inexorably linked to the rise of Arab nationalism as the dominant ideology in the area.

CHAPTER SIX

CONSOLIDATING ARAB NATIONALISM:
THE EMERGENCE OF "ARAB" EGYPT

When Gamal 'Abd al-Nasir returned to Egypt after the fiasco of Palestine, his first thoughts were not on Arab nationalism; they were focused instead on Egypt—on the corruption of its political and social order, and on the continued dominance of the British in its political life. Indeed, this paramount concern with Egypt's domestic affairs was prevalent in Nasir's thoughts even as he was executing his "Arab nationalist" duty in Palestine. "We were fighting in Palestine," Nasir would later reminisce, "but our dreams were in Egypt. Our bullets were directed at the enemy lurking in the trenches in front of us, but our hearts were hovering round our distant mother country, which was a prey to the wolves that ravaged it. . . . We spoke of nothing but our country and how to deliver it."[1] At one time, when Nasir and his unit were trapped by the Israelis, he saw this predicament as a metaphor for Egypt's own entrapment: "What is happening to us here is a picture in miniature of what is happening in Egypt."[2] Nasir was disgusted

[1] Quoted in Patrick Seale, *The Struggle for Syria: A Study of Post-War Arab Politics, 1945–1958* (New Haven, Connecticut: Yale University Press, 1986), p. 192.

[2] Joachim Joesten, *Nasser: the Rise to Power* (Westport, Connecticut: Greenwood Press Publishers, 1974), p. 81; also Jean Lacouture, *Nasser: A Biography* (New York: Alfred A. Knopf, 1973), pp. 64–66.

with the incompetence of the Egyptian High Command, and sick-
ened by the corruption of governmental departments responsible
for supplying weapons "which were frequently more dangerous to
the user than to the enemy."[3] Such ideas were hardly unique to
Nasir; they were on the minds of many of the Egyptian army officers, who returned to Egypt defeated and humiliated, echoing in
their hearts the exhortation of one of their fallen comrades to "remember that the real battle [was] in Egypt."[4]

Nasir, then, was first and foremost an Egyptian patriot. When
he fretted over the area's social and political ills, he thought essentially of Egypt. When he searched for ways of deliverance from
British imperialism, his concern was directed primarily at Egypt,
even though other Arab countries suffered the same fate. If other
Arabs came to mind, it was only in ways to help bring about
Egypt's salvation.[5] One reason for pushing the Arab dimension to
the margins of his concerns was the practical consideration that
Egypt, with all of its internal problems, could ill-afford to be mired
into the turbulence of Arab politics. But there was also another,
perhaps more fundamental reason: Nasir was simply echoing the
dominant political sentiments of his countrymen. It is true, as we
have seen, that the Arab ideological trend had gathered momentum
in Egypt, especially after the 1936–1939 Arab revolt in Palestine;
it is equally true, however, that Arab nationalism did not achieve
ideological primacy in Egypt. Egyptian, rather than Arab, nationalism continued to be the dominant ideology. Its roots dug so deep
into the Egyptian soul that even by the end of the 1950s, the decade
that witnessed the greatest triumphs of Arab nationalism under
Egypt's own leadership, observers would note Egyptian indifference to the Arab identity. The Syrian Salah al-Din Bitar, who along
with Michel Aflaq, founded the Arab nationalist Ba'th Party, and
who became a member of the first cabinet of the United Arab Re-

---

[3] Anthony Nutting, *Nasser* (London: Constable, 1972), p. 28.

[4] Peter Mansfield, *Nasser's Egypt* (Harmondsworth, Surrey: Penguin Books, 1965),
p. 39.

[5] Robert Stephens, *Nasser: A Political Biography* (New York: Simon and Schuster, 1971),
pp. 85–87.

public (UAR), which was formed in 1958 through the organic union of Egypt and Syria under Nasir's leadership, stated categorically that Nasir's conversion to Arab nationalism only began around 1953–1954, adding that "the Arab idea never went very deep in Egypt."[6] Even if Bitar's evaluation could be dismissed as an invective by a disillusioned Syrian (which he certainly became by the last years of the union), then the words of Muhamed Hasaneen Haykal, Nasir's confidant and the most influential Egyptian journalist of the Nasirist era, are less easy to dismiss. Reflecting on the eventual failure of the UAR, Haykal wrote candidly:

> In Egypt, the Arab people had not reached the stage of complete mental readiness for Arab unity. The centuries of Ottoman tyranny had isolated the Arab people to the west of the Sinai (Egypt and North Africa) from the remaining Arab people to the east of the Sinai (the Fertile Crescent and the Arabian Peninsula). After the awakening which occurred during Napoleon's rule, Egypt, overwhelmed by this awakening was unable to shift its attention from its own soil so that it can look across the Sinai and discover its Arab position.[7]

The Egyptians' concerted, at times even obsessive, focus on their country was made even more intense by the visible presence of the British in their "beloved" Egypt. The 1936 Anglo-Egyptian Treaty had stipulated the maintenance of a British military garrison in the Canal Zone to ensure the security of British imperial communications.[8] By 1951, the number of British troops had reached 75,000.[9] Their military presence was felt in the major urban centers as well, particularly during the World War II years. Indeed, not until 1946 would the British evacuate the most visible historical monument in Cairo dominating the city's skyline, the Great Citadel of Salah al-

---

[6] Seale, *The Struggle for Syria*, p. 311.

[7] *Al-Ahram* (Cairo), November 3, 1961.

[8] P. J. Vatikiotis, *The History of Modern Egypt: From Muhammed Ali to Mubarak*, 4th ed., (Baltimore: Johns Hopkins University Press,1991), p. 293.

[9] Jacques Berque, *Egypt: Imperialism and Revolution* (New York: Praeger Publishers, 1972), p. 669.

Din al-Ayyubi.[10] Along with their military presence, the British exercised an inordinate influence over the political process. Which Egyptian could forget the humiliating events of February 1941, when the British ambassador surrounded the Royal Palace with British tanks and forced King Farouk to appoint the pro-British Nahas Pasha as prime minister?

To be an Egyptian patriot then was to struggle to cleanse Egypt of the British presence and to safeguard Egypt's territorial integrity. It was to achieve these two goals that the army rose against the monarchy in July 1952. The leader of the coup was General Muhamed Neguib, but real power rested with an eleven-man committee of junior officers, whose acknowledged leader was Colonel 'Abd al-Nasir. They set out immediately to reform (and eventually transform) Egypt's political and economic systems. In this initial period of the revolution, they showed no interest in Arab affairs. But they did have one extraterritorial goal, namely uniting Egypt with its southern neighbor, Sudan. To Arab nationalists, this might have qualified as a concern that went beyond the declared parochial interests of Egypt's new rulers. But to the Egyptians, the integration of Egypt and Sudan was a "domestic" issue, conceived locally as the "unity of the Nile valley."

Sudan had been officially regarded as an indivisible part of Egypt since the early nineteenth century. However, real control of the territory passed on to Britain after the latter's occupation of Egypt in 1882. British political paramountcy in Sudan was later legitimized through the 1899 accord with Egypt, in which the Egyptians recognized Britain's suzerainty over Sudan. With Britain showing signs of flexibility over the Sudanese issue, Nasir and the new junta set out to influence Sudanese public opinion. Large sums of money were spent and intense propaganda used to reorient Sudanese perceptions northward toward Egypt. All this effort, however, was to no avail. The Sudanese seemed as hostile to the possibility of Egyptian domination as they were to existing British control. And indeed, they were eventually to opt for complete independence,

[10] Ibid., p. 581.

which to Nasir represented "a great personal tragedy."[11] With very limited options, the Egyptians accepted the Sudanese decision. Like earlier efforts in the Fertile Crescent, this endeavor to unite two Arabic-speaking countries came to a disappointing end.

With the collapse of the Sudanese initiative, Nasir and his comrades refocused their energies on ridding Egypt of British political influence and military presence. This translated into a vehement campaign against Britain and its Western allies. And it was in this essentially anti-imperialist stance that Arab nationalism found its most vibrant voice. One is almost tempted to say that Nasir slid into Arab nationalism through the back door of anti-imperialism. Nasir had not seriously thought of Arab nationalism as an autonomous category in the way Sati' al-Husri conceived of it. When he thought of it, it was primarily as a means to achieve some other goal or value, and in that period, the primary goal and paramount value was the struggle against British and Western imperialist policies. Reflecting on his experience in the Palestine war, Nasir wrote that not only Egypt, but the whole region was the object of imperialist designs, and in that case, it made great sense to him that the region should have at a minimum a unity of effort and purpose to fight the imperialist enemies collectively.[12] So when in 1953 the idea of a Western alliance threatened to isolate Egypt, Nasir began to shift the ideological and political attention of his political order from Egypt to the wider Arab world. And when he did, he found a ready and receptive audience among the peoples of the Arab world.

The Arab world was undergoing major demographic and social changes, some of which were occurring at a bewildering speed. Rapid population growth, changes to traditional economic relations, accelerated migrations from rural to urban areas, and the spread of modern public education had produced a social and intellectual milieu that was ready for revolutionary picking. The most consequential of these changes occurred in education. In Egypt, students in secondary schools increased from 15,000 in 1933 to 41,000

[11] *Daily Telegraph* (London), July 11, 1955.
[12] Premier Gamal Abdul Nasser, *Egypt's Liberation: The Philosophy of the Revolution* (Washington, D.C.: Public Affairs Press, 1955), p. 103.

in 1951.[13] As late as 1939–1940, there were only 4,000 pupils in seven Syrian state secondary schools; by 1955–1956, Syria could boast 258 state secondary schools with an enrollment of 60,000 pupils.[14] In Iraq, only 200 students received a secondary education in 1920, yet by 1958, there were 74,000 students in secondary schools.[15] In this, the educational benefits were not confined to the politically dominant Sunni population; they accrued to the Shiites as well.[16] This was reflected in the expansion of higher education, where in 1951, 1,091 students received degrees from nine different colleges.[17] True, even these dramatic improvements constituted no more than between 25 and 35 percent of all school-age children, nevertheless, they contributed significantly to the expansion of a literate and politically aware middle class, which actively assumed a leadership role in the propagation of radical nationalism. As we shall see, much of the political turbulence that characterized the 1950s was fomented by countless street demonstrations and riots begun by student populations, and supported, in many cases vigorously, by other sectors of the middle class, particularly and most consequentially the officer corps of the armed forces. Of course, the process of social change, including the expansion in education, had started in the interwar years, but its consequences—social tension, political restlessness, and a broader awareness that challenged traditional political ideas and practices—peaked in the 1950s.

The students and other members of the middle class—the custodians of radical nationalist ideas—were the very people who would become Nasir's nationalist generation, his foot soldiers, ever ready to do his bidding, all in the service of Arab nationalism. Like their hero, however, the primary focus of their rebelliousness in the early

[13] These figures are obtained from Joseph S. Szyliowicz, *Education and Modernization in the Middle East* (Ithaca, New York: Cornell University Press, 1973), pp. 187–188, and M. E. Yapp, *The Near East Since the First World War* (London: Longman, 1996), pp. 62–63.

[14] Ibid., p. 102.

[15] Ibid., p. 76.

[16] Phebe Marr, "The Development of a Nationalist Ideology in Iraq, 1920–1941," *The Muslim World*, vol. 75, no. 2 (April 1985): 100.

[17] Fahim I. Qubain, *Education and Science in the Arab World* (Baltimore: Johns Hopkins University Press, 1966), p. 221.

part of the 1950s was imperialism[18]—the maddening spectacle of foreign troops and personnel on their soil,[19] the fear of continuing colonialist and imperialist hegemony over the area, the perception that many of the indigenous leadership were but puppets in the hands of exploitative foreigners, and the unshakeable belief that Israel was the illegitimate offspring of perfidious imperialist conspiracies against the Arab world. This almost axiomatic belief in the essential ill will of the West was of course given an added edge by the increasing rigidity of the Cold War. What the West thought of as a security arrangement, educated and politically aware Arabs would interpret as a Western conspiracy. For Nasir, British presence on Egyptian soil made it unthinkable for Egypt to enter into security arrangements with the West. But Egypt could not resist Western pressure on its own. To mount an offensive against Western alliances, Egypt would need to tap the burgeoning Arab anti-imperialist revolutionary potential. And to do that effectively, Nasir knew that he had to reorient Egypt toward the Arab nationalist path.

John Foster Dulles, the U. S. secretary of state, brought the idea of a defense alliance against Soviet ambitions in the region to Cairo in May 1953. But the American's goals contrasted sharply with those of the Egyptians. Nasir and the other members of the military junta were not in the least concerned about threats from the Soviet Union, which, as Nasir reminded Dulles, was "five thousand miles away."[20] Rather, they tried to impress on Dulles that it was the British "occupation" of the Suez Canal that in their calculation represented the main threat not just to Egypt's stability, but also to the legitimacy and possible survival of the country's military leaders. When Dulles left Cairo, he took with him what was at best a lukewarm Egyptian response to his initiative.

[18] See Walid Khadduri, "al-Qawmiya al-'Arabiya wa al-Dimuqratiya: Muraja'a Naqdiya," (Arab nationalism and democracy: a critical review), *al-Mustaqbal al-'Arabi*, no. 228 (February 1998): 38.

[19] In the early 1950s, all of North Africa, Sudan, the Gulf, and South Yemen were colonial possessions; and British troops were stationed in Egypt and Iraq. Only Saudi Arabia, North Yemen, Syria, Lebanon, and Jordan were free of foreign presence, even though the commander of the Jordanian armed forces was British.

[20] Nasir's interview with *The Sunday Times* (London), June 24, 1962.

The Egyptians, however, knew that this would not be the end of the affair. They believed that other states in the region, particularly Iraq, Jordan, and Lebanon, would more than likely join such an alliance, and if they did, Syria would be encircled and perhaps pressured into joining as well. This inevitably would lead to the political and strategic isolation of Egypt from the region. It was obvious to Egypt's leadership that rebuffing Dulles was not enough; Arab states had to be actively discouraged from entering into such alliances. Not surprisingly, an Egyptian campaign to galvanize the citizens of other Arab states against Western alliances had to tap the most readily acceptable bond that drew Egyptians and the other Arabs together, that of Arab nationalism—the notion that, politically divided as they were, the Arabs still constituted one indivisible nation, and thus in the words of Egypt's radio station "Voice of the Arabs," "what impacted one part of this nation would by definition impact the other parts."[21] If Arab governments were to complain that Nasir and the Egyptian leaders were interfering in their countries' internal affairs, the bonds of "Arab nationalism" and membership of the "Arab nation" would be invoked by the Egyptian leaders to justify their policies.

The phenomenal speed with which Arab nationalism became the predominant radical, on the whole anti-Western, ideology in the region in the 1950s resulted in large measure from Egypt's onslaught against Western alliances. And Egypt's undoubted success was aided substantially by two factors: the country's own capabilities, and Nasir's committed leadership and single-minded pursuit of his goals.

Egypt was endowed by nature to be the most important Arab state. Geographically, it constituted a bridge between the eastern and western parts of the Arab world, and unlike other Arab states whose legal status rested on artificial boundaries drawn up by old colonial powers, Egypt had been a distinct geographical unit for over four thousand years. Egypt also had the largest population of

[21] British Broadcasting Corporation, *Summary of World Broadcasts: Part IV, The Arab World, Israel, Greece, Turkey, Iran* (hereafter cited as *SWB*), London, July 21, 1954, p. 3.

Egypt's Exports to and Imports from Arab Countries of Books, Films, and Newspapers, 1957

Medium	Imports (1,000 kg)	Exports (1,000 kg)
Books	104.8	1,421.0
Films	1.9	10.0
Newspapers	64.5	498.8
Total	171.2	1,929.8

Source. A. I. Dawisha, *Egypt in the Arab World: The Elements of Foreign Policy* (London: Macmillan, 1976), pp. 176–177.

all Arab countries. In 1958, it constituted 35 percent of the total population of all Arab states.[22] Due to the post-Napoleonic renaissance in Egypt, which opened the country and its population to Western civilization a full century before the rest of the Arab world, Egypt enjoyed a pronounced cultural and intellectual preeminence in the region (see the above table). In 1947, for example, Cairo boasted fourteen daily newspapers and twenty-three weeklies, a number of which were distributed in other Arab countries. Egypt was the only Arab country with a viable film industry, and Egyptian movies in the 1940s and 1950s competed vigorously with their Western counterparts in Arab movie theaters. Kemal al-Shenawy was as beloved a heartthrob as Clark Gable or Tyrone Power; Isma'il Yassin was a bigger comedic name than Bob Hope or Danny Kaye, and Fatin Hamama and Layla Murad were far more popular leading ladies than Vivien Leigh or Doris Day. In song and music, Egypt had no rival. Egyptian singers and musicians were household names throughout the region, the most beloved and revered of whom was the majestic Umm Kulthum, an Arab icon, whose legendary five-hour concerts on the first Thursday of the month gathered people around their radio sets in Baghdad, Damascus, Casablanca, Amman, and other cities throughout the Arab world. Umm Kulthum reigned supreme, the unrivaled queen of Arab song, transcending inter-Arab conflicts, until her death on February 3, 1975.

[22] A. I. Dawisha, *Egypt in the Arab World: The Elements of Foreign Policy* (London: Macmillan, 1976), p. 80.

During the two weeks she spent in the hospital before her death, radio stations across the Arab world broadcast periodic bulletins of her condition, and on the news of her death regularly scheduled programs were replaced by Quranic recitals.[23] In addition to Umm Kulthum, other Egyptian singers and songwriters, such as 'Abd al-Halim Hafiz, Nejat al-Saghira, and Muhamed 'Abd al-Wahab established renowned reputations and were universally beloved throughout the Arab world. Indeed, non-Egyptian singers, such as the Syrians Farid al-Atrash and Asmahan, the Lebanese Sabah, and the Algerian Warda al-Jazai'riya, became household names in the Arab world only after they worked and settled in Egypt.[24] These singers, as well as the predominance of Egyptian films, made "Egyptian" the only universal Arabic dialect in the region.

These objective elements of Egypt's centrality in the Arab world had, over time, made an imprint on the attitudes of the other Arabs. As we have seen, Sati' al-Husri, even though a Syrian, whose intellectual output occurred primarily in Iraq, nevertheless accepted unequivocally Egypt's centrality in the Arab world, declaring it to be the only possible leader of Arab nationalism.[25] And this perception was prevalent in the Arab world. As one Syrian official put it, "The Arabs have always considered Egypt as the headquarters of Arab nationalism due to its geographic, social and cultural position."[26] Echoing this sentiment, an Iraqi nationalist leader insisted that Egypt was "a strong foundation and a vital and sure base for the Arab nation." He added that Iraq could not act as such a base, because Iraq did not "possess the capability to assume this posi-

[23] For an excellent study of the life and times of Umm Kulthum, see Virginia Danielson, *The Voice of Egypt: Umm Kulthum, Arabic Song and Egyptian Society in the Twentieth Century* (Chicago: University of Chicago Press, 1997).

[24] Of course, there were a few singers who established an Arab-wide reputation without having to work in Egypt. The Lebanese folksinger Fayrouz comes readily to mind. But she would be the exception rather than the rule.

[25] Abu Khaldun Sati' al-Husri, "Dawr Misr fi al-Nahdha al-Qawmiya al-'Arabiya," (Egypt's role in Arab nationalist renaissance) in his *Abhath Mukhtara fi al-Qawmiya al-'Arabiya* (Selected studies in Arab nationalism) (Beirut: Markaz Dirasat al-Wuhda al-'Arabiya, 1985), p. 105.

[26] Al Jumhuriya al-'Arabiya al-Muttahida, *Mahadhir Jalsat Mubahathat al-Wuhda* (Proceedings of the meetings on unity discussions) (Cairo: National Printing and Publishing House, 1963), p. 74.

tion." However, "it was well within Egypt's capability."[27] This entrenched belief in Egypt's dominance and centrality meant that other Arabs would be wary of pursuing any project that would not, at a minimum, receive Egypt's blessings. For instance, the Syrian Michel Aflaq, who founded the Ba'th Party, conceded that there could be no Arab unity without Egypt because "she could and would successfully oppose any movement toward Arab unity which excluded her."[28] In the same vein, Egypt's threat to withdraw from the Arab League in August 1962 prompted President Fuad Shihab of Lebanon to appeal to Nasir to change his mind on the grounds that "the league will have no value if [Egypt] withdrew from it," since Egypt was the League's "biggest and strongest member state."[29] Most tellingly, was the admission of King Faysal of Saudi Arabia, who at various times had been the linchpin of the anti-Nasirist forces in the region, to Nasir that his father, King 'Abd al-'Aziz, the founder of Saudi Arabia, had given his children one piece of advice: "He told us to pay attention to Egypt's role, for without Egypt, the Arabs throughout history would have been without value."[30] These attitudes point to the firm belief held by Arabs that Arab nationalism could only flourish with Egypt's active involvement. The committed nationalist might have believed that an Arab nation, united in thought and action, was a revolutionary juggernaut that would sweep aside all doubters and enemies in its victorious march toward independence and progress. But the believer also knew that Iraq, Syria, Jordan, or Saudi Arabia could not be the driving engine of this juggernaut; only Egypt could fill this role.

The problem for the nationalists, as we have seen, was that while Egypt possessed the capabilities to lead the Arab nationalist movement, its heart was not really in it. And this was true well into the Nasirist era. The high school history curriculum for the academic year 1953–1954, which was developed under the auspices of the

[27] Ibid., p. 37.
[28] Quoted in Seale, *The Struggle for Syria*, p. 311.
[29] *Al-Ahram* (Cairo), September 9, 1962.
[30] *Al-Ahram* (Cairo), January 10, 1970.

revolutionary regime to replace the existing curriculum taught under the monarchy, had precious few references to the Arab nation or to Arab nationalism. It concentrated instead on Egypt's stellar role in world history—its inimitable contribution to "the building of world civilization," its historically enshrined identity, and its immense achievements which "outdistanced all other nations (*Umam*),"[31] the implication being that Egypt was itself a full-fledged nation. The Liberation Rally, established in 1953 as the unitary political organization of the postmonarchical political system, said nothing of Arab unity, but merely called for "strengthening ties with the Arab peoples."[32] It is instructive to note here the pointed reference to the multiple Arab peoples (*al-Shu'ub al-'Arabiya*), at the expense of the expression used by Arab nationalists of one Arab people (*al-Sha'ab al-'Arabi*). While accepting that they had special and long-standing ties with the other Arabs, Nasir and the new Egyptian leaders continued to feel and express the same sense of cultural individualism and national exceptionalism that characterized the attitudes and policies of the *ancien regime*.

Riad Taha, an influential Lebanese journalist who was close to Nasir in the 1950s, relates that the discussions which preceded the promulgation of the 1956 Egyptian constitution were replete with references to the "Egyptian nation." Taha claims that only after his own personal appeal to Nasir was an article inserted proclaiming the Egyptian people to be "part of the Arab nation." Yet even then, the article was contradicted by other references in the constitution in which the term "nation" was attached to "Egypt."[33] These seemingly entrenched "Egyptianist" attitudes meant that the abundance of capabilities at Egypt's disposal to lead the Arab world were balanced with a pronounced lack of will to undertake a leadership role—that is until Nasir concluded that the most effec-

[31] Quoted in Eberhard Kienle, "Arab Unity Schemes Revisited: Interest, Identity, and Policy in Syria and Egypt," *International Journal of Middle East Studies*, vol. 27, no. 1 (February 1995): 63.

[32] Ibid.

[33] Riad Taha, *Qissat al-Wuhda wa al-Infisal: Tajribat Insan 'Arabi Khilal Ahdath 1955–1961* (The story of unity and secession: the experience of an Arab person during the events of 1955–1961) (Beirut: Dar al-Afaq al-Jadida, 1974), pp. 40–41.

tive means to combat the Western powers in their effort to isolate Egypt by enlisting Arab countries into anti-Soviet military alliances was to appeal to the Arab people through the shared agency of Arab nationalism. It was then that Nasir decided to subsume Egypt's identity within the overall Arab identity.

This dramatic conversion to the cause of Arab nationalism, in which Nasir was to use Egypt's extensive capabilities, particularly its unquestionable cultural dominance, was to be transmitted to the rest of the Arab world through the medium of radio. Like no other Egyptian or Arab leader before him, or among his contemporaries, Nasir recognized the immense power of radio, a power which, as a dazzling orator, he had used vigorously and effectively. From early in the regime's tenure, Nasir devoted considerable financial resources to the expansion of public broadcasting. The "Voice of the Arabs" started its radio transmissions to the Arab world in July 1953. The timing is instructive. Less than two months earlier, Nasir had rejected the idea of a Western alliance submitted to him by John Foster Dulles, becoming convinced in the process that the U. S. secretary of state would pursue other, possibly more pliant, Arab countries. The creation of the "Voice of the Arabs" was thus a function of Nasir's utilitarian approach to Arab politics rather than an affirmation of his ideological commitment to the Arab idea. The transmission time of the new station was increased threefold in January 1954, and it declared unequivocally that "the Voice of the Arabs speaks for the Arabs, struggles for them and expresses their unity."[34] On another occasion, the Arabs were reminded that Egypt was "in the service of the Arab nation and its struggle against Western imperialism and its lackeys in the Arab world."[35] The language should have warned Arab leaders of things to come. The radio station became Nasir's main vehicle in propagating his views, which on many occasions contrasted sharply with the views of other Arab leaders. Egypt's domestic service, "Radio Cairo," was similarly expanded to cover much of the Arab world,

[34] *SWB*, January 12, 1954, p. 4.
[35] *SWB*, February 8, 1954, p. 5.

and together with the "Voice of the Arabs" became primary agents of instability in countries such as Iraq, Jordan, and Lebanon.

The expansion in Egyptian public broadcasting was large and rapid. The daily transmission of the "Voice of the Arabs" grew from thirty minutes in 1953 to just short of twenty-four hours in the 1960s.[36] In the same period, the domestic program, now broadcasting throughout the Arab world, increased its daily transmission from eleven hours to twenty.[37] The country's radio transmission power which stood at 72 kilowatts in 1952 had risen to 1,624 kilowatts ten years later.[38] Indeed, in terms of weekly program output, Egypt in 1960 ranked as the sixth largest international broadcaster, preceded only by the United States, the Soviet Union, China, West Germany, and Britain.[39] Thus, in the course of a few years, Nasir had transformed Egypt's broadcasting system into a potent propaganda weapon, whose considerable success, especially in the 1950s, played a major role in projecting and later cementing Egypt's and Nasir's leadership of the Arab nationalist movement.

Three factors contributed to this success. The very fact of Egypt's cultural hegemony meant that audiences were naturally drawn to the Egyptian radio station. Nothing that the other Arabs would produce in plays, soap opera, comedic programs, and the arts could even remotely match the sophistication of Egyptian programming. In music, as we have seen, Cairo was supreme, its concerts unrivaled, its artists legendary. At various times, these artists rendered songs in praise of Nasir and his ideological message. Umm Kulthum was particularly close to Nasir,[40] and sang no less than 31 "patriotic" songs, a number of them extolling Nasir himself.[41] Similarly, the most renowned Arabic male singer/composer,

---

[36] Douglas A. Boyd, *Broadcasting in the Arab World: A Survey of the Electronic Media in the Middle East*, 2nd ed. (Ames: Iowa State University Press, 1993), p. 28.

[37] Ibid., p. 21.

[38] Boyd, *Broadcasting in the Arab World*, p. 35.

[39] Ibid., pp. 32–33.

[40] See Hanafi al-Nahlawi, *'Abd al-Nasir wa Umm Kulthum: 'Ilaqa Khassa Jiddan* ('Abd al-Nasir and Umm Kulthum: a very special relationship) (Cairo: Markaz al-Qada li al-Kitab wa al-Nashr, 1992).

[41] Virginia Danielson, "Performance, Political Identity and Memory: Umm Kulthum and Gamal 'Abd al-Nasir," in Sherifa Zuhur, *Images of Enchantment: Visual and Performing*

Muhamed 'Abd al-Wahab, sang a hugely popular ode with the refrain of *ya Gamal, ya Gamal* (O' Gamal, O' Gamal). For the officials, it remained a simple matter of inserting political programming in the midst of this rich cultural tapestry.

The second reason for Egyptian primacy in radio propaganda was that other Arab countries were too slow to understand the power of the radio. By the time they embarked on upgrading their own transmissions, they were lagging far behind Egypt. So during the crucial years of the 1950s and 1960s, they simply were not able to match Egypt's transmission power. Their own services were so rudimentary that they were unable to lure listeners away from Egyptian programming. Moreover, they had virtually no jamming capability. Even Iraq, which in the mid-1950s was Egypt's main competitor in the area, "did not have sufficient transmitter power to cover its own country completely with an Arabic service, much less to reach neighboring Arab countries with a reliable signal."[42]

Finally, the success of Egypt's radio propaganda was also a function of Nasir's own oratorical brilliance. A dazzling public speaker who mesmerized his listeners and kept them in rapt attention throughout the duration of his usually long speeches, Nasir had a knack for creatively manipulating the Arabic language, a linguistic medium ideally suited for arousing emotions, to produce the desired response from his audience. He had great command of classical Arabic, but was not afraid to intersperse colloquial Egyptian to imprint into the consciousness of his listeners a "folksy" image of himself, that of the common man. If one word is associated in the minds of people with Nasir's oratory, a word that was repeated over and over again in his speeches, it was *karameh*, dignity. For the millions of common folk in Egypt and the rest of the Arab world who for years had suffered untold indignities at the hands of the colonizers, *karameh* would find a sure resonance in their hearts. And when all was said and done, Nasir's message of reclaiming the Arabs' glorious past and setting its brilliance against

---

Arts of the Middle East (Cairo: The American University in Cairo Press, 1998), pp. 121–122.

[42] Boyd, *Broadcasting in the Arab World*, p. 121.

the sorry contemporary conditions of subservience to the foreigners was the kind of message that fit right into the turbulent milieu of the times. Nasir used the device that had become the stock-in-trade of all nationalists: he made "use of the past in order to subvert the present."[43] And there were precious few arguments of equal emotional power that supporters of the West could muster in response.

Egypt's propaganda claims were accompanied by concrete policies designed to make these claims credible. Nasir and his administration moved on a number of fronts to enhance Egypt's objective capabilities. The new government vigorously undertook to spread education to all sectors of society. At one time it opened new schools at the rate of two every week, so that between 1953 and 1958, the student population rose by a staggering 50 percent, accompanied by a 57 percent rise in the number of teachers.[44] Even though Egypt needed its teachers to service the huge expansion in education, the government continued, indeed increased, the country's traditional export of teachers to schools of other Arab countries. Egyptian teachers were now not just a living testimony to Egypt's primacy, but also to Nasir's policies and principles.

Parallel to the pursuit of cultural supremacy, Nasir made every effort to maintain Egypt's military dominance. Cognizant that perceptions of military power are crucial to the exercise of political influence, Nasir would ensure that other Arabs were aware of the power of the Egyptian army. In 1961, Nasir proudly reminded King Husayn of Jordan that the power of Egypt's army was such that it would "satisfy the hopes of every Arab," a fact that attested to Egypt's determination "to undertake [its] responsibility toward the common enemy of the Arab nation."[45] And this was no idle boast; for Nasir pumped significant resources into the military. In 1957, Egypt's defense expenditure stood at $264 million, while the combined expenditure of Syria, Iraq, and Jordan totaled $156

[43] Elie Kedourie, *Nationalism* (London: Hutchinson University Library, 1961), p. 75.

[44] United Nations, Department of Economic and Social Affairs, *Statistical Yearbook, 1955*, p. 570; and *Statistical Yearbook, 1960*, p. 578.

[45] *Al-Ahram* (Cairo), March 31, 1961.

million.[46] It was hardly surprising then that the Algerian leader Ahmed Ben Bella would first come to Cairo to seek Nasir's counsel before announcing the Algerian revolution against France.[47] Indeed, the first communiqué of the Algerian National Liberation Front, announcing the birth of the revolution against France on November 1, 1954, was broadcast on Egypt's "Voice of the Arabs."[48] Ben Bella's initiative, that of traveling to Cairo to seek Nasir's support, was to be repeated time and again by countless Arab leaders in years to come.

The weight and centrality of Nasir's Egypt in the Arab world can be ascertained by an examination of the various unity schemes in the Arab world during Nasir's leadership between 1954 and 1970. Of the eight proposed and/or attempted unity schemes involving Egypt, three were initiated by Syria, three by Iraq, and two by Yemen.[49] These initiatives were undertaken not necessarily because of the leaders' abiding belief in Arab unity (although there certainly was an element of that), but because these unity initiatives tended to have an immediate and significant impact on the legitimation of these leaders in their respective countries. And this should tell us something about the elevated status of Egypt and its charismatic leader in the eyes of the Arabs, leaders and citizens alike.

Nasir's Egypt was by no means loved by all; some resented it, others feared it. But loathed or revered, its leadership of revolutionary Arab nationalism from the mid-1950s until Nasir's death in October 1970 was acknowledged by friend and foe. Muhamed Fadhil al-Jamali, who at various times had been Iraq's prime minister or foreign minister during the 1950s, the period of intense Iraqi-

---

[46] United Nations, *Statistical Yearbook, 1960*, pp. 509–535.

[47] Fuad Matar, *Bisaraha 'An 'Abd al-Nasir: Hiwar ma'a Muhamed Hasaneen Haykal* (Candidly about 'Abd al-Nasir: a conversation with Muhamed Hasaneen Haykal) (Beirut: Dar al-Qadhaya, 1975), p. 105.

[48] Ahmad Hamroush, *Qissat Thawrat 23 Yuliyu, al-Jusi' al-Rabi': 'Abd al-Nasir wa al-'Arab* (The story of the July 23 revolution, volume 4: 'Abd al-Nasir and the Arabs) (Cairo: Dar al-Mawqif al-'Arabi, 1983), p. 363.

[49] Dawisha, *Egypt in the Arab World*, p. 134; also Kienle, "Arab Unity Schemes Revisited," pp. 54–55.

Egyptian enmity, claims to have been the first to coin the phrase *Nasirism*.[50] He used it in a major address to the United Nation's General Assembly in 1958, in which he accused the Egyptian leader of mounting a campaign to destabilize other Arab states that happened not to see eye to eye with him on certain issues and policies. Jamali's argument rested on a main pillar of international law, that of the inviolability of state sovereignty. Iraq had the unquestioned sovereign right, Jamali asserted, to pursue its national interest without the interference of other states. Beyond the strictures of international law, the Charter of the League of Arab States, a document to which all Arab states were expected to adhere, insisted on total respect for the independence and sovereignty of each Arab state, and its right to pursue its own foreign policy.[51] To these accusations, Nasir had a ready and potent retort emanating from, by that point, his wholesale and wholehearted espousal of Arab nationalism.[52] Nasir's position, loudly declared and gleefully transmitted over the airwaves, gave revolutionary Arab nationalism the pride of place in determining Egyptian Arab and foreign policy. Arab nationalism, Nasir argued, took precedence over any other consideration, even state sovereignty. Since Arab nationalism was the primary ideological and emotional identification of every Arab, then, according to Nasir, Egypt had not just the right, but the duty to intrude into the affairs of other countries that were not conducting themselves in accordance with Arab nationalist principles. Nasir's Egypt then had a dual role—that of a traditional state and that of the revolutionary entity serving the higher interests of Arab nationalism. Muhamed Hasaneen Haykal, Nasir's confidant and editor of the influential newspaper, *al-Ahram*, elucidated this Egyptian duality of roles:

[50] Muhamed Fadhil al-Jamali, *Safahat min Tarikhina al-Mu'asir* (Pages from our contemporary history) (Cairo: Dar Su'ad al-Sabah, 1993), p. 197.

[51] Michael N. Barnett, *Dialogues in Arab Politics: Negotiations in Regional Order* (New York: Columbia University Press, 1998), p. 80.

[52] *Al-Ahram* (Cairo), March 5, 1958. By the end of the 1950s, Nasir was eulogized by his propaganda machine as "the symbol of Arab nationalism [which represented] immediate unity." *SWB*, April 29, 1960.

We should distinguish between two things: Egypt as a state and as a revolution. . . . If as a state, Egypt recognizes boundaries in its dealings with governments, Egypt as a revolution should never hesitate to halt before these boundaries, but should carry its message beyond the borders in order *to initiate its revolutionary mission for a unitary Arab future.* . . . We should do our best to cooperate with governments, *but we should refrain from extending such cooperation if it were to affect the people's movements.* This policy must be pursued whatever the consequences or the difficulties may be.[53] (italics added)

In Egyptian perceptions, Arab nationalism by the beginning of the 1960s had moved a long way from its conception a decade earlier. Then it had been merely a topic of argument and dialogue among intellectuals, or a convenient policy goal to which self-interested politicians would pay lip service. Under the now committed leadership of Egypt under Gamal 'Abd al-Nasir, Arab nationalism became a revolutionary movement which would resonate among the mass of Arab people regardless of the political divisions of the world that these people inhabited. At this point, most Arabs could not conceive of the Arab nationalist movement without the leadership of Egypt and its charismatic leader.

The immense upsurge in the popularity of Arab nationalism once Nasir put his charisma and Egypt's weight behind the concept in the 1950s was bound to have an impact on other radical movements and parties. Those who shared Nasir's views would see their fortunes rise, and those who did not would suffer setbacks and reverses and, on occasion, extinction.

Sharing Nasir's views on Arab nationalism was the Ba'th Party, which as we have seen was formally founded in 1947. The Party was the brainchild of two young Syrian intellectuals, Michel Aflaq and Salah al-Din Bitar, who had formed a close friendship while studying in Paris in the 1930s. Aflaq, who assumed the role of the Party's philosopher, spent his entire career asserting the validity of the notion of "an indivisible Arab nation." This nation, according

[53] *Al-Ahram* (Cairo), December 29, 1961.

to Aflaq, had been forcibly divided by colonialism and imperialism, a division that had led to a degeneration of the Arab spirit. The major goal of the Ba'th Party was to reverse this trend and rejuvenate the Arab will so that it could become the living instrument for the creation of "one Arab nation with an eternal mission."[54] The Arab nation was in such dire straits that the need for rejuvenation was immediate, and could not be left to a gradual, evolutionary transformation. Hence, as with Nasir, "revolution" figured prominently in Aflaq's ideas.

This revolutionary bent was intensified in 1953 through the merger of the Ba'th with the Arab Socialist Party under the leadership of Akram Hourani. Hourani's political influence emanated from a power base centered on the agricultural region around the Syrian city of Hama, where he had organized successful peasant revolts against the large landowning families.[55] He had a genius for clandestine organizational activity, and had established extensive contacts inside the armed forces.[56] Whereas Aflaq thought of revolution primarily in theoretical and philosophical terms, Hourani's own revolutionary experience gave the concept a more concrete manifestation. After the merger, the Party's name was changed to the Arab Socialist Ba'th Party. Aflaq became its secretary-general, responsible for ideological direction. But Hourani soon established himself as the real leader, around whom gathered professionals, students, and army officers "who were among some of the most candescent of the generation that grew up in the waning years of the mandate period and the dawning of the independence era."[57]

---

[54] For a concise exposition of Aflaq's ideas, see Leonard Binder, *The Ideological Revolution in the Middle East* (New York: John Wiley and Sons, Inc., 1964), pp. 154–197; for the early history, organization, and rise in political influence of the Ba'th Party, see John Devlin, *The Ba'th Party: A History from its Origins to 1966* (Stanford, California: Hoover Institution Press, 1976); also Kamel Abu Jaber, *The Arab Ba'th Socialist Party: History, Ideology and Organization* (Syracuse, New York: Syracuse University Press, 1966).

[55] Patrick Seale, *Asad of Syria: The Struggle for the Middle East* (Berkeley: University of California Press, 1988), pp. 41–43.

[56] Salah Nasr, *'Abd al-Nasir wa Tajribat al-Wuhda* (Abd al-Nasir and the experience of unity) (Beirut: al-Watan al-'Arabi, 1976), p. 51.

[57] Ahmad 'Abd al-Karim, *Hisad: Sineen Khasiba wa Thimar Mura* (Harvest: fertile years and bitter fruit) (Beirut: Bisan li al-Nashr wa al-Tawzi', 1994), p. 201.

Hourani recruited heavily from among the ranks of the military and educational institutions. By 1954, the Baʻth had succeeded in establishing a political presence in the country. In that year's election, party members won thirteen seats in the 141-seat National Assembly.[58] Even though it could not match the traditional politicians who won the lion's share of the parliamentary seats, this was still an impressive tally for a party that did not officially exist a decade earlier.

In the early 1950s, the Party embarked on expanding its activities beyond Syria, concentrating its effort in the neighboring Hashemite monarchies of Iraq and Jordan. Working clandestinely (not surprisingly, neither government welcomed the revolutionary philosophy of the Baʻth), the Party saw a steady, if not spectacular, rise in its membership. Its political fortunes were aided by Nasir's nationalization of the Suez Canal and the subsequent tripartite attack on Egypt. In October 1956, at the height of the Suez crisis, two Jordanian Baʻthists won parliamentary seats in what was probably the freest election Jordan had yet known. The Baʻthists could have won more seats had their Arab nationalist program not competed with that of the National Socialist Party under Sulayman Nabulsi, who was perceived in Jordan as a strong admirer of Nasir.[59]

In Iraq, Baʻthist clandestine activities began in 1951, but recruitment proceeded slowly due to intense governmental repression and the competition provided by a long-established clandestine Communist Party. The Party's growth accelerated after 1954, coinciding with Nasir's onslaught against the Western alliance system which soon was to be centered in Baghdad. As in Jordan, the Party received its greatest boost after the Suez crisis,[60] as its Arab nationalist principles echoed those of the charismatic Nasir, who by then had become the acknowledged leader of the Arab nationalist movement. By the time of the Iraqi revolution in July 1958, the Baʻthists

[58] Malik Mufti, *Sovereign Creations: Pan-Arabism and Political Order in Syria and Iraq* (Ithaca, New York: Cornell University Press, 1996), p. 71.

[59] Devlin, *The Baʻth Party*, p. 103.

[60] Abu Jaber, *The Arab Baʻth Socialist Party*, p. 53.

had become a recognized element of the "progressive" forces that were instrumental in the demise of the Iraqi monarchy. And indeed, Fuad al-Rikabi, the secretary-general of the regional command (the Iraqi branch) of the party entered the first cabinet of the Iraqi Republic.

Even more so than the Ba'th, the Arab Nationalists Movement (ANM), which was formed in 1951 by a number of Palestinian students and professionals under the leadership of the Christian Palestinian, George Habash,[61] tied its political fortunes to Nasir, following his lead through much of the 1950s and 1960s. Indeed, unlike the Ba'th, which at various times in the 1960s broke with Nasir, attacking him and his policies vehemently, and advocating a different Arab nationalist path, the ANM remained on the whole loyal to Nasir and his brand of Arab nationalism right until the disastrous Arab defeat in the June 1967 Six Day War.[62] It was as though the ANM saw itself as an arm of Nasirist policies, working at the grassroots level, spreading Arab nationalist doctrine, particularly in Palestine, Iraq, the Gulf, and South Arabia.[63] Undoubtedly, this close, almost symbiotic, association with Nasir was beneficial to the ANM; Nasir's triumphs were theirs, and his charisma benefited their organization. But this association also had its costs. Nasir's defeats reflected badly on the ANM. It is hardly coincidental that the organization began to atrophy in the mid-1960s when Nasir's Egypt suffered a number of setbacks in the Arab world. Indeed, the ANM disintegrated as a unified movement in the wake of the Six Day War. Moreover, its close association with Nasir robbed it of a separate identity. What need was there for someone

[61] Habash later was to form the Popular Front for the Liberation of Palestine (PFLP), which gained international notoriety by masterminding a series of high-profile airplane hijackings during the 1970s, the most infamous of which occurred in Jordan in September 1970, which led to the Jordanian civil war that became known to Palestinians as "Black September." After the 1970 debacle, Habash headquartered the PFLP in Damascus, and remained a nemesis of the Palestinian Liberation Organization leader, Yasir Arafat.

[62] See 'Abdallah Saloom al-Samarai', "Harakat al-Qawmiyeen al-'Arab wa Dawruha fi al-Wa'yi al-Qawmi," (The Arab nationalists movement and its role in national consciousness), al-Mustaqbal al-'Arabi (Beirut), no. 84 (February 1986): 75–99.

[63] 'Abd al-Karim, Hisad: Sineen Khasiba wa Thimar Mura (Harvest: fertile years and bitter fruit), p. 247.

who already identified himself as a Nasirist or Arab nationalist to join the ANM? Perhaps this is why the ANM never achieved the later political prominence of the Ba'th, which had always been jealous about preserving its own separate political identity. On balance, however, the association with Nasir was ultimately beneficial to the ANM. It is highly unlikely that the mass base of the organization would have grown had it not been for Nasir's charismatic propagation of Arab nationalism.

On the opposite end of the political spectrum, the political groups and parties that did not share the ideological proclivities of Egypt's leader saw a considerable decline in their political fortune. While the death of Antun Sa'ada was a major blow to the Syrian National Party (SNP), the party itself continued to organize and recruit new members attracted to the idea of "Greater Syria." In the first half of the 1950s, the SNP was probably the Ba'th's main rival, as both scrambled to clandestinely recruit adherents from the same societal base. As a result, great enmity developed between the two parties. In March 1955, as the Nasir-led Arab nationalist onslaught against Western military alliances gathered momentum, and was beginning to galvanize Arab public opinion, the SNP was implicated in the assassination of 'Adnan Maliki, a popular Ba'thist officer. Rumors were abound that the SNP was working with Western intelligence against the Communist Party and Nasirist and Ba'thist Arab nationalism in Syria.[64] From then on, its activity was severely curtailed by a witch-hunt against party members undertaken by Arab nationalist officials that succeeded in ultimately driving the SNP out of Syria.[65] But beyond the political persecution, the Party's days were already numbered in Syria; it had been overtaken by the upsurge in pro-Egyptian Arab nationalist sentiment that occurred in the mid-1950s.[66]

[64] Michael C. Hudson, *Arab Politics: The Search for Legitimacy* (New Haven, Connecticut: Yale University Press, 1977), p. 257.

[65] 'Abd al-Karim, *Hisad: Sineen Khasiba wa Thimar Mura* (Harvest: fertile years and bitter fruit), p. 245; Nasr, *'Abd al-Nasir wa Tajribat al-Wuhda* (Abd al-Nasir and the experience of unity), p. 68.

[66] Albert Hourani, *Arabic Thought in the Liberal Age, 1798–1939* (London: Oxford University Press, 1970), pp. 317–318.

Another party that came up against the Nasir-led Arab nationalist movement was the Iraqi Communist Party. Up until the mid-
1950s, the party was at the forefront of clandestine activities
against the monarchical regime, dwarfing the Ba'th and other Arab
nationalist and "progressive" groups. The Communists had been
responsible for a number of antigovernment uprisings in various
Iraqi towns and cities, including the famed *al-Wathba*, "the most
formidable mass insurrection in the history of the monarchy."[67] *Al-
Wathba* lasted for eleven days in January 1948, and resulted in
between 200 and 300 dead. But it did bring about the abrogation
of a major treaty with Britain and the fall of the government responsible for the treaty. Saleh Jaber, the Iraqi prime minister, beat
a hasty and unceremonious retreat to his tribal domain and from
there escaped to England. As late as 1956, the Communists were
able to mount two mass insurrections in the city of Najaf and the
town of Hayy. A secret police document confided that Communism
in Hayy had "penetrated among all classes."[68] Both insurrections
were ultimately suppressed by government forces with great difficulty and not inconsiderable loss of life.

During this period of vigorous underground activity by the
Communists, the Ba'th Party was working merely to establish some
presence among the country's opposition forces. Yet by 1958, at
the time of the Iraqi revolution, Ba'thists and other Arab nationalists could legitimately claim to have balanced the power of the
Communists. And even though the Communists seemed to have
the upper hand in the first two years of the Iraqi Republic, they
were soon to be swept aside by the gathering nationalist tide. The
Communists, who were then the tolerated allies of Iraq's dictator,
'Abd al-Karim Qasim, must have seen the writing on the wall,
when in 1962, the Iraqi Ba'th Party, officially banned and working
underground, was able to organize a huge demonstration in Bagh-

[67] Hanna Batatu, *The Old Social Classes and the Revolutionary Movements of Iraq: A
Study of Iraq's Old Landed and Commercial Classes and of its Communists, Ba'thists, and
Free Officers* (Princeton, New Jersey: Princeton University Press, 1978), p. 545. Using secret
police and Communist Party documents, Batatu provides a graphic description of this massive insurrection, pp. 545–566.
[68] Ibid., p. 756.

dad to welcome the Algerian leader Ahmad Ben Bella on his first visit to Iraq. In defiance of the government, the thousands of demonstrators hoisted banners that carried the slogan:[69]

| *Ben Bella ahlan beek* | Ben Bella welcome to you |
| *Hizb al-Ba'th yehayeek* | The Ba'th Party greets you |

A few months later, the Ba'th Party, supported by other Arab nationalists, was able to mount a successful military coup that spelled the beginning of the end for the Iraqi Communists. And indeed, by the mid-1960s, the once most powerful underground organization in Iraq had been reduced to a mere skeleton of its former self—a sorry collection of old-timers, unable to infuse much needed young blood into the Party, cognizant of the fact that the present held precious few opportunities, and the future fewer still.

The Iraqi Communist Party, much like other groups and organizations that did not partake in the Arab nationalist idea, simply could not withstand the gathering force of the nationalist tide. This tide sprung to life in the early days of 1955, when Gamal 'Abd al-Nasir decided to take on the propagators and supporters of the Baghdad Pact.

[69] 'Ali Karim Sa'id, *Iraq 8 Shibat 1963: Min Hiwar al-Mafahim ila Hiwar al-Dam; Muraja'at fi Dhakirat Taleb Shabib* (Iraq 8 February 1963: from a dialogue over norms to a dialogue of blood; reviews in the memory of Taleb Shabib) (Beirut: Dar al-Kunuz al-Adabiya, 1999), p. 49.

CHAPTER SEVEN

ARAB NATIONALISM ON THE MARCH, 1955–1957

If specific events were to be picked as signposts in the spectacular forward march of Arab nationalism during the 1950s, the three that stand out are the 1955 Baghdad Pact, the 1956 Suez Crisis, and the birth of the United Arab Republic (UAR) in 1958. While Egypt's perceived victory in the Suez Crisis and the merger of Egypt and Syria into the UAR constituted perhaps the two singular events that truly galvanized Arab public opinion behind the ideas and symbols of Arab nationalism, it was the Baghdad Pact which was the defining event that triggered a chain of political initiatives and responses that ultimately were to mark the period as the nationalist era. It was in this era that large segments of the educated populace, bewitched by the power of the Arab idea and seduced by the charisma of Gamal 'Abd al-Nasir, came to believe passionately, albeit naïvely as it turned out, in the unquestionable and inevitable triumph of Arab nationalism. And indeed if nothing else, it was the Baghdad Pact that brought Egypt fully, unequivocally, and vigorously into the very heart of Arab politics.

It all began innocuously enough in May 1953. John Foster Dulles, the U. S. secretary of state, paid a visit to Cairo to muster support for a Western defense alliance which would be based on the Middle East and would link with the North Atlantic Treaty Organization (NATO) to its west and a projected Southeast Asian alliance (formed in 1954) to its east. These alliances were part of a grand security design known as the policy of Containment, which was meant to keep the Soviets and other Communists at bay. Nasir and his colleagues, however, were lukewarm to the idea. As he would later say in an interview, Nasir could not take seriously the American contention that a threat to the region would emanate from a power "whose forces were five thousand miles away."[1] A more serious objection related to the whole question of the balance of power in such an alliance. Nasir explained to Dulles:

> If a small state entered an alliance with a large state, then dominance and leadership will reside with the larger state, and the small state will become nothing but a subservient entity good only for taking orders. We therefore believe that defense of our region should emanate from the region itself without the participation of a foreign country.[2]

Dulles left Cairo empty-handed but relations did not seem particularly strained. This, however, soon was to change. Faced with Egypt's rejection of the American project, the dogged and intractable American secretary of state shifted his attention to Baghdad, where the virulently pro-Western Iraqi government endeavored ceaselessly to project Iraq as the balancing pole to Egypt in the Arab world. In January 1954, the United States, in response to an Iraqi request for military aid, used language that seemed to tie American approval to Iraq's participation in a "regional security arrangement."[3] Given the political orientation of Iraq's political elite, particularly of its strongman, Nuri al-Sa'id, it was a forgone

---

[1] *The Sunday Times* (London), June 24, 1962.

[2] Quoted in Fikrat 'Abd al-Fattah, *Siyasat al-'Iraq al-Kharijiya fi al-Mintaqa al-'Arabiya, 1953–1958* (Iraq's foreign policy in the Arab region, 1953–1958) (Baghdad: Wizarat al-Thaqafa wa al-I'lam, 1981), p. 333.

[3] Elie Podeh, *The Quest for Hegemony in the Arab World: The Struggle Over the Baghdad Pact* (Leiden: E. J. Brill, 1995), p. 64.

conclusion that the Baghdad government would respond favorably to the American proposal.

From around the fall of 1954, Nuri al-Saʻid began the process that would eventually end in the announcement of the Baghdad Pact. First, he had to ensure domestic compliance. He therefore called an election in September 1954 which was so rigged that no less than 100 of the 135 members of the new parliament were avid Nuri supporters. Indeed, only 23 seats were contested; the rest were won unchallenged.[4] Having ensured domestic compliance, Nuri traveled to Cairo to discuss with Nasir security arrangements for the region. The meeting stalemated with Nasir reiterating his position that regional security should fall on the Arab countries themselves, and Nuri insisting that only with the help of the Western powers could Iraq and the region prevent Soviet and Communist aggression.[5] The problem was that while Nasir emphasized Arab neutrality in the ideological and political struggle between the superpowers, Nuri could not conceive of a political path for the Arabs that was divorced from the West. He later wrote that in the meeting, Nasir

> failed to understand that the West would not tolerate Russian influence in the Middle East. He failed to understand that the West would not grant the Arabs the luxury of neutralism, that this area is too decisively vital for that sort of foolishness. He failed to understand that the Middle East is inextricably tied to the West economically—there is no other bigger market for Arab oil, for example. Despite a soldier's background, Nasser overlooked the military reality of Russia's incapacity to defend the Arabs if they made an enemy of the West.[6]

[4] K. al-Husri, "The Iraqi Revolution of July 14, 1958," *Middle East Forum*, vol. 41 (1965): p. 27.

[5] Kennet Love, *Suez: The Twice Fought War* (New York: McGraw Hill, 1969), pp. 195–196; Podeh, *The Quest for Hegemony in the Arab World*, p. 88; and ʻAbd al-Fattah, *Siyasat al-ʻIraq al-Kharijiya* (Iraq's foreign policy in the Arab region), pp. 308–311.

[6] Nuri al-Saʻid's article appeared posthumously in *Life*. This specific quote from the article is taken from Robert Stephens, *Nasser: A Political Biography* (London: Allen Lane / Penguin Press, 1971), p. 149.

At the end of the meeting, Nasir, probably more in frustration than agreement, told Nuri that he was free to do what he thought was best for Iraq,[7] but that he should not rush into any deal with the West. Nuri, on the other hand, believing that he had made his position clear to Nasir, and that the Egyptian leader would not object too strenuously if Iraq went ahead with its plans, decided that it was time to act.

In early January 1955, during a visit by the Turkish prime minister, Adnan Menderes, an announcement was made that Iraq and Turkey intended to enter into a military alliance soon. This apparently came as a great surprise to Nasir and the Egyptian leaders. Nasir had thought that he had extracted a promise from Nuri not to make a significant move in the direction of an alliance with the West without first consulting with Cairo.[8] In response, Nasir called a meeting of Arab prime ministers in Cairo with the intention of condemning the proposed Iraqi action. But the most that the prime ministers were able to agree on was to dispatch a delegation to Iraq to persuade Nuri to change course or, at a minimum, to postpone the pending treaty. The delegation included Colonel Salah Salem, a senior member of Egypt's ruling group. Nuri would not budge, and his parting words to Salem were: "I am not a soldier in 'Abd al-Nasir's army. Please tell him that I will not obey his orders."[9] And indeed he did not. On February 25, 1955, Iraq signed a security treaty with Turkey, which became known as *Mithaq Baghdad*, the Baghdad Pact. The treaty was designed to be the first step of a regional security alliance involving Pakistan and Iran and the possible future membership of the United States and Great Britain. Nuri immediately invited other Arab countries to join.

[7] Phebe Marr, *The Modern History of Iraq* (Boulder, Colorado: Westview Press, 1985), p. 117. Marr got this information from an interview with Najib al-Rawi, the then-Iraqi ambassador to Cairo, who attended the Iraqi-Egyptian meeting. It is, however, important to note that the interview was conducted fourteen years after the meeting, and it is not clear whether al-Rawi had taken notes of the meeting or was speaking from memory.

[8] 'Abd al-Latif al-Baghdadi, *Mudhakarat 'Abd al-Latif al-Baghdadi, al-Jusi' al-Awal* (Memoirs of 'Abd al-Latif al-Baghdadi, volume one) (Cairo: Al-Maktab al-Musri al-Hadith, 1977), p. 200.

[9] Ahmad 'Abd al-Karim, *Hisad: Sineen Khasiba wa Thimar Murra* (Harvest: fertile years, bitter fruit) (Beirut: Bisan li al-Nashr wa al-Tawzi', 1994), p. 271.

Egypt's response was expeditious and resolute. On the political level, Cairo moved to secure its own diplomatic position in the region and to isolate Iraq politically. In early March, less than two weeks after the formal announcement of the Baghdad Pact, Egypt formed its own alliance with Syria, which was endorsed by Saudi Arabia, the traditional nemesis of the Hashemites. It was pointedly claimed that the alliance was only the first step in the wider integration of the Arab world.[10] To prove a point, Nasir dispatched Egyptian forces to be stationed on Syria's borders with Iraq and Turkey. These moves were cemented later on in the year when, in the name of Arab nationalism, the Egyptian-Syrian Mutual Defense Pact was signed, to be followed a week later by another pact with Saudi Arabia which Yemen joined. The moves represented Nasir's determined efforts to politically isolate Iraq and to exhibit in a concrete fashion to Arab public opinion that there were Arab alternatives to Western alliances. Yet Nasir knew that this in itself would not be enough to ensure that the balance of forces would continue to be in Egypt's favor.

So in addition to diplomacy, Cairo unleashed an intense propaganda campaign against the Baghdad Pact, against those who signed it, and the others who were contemplating signing it. The campaign was waged through the "Voice of the Arabs," which, as we have seen, dominated the airwaves of the region. Iraq lacked the capacity to take the war of words to Egypt, and possessed only limited capacity to jam the Egyptian broadcasts in its own backyard. So unlike Egyptians who heard only one message, that of Nasir, Iraqis were exposed to two: on the one hand, their own leaders appealed to them to uphold the status quo and to continue along the old path of relationships and dependence on the protection of the Great Powers; on the other hand, Egypt appealed for self-sufficiency and for dependence on one's self against the greed and ill will of the foreigner. Regardless of the merits of the two messages, it was a foregone conclusion as to which of the two positions would win the hearts and minds of the Arab populace, or at

[10] *Al-Ahram* (Cairo), March 10, 1955.

least of its politically influential segment, the rapidly expanding middle class—professionals, army officers, merchants, and, crucially in this period, college and high school students, who quickly became Nasir's foot soldiers in their respective countries.

Egypt's propaganda was highly incendiary, using the semantic properties of the Arabic language to foment the emotions and "to boil the blood"[11] of its target populations. It was no coincidence that its most susceptible targets were the young, who were open more readily to emotional appeals than to rational argument. At the prompting of Egypt's leadership, the "Voice of the Arabs" launched an onslaught against Iraq's government over the Baghdad Pact and other alleged infidelities to the nationalist cause, and took to calling Nuri al-Sa'id "a traitor."[12] There was no need for further elaboration: Was it not absolutely clear to the listeners in Baghdad and other Iraqi cities that the characterization simply defined Nuri's dependence on foreign powers to the detriment of the Arab cause? Moreover, the "Voice of the Arabs" found Nuri's proclivity to the foreigner not at all surprising, for was Nuri himself not of "Turkish descent,"[13] and was he not dispersing Iraqi Arab officers and replacing them with "Turkoman officers to ensure the subjugation of the Iraqi army and to force it to be loyal to imperialist obligations.'?[14] Such allegations, where the standards for precision are at best nebulous, clearly illustrate the attractiveness of propaganda to political leaderships. Take this case of Nuri's alleged "Turkish descent," which the "Voice of the Arabs" enunciated as an accepted truth in no need of further elaboration, to say nothing of corroboration. The truth is far more complex. Nuri's family traced its ancestry and residence in Baghdad back to over three centuries to an Arab patriarch who married a Turkish woman from Constantinople. For the next three hundred years, the family lived continuously in Iraq and was accepted and respected as Arab. Nuri

[11] *Al-Ahram* (Cairo), February 18, 1957.

[12] Al-Baghdadi, *Mudhakarat 'Abd al-Latif al-Baghdadi* (Memoirs of 'Abd al-Latif al-Baghdadi), p. 200.

[13] The British Broadcasting Corporation, *Summary of World Broadcasts, Part IV: The Arab World, Israel, Greece, Turkey, Iran* (hereafter cited as *SWB*), March 7, 1957, p. 3.

[14] *SWB*, May 3, 1958, p. 1.

himself was a prominent commander of the successful 1916 Arab revolt against the Ottoman Turks.[15]

Nuri and the Iraqi government did not remain quiet; they retaliated, mincing no words. But in this mammoth struggle over the right to define the Arab national interest, Iraq was fighting a losing battle. It lacked the seductive appeal of Egypt's message, it was no match for Cairo's airwave capability, and it had no one of Nasir's charisma and mounting prestige in the Arab world.

Nasir's aura was boosted further through the emergence of a world movement of leaders who rejected alliances with either the United States or the Soviet Union, seeking instead a nonaligned position. The movement's first major meeting took place in the Indonesian city of Bandung in April 1955. In this conference, Nasir joined some of the most prominent Third World leaders of the time, including Marshal Tito of Yugoslavia, Prime Minister Nehru of India, Premier Chou En-Lai of China, and President Sukarno of Indonesia, all of whom endeavored to stake out for their countries a neutralist position between the two seemingly irreconcilable positions of East and West in those highly combustible Cold War years of the 1950s. As an international event, the meeting in Bandung attracted intense world scrutiny. Bandung confirmed in the minds of Arabs Nasir's contention that Arab leaders *can* pursue policies that are independent of the West. Even more relevant to our topic, Nasir's words were treated by the other leaders as well as the media as representing not just Egypt, but the Arab world. When he spoke, he spoke with the confidence and demeanor of someone who knew that he had the Arab populations behind him. He was becoming increasingly comfortable with his new role as the leader of Arab nationalism, and the main propagator of its message which prescribed the independence of the Arabs from all foreign interests and ideologies.

If some Arabs thought that Nasir's "independent" position entailed a rich glossary of words, but lacked any substance, Nasir

---

[15] See Waldeman J. Gallman, *Iraq Under General Nuri: My Recollections of Nuri al-Sa'id, 1954–1958* (Baltimore: Johns Hopkins University Press, 1964), pp. 9–12; also Lord Birdwood, *Nuri As-Said: A Study in Arab Leadership* (London: Cassell, 1959), pp. 8–9.

was soon to confound them. On September 27, 1955, he signed an arms deal with Czechoslovakia, breaking Western monopoly over the sale of arms in the region. Admittedly, this was not the first arms deal with a Soviet bloc country signed by an Arab state. Syria had already received a few arms from the Soviet bloc, which had created some concern in Western capitals. But the announcement of the Czech arms deal involving the most powerful Arab country, signed by a man increasingly perceived as the charismatic leader of the Arab nationalist march, was bound to create severe consternation bordering on panic among the Western powers and their allies in the area.

The roots of the Czech arms deal lay primarily in the Arab-Israeli conflict. It was not just pro-Western Arab leaders who were becoming wary of Nasir's mounting popularity among their populations. The Israelis also worried about the possible deleterious consequences of the rising tide of militant Arab nationalism under Nasir's leadership on their young country. There were already some infiltrations into Israel from Egypt carried out by Palestinian and Egyptian commandos calling themselves the *fedayyin* (martyrs). David Ben-Gurion, the father of the state of Israel, was especially irked. He was convinced that the Israelis had to teach Nasir a lesson, perhaps even remove him from power. "It is definitely possible to topple him," Ben-Gurion told his cabinet colleagues, "and it is even a *mitzvah* [a sacred obligation] to do so. Who is he anyway, this Nasser-Shmasser?"[16] One way to undermine the popularity of the Egyptian president among the Arabs was to show him up as militarily impotent. This way he would be cut down to size from the leader of Arab nationalism to a mere Nasser-Shmasser. So on February 28, 1955, Israeli forces led by Ariel Sharon (later to be elected Israeli prime minister in February 2001) launched a massive raid on the Egyptian-controlled Gaza Strip, destroying its military headquarters, killing thirty-eight soldiers, and wounding thirty-one.

---

[16] Quoted in Avi Shlaim, *The Iron Wall: Israel and the Arab World* (New York: W. W. Norton & Company, 2000), pp. 135–136.

Nasir was just as aware of the deleterious impact of the raid on his image as the dynamic leader of an ascendant nationalist movement. He had indeed tried to buy weapons from the British and the Americans but all he got were a few Centurion tanks which in no way matched the substantial arms deliveries Israel was beginning to receive from the French.[17] And the Americans flatly refused a $27 million arms request from Nasir on the flimsy grounds that Egypt was unable to pay for them in hard currency.[18] So during the Bandung Conference, Nasir approached the Chinese premier, Chou En-Lai, and inquired as to whether China would be prepared to sell Egypt arms. Chou En-Lai declined, citing China's own dependence on Russian arms, but promised to pass Egypt's request to the Soviets, who did not take long to agree.[19] The Czech arms deal was basically a deal with the Soviets that used Czechoslovakia as an intermediary.[20]

The arms deal allowed for the first real penetration by the Soviet Union into Arab and Middle East politics, which was to diametrically change the balance of forces in the area. From then on the West lost its monopoly over security (and eventually political) affairs of the region, which in Arab eyes became the ultimate vindication of Nasir's argument for Arab independence. Even Jordan's King Husayn, hardly a disciple of Nasir, would admit to the wider impact of the arms deal:

> Then the bombshell fell on the Arab world [when] Nasser announced his now historic arms deal with the Soviet bloc. In an instant, everything changed. Hundreds of thousands of Jordanians, listening avidly to the propaganda on Cairo Radio, saw in Nasser a mystical sort of savior and . . . their best bet for their future against Israel. [All] they saw was . . . that Nasser was the first Arab states-

[17] Stephens, *Nasser: A Political Biography*, p. 157.
[18] Humphrey Trevelyan, *The Middle East in Revolution* (London: Macmillan, 1970), pp. 27–28.
[19] 'Abd al-Karim, *Hisad: Sineen Khasiba wa Thimar Murra* (Harvest: fertile years, bitter fruit), p. 276.
[20] Karen Dawisha, *Soviet Foreign Policy Towards Egypt* (London: Macmillan, 1979), p. 11.

man really to throw off the shackles of the West. I must admit I
sympathized with the point of view to a great extent.[21]

Indeed Husayn's own parliament cabled Nasir a unanimous resolution, whose language clearly illustrates the image of Nasir held
by the Arab populations: "The Jordanian Chamber of Deputies
congratulates you, the soul of Arabism, and supports you in all
your efforts in securing arms without any restrictions or conditions
for the defense of the Arab countries."[22] Not only was Nasir described as the *soul of Arabism* in a country whose king also lay
claim to the same designation, but the deputies saw the arms deal
as enhancing not necessarily the security of Egypt but *the defense
of the Arab countries*.

Thus there was much rejoicing in the Arab world. The people
who took to the streets in Damascus, Baghdad, Amman, and even
the cities of the conservative and less developed Gulf protector-
ates,[23] saw in the Czech arms deal not just an assertion of Egyptian
independence, but an Arab victory over "imperialism" and its "illegitimate offspring," Israel. Not one for an understatement, the
"Voice of the Arabs" trumpeted the deal for months afterward as
a momentous juncture in the historical march of Arab nationalism.

If by now some Arab leaders still doubted the adulation of Nasir
felt by their own citizens, the events surrounding Jordan's efforts
to join the Baghdad Pact were to erase any such doubts summarily.
King Husayn had been cool to the idea of joining the Iraqi-Turkish
alliance because he believed that Jordan would "get nothing additional out of it except abuse from Egyptian propaganda."[24] But
frustrated by their inability to draw other Arab countries into the
Pact, and fearing that they were losing the battle against Nasir and
his propaganda, Iraq, Turkey, and Britain made a concerted effort

[21] His Majesty King Hussein 1, *Uneasy Lies the Head* (New York: Bernard Geis Associates, 1962), pp. 106–107.
[22] Peter Snow, *Hussein: A Biography* (New York: Robert B. Luce, Inc., 1972), p. 74.
[23] Riad Taha, *Qissat al-Wuhda wa al-Infisal: Tajribat Insan 'Arabi Khilal Ahdath 1955–
1961* (The story of the unity and separation: the experience of an Arab person during the
events of 1955–1961) (Beirut: Dar al-Afaq al-Jadida, 1974), p. 61
[24] Quoted in Podeh, *The Quest for Hegemony in the Arab World*, p. 174.

to bring the pro-Western Hashemite Jordan into their agreement. Iraq promised financial aid,[25] Turkey hinted at bolstering Jordan's defense against Israel and Syria,[26] and Britain offered 5.5 million pounds sterling in arms, more aid for industrial and energy development, and a promise to revise the Anglo-Jordanian treaty.[27] Britain dispatched its chief of staff, Sir Gerald Templer, in early December 1955 to present the aid package to the Jordanians and to discuss the mechanics of Jordan's membership in the pact. Egypt immediately unleashed a violent verbal onslaught against the Templer mission, and the country witnessed a wave of riots, demonstrations, and strikes that shook the very foundation of Husayn's political order.[28] Interesting enough, the most telling and vivid description of the political crisis in Jordan that followed the Templer mission is told by the king himself:

> Without warning, the Egyptians launched a heavy barrage of propaganda against Jordan. Within a matter of hours Amman was torn by riots as the people, their senses blurred by propaganda, turned to Nasir, the new *mystique* of the Arab world . . . I stuck to my guns. Under pressure, Sa'id Mufti, the premier—a good man, but old—resigned and the government fell. Immediately, the rioting flared up again. By innuendo, the ministers who had resigned let it be known they had only taken this extreme step through patriotic motives and that perhaps Cairo was right about a "sell-out to imperialism and the Jews". . . . As the mob roamed the streets, I brought Hezza Pasha Majali. . . . He announced publicly that he was in favor of the Baghdad Pact, and between us, this great patriot and I did every-

---

[25] Isma'el Ahmad Yaghi, *al-'Ilaqat al-'Iraqiya al-Urduniya, 1941–1958* (Iraqi-Jordanian relations, 1941–1958) (Cairo: Dar al-Sahwa li al-Nashr, 1988), p. 40.

[26] Podeh, *The Quest for Hegemony in the Arab World*, pp. 175–176

[27] Michael B. Oren, "A Winter of Discontent: Britain's Crisis in Jordan, December 1955–March 1956," *International Journal of Middle East Studies*, vol. 22 (1990): 176.

[28] Uriel Dann, *King Hussein and the Challenge of Arab Radicalism: Jordan, 1955–1967* (New York: Oxford University Press, 1989), pp. 28–29; Snow, *Hussein: A Biography*, pp. 76–79; Oren, "A Winter of Discontent," pp. 176–178; al-Baghdadi, *Mudhakarat 'Abd al-Latif al-Baghdadi* (Memoirs of 'Abd al-Latif al-Baghdadi), p. 201; al-Fattah, *Siyasat al-'Iraq al-Kharijiya fi al-Mintaqa al-'Arabiya* (Iraq's foreign policy in the Arab region), pp. 360–363; Michael N. Barnett, *Dialogues in Arab Politics: Negotiations in Regional Order* (New York: Columbia University press, 1998), pp. 116–119.

thing we could. But we were virtually helpless. . . . Still we might have held on, but on December 19, the Minister of Interior and two others of Majali's government resigned. Majali tried to find replacements but in vain. There was nothing I could do but dissolve the government . . . with the promise of elections in three or four months. . . . The Jordanian High Court ruled the decree was unconstitutional and the old deputies had to be reinstated. Now all hell broke loose. Riots such as we had never seen before . . . disrupted the entire country. This time bands of arsonists started burning government offices, private houses, foreign properties. I had no alternative but to call out the Legion (army), who with tear gas and determination met force with force. I imposed a ten-day curfew on the country.[29]

In addition to calling the Jordanian army to restore order in the streets of the Jordanian cities, the position of the king had become so precarious that he also was compelled to ask for Iraqi troops.[30] Indeed, panic had spread to Whitehall. Britain's prime minister, Anthony Eden, dispatched two parachute battalions and a battalion of Highland Light Infantry to Cyprus. He also ordered the armored regiment at Aqaba to move closer to Amman.[31] Finally, yet another hastily appointed prime minister, Samir Rifa'i, conceded that the Jordanian government no longer contemplated joining the Baghdad Pact. Only then was calm restored, and life returned to normal. Nasir had won, and won big. He had imposed his will on a recalcitrant Arab leader not through military force, but through manipulating the sentiments of that leader's own population. And those sentiments were aroused by Nasir's invocation of Arab nationalism.

The Jordanian events not only stopped the Hashemite kingdom from entering the Baghdad Pact, but it also sent a message of dire warning to any other Arab country that might have been contemplating joining the Western-inspired alliance. And indeed, the

[29] Hussein, *Uneasy Lies the Head*, pp. 110–112.
[30] Yaghi, *al-'Ilaqat al-'Iraqiya al-Urdiniya* (Iraqi-Jordanian relations), p. 41.
[31] Snow, *Hussein: A Biography*, p. 79.

Baghdad Pact never expanded in the Arab world and was finally put to rest in 1959 when the new republican government of Iraq withdrew its membership. The Pact was to be given another life as the Central Treaty Organization (CENTO), with regional membership limited to Turkey, Iran, and Pakistan. However, lacking the involvement of any country from the Arab "core," CENTO was a mere shadow of what Dulles and the original planners had hoped to achieve.

Egypt's victory had much to do with Nasir's charisma (or his *mystique* as King Husayn put it in his memoirs) and Egypt's overwhelming preponderance in the battle of the airwaves. But success would not have come so readily had it not been for the power of the message. The Jordanian events of December 1955 constituted the first actual illustration of the power of Arab nationalism. Indeed a rational assessment of Jordanian national interest supports Husayn's position. Britain had pledged to embark upon a quantitative and qualitative improvement of the Jordanian armed forces, and along with Iraq, promised Jordan badly needed economic aid. There was also a commitment to revise the Anglo-Jordanian treaty in Jordan's favor. But it was not rationality, the national interest, or power politics that drove the Jordanian rioters; it was the emotional and mystical power of Arab nationalism, articulated by a charismatic leader, that brought the Jordanians onto the streets. The struggle over the Baghdad Pact ushered in a period in the history of the region in which Arab nationalism became the uncontested ideological force among citizens of the countries and areas that called themselves Arab.

The post Baghdad Pact era brings to mind Benedict Anderson's definition of a nation as an imagined community:

It is *imagined* because the members of even the smallest nation will never know most of their fellow members, meet them, or even hear of them, yet in the minds of each lives the image of their communion.[32]

---

[32] Benedict Anderson, *Imagined Communities: Reflections on the Origins and Spread of Nationalism* (New York: Simon and Schuster, 1993), p. 6.

During the few years that followed the Baghdad Pact, particularly 1955–1958, which represent the apex of the Arab nationalist tide, an Iraqi lawyer, a Jordanian student, a Bahraini poet, a Syrian doctor, and a Moroccan businessman would not have known one another by name or profession, but by adhering to the Arab nationalist creed, they were indeed but one fraternity, sharing in convictions and aspirations. Such individuals would not have known of each other's existence, and, given the wide regional variations in the dialects of the Arabic language, might not have conversed easily had they met, but in these few and fateful years, they belonged to one another spiritually, for indeed, *in the minds of each lived the image of their communion.*

The old world was crumbling: traditional values and customs were questioned, old patterns of authority were coming increasingly under attack, and Nasirist Arab nationalism was leading the assault everywhere in the Arab world, even in its remotest areas and most traditional parts. R. Stephen Humphreys relates the experience of a young British scholar:

> A friend and I were in Seyyum, one of the ancient towns of the great eastern wadi of Hadhramaut (in Yemen), dominated by a highly influential clan of sherifs, descendants of the Prophet Muhammad. . . . Two young men of that family met us in the street . . . the green band around their turbans . . . signified their holiness and the precedence of their position. . . . The fullness of sanctity and a ritualized sense of gracious order and harmony were added to when a student of mine encountered in the street stooped respectfully to kiss the young sherifs' hands as we passed. . . . A day later I met the student, a boy in his late teens like myself. He delivered [a] blow. "We kiss their hands now," he said, "but just wait till tomorrow." He was a Nasserist . . . he belonged to a cultural club in which most of the young men were sympathizers with the cause of the Egyptian President. The cause was identified as that of all Arabs against imperialism and the control of conservative and reactionary forces.[33]

---

[33] R. Stephen Humphreys, *Between Memory and Desire: The Middle East in a Troubled Age* (Berkeley: University of California Press, 1999), pp. 135–136.

Arab nationalism was also making inroads into some of the most intractable communal divides. Take the case of the pronounced Sunni-Shiite divide in Iraq. As the country secularized, and the influence of religious schools waned,[34] more Shiite Iraqis participated in the body politic. Some worked within the system and rose to positions of political prominence, others joined the underground political opposition. During the 1940s and early 1950s, many of the Shiite youth gravitated away from the Arab nationalist groups and toward the Communist Party.[35] One of the reasons for this was Shiite concern that Arab nationalism was essentially a Sunni project aimed at uniting the Arab states, whose populations were predominantly Sunni, thus rendering the Iraqi Shiites (a majority in Iraq) an insignificant minority. But if there was one period where this sectarian divide was at its lowest, it was during the 1950s, and particularly in this 1955–1958 period. It was not as though all Shiites became ardent nationalists, but more of them joined the nationalist ranks, be it as Nasirists, Qawmiyeen 'Arab (Arab nationalists), or Ba'thists. Indeed, of the seventeen members of Iraq's Ba'th Party leadership in the 1950s, eight were Shiites, including the secretary-general, Fuad al-Rikabi.[36] More significantly, as nationalists, especially in the mid-1950s, their identity was increasingly defined by their nationalism, so that their sectarian affiliations became unimportant, not worth even inquiring about. Taleb Shabib, the first foreign minister in the Ba'thist government that took over power from 'Abd al-Karim Qasim in February 1963, says that members of the party command never discussed, indeed were unaware of, each other's sectarian denominations.[37]

---

[34] At the turn of the twentieth century, over 8,000 students attended Shiite *madrasas* (religious schools) in Iraq's holy Shiite city of Najaf. By 1957, the number had dwindled to 1,954. See Yitzhak Nakash, *The Shi'is of Iraq* (Princeton, New Jersey: Princeton University Press, 1994), p. 254

[35] See Liona Lukitz, *Iraq: The Search for National Identity* (London: Frank Cass, 1995), pp. 151–153.

[36] Hanna Batatu, *The Old Social Classes and the Revolutionary Movements of Iraq: A Study of Iraq's Old Landed and Commercial Classes and of its Communists, Ba'thists and Free Officers* (Princeton, New Jersey: Princeton University Press, 1978), pp. 1216–1218.

[37] See 'Ali Karim Sa'id, *'Iraq 8 Shibat, 1963: Min Hiwar al-Mafahim ila Hiwar al-Damm, Muraja'at fi Dhikrayat Taleb Shabib* (Iraq of 8 February, 1963: from a dialogue over norms

The next momentous event contributing to the upward march of the Arab nationalist movement was the 1956 Suez Crisis—Nasir's nationalization of the Anglo-French owned Suez Canal Company and the ensuing invasion of Egypt by Israel, Britain, and France. The crisis could be traced back to the efforts by Nasir and his colleagues to build the Aswan Dam, which since the first year of the Egyptian revolution had been the major development scheme planned by the new regime. The Dam had been constantly trumpeted as the symbol of a new dynamic and industrialized Egypt. As it was conceived, the Dam would extend continuous irrigation to Upper Egypt, enabling over 125 million acres of arid land to be cultivated. The Dam would also provide the necessary electric power to fulfill the extensive industrialization program that Nasir hoped would give Egypt complete self-sufficiency and help it catch up to the "advanced and industrial" West. In December 1955, the United States, Great Britain, and the World Bank offered to assist Egypt in building the Dam. This offer was accompanied, however, by several conditions, including World Bank supervision of Egypt's budget and its balance of payments, as well as an Egyptian commitment not to seek aid from Communist sources. Nasir balked at such stipulations, which amounted, in his opinion, to foreign control over Egypt's economy and foreign policy. The United States and Britain, on the other hand, had decided at the time the offer was made that Nasir's response to the conditions attached to the offer would be an important factor in assessing future prospects for his cooperation with the West.[38] As Nasir hesitated and demurred through the early months of 1956, Dulles and Britain's prime minister, Anthony Eden, the Czech arms deal still fresh in their minds, decided that the Egyptian leader was surreptitiously negotiating a separate deal with the Soviet Union. Then two events occurred that were to finally deal a deathblow to the Western offer of aid.

In March 1956, King Husayn of Jordan dismissed John Glubb, the British commander of the Arab Legion, Jordan's armed forces.

---

to a dialogue of blood: reviews in the memory of Taleb Shabib) (Beirut: Dar al-Kunuz al-'Adabiya, 1999), pp. 307–314.

[38] Anthony Eden, *Full Circle* (London: Cassell, 1960), p. 335.

The king obviously had been stung by Egyptian radio attacks during the Templer affair, and the radio's constant taunting of Husayn for allowing an Englishman to command the army of his Arab country. Was this not the irrefutable proof, Egyptian radio asked repeatedly, that Jordan was nothing more than Britain's handmaid? The king realized that as long as Glubb was his army chief, he would continue to be the punching bag of Egypt's propagandists. Beyond that, the Sandhurst-trained young monarch, who fancied himself as a military man, became increasingly jealous of Glubb and his ubiquitous control of the Legion—hence, Glubb's sudden and unceremonious dismissal.

Whatever the reason for Glubb's dismissal, Eden blamed it entirely on Nasir.[39] From then on, Eden was determined to rid the world of this new menace to British and Western interests. When the minister of state for foreign affairs, Anthony Nutting, sent him a memo citing the possibility of political chaos in Egypt if Nasir were to be removed, and suggesting instead various means for politically neutralizing the Egyptian leader, Eden called him on the phone, shouting: "[W]hat's all this poppycock you've sent me? . . . what's all this nonsense about isolating Nasser, or 'neutralizing' him, as you call it? I want him destroyed, can't you understand? I want him removed. . . . And I don't give a damn if there's anarchy and chaos in Egypt."[40]

If the dismissal of Glubb brought Eden's ire upon Nasir, then Egypt's recognition of the People's Republic of China in May 1956 was to incur the wrath of John Foster Dulles. 'Abd al-Latif al-Baghdadi, a senior member of Egypt's political elite, relates that Egypt, having placed itself firmly in the nonaligned camp, could no longer go along with the American charade of positing the government of

[39] The announcement of Glubb's dismissal came when the British foreign secretary, Selwyn Lloyd, who was in Cairo, was returning from dinner with Nasir. Lloyd thought that Nasir had known about the news from Amman all along and had kept it from him to mock and humiliate him and Britain. Nasir, however, had been as surprised as everyone else by the news of Glubb's removal, which resulted from mounting "personal jealousies and antagonisms" between the king and his British army commander. See Stephens, *Nasser: A Political Biography*, pp. 179–180.

[40] Anthony Nutting, *No End of a Lesson* (London: Constable, 1967), pp. 34–35.

the tiny island of Formosa (later to be named Taiwan) as the real
and legitimate representative of the Chinese people. Moreover, the
Soviet leader, Nikita Khrushchev, had declared his willingness to
join the West in an arms control regime in the Middle East. In case
this were to happen, Egypt felt that recognition of China would
give the Soviets the necessary camouflage to send arms to Egypt
through a third channel, namely China.[41] Dulles, however, had little time for such reasoning. He viewed Egypt's recognition of China
as further proof of Nasir's irreversible tilt toward the Communist
world. On July 19, 1956, the offer of assistance to Egypt was officially withdrawn because "the ability of Egypt to devote adequate
resources to assure the project's success has become more uncertain
than at the time the offer was made."[42] It was not just a rejection,
but a humiliating public slap in the face, implying Egypt's lack of
credit worthiness.

Infuriated, Nasir, in a major speech a week later, declared that
since the West was unwilling to help finance the Aswan Dam, Egypt
had no alternative but to raise the money on its own. This could
only be achieved by nationalizing the Suez Canal Company. A law
nationalizing the Anglo-French company followed, with Nasir
pointedly reminding his ecstatic audience that the moment should
be cherished not only by Egyptians but by all Arabs for it was an
affirmation of Arab sovereignty, dignity, and pride, and a victory
for the Arabs and their triumphant nationalism over the perfidious
forces of colonialism and imperialism.

The decision was not as spontaneous as it might have seemed.
Nasir had spent the week after Dulles's announcement of the withdrawal of the American aid offer for the Dam trying to assess the
possible international responses to the nationalization of the Suez
Canal Company, and whether these warranted a delay or even an
abandonment of the decision.[43] He concluded that Dulles, while

[41] Al-Baghdadi, *Mudhakarat 'Abd al-Latif al-Baghdadi* (Memoirs of 'Abd al-Latif
al-Baghdadi), pp. 315–316.

[42] N. Frankland and V. King, eds., *Documents on International Affairs, 1956* (London:
Oxford University Press, 1959), pp. 69–70.

[43] See Salah Nasr, *'Abd al-Nasir wa Tajribat al-Wuhda* ('Abd al-Nasir and the experiment
of unity) (Beirut: al-Watan al-'Arabi, 1976), pp. 85–87.

sharing Eden's concerns, was not eager to use military means, but preferred economic and financial pressures on Egypt. As for the French, Nasir was confident that they were so mired in the escalating violence of the Algerian revolution that they simply would not be able to muster additional forces for a military operation against Egypt. And he never entertained the possibility of an Israeli involvement in an attack on Egypt. But that was not his assessment of British responses. Nasir was certain that Eden would contemplate military action; but on analyzing the existing geostrategic situation of Britain's military power in the region, he felt that, in light of Egypt's dire financial needs, the risk was worth taking. In an interview six years later, he expounded on his thinking at the time:

> Basically, [the problem] became a simple one. There could be no question of shelving the plan: the money had to be found; and the only means I had of increasing the national revenue by any marked degree, was by nationalizing the Suez Canal [Company]. I knew that I was taking a calculated risk. I knew of my personal experience of Anthony Eden that he would feel bound to take action to protect British interests; but I was almost certain, too, that Britain did not have enough troops in Kenya, Cyprus or Aden, their nearest bases to carry out an attack. I believed that, in the time needed for him to mobilize sufficient forces, it would be possible for us to reach a peaceful solution.[44]

Nasir miscalculated. Eden responded by colluding with the French (upset over Egypt's support for the Algerian revolution) and the Israelis (who sought an end to fedayyin raids into Israel). The purpose of this collusion was to reclaim Western sovereignty over the canal, defeat Egypt militarily, and thus undermine Nasir's prestige and leadership of the Arab nationalist movement. The tripartite attack began on October 29 with the Israeli invasion of Sinai, followed the next day by a prearranged Anglo-French ultimatum to both parties to stop fighting within twelve hours and to withdraw their forces ten miles from either side of the Canal, so as to

---

[44] *Sunday Times* (London), June 24, 1962.

allow Anglo-French forces to move in between the two combatants. The ultimatum, which effectively called on the Egyptians to withdraw their forces over 100 miles, allowing the Israelis to advance all the way to the Canal with no resistance, seemed to Nasir so fantastic that he initially believed it to be a bluff.[45] But on October 31, British and French aircraft began bombing Egyptian airfields. The objective was not just to restore Anglo-French ownership of the Suez Canal Company, but to topple Nasir. Immediately after the first bombing raid, a British radio station in Cyprus appealed to Egyptians to rise against Nasir, who, according to the radio announcer, had gone "mad and seized the Suez Canal . . . rejected a fair solution . . . exposed you to Israeli attacks . . . betrayed Egypt . . . [and] adopted dictatorship."[46] Within less than twenty-four hours, the attackers had succeeded in neutralizing Egypt's air bases. On November 4, British and French paratroopers landed in Port Sa'id on the Mediterranean end of the Canal, and two days later, after heavy fighting and Egyptian casualties between 650–1,000 dead, the town was in the hands of the invaders. Immediately, a British armored column began advancing down the Canal in the direction of Isma'ilia and Suez, the two other major Canal cities. At that point, the Egyptians became convinced that the Anglo-French forces were set on moving on Cairo. In an emergency meeting, Nasir and his colleagues decided to take poison rather than risk the national humiliation of capture by the invaders. But 'Abd al-Latif al-Baghdadi, a senior member of the leadership was missing from the meeting, so an emissary was sent to find him and bring him to the meeting while another member of the leadership was dispatched to bring back the necessary poison. As Nasir and his colleagues waited for Bahgdadi to make an appearance and for the poison to be brought, news from New York, indicating British and French agreement to halt all hostilities, arrived in Cairo.[47]

[45] Sayed Mare'i, *Awraq Siyasiya* (Political papers) (Cairo: al-Maktab al-Musri al-Hadith, 1978), p. 357.

[46] Anthony Nutting, *Nasser* (London: Constable, 1972), p. 174.

[47] As told by Baghdadi, and related in Fathi Radwan, *72 Shahran Ma'a 'Abd al-Nasir* (72 months with 'Abd al-Nasir) (Cairo: Dar al-Huriya, 1986), p. 96.

The sudden change of fortune for Nasir and Egypt was naturally trumpeted by Egyptian propaganda as a direct result of Egypt's valiant resistance. But in fact it was Washington that played the decisive role. President Eisenhower and Secretary of State Dulles had warned against the use of force, and were furious at not having been consulted by the British and the French; indeed, they felt that they had been deliberately deceived by Eden and the French prime minister, Guy Mollet. Moreover, they were concerned that the crisis in Suez would drag them into a possible nuclear conflict with the Soviets. The British and French desperately needed American financial help to offset the extra cost of alternative oil supplies after the Egyptians blocked the Suez Canal by sinking ships in it, and the Syrians blew up pipelines carrying British-owned petroleum from the oil fields of Iraq to the Mediterranean port of Latakiya. The Americans, however, let it be known that any financial help was contingent on the cessation of hostilities. The immediate consequence was a run on sterling in international financial markets, and coupled with a chorus of global condemnation, even from close and long-standing allies, the British and French had little alternative but to halt the invasion. Away from public posturing, Nasir conceded Washington's decisive role. In the first ministerial meeting after the collapse of the invasion, Nasir acknowledged the role of the United States and its president in foiling the "tripartite conspiracy." He told the assembled ministers that it was "Eisenhower who played the greatest and most decisive role in standing up to Britain, France and Israel, even though the conspiracy took him by surprise in the middle of his election campaign for a second term, in which he was in need of Jewish votes. . . . But Eisenhower completely disregarded all this, and stood decisively and resolutely by Egypt."[48] The lack of American support spelled the beginning of the end for the ill-fated Anglo-French operation, which was eventually to conclude in the ignominious evacuation of all their troops from Egypt by December 22, 1956, without the achievement of any of their objectives.

[48] Mare'i, *Awraq Siyasiya* (Political papers), p. 362.

Militarily, Nasir's much trumpeted armed forces had lost the war summarily. But politically in Egypt and in the Arab world Nasir had secured a famous and resounding victory. "With the Suez Canal Crisis," writes John Badeau, "Nasser suddenly filled the Middle Eastern horizon, becoming a regional hero. To restless and frustrated Arab nationalists he indeed seemed a second Saladin, turning the table on Western imperialism."[49] Indeed, Arabs gave Nasir their overwhelming support throughout the duration of the crisis. Arab cities simply erupted in anti-Western demonstrations and riots. People took to the streets shouting the name of Nasir as the symbol of Arab steadfastness against the forces of imperialism. Petroleum pumps in Iraq, Syria, and Saudi Arabia were sabotaged,[50] and there was a grassroots effort to boycott British and French merchandise.[51] Governments under this intense popular pressure brought their policies as far as they could behind Egypt. Syria and Saudi Arabia broke relations with Britain and France. Syrian troops moved into Jordan and linked with Jordanian units,[52] after which the Syrian and Jordanian governments offered to send troops to help Egypt, but Nasir declined, at which point Jordan's Arab Legion seized some of the British army stores in Amman. The recently elected nationalist government of Sulayman Nabulsi brought Jordan into a military pact with Syria and Egypt, and in January 1957, the "Treaty of Arab Solidarity" was concluded among Egypt, Jordan, Saudi Arabia, and Syria for a period of ten years.[53]

---

[49] From John Badeau's introduction to Nasir's book, *The Philosophy of the Revolution* (Buffalo, New York: Economica Books, 1959), p. 14.

[50] Ahmad Hamroush, *Qissat Thawrat 23 Yuliyu , al-Jusi' al-Rabi'i: 'Abd al-Nasir wa al-'Arab* (The story of the July 23 revolution, 4th volume: 'Abd al-Nasir and the Arabs) (Cairo: Dar al-Mawqif al-'Arabi, 1983), pp. 20–21.

[51] Taha, *Qissat al-Wuhda wa al-Infisal* (The story of the unity and separation), pp. 46–48.

[52] Abd al-Karim, *Hisad: Sineen Khasiba wa Thimar Murra* (Harvest: fertile years, bitter fruit), pp. 340–341.

[53] As it turned out, a ten-year treaty was wishful thinking. The Jordanian monarch had been wary of Nasir's immense popularity among the citizens of Jordan, especially the Palestinians, and feared the destabilizing impact of Arab nationalism on his own rule. He was right. In April 1957, he managed to foil an attempted coup by Arab nationalist officers of the Arab Legion who admired Nasir and thought of their king as too dependent on Britain and the other enemies of Arab nationalism. By the end of 1957, the Saudi monarch, Sa'ud

But the most consequential impact of the Suez Crisis occurred in Iraq. Nuri al-Sa'id, Nasir's main nemesis in the Arab world, had known beforehand of the impending attack on Egypt, and, in a meeting with the British, had in fact advocated it.[54] Nuri was so elated with the first news of the attack that he instructed the radio station to play a then popular love song entitled, *al-postakiya ish-taku min kithrat marasili* (The Postmen Complained about the Abundance of My Letters). The song was not a reflection of Nuri's romantic disposition; it was a patronizing and backhanded reference to Nasir's father who had been employed as a lowly post office clerk.[55] Nevertheless, realizing the inevitable public anger, Nuri felt obliged to condemn the Anglo-French action as a flagrant collusion with Israel. The Iraqi government made a show of refusing to sit with Britain in a Baghdad Pact meeting, and diplomatic relations with France were severed. Yet this circumspect response hardly placated the seething populace, who took to the streets in huge numbers.[56] Riots erupted in Iraq's three main cities of Baghdad, Basrah, and Mosul, and in the Shiite cities of Kufa, Najaf, and Hillah, where the Communists were particularly strong.[57] The situation deteriorated so badly in Najaf that a battalion of special forces from Mosul, all of whose members were Sunnis, was sent to bolster the overmatched police and restore order in the city.[58] In Baghdad,

---

bin 'Abd al-'Aziz, had become convinced that Nasir's propagated Arab nationalism could not but eventually be a fatal threat to his family's political survival. By 1958, Jordan and Saudi Arabia had joined Iraq in becoming Egypt's main enemies.

[54] Tawfiq al-Suwaydi, *Mudhakarati: Nisf Qarn min Tarikh al-'Iraq wa al-Qadhiya al-'Arabiya* (My memoirs: half a century of the history of Iraq and the Arab undertaking) (Beirut: Dar al-Kitab al-'Arabi, 1969), p. 552.

[55] Conversations with the author's father, Royal Iraqi Air Force Colonel 'Isam Dawisha, and with the then-Commander-in-Chief of the Royal Iraqi Air Force, Brigadier Kadhim 'Abadi.

[56] See Naji Shawkat, *Sira wa Dhikrayat Thamaneena 'Aman, 1894–1974* (Biography and memoirs of eighty years, 1894–1974) (Baghdad: Maktabat al-Yaqdha al-'Arabiya, 1974), p. 587; see also on the same subject 'Abd al-Jabbar 'Abd Mustafa, *Tajribat al-'Amal al-Jabhawi fi al-'Iraq Beina 1921–1958* (The experiment of oppositional work in Iraq between 1921–1958) (Baghdad: Manshurat Wizarat al-Thaqafa wa al-Funoon, 1978), pp. 245–246.

[57] Halim Ahmad, *Mujaz Tarikh al-'Iraq al-Hadith, 1920–1958* (A short history of modern Iraq, 1920–1958) (Beirut: Dar Ibn Khaldun, 1978), pp. 108–109.

[58] Abd al-Razzaq al-Hasani, *Tarikh al-Wizarat al-'Iraqiya, al-Jusi' al'Ashir* (The history of Iraqi cabinets, volume 10) (Baghdad: Dar al-Shu'un al-Thaqafiya al-'Amma, 1988), pp. 113–114. Also, Sa'id, *'Iraq 8 Shibat, 1963* (Iraq of 8 February, 1963), p. 91.

in just two days of rioting, 378 demonstrators were arrested.[59] The
Iraqi government was compelled to impose martial law. Even so,
Nuri felt that he could not guarantee Iraqi stability for more than
a few days. The British ambassador reported to his government that
he had never seen Nuri "more deeply discouraged and depressed;"[60]
and in a Baghdad Pact meeting, Turkish prime minister, Adnan
Menderes, thought that Iraq's leaders were in a state of "near
panic."[61] Recognizing that the imperatives of this new era necessitated unequivocal and public adherence to Arab nationalism, Nuri
went on the radio on November 23, 1956, to emphasize to his people his strong and long-standing Arab nationalist credentials:

> Compatriots; you have known me as a struggling young man who
> advocated and worked for the independence of the Arabs and their
> unity and for raising the prestige of the Arab at a time when the
> word "Arab" would have cost the speaker his neck. This was at a
> time when those who are today advocating nationalism were pros-
> trating themselves at the feet of the oppressors and the imperialists
> and accusing us of treason and atheism. I have been exposed to
> danger more than once, and proceeded on my way seeking nothing
> but the independence of the Arabs, the glory of the Arabs and the
> dignity of the Arabs. . . . The call to Arab nationalism is not acciden-
> tal to me, but is my very being. I am proud of it and I strive to
> promote it and to safeguard it whether I am inside or outside the
> government.[62]

Along with such nationalist appeals to his own people, Nuri went
beyond the borders of Iraq, and tried to promote his point of view
at the expense of Nasir's Egypt. He did this by intensifying his
government's policy, which had started earlier, of buying off as
many Arab newspapers and magazines as he could. For example,
one thousand Jordanian dinars were paid to Huza' al-Majali to

---

[59] 'Abd Mustafa, *Tajribat al-'Amal al-Jabhawi fi al-'Iraq* (The experiment of oppositional
work in Iraq), p. 246; Al-Hasani, *Tarikh al-Wizarat al-'Iraqiya* (The history of Iraqi cabinets), p. 113.
[60] Podeh, *Quest for Hegemony in the Arab World*, p. 212.
[61] Ibid., p. 216.
[62] Ibid., p. 220.

establish the anti-Nasir magazine *Sawt al-Urdun* (The Voice of Jordan). Similarly, in order to confront the Nasirist tide in Syria, the Iraqi consulate in Damascus paid over eleven thousand Syrian lires on a monthly basis to two newspapers and two magazines.[63]

But to no avail! The Arab nationalist creed by now had become inexorably linked in the minds of the Arab people to the person of Gamal 'Abd al-Nasir. And this seems to have necessitated some rewriting of history on the part of Egypt's political elites, who only three to four years earlier had seen and presented themselves as Egyptian patriots, speaking little of Arab nationalism. In an article in Cairo's influential *al-Ahram* in March 1957, Anwar al-Sadat, an original member of the Free Officers, later to succeed Nasir to the presidency, declared:

> There was nothing behind our coup other than Arab nationalism ... which awakened a new historical development. ... We must nurture this link between the people of the Arab nation ... for when the revolution occurred in Egypt, it rendered the Arab nation one nation, sharing one history and claiming one destiny.[64]

By the end of 1956, in any part of the Arabic-speaking world, Arab nationalism had become the dominant ideology, and Nasir had been anointed as its leader and keeper of its conscience. A poignant illustration of this occurred during the first truly free elections in Jordan in late 1956. One Muslim candidate gave a speech to a gathering at the venerated al-Aqsa mosque in Jerusalem (which until June 1967 was under Jordanian control). At the conclusion of his speech, his audience, all devout Muslims, asked him: "Does Nasir support you?" He replied that he did not know. The result was the election of a Christian Communist candidate who belonged to a grouping supported by Nasir.[65] There can be little doubt that Nasir's charisma, bolstered by his perceived victory in the Suez

[63] See Fattah, *Siyasat al-'Iraq al-Kharijiya fi al-Mintaqa al-'Arabiya* (Iraq's foreign policy in the Arab region), pp. 225–226.

[64] Quoted in P. J. Vatikiotis, "Dilemmas of Political Leadership in the Arab Middle East: The Case of the UAR," *American Political Science Review*, vol. 55, no. 1 (March 1961): 108.

[65] Hamroush, *Qissat Thwrat 23 Yuliyu* (The story of the July 23 revolution), p. 22.

Crisis, and given expression by Egypt's unrivaled primacy over the airwaves, contributed in no uncertain terms to the phenomenal ascent of the Arab national idea in these few years. The expression *al-Umma al-'Arabiya min al-Muhit al-Atlasi ila al—Khalij al-'Arabi* (the Arab nation from the Atlantic Ocean to the Arabian Gulf) gained increasing currency and was frequently invoked in speeches, articles, and conversations. It was put in poetic form, and very quickly was on the lips of euphoric nationalist crowds throughout the Arab world:

minal khalij al-thai'r	From the rebellious Gulf
ilal muhit al-hadir	To the roaring ocean
Labaika 'Abd al-Nasir	At your service, 'Abd al-Nasir

The universal popularity of this poetic slogan was attested to by a group of senior officers in Iraq's Royal Air Force who went to Morocco on an official visit in 1957. To Iraqis, Morocco seemed as culturally distant as it was geographically remote. The officers, therefore, were truly taken aback when they heard this poetic slogan recited by Moroccans from various professions, including army officers. The Iraqi officers returned to Iraq convinced not only of the eventual victory of Nasir over Nuri al-Sa'id, but also of the inevitable triumph of Arab nationalism in its mission to create a unitary Arab state under Nasir's leadership.[66]

As more people began to believe, romantically perhaps, in the "indivisibility of the Arab nation" and Nasir's leading role within it, and as the Egyptians themselves began to shed their earlier insularity, and state publicly their full adherence to the Arab nationalist creed, Cairo was bound to become the target of other Arabs desiring unity. And so it fell on the Syrians, enthusiastic Arabists who happened to be wracked by internal divisions, to demand that Egypt stand by what it had been preaching and join Syria to establish one unitary state.

[66] Conversations with the author's father, Air Force Colonel 'Isam Dawisha.

CHAPTER EIGHT

THE APEX OF ARAB NATIONALISM: THE UNITED ARAB REPUBLIC AND THE IRAQI REVOLUTION, JANUARY–SEPTEMBER 1958

The United Arab Republic (UAR), formed by the fusion of Egypt and Syria on February 1, 1958, came as a stunning surprise to most Arabs and non-Arabs. No one whose expectations were shaped by rational assessment could think that an organic unity between two Arab states was at all possible in such a short space of time. It was not the actual unity that was so surprising; Arab nationalists fervently believed in the *eventual* amalgamation of Arab countries. But no one (not even the main participants, as we shall see) was prepared for the breathless pace at which events were to unfold.

The Syrians, who demanded from Gamal 'Abd al-Nasir, and ended up getting, an organic form of unity in 1958, had made earlier proposals for looser forms of union with Egypt. As early as the spring of 1955, ostensibly as a response to the Baghdad Pact, Khalid al-'Azm, the then-prime minister of Syria, proposed the integration of the two armies, economic and financial cooperation between the two countries, and greater collaboration in foreign affairs.[1] The Egyptians, it seems, were not ready to even contemplate such a proposal.[2] Nor were the Egyptians more forthcoming in the summer of 1956 when the Syrians tried again to discuss unity.[3] As late as the spring of 1957, Nasir told a Lebanese journalist, who was a fervent Arab nationalist, that any unity project among Arab states would be met with vigorous resistance by the British and the Americans, and even the Soviet Union might not be agreeable to such an idea.[4] Nasir preached Arab nationalism and was cognizant of its ultimate goal, but obviously was enough of a realist to appreciate the many obstacles to its actual realization. And in any case, the balance of political power in the Arab world was firmly in favor of Nasir in the wake of the Suez Crisis, a balance of forces that saw Syria, Jordan, and Saudi Arabia allied with Egypt. Nasir had no reason to frighten off the Jordanian and Saudi monarchs by elevating "Arab unity" from the realm of aspirational rhetoric, where it had until then resided, into the sphere of actual policy making.

The momentum, however, began to change in the summer of 1957, a change brought about as much by external factors as internal ones. As the post-Suez Arab nationalist tide swept through every street, alley, and coffee shop in the Arab countries, and as Nasir appeared to be the sole custodian of the Arab nationalist mantle, using it at will to appeal to Arab mass opinion over the heads of their increasingly beleaguered governments, some of his political allies began to reassess their positions. This was especially

[1] Khalid al-'Azm, *Mudhakarat Khalid al-'Azm, al-Mujalad al-Thalith* (The memoirs of Khalid al-'Azm, volume three) (Beirut: al-Dar al-Muttahida li al-Nashr, 1973), p. 145.

[2] Mahmud Riad, *Mudhakarat Mahmud Riad, 1948–1978, al-Jusi' al-Thani* (The memoirs of Mahmud Riad, 1948–1978, volume two) (Cairo: Dar al-Mustaqbal al-'Arabi, 1986), p. 108. Riad, who was Egypt's ambassador to Damascus, felt that 'Azm's initiative was motivated less by 'Azm's commitment to Arabism and more by personal political ambitions. *Ibid.*, p. 107.

[3] James Jankowski, "Arab Nationalism in 'Nasserism' and Egyptian State Policy, 1952–1958," in *Rethinking Nationalism in the Arab Middle East. eds.* James Jankowski and Israel Gershoni. (New York: Columbia University Press, 1997), pp. 162–163.

[4] Riad Taha, *Qissat al-Wuhda wa al-Infisal: Tajribat Insan 'Arabi Khilal Ahdath 1955–1961* (The story of the unity and separation: the experience of an Arab person during the events of 1955–1961) (Beirut: Dar al-Afaq al-Jadida, 1974), p. 73.

true of the Saudi and Jordanian kings. King Saud had allied his country with Egypt against Iraq because of his family's historical enmity to the Hashemites. After all, it was only after the expulsion of the Hashemites from al-Hejaz, that Saud's father was able to establish the Kingdom of Saudi Arabia, and Saud suspected that the Hashemites had neither forgotten their misfortune, nor relinquished their claim to his country. Thus his proximity to Nasir was political and strategic, hardly based on a convergence of their belief systems. On the Jordanian front, King Husayn had allowed the nationalist government of Sulayman al-Nabulsi, popularly elected in October 1956, to direct Jordan's foreign policy, which predictably came to follow the lead of Nasir's Egypt. For a while Husayn did not appear to mind, seemingly enjoying the peaceful respite provided by a friendly "Voice of the Arabs." But the honeymoon could not last. The conservative and status quo bases of the two countries were diametrically opposed to the radical and revolutionary tenets of Arab nationalism. The peace was little more than a truce waiting to be broken.

The first signs of a potential change in Saudi policy occurred in November 1956, when King Saud attended a conference of Arab heads of state in Beirut. Called by the pro-Western Lebanese president, Camille Chamoun, the conference highlighted the precariousness of the monarchies and the status quo republics in the wake of the Suez Crisis and the ascendancy of revolutionary Arab nationalism. Saud also had an opportunity to meet privately with Iraq's King Faysal II, in which both pledged to overcome the traditional Saudi-Hashemite enmities.[5] But what was most consequential in radically changing Saudi foreign policy was a sustained U. S. initiative, launched in January 1957 by President Eisenhower in his State of the Union address, which was later to become known as the "Eisenhower Doctrine." It pledged American assistance, including the dispatch of armed forces, to nations requesting American help "against overt aggression from any nation controlled by interna-

[5] See 'Abd al-Razzak al-Hasani, *Tarikh al-Wizarat al-'Iraqiya, al-Jusi' al-'Ashir* (The history of Iraqi cabinets, volume ten) (Baghdad: Dar al-Shu'un al-Thaqafiya al-'Amma, 1988), p. 106.

tional communism."[6] That same month, ARAMCO, the American oil company responsible for Saudi oil productions, arranged for King Saud to visit Washington in the hope that he would be persuaded to rally the anti-Nasirist forces in the area.[7] And they succeeded famously.

The first discernible shift in Saud's political orientation occurred in April 1957 when he sent troops to Jordan to help King Husayn against his pro-Nasir prime minister, Sulayman al-Nabulsi. First in his cordial meeting with King Faysal II of Iraq and now in his decision to come to the aid of the Jordanian monarch, Saud had finally decided (probably also with American prompting) that the long-standing and often bitter rivalry between the Saudis and the Hashemites was now superceded by the shared interest of all the status quo leaders in the area in combating the destabilizing impact of the radical and Nasir-propagated Arab nationalism.

Saud's change of heart was not entirely motivated by consideration of personal interest and political survival. There was also an ideological dimension. The product of a radically different environment from that of Egypt, Saud's understanding of Arab nationalism was bound to be markedly different from that of Nasir's. As one analyst observed:

> To the Saudi rulers, their Arabness was such a self-evident fact that no theoretical elaboration was needed. Being of tribal stock, they thought of themselves as the real ethnically pure Arabs. While they recognized the special ties among Arab countries, they attributed them as much to religion and proximity as to Arabism. They did not recognize the mystical links emanating from Arab nationalism. If unity was to be the goal, it should be based on Islam, rather than Arabism.[8]

Whether resulting from political interest or ideology or a combi-

---

[6] P. E. Zinner, ed., *Documents on American Foreign Relations, 1957* (New York: Harper and Brothers, 1958), p. 201.

[7] Erskine B. Childers, *The Road to Suez* (London: Macgibbon and Kee, 1962), p. 313.

[8] Ghazi A. Algosaibi, *The 1962 Revolution in Yemen and its Impact on the Foreign Policy of the UAR and Saudi Arabia* (Unpublished University of London Ph.D. thesis, 1970), p. 272.

nation of both, the change in Saud's Arab policy was a major coup for the Eisenhower administration. After all, throughout the conflict over the Baghdad Pact, the debate over the Czech arms deal, and the Suez Crisis, Saudi Arabia was Egypt's staunchest ally. Indeed, its policies in the region followed that of Egypt so closely that, to one observer, Saudi Arabia seemed to be "well on the way of becoming Egypt's most valuable colony."[9] Washington must have savored Saud's change of heart, which was so extreme that in March 1958, Nasir disclosed that Saud had attempted to assassinate him to stop the union between Egypt and Syria.[10]

In Jordan, King Husayn had become increasingly wary of the foreign policy direction his popularly elected prime minister was taking. The pro-Nasir Sulayman al-Nabulsi was advocating establishing diplomatic relations with the Soviet Union, accepting foreign aid from Moscow, and refusing any aid from the United States, due to the latter's "effort to undermine Arab unity and to isolate 'Abd al-Nasir."[11] These policies, and his frequent pro-Nasir statements, won Nabulsi great popularity inside Jordan, but not with the king. On April 10, 1957, Husayn dismissed Nabulsi and promptly requested military help from Iraq and Saudi Arabia. For the next two weeks, massive civil disturbances plagued the country, and Husayn survived two "coups" against him from pro-Nabulsi / Nasir officers in the Jordanian army.[12] The rioters were urged on by the "Voice of the Arabs" and "Radio Cairo," which blamed the dismissal of Nabulsi and the consequent deterioration in the security situation on the king and the other "agents of imperialism

[9] G. A. Lipsky, et al., *Saudi Arabia* (New Haven, Connecticut: Hraf Press, 1959), p. 201.

[10] Robert Stephens, *Nasser: A Political Biography* (London: Allen Lane / Penguin Press, 1971), pp. 261–262.

[11] Salah Nasr, *'Abd al-Nasir wa Tajribat al-Wuhda* ('Abd al-Nasir and the experiment of unity) (Beirut: al-Watan al-'Arabi, 1976), p. 103.

[12] His Majesty King Hussein I, *Uneasy Lies the Head* (New York: Bernard Geis Associates, 1962), pp. 165–183. To what extent these were real "coups" or just an exercise in muscle flexing in a chaotic situation is open to question. See Uriel Dann, *King Hussein and the Challenge of Arab Radicalism: Jordan, 1955–1967* (New York: Oxford University Press, 1989), pp. 54–59; also Robert Satloff, *From Abdullah to Hussein: Jordan in Transition* (New York: Oxford University Press, 1994), pp. 164–168.

in the Palace."[13] In the midst of the chaos, John Foster Dulles, the U. S. secretary of state, pointedly invited Husayn to ask for American help. Immediately, the king called a press conference, where he angrily denounced Nasir, accusing Egypt of being behind the riots and the two abortive coups.[14] He then declared martial law and embarked on a mass arrest of Nabulsi elements in the army and in the country. The United States followed this action with military and economic aid worth $70 million. In Washington, a State Department spokesman coolly called attention to the obvious connection between Husayn's press conference, the Dulles statement, and the Eisenhower Doctrine.[15] Nasir retorted by unleashing a propaganda campaign so violent in tone and content that it led the beleaguered king to sever diplomatic relations with Egypt in June.

The Arab balance of political forces in the summer of 1957 was somewhat of a mixed bag for the acknowledged leader of Arab nationalism. On the mass public level, Arab nationalism was supreme, unrivaled by any other ideology, and consequently no Arab leader could even touch Nasir's universal popularity. But the champion of the Arab nationalist tide was not exactly the flavor of the month with the political leaderships of the Arab countries. His only active political ally was Syria, and in the summer of 1957, Syria was mired in an ominous international crisis. In August, the defense minister, Khalid al-'Azm, the patriarch of a prominent landowning family, yet a declared socialist, concluded a major agreement for military and economic aid with Moscow. He followed this with the appointment of 'Afif al-Bizri, an officer with pronounced Communist sympathies, as the country's chief of staff. The Americans, afflicted during this intense Cold War era

[13] British Broadcasting Corporation, *Summary of World Broadcasts, Part IV: The Arab World, Israel, Greece, Turkey, Iran* (hereafter cited as *SWB*), April 19, 1957, p. 2. This accusation was repeated almost on a daily basis over the following two months.

[14] There was indeed some truth to the king's accusation. According to a senior Egyptian intelligence officer, anti-king pamphlets, accusing him of collaborating with the Americans, which appeared in the streets of Amman, Jerusalem, and other Jordanian cities, originated in Cairo. See Nasr, *'Abd al-Nasir wa Tajribat al-Wuhda* ('Abd al-Nasir and the experiment of unity), p. 103.

[15] H. B. Westerfield, *The Instruments of American Foreign Policy* (New York: Thomas Y. Crowell Company, 1963), p. 479.

with what could only be described as Communist neurosis, and egged on by the anti-Nasirist forces in the area, became convinced of an impending Communist takeover in Syria. A meeting of the Baghdad Pact in Ankara, attended by Loy Henderson, a high-level official of the U. S. State Department, agreed that "the present regime in Syria had to go; otherwise the takeover by the Communists would soon be complete."[16] Turkish troops moved along the Syrian border in September, and the Turkish government hinted that it would not tolerate the Communists taking over power in Syria.

Nasir had to take a stand in defense of his only remaining radical ally. He unleashed a barrage of propaganda against the United States and its "stooges" in the Arab world. For over two weeks, Egyptian radio maintained a relentless verbal onslaught against "American imperialism" and its alleged clients and supporters among the Arab governments. For good measure, Nasir dispatched a military contingent to Syria to aid in its defense. As a military deterrent, it was of little value, but in its symbolism, it had an electrifying impact on Arab public opinion. It portrayed Nasir as the unwavering defender of Arab nationalist principles, sharply contrasting him with the other Arab leaders who, in their support of non-Arab Turkey against Syria, confirmed in Arab perception their seemingly tepid commitment to Arab nationalism. By early September, Nasir's political strategy was beginning to pay dividends, as the other leaders, now fully cognizant of the political cost of their stance, began feverishly to reassess their policies. One by one, Arab leaders, who had favored the American position, beat a hasty retreat. The Jordanian foreign minister declared that it was never Jordan's intent to interfere in Syria's domestic affairs; the Iraqi premier, in a statement that must have hurt mightily, announced "complete understanding with the Syrian President;"[17] and the Saudi king sent a message to the baffled and dejected American president

---

[16] Dwight D. Eisenhower, *The White House Years*, vol. 2: *Waging Peace* (New York: Doubleday, 1965), p. 197.

[17] Patrick Seale, *The Struggle for Syria: A Study of Post-War Arab Politics, 1945–1958* (New Haven, Connecticut: Yale University Press, 1986), p. 303.

urging caution and moderation. As the crisis subsided, it was obvious to one and all that Egypt and Syria had won the day. In the
ensuing euphoria, Anwar al-Sadat, the then-speaker of Egypt's Parliament, headed a parliamentary delegation on a visit to Damascus,
at the conclusion of which the Syrian Parliament voted unani-
mously for immediate union with Egypt.

If the Syrians thought that the champion of Arab nationalism
would jump at their offer, they were soon to be disappointed. Nasir
was skeptical. To a Syrian delegation, he expressed his concern
over the proclivity of the Syrian armed forces for constant interference in their country's domestic politics. He told the Ba'thist Salah
Bitar: "I have spent the last five years distancing the Egyptian army
from politics."[18] He also sent an emissary to Damascus to explain
his seeming reluctance to join politically with Syria. The same objections about the Syrian army were voiced, but further concerns
were transmitted to the Syrians; concerns about the incompatibility
of the two economies and the political imbalance between two different party systems.[19] It was obvious that during these highly emotional times, Nasir was trying to keep a level head about a project
that could have momentous and unforeseen consequences. Realizing the depth of Nasir's reservations about a possible unity with
Syria, the Syrian leaders went all out to force his hand, not only
because of their commitment to the Arab nationalist creed, but also
because unity with Egypt had become the only means to preserve
unity within Syria itself.

The end of 1957 saw a near paralysis of political life in Syria.
The crisis of late summer had all but abated, but had left in its
wake three forces competing against one another: the conservative
feudalist and financial classes, the Arab nationalists, Ba'thists or
Nasirists, and the Communists and their sympathizers. These divisions probably would not have been so critical had they not been

---

[18] Ahmad Hamroush, *Qissat Thawrat 23 Yuliyu, al-Jusi' al-Rabi': 'Abd al-Nasir wa al-
'Arab* (The story of the 23 July revolution, volume 4: Abd al-Nasir and the Arabs) (Cairo:
Dar al-Mawqif al-'Arabi, 1983), p. 42.

[19] Nasr, *'Abd al-Nasir wa Tajribat al-Wuhda* ('Abd al-Nasir and the experiment of unity),
p. 118.

mirrored within the ranks of the military, where there was such diffusion of power that no one group could impose its will on the others and restore order.

From all these competing groups, the Ba'th Party stood out as the one organized institution that had consistently and genuinely agitated for the political unity of the "Arab nation." Cognizant of the paralysis that had mired Syria's political circles, which contrasted with the mounting public clamor for some kind of action in the direction of union with Nasir's Egypt, the Ba'th drafted in December a project for federal union. The drafting of the document came as no surprise to Ba'thist supporters or to other Arab nationalists. What was surprising was the tone of the document and the kind of union proposed. A "federal union" might have been a considerable step forward at a time when the Arab world was wracked with political divisions and acrimonious recriminations. But to fervent Ba'thists and other Arab nationalists, anything but an organic unity of what they considered to be "the artificially separated regions of the eternal and indivisible Arab nation" was an anemic alternative indeed. The Ba'thist leaders, however, had their reasons, which were grounded less in ideological yearnings and more in political realities. As Michel Aflaq explained:

> We wanted two things which may seem contradictory. On the one hand, we wanted a federal state strong enough and centralized enough to stand firm against the maneuvers of opponents at home and foreign governments abroad. The federal institutions would have to be more than a facade. . . . But our wish for a strong government was tempered by a second consideration. We wanted a federation to make allowances for the different political histories of the two countries. We believed that a sensitivity to local traditions was not only in the interests of the proposed union itself, but was also essential to make it attractive to other Arab countries. In our project we provided, for instance, for effective local parliaments and governments in each province.[20]

[20] Seale, *The Struggle for Syria*, p. 318.

In retrospect, this might have been a better and more workable prototype for union than the one eventually agreed on, but no sooner had it been drafted, than it had been overtaken by events. The Communists and their sympathizers were loathe to allow the Ba'thists to take the initiative, even though they favored an even looser federation in which their party would continue to operate legally. Their tactic was simple: up the ante, and demand total organic unity. In the one-upmanship game that characterized factionalized Syrian politics at the end of 1957, the Communists would outbid the Ba'th, yet remain secure in the knowledge that Nasir, who had shown himself to be against even a loose federation, would reject the proposal out of hand. But in trying to outmaneuver the Ba'th, the Communists ended up outmaneuvering themselves, for they were unprepared for the rapid unfolding of events spearheaded by a public driven to frenzy by all the talk and promises of union with Egypt. 'Afif al-Bizri, Syria's chief of staff and a Communist sympathizer, explains well the developing situation, in which the political parties' outbidding of each other interacted with the volatile sentiments of the Syrian public, with the result of inducing the Syrian officers to travel to Cairo and literally hand over their country to Nasir. Bizri maintains that none of the Syrian politicians really wanted unity. In fact,

> ... no one wanted unity. Even 'Abd al-Nasser didn't want it. ... So I ... waited for the appropriate moment and said: now we will offer unity to 'Abd al-Nasser. Since they're all saying, unity, unity, unity. Nobody would dare to say no, we don't want it. The masses would rise against them. I mean we followed the masses. The crowds were drunk. ... Who at that hour could dare say we do not want unity? The people would tear their heads off.[21]

Bizri and the military had decided to take matters into their own hands. On January 11, 1958, fifteen officers, led by Bizri, informed the Egyptian military attaché in Damascus of their intention to go

---

[21] Quoted in Malik Mufti, *Sovereign Creations: Pan Arabism and Political Order in Syria and Iraq* (Ithaca, New York: Cornell University Press, 1996), p. 91.

to Cairo, and then immediately boarded a military plane and headed to Egypt. No Syrian politician was told of the trip until the officers had arrived in Cairo. Informed about the Syrian initiative, Egypt's ambassador to Syria, Mahmoud Riad, drove to the Presidential Palace to discuss the rapidly developing situation with Syria's president, Shukri al-Quwatly. Understandably, Quwatly was incensed, accusing Riad of complicity, and repeatedly characterizing the action by Bizri and the other officers as a military coup. He told Riad pointedly that only the Syrian government had the authority to make a decision on unity.[22] Syria's politicians could hardly be expected to get excited about a unity that would be bound not only to make Syria a satellite of Egypt, but also to push Syria's political leaders out onto the margins of political life in their own country.

Interesting enough, the Egyptian leaders were just as wary about the proposed unity as their Syrian counterparts.The entire upper echelon of Egypt's policy-making elite advised Nasir against what appeared to be a headlong dive into unitary schemes. Intelligence officers offered a gloomy prognosis of Syria's stability, citing the inordinate political power of the military officers and their regular interventions in the political process. Some of Nasir's most senior colleagues emphasized the incompatibility of the two political systems. Egypt had banned political parties, creating the unitary and closely controlled National Union; Syria had a multiparty system, which spanned the ideological spectrum from the far left to the far right. The Ba'th and the Communist parties in Syria were active and well organized, and it was an open question as to whether they would accept a life of political anonymity. If anything, the chances were that very quickly they would become a source of intrigue and conspiracy.

Then there was the absence of a common geographic border. Not only that but in between the two segments of the proposed unitary state lay none other than the state of Israel. Overall, the

[22] Ibid., p. 92.

political and geostrategic obstacles seemed daunting.[23] The economic conditions did not offer great hopes either. In Egypt, the
currency was the pound, and the economy was shifting purposefully toward central planning, whereas in Syria, the currency was
the lira, with an economy based primarily on freewheeling business
practices and transactions.[24] The Egyptians were thus worried that
Syria's smaller economy would become a burden on Egypt's trea-
sury. And then there were those Egyptian leaders with Islamist
tendencies, prime among them Kemal al-Din Husayn, who seemed
to find the existence of Christians in leadership roles in Syria somewhat unpalatable. When asked his opinion about unity with Syria
by Nasir, Husayn replied: "I do not trust them. . . . The Ba'thist
leaders at present are agents. And Michel Aflaq and Antun Sa'ada
are the biggest agents. And they are working against Islam."[25] Perhaps the most telling advice came from Fathi Radwan, another
member of Nasir's inner circle. Radwan cautioned his president:
"Tomorrow, you are going to become the President of the Syrian
state, and you have not even put your foot in it, nor do you know
much about it, nor have you given this step much thought."[26] Nasir
readily agreed, for he related to Radwan a conversation he had
with Salah Bitar, the Ba'thist leader and Syria's foreign minister,
who had joined the negotiations in Cairo on January 16 and who
was trying to encourage Nasir to accept the Syrian proposals.
"Bitar told me," Nasir said, "when a person prepares to dive into

[23] See Hamroush, *Qissat Thawrat 23 Yuliyu* (The story of the 23 July revolution), pp.
43–45; Nasr, *'Abd al-Nasir wa Tajribat al-Wuhda* ('Abd al-Nasir and the experiment of
unity), pp. 124–125.
[24] Sayed Mare'i, *Awraq Siyasiya* (Political papers) (Cairo: Al-Maktab al-Misri al-Hadith,
1978), pp. 392–393. Mare'i was the UAR's Central Minister for Agriculture.
[25] Samir Gawhar, *al-Samitun Yatakalamun: 'Abd al-Nasir wa Madhbahat al-Ikhwan*
(The silent speak: Abd al-Nasir and the massacre of the [Muslim] brothers) (Cairo: al-Maktab al-Misri al-Hadith, 1975), p. 112. The interesting observation about this quote is that
Michel Aflaq, the committed believer in Arab unity, had nothing in common with the virulently *Syrian* nationalist Antun Sa'ada, who in any case had been executed in 1949! It is
only because the two were Christians, supposedly "working against Islam," that Husayn
would lump them together.
[26] Fathi Radwan, *72 Shahran ma'a 'Abd al-Nasir* (72 months with 'Abd al-Nasir) (Cairo:
Dar al-Huriya, 1986), p. 104.

a swimming pool, he has an initial fear of the water, but this fear
disappears once he has jumped into the water. So I told him,
Brother Salah, what scares me is that I may be jumping into an
empty pool."[27] Given all these apprehensions and concerns, it is
not clear whether the Syrian officers, who took off for Cairo on
January 11, really understood what a tough sell they had on their
hands.

The officers who flew to Cairo represented a true microcosm of
the military's factionalized state. There were Ba'thists, Nasirists,
Communist sympathizers, and representatives of the feudal / mer-
chant oligarchy. As Nasir would later comment, the Syrian army
seemed to be "divided into clans and parties."[28] But divided ideo-
logically as they were, they now put up a united front in waving
all the Egyptian objections aside, telling Nasir categorically that
without unity, Syria would implode. The Arab nationalists among
them also hinted that Syria was on the verge of falling into the
hands of the Communists. With that, the Syrians left Nasir with
no option. He was effectively cornered. He was after all the "hero"
of Arab nationalism, the man who, to the applause, adulation, and
eternal gratitude of every Arab nationalist, came to Syria's aid only
a few months earlier when it faced "imperialist" threats from Turkey, Iraq and the United States. How could he now abandon it to
internal disintegration and political ruin? Could the prophet of
Arab nationalism turn a deaf ear to these urgent appeals made in
the very name of Arab nationalism? Nasir, his options severely limited by the Arab nationalist discourse, which had shaped his political relations with the rest of the Arab world since 1955, had little
choice but to accept, but against his better judgment. He was later
to expound on the dialogue that shaped the negotiations:

> I told them: let us pave the way for unity because unity needs prepa-
> ration, because unity is tantamount to troubles and problems, and
> because it is an inter-mixture. I said this but they told me: where are
> the aims that you have advocated? Where are the aims that you have

---

[27] Ibid.
[28] Stephens, *Nasser: A Political Biography*, p. 274.

proclaimed? Will you go back on those aims? . . . will you leave Syria to be torn by strife? Will you let Syria be lost? I said: Never. To me . . . it is a sector of the Arab homeland in which I have laid my faith. I said: I agree to unity.[29]

Having received Nasir's agreement, the Syrian officers flew back to Damascus, and in a move which should have forewarned Nasir, informed the Syrian cabinet of what had transpired in Cairo, and commanded them to get ready to go to the Egyptian capital. On January 31, the officers, under the direction of 'Afif al-Bizri, assembled the cabinet and put them on a plane headed for Cairo. Khalid al-'Azm describes bitterly the brazen manner by which the army officers imposed their will on the politicians, some of whom, such as 'Azm, had reservations about Nasir's style of personalized rule. "The officers herded us like sheep," 'Azm relates, "and put us on a plane which took all of us—the President, Ministers and senior army officers—to Cairo, where meetings were held in al-Qubba Palace which ended with signing the unity agreement . . . then they flew us back the following day into a military airfield, where they gave us a lunch of rice, meat and a piece of bread that was served on a metal plate."[30] This must have been particularly galling to a wealthy aristocrat such as 'Azm, even with his announced leftist leanings. Patrick Seale confirms the military's high-handedness. He writes that Bizri literally ordered the members of the Cabinet into the departing plane, and to the more recalcitrant of the group, he was supposed to have said: "there are two roads open to you: one leads to Mezza (a notorious prison); the other to Cairo."[31] They promptly decided to take the high road to Cairo. The following day, February 1, 1958, the amalgamation of Egypt and Syria into the United Arab Republic (UAR) was proclaimed.

While Nasir was pushed into the union against his better judgment, he nevertheless made sure that a united state would be established only in accordance with his terms, not those of the Syrians.

---

[29] *SWB*, September 29, 1961, p. 9.
[30] Al-'Azm, *Mudhakarat Khalid al-'Azm* (The memoirs of Khalid al-'Azm), pp. 197–198.
[31] Seale, *The Struggle for Syria*, p. 323.

He insisted on a comprehensive merger in which the Syrian political system would be fused into that of Egypt, adopting the latter's political and social institutions. This meant that all political parties had to be dissolved, the Syrian army had to withdraw from politics, the two economies had to be blended, and state control and agricultural reform had to be extended to Syria.

The Syrian politicians naturally were hardly thrilled by Nasir's conditions. The conservatives and Communists knew that theirs was the bleakest future; their equivalents in Egypt had fared not well at all in the kind of society Nasir was building in Egypt. Even the Ba'thists were anything but ecstatic about the dissolution of their party, and they made desperate efforts to backtrack into their original federal proposal.[32] Over secret deliberations, the various factions within the Syrian cabinet got together and came up with a counterproposal which emphasized the "federal" nature of the union, thus giving each country greater autonomy than Nasir had proposed. But the Syrians now were clutching at straws, and they knew it. At this late stage of the process, there was no turning back, unless, to quote Bizri's chilling words again, they wished to have "their heads torn off" by the people. The entire Arab world followed the progress of the talks fervently, and with mounting frenzy, demanding immediate unity, and expecting it to be on Nasir's terms. So when Nasir flatly rejected the Syrian revised draft, insisting that only his conception of the union was on the table, the Syrian parties and politicians had no choice but to sign on the dotted line.

Arabs everywhere heard the news of the merger with stunned amazement, which quickly turned into uncontrolled euphoria. Spontaneous celebrations occurred in many parts of the Arab world, and people congratulated one another in their homes, on the streets, and in their offices. One influential Arab journalist described the announcement of the UAR as "the greatest hour in the history of the Arabs since the . . . victories of Salah al-Din [al-Ayyubi]."[33] The outpouring of public support for the UAR attained

---

[32] Mufti, *Sovereign Creations*, pp. 93–94.
[33] Taha, *Qissat al-Wuhda wa al-Infisal* (The story of the unity and separation), p. 101.

its greatest expression in Syria. Akram al-Hourani, a Ba'thist leader and the president of Syria's Chamber of Deputies (Parliament) describes vividly the elation that engulfed Damascus in the days that followed the proclamation of the UAR.[34] He writes that Damascus was immediately invaded by hordes of people from Aleppo, Hama, Homs, Latikiya, and other Syrian districts. Along with their Damascene compatriots, they filled every street and every square of their capital. Unable to contain their joy, they sang, listened to impromptu patriotic orations, danced the *dabka* (Syrian folk dance), and made up instant poetic slogans that were rhythmically sung and repeated by all. The following are a few of these poetic slogans. They are interesting in the sense that they reflected the political proclivities of the Syrian public in those heady days:

wahdat Misr wa Suriya	the unity of Egypt and Syria
jisr al-wuhda al-'Arabiya	is the bridge of Arab unity
shawka bi 'ayn al-raj'iya	and a thorn in the eye of reaction
dhid al-isti'mar wahlaful	against imperialism and its
al-'askariya	military alliances

To emphasize the secular nature of Arab nationalism, and its egalitarian promise of social justice, the frolicking multitude would chant:

badna wuhda 'Arabiya	we seek Arab unity
Islam wa Nisraniya	of Islam and Christianity
wa 'adala ijtima'iya	and social justice

Of course, the unity of Egypt and Syria brought to mind other pressing Arab concerns. Foremost among these was the four-year old Algerian revolution against French colonialism, which claimed the following chant:

huriya lil Jaza'ir	freedom to Algeria
lil watan al-'Arabi al-	to the revolutionary Arab
Tha'ir	homeland

[34] *Al-Quds al-'Arabi* (London), May 29–30, 1999. This paper serialized Hourani's memoirs. This particular issue contained the 85th installment.

And how could this repertoire be complete without reference to the one man who by then had constituted in the minds of this nationalist generation the most detested enemy of Arab nationalism:

khai'n ya Nuri al-Sa'id   traitor, O' Nuri al-Sa'id
sha'bina mithlal hadid   our people are (made) of steel

These and other largely spontaneous chants and slogans were at the heart of the festivities that lasted several days, invariably continuing through the night. No wonder then that the referendum in the two countries registered almost unanimous approval of the new united state, 99.25 in Syria and 99.8 in Egypt. Some have disputed these figures. Khalid al-'Azm, a bitter foe of the union, alleges that ballot boxes were illegally stuffed with ballots, to the extent that in some districts, the ballots exceeded the number of registered voters.[35] Be that as it may, and indeed it was in the interest of the new political leadership to portray the union as universally supported, the UAR, without a shadow of doubt, commanded the overwhelming and ecstatic support of the vast majority of Syrians. However, in the case of Egypt, where Arab national awareness lagged considerably behind that of Syria, the figure could indeed have been inflated by the centralizing regime.

Having been told of the public delirium in Syria, Nasir arrived unannounced in Damascus on the morning of February 24, and headed straight to the house of President Shukri al-Quwatly. As news of Nasir's arrival spread, vast numbers of people of all ages left their workplaces and homes, some still in their nightdresses, and made their way to Quwatly's house. "It was an awesome sight," recalls Hourani, "this sea of colliding humanity which gathered with astonishing speed."[36] When the two presidents and the other dignitaries decided to move from Quwatly's residence to the official guesthouse, which was a mere 150 yards away, they were mobbed by the people whose numbers had swelled from the thou-

---

[35] Al-'Azm, *Mudhakarat Khalid al-'Azm* (The memoirs of Khalid al-'Azm), pp. 163–165.
[36] *Al-Quds al-'Arabi* (London), May 29–30, 1999.

sands to the hundreds of thousands.[37] Even though the official car
was ringed by soldiers, the crush was such that Quwatly nearly
fainted. And a distance that could be walked in less than five minutes, took the official open-air car over two hours to cover.[38] Nasir
and the Egyptian entourage stayed in the presidential guesthouse
for a week, during which hundreds of speeches were made to the
adoring multitude camped outside. Anwar al-Sadat was a member
of Nasir's entourage. He wrote in his autobiography:

> I really feel incapable of describing that week. It was like a constant
> delirium—a stream of [speeches] that flowed day and night. . . . The
> crowds could not get enough and seemed to grow increasingly fren-
> zied. All that was said was hailed, applauded, celebrated. People
> chanted and screamed and called for more. For a whole week the
> crowds besieged the Guesthouse. They camped outside in the wide
> square, eating, drinking, and sleeping in the open air.[39]

The tumultuous welcome affected even Nasir himself. Three
weeks earlier, in a speech to the Egyptian National Assembly, he
had struck a note of caution advising the Egyptians not to be swept
by the emotions and excitement of the present into underestimating
the inevitable problems that lay ahead.[40] But now in Damascus,
where the city's public squares had been transformed into something akin to areas of public worship, Nasir could not but be
moved by the adulation that surrounded him. He threw caution to
the wind, and to the thunderous jubilation of the crowd, he publicly avowed his commitment to a broader unity of all the Arab

[37] Fuad Matar, *Bisaraha 'an 'Abd al-Nasir: Hiwar ma'a Muhamed Hasaneen Haykal*
(Frankly on 'Abd al-Nasir: a conversation with Muhamed Hasaneen Haykal) (Beirut: Dar
al-Qadhaya, 1975), p. 137.

[38] Al-'Azm, *Mudhakarat Khalid al-'Azm* (The memoirs of Khalid al-'Azm), p. 165; see
also the recollections of Akram al- Hourani in *al-Quds al-'Arabi*, May 29–30, 1999; Matar,
Bisaraha 'an 'Abd al-Nasir (Frankly on 'Abd al-Nasir), p. 137; Hamroush, *Qissat Thawrat
23 Yuliyu* (The story of the 23 July revolution), p. 58. Hamroush relates that at some point
during Nasir's visit to Aleppo, Nasir's car was carried on peoples' shoulders.

[39] Anwar Sadat, *In Search of Identity: An Autobiography* (New York: Harper and Row,
1977), p. 152.

[40] The United Arab Republic, *President Gamal Abd al-Nasser's Speeches and Press Interviews, 1958* (Cairo: Information Department, n.d.), p. 27.

people.[41] It might have been a statement born out of the heady emotions of that moment, but the impact of his words went beyond the limited confines of Damascus, or Syria.[42]

Most troubling for the West was the response in Iraq, the citadel of the anti-Nasirist forces in the area. 'Abd al-Karim al-Uzri, a pillar of the monarchical political order and frequent cabinet member, describes in his memoirs the response at the popular level and among the ruling elite:

> [The UAR] generated among the educated and politically aware Iraqis an overwhelming sense of exuberance and ardor, and resuscitated within them aspirations, the realization of which they had considered to be no more than a dream. . . . [The formation of the UAR] also engendered extreme bitterness against the existing Iraqi political order for isolating Iraq from the Arabist tide, and distancing it from the unifying Arab nationalist movement. The unity between Egypt and Syria also caused a wave of fear and confusion among Iraq's rulers, the Western supporters of Iraq, some of the neighboring countries, and members of the Baghdad Pact, because of the immense dangers this unity would bring not only to Iraq, but also to the Hashemite Kingdom of Jordan and to Western interests in the area generally.[43]

The elation among Iraq's middle class—students, professionals, businessmen, army officers, and so forth—was such that immense political risks were taken simply to register approval of the Egyptian-Syrian merger. Defying Nuri al-Sa'id and his feared security apparatus, a number of prominent Iraqi politicians, journalists, and academics sent a congratulatory telegram to Nasir, in which

[41] For the full text, see *ibid.*, pp. 28–45.

[42] See Naji 'Abd al-Nabi Bazzi, *Suriya: Sira' al-Istiqtab: Dirasa wa Tahlil li Ahdath al-Sharq al-Awsat wa al-Tadakhulat al-Duwaliya fi al-Ahdath al-Suriya, 1917–1973* (Syria: the struggle of polarization; a study and analysis of Middle Eastern affairs and international interventions in Syrian affairs, 1917–1973) (Damascus: Dar Ibn al-'Arabi, 1996), pp. 304–305; see also Ahmad 'Abd al-Karim, *Hisad: Sineen Khasiba wa Thimar Murra* (Harvest: fertile years and bitter fruit) (Beirut: Baysan, 1994), p. 387.

[43] 'Abd al-Karim al-Uzri, *Tarikh fi Dhikrayat al-'Iraq, 1930–1958* (History in the memoirs of Iraq, 1930–1958) (Beirut: Markaz al-Abjadiya li al-Saff al-Taswiri, 1982), p. 544.

the birth of the UAR was described as "signifying a new era in the history of the Arab nation [whose] primary interest is to serve Arab nationalism."[44] This public and pervasive endorsement of the UAR left the country's rulers in a state of near despair. According to Britain's Ambassador to Iraq, Crown Prince 'Abd al-Ilah believed "that if the present trend of events, both inside Iraq and in the neighboring countries, continued without further check, the situation would crumble irretrievably within a period of months and certainly before the end of the year. The impact of Nasser's success and propaganda would prove too strong."[45] Uzri too found the crown prince "in a state of great fear and panic," telling Uzri that the UAR "constituted a dangerous challenge to Iraq and a threat to its existence."[46] 'Abd al-Ilah tried feverishly to induce the other members of the Baghdad Pact not to recognize the UAR on the grounds that "the Egyptian-Syrian union was aimed not only against Iraq's interest, its security and its national goals, but also against its foreign policy, embodied in the country's membership of the Baghdad Pact."[47] But the crown prince was to be disappointed. Unpalatable as it might have been to the anti-nationalist forces, the UAR nevertheless had already been formed, was accorded enthusiastic domestic support, and had received diplomatic recognition from countries such as the United States and Saudi Arabia. The Baghdad Pact countries therefore went ahead and recognized the UAR. As for Iraq, its recognition came only after the July 1958 revolution.

The great consternation felt by Iraq's rulers was more than echoed by Jordan's King Husayn, saddled as he was by a large and radicalized Palestinian population. Immediately after the formation of the UAR, King Husayn initiated a series of meetings with the Iraqi leaders which resulted in the creation of a federation to be named "The Arab Union" on February 14, 1958. In the first

[44] Fikrat Namiq 'Abd al-Fattah, *Siyasat al-'Iraq al-Kharijiya fi al-Mantaqa al-'Arabiya, 1953–1958* (Iraq's foreign policy in the Arab region, 1953–1958) (Baghdad: Dar al-Rashid li al-Nashr, 1981), pp. 214–215.

[45] Mufti, *Sovereign Creations*, p. 104.

[46] Al-Uzri, *Tarikh fi Dhikrayat al-'Iraq* (History in the memoirs of Iraq), p. 550.

[47] Al-Hasani, *Tarikh al-Wizarat al-'Iraqiya* (The history of Iraqi cabinets), p. 205

communiqué which announced the Hashemite union, the citizens of the new federated entity were reminded that it was the Hashemites (and by implication, not 'Abd al-Nasir) who were the real custodians of Arab nationalism, since it was Jordan's Husayn and Iraq's Faysal who were the inheritors of the 1916 "Great Arab Revolt" and "its eternal nationalist message." The two Hashemite kings constituted "the flame that would guide the Arab nation in its march toward its declared aspiration of comprehensive and universal unity."[48] The wording of the declaration is a testimony to the political sentiments and sensibilities of that era. In a political milieu in which Arab nationalism reigned supreme, it is understandable that the two monarchies would resort to the only relevant political vocabulary of the time.

But they were fighting a losing battle. Their union was little more than "an admission of their [own] weakness."[49] It was evident from the discussions that preceded the announcement of the "Arab Union" that Amman and Baghdad were mounting an almost desperate rearguard action to hold the line against Nasir's seemingly unstoppable Arab nationalist juggernaut. Thus, the Jordanian foreign minister reminded the other participants that "Egypt's rulers . . . have expanded their goals, and have advocated a revolutionary philosophy which extended [beyond Egypt] to the Arab and Islamic worlds. It is therefore the duty of the governments of Iraq and Jordan to hold the line, for Jordan was their first target since it was the bridge that would take them to Iraq and Saudi Arabia."[50] The problem was that the Union lacked public support. In contrast to the popular euphoria that greeted the founding of the UAR, the "Arab Union" was met with universal silence and lassitude.[51] And

---

[48] Al-Uzri, *Tarikh fi Dhikrayat al-'Iraq* (History in the memoirs of Iraq), p. 545.

[49] Naji 'Allush, *al-Thawra wa al-Jamahir: Marahil al-Nidhal al-'Arabi wa Dawr al-Haraka al-Thawriya, 1948–1961* (The revolution and the masses: the stages of the Arab struggle and the role of the revolutionary movement, 1948–1961) (Beirut: Dar al-Tali'a li al-Tiba'a wa al-Nashr, 1973), p. 84.

[50] The quote is taken from the minutes of the meetings which preceded the announcement of the "Arab Union". The quote appears in al-Fattah, *Siyasat al-'Iraq al-Kharijiya* (Iraq's foreign policy in the Arab region), p. 475.

[51] Ismael Ahmad Yaghi, *al-'Ilaqat al-'Iraqiya al-Urduniya, 1941–1958* (Iraqi-Jordanian relations, 1941–1958) (Cairo: Dar al-Sahwa li al-Nashr, 1988), p. 55.

indeed, the Hashemites themselves knew only too well that they had long lost the popularity contest; a realization which only intensified their rage at the UAR. This was more than evident in the exchange of letters between Nasir and Iraq's crown prince, 'Abd al-Ilah, after the formation of the Arab Union. Even though the Hashemites had not recognized the UAR, Nasir dispatched a warm congratulatory letter immediately after the announcement of the Arab Union. Nasir's letter spoke of his confidence that the Arab Union would add strength to the Arab nation and would be a shield against that nation's enemies. Nasir also called the formation of the Arab Union a proud day for Arab nationalism.[52] 'Abd al-Ilah, writing on behalf of the young King Faysal responded by first thanking Nasir, then reiterating the alleged long series of struggles that the Hashemites had waged on behalf of Arab nationalism which was bound to lead the Arabs to comprehensive unity. He ended the letter by asking the Almighty's help in granting success and prosperity to all Arabs and Muslims.[53] No mention of the UAR was made.

'Abd al-Ilah's response is indicative of the psychological landscape in which the Arab Union was born. The Hashemite initiative was defensive rather than creative, born not out of exuberance, but out of fear. The Union's discourse might have been dressed in Arab nationalist sentiment, but its actuality was different: it was a political venture, based on an institutional marriage, designed to mount a diplomatic and strategic counterpoint to Nasir in the region. It was meant to safeguard and reinforce not just the security and safety of the two kingdoms, but also of the other states threatened by the popular appeal of Arab nationalism, which was aided vigorously by Egypt's propaganda, as well as on occasions by its intelligence services. One such threatened state was Lebanon with its highly polarized sectarian society.

Lebanon's political order was based on the "Pact of 1943" between Christian and Muslim leaders, which divided governmental responsibilities among the two religious communities. This tenu-

---

[52] Al-Hasani, *Tarikh al-Wizarat al-'Arabiya* (The history of Iraqi cabinets), p. 203.
[53] Ibid., pp. 203–204.

ous arrangement worked as long as the system did not come under any external strain. But the rise of Arab nationalism undermined the delicate balance, since the country's politically dominant Christian community saw in Arab nationalism and its ultimate goal of comprehensive Arab unity the dissolution of their separate identity and the loss of their political independence. It thus came as no surprise that the responses of the two communities to the announcement of the UAR were radically different. In general, most Muslims rejoiced: many Muslim schools held celebratory rallies, and demonstrations in support of the new unified state were held throughout Lebanon despite governmental bans. Delegation after delegation crossed over to Syria to congratulate its leaders on the "historic decision." Most of the Christians, however, were simultaneously and feverishly reiterating their faith in, and hopes for, the maintenance of Lebanon's sovereignty.

This increasing polarization erupted into a full-fledged civil war in May 1958, which President Camille Chamoun and his foreign minister, Charles Malik, both Christians, blamed entirely on the UAR and its leaders. It seems that Malik, troubled by the vexatious spectacle of hordes of Lebanese arriving in Damascus and shouting for Arab unity under Nasir's leadership,[54] had taken it upon himself to be the first line of defense against the irredentist Nasirist tide. It was Malik who convinced Chamoun to go to the United Nations Security Council, citing UAR interference in Lebanon's internal affairs. In his address to the Security Council, Malik alleged that the interference was conducted through a large supply of arms to antigovernment forces, training of subversive elements in Syria, participation of UAR nationals in the civil war, and employment of hostile press and radio campaigns against Lebanon's government.[55] As it turned out, United Nations' observers who were sent to Lebanon vitiated Malik's claims of arms supply or personnel infiltration

---

[54] Nadim Dimashqiya, *Mahattat fi Hayati al-Diblomasiya: Dhikrayat fi al-Siyasa wa al-'Ilaqat al-Duwaliya* (Stations in my diplomatic life: memoirs of politics and international relations) (Beirut: Dar al-Nahar li al-Nashr, 1995), pp. 120.

[55] The bitter and somewhat rambling speech can be found in Fahim Qubain, *Crisis in Lebanon* (Washington, D.C.: The Middle East Institute, 1961), pp. 181–196.

from the UAR. But that was not necessarily Malik's goal. What he and Chamoun were really after could be discerned from the complaint's conclusion, which characterized UAR activity as representing "a danger to international peace and security."[56] These were the very words used in the Eisenhower Doctrine, and as Malik was careful to link UAR action to international Communism,[57] his appeal was meant to specifically target the United States and its allies, particularly members of the Baghdad Pact.

Not surprisingly, the country that took up the challenge was Iraq. As the only Arab member of the Baghdad Pact, Iraq would naturally take a proactive stance on the matter. And in any case, the possibility of Lebanon's disintegration, or worse its absorption by the UAR, had to be a matter of immense concern for the Iraqi leadership. Indeed, Iraq's foreign minister, Fadhil al-Jamali, was dispatched to the United Nations and worked closely with Charles Malik, delivering a speech that asserted Iraq's wholehearted support for Lebanon against the scourge of "Nasserism."[58] Nuri al-Sa'id followed this diplomatic move by calling an emergency high-level meeting of the Baghdad Pact to be held in Istanbul on July 14. Simultaneously, he ordered army units to move into northern Jordan near the border of Syria and Lebanon.

But when the Baghdad Pact meeting convened, Iraq's seat was vacant, and the army units never arrived in Jordan. The units, stationed about 90 miles northeast of Baghdad, stopped their journey to Amman short, occupying instead the Iraqi capital, and with the collaboration of other army units toppled the monarchical political order, killing Nuri al-Sa'id, King Faysal II, Crown Prince 'Abd al-Ilah, and the other members of the royal family, and proclaimed the birth of the Iraqi Republic. In one dramatic, albeit gruesomely bloody, day, Nasir witnessed the demise of his greatest antagonist

[56] See Fawzi Abu Diab, *Lubnan wa al-Ummam al-Muttahida* (Lebanon and the United Nations) (Beirut: Dar al-Nahdha al-'Arabiya, 1971), p. 139.

[57] Dimashqiya, *Mahattat fi Hayati al-Diblomasiya* (Stations in my diplomatic life), p. 121–122.

[58] Muhamed Fadhil al-Jamali, *Safahat min Tarikhina al-Mu'asir* (Pages from our contemporary history) (Cairo: Dar Su'ad al-Sabah, 1993), p. 197.

and most capable foe. Revolutionary Arab nationalism had achieved yet another remarkable triumph. And surely more were on the way, or so everyone believed.

The odds-on favorite to be the next to fall prey to the Arab nationalist avalanche was Hashemite Jordan. The Arab Union, the very arrangement fashioned by King Husayn for his own protection, lay in ruins, smothered in the blood of those who, like him, had dared to confront Nasir and Arab nationalism. In sheer desperation, he tried to decouple the man from the movement: "We want Nasir to know that Arab nationalism was born before he was."[59] True. But in the political milieu of the time, these were hollow words, the words of a man seemingly enveloped by a sense of hopelessness, of a relic of the "reactionary past" trying to cast aspersions on the man of the hour, the acknowledged hero of triumphant Arab nationalism. To most Arabs and indeed non-Arabs, it was a foregone conclusion that Husayn was doomed. In his biography of the king, the British journalist, Peter Snow, who reported from Amman in the wake of the Iraqi revolution, describes vividly the mood and expectations of those days:

> [P]eople expected to wake up each morning to hear that [the King] had been assassinated. Talk of conspiracy was everywhere. There were a number of bomb explosions, a large number of arrests and a ruthless clampdown by Hussein's security forces. Censorship was imposed on the press. Those were some of the most tense days the King ever had to endure. Journalists, many of whom had to leave the country to file their reports, told of open public support for President Nasir and the widely held assumption that Jordan would follow Iraq into the revolutionary camp.[60]

Even the U. S. government seemed to share in the general sense of doom surrounding the king's prospects. A directive by the United

---

[59] Quoted in Michael N. Barnett, *Dialogues in Arab Politics: Negotiations in Regional Order* (New York: Columbia University Press, 1998), p. 134.

[60] Peter Snow, *Hussein: A Biography* (New York: Robert B. Luce, Inc., 1972), pp. 128–129.

States National Security Council stated that "the indefinite continuance of Jordan's present political status has been rendered unrealistic by recent developments." The directive went on to recommend "in the face of the irresistible forces of nationalism, anti-monarchism, and anti-colonialism, the most that could be hoped for was an orderly devolution leading to Hussein's dignified withdrawal and an agreed absorption of Jordan by its Arab neighbors."[61]

Realizing perhaps that his hours were numbered if he did not act swiftly, Husayn requested British military aid. Prime Minister Harold Macmillan decided on an immediate airlift of fifteen hundred troops from Cyprus to Amman. But they had to fly over the airspace of the normally recalcitrant Israelis. However, as it turned out, Israeli approval was never in doubt, since in the words of Foreign Minister Golda Meir, the Israelis prayed "three times a day for King Hussein's safety and success."[62] On July 17, British paratroopers landed in Amman, their numbers swelling eventually to four thousand. They stayed in Jordan until the king deemed the dangers to have dissipated. While undoubtedly the presence of the troops bolstered immeasurably the tottering monarchy, they nevertheless represented for the king a humiliating affirmation of Egypt's claims that "imperialism" was in the service of Arab "reactionary" leaders in their efforts to save themselves from the wrath of Arab nationalism and its committed disciples all over the Arab world. Egypt had made the same derisive accusation two days earlier when American troops landed in Beirut, the capital of Lebanon, to save that other hapless "reactionary" leader, Camille Chamoun.

In Iraq, the new revolutionary government under the leadership of General 'Abd al-Karim Qasim and Colonel 'Abd al-Salam 'Aref promptly reversed its predecessor's policies, declaring itself to be part of the Arab nationalist struggle. Its first foreign policy act was the recognition of the UAR. A mere five days after the coup, on July 19, Colonel 'Aref led a high-level Iraqi delegation to Damascus

---

[61] Dann, *King Hussein and the Challenge of Arab Radicalism*, p. 93.

[62] Quoted in Avi Shlaim, "Israel, the Great Powers, and the Middle East Crisis of 1958," *The Journal of Imperial and Commonwealth History*, vol. 27, no. 2 (May 1999): 185.

where he met with Nasir. In a number of public speeches to huge and ecstatic crowds both characterized the Iraqi revolution as a crowning achievement of Arab nationalism. And in this the two leaders were simply responding to peoples' sentiments, for this was indeed the main theme of the slogans thundered by the crowds that filled the streets of Damascus once news of the Iraqi revolution reached Syria's capital.[63] And the Syrian demonstrators themselves were only echoing their brethren in Iraq who filled the streets, and who, in their frenzied chants, promised themselves to Nasir as his flock, his loyal cavalry.[64] So it was hardly a surprise when, in the meetings between Nasir and the Iraqi delegation, 'Aref expressed his hope that "Iraq would soon join the UAR."[65] And the crowds that filled the streets sang and danced and expected nothing less.

If an analyst could legitimately step back and isolate one specific period, be it a week, a month, a year, from the ongoing procession of historical development, and point to this period in time as the very apex, the flowering climax, of whatever historical story he or she is telling, then the period after the Iraqi revolution, short-lived as it turned out to be, represented the very peak of the relentless upward rise of Arab nationalism. In that brief historical moment, the jubilant and energized masses genuinely and fervently believed that they had witnessed the final and ignominious defeat of those they considered to be the enemies of Arab nationalism. Moved by this victorious spirit, they could now hope, for the first time in almost five hundred years, to turn their glorious past into a glittering and heroic future. The process would begin by the entry of Iraq into the UAR, which was accepted as a foregone conclusion, and this would constitute the rock upon which Nasir would build the

---

[63] See, for example, Taleb Mushtaq, *Awraq Ayami,1900–1956, al-Jusi' al-Awal* (Papers of my days, volume one) (Beirut: Dar al-Tali'a li al-Tiba'a wa al-Nashr, 1968), pp. 563–568.

[64] Hanna Batatu, *The Old Social Classes and the Revolutionary Movements of Iraq: A Study of Iraq's Old Landed and Commercial Classes and of Its Communists, Ba'thists and Free Officers* (Princeton, New Jersey: Princeton University Press, 1978), p. 816.

[65] Majid Khadduri, *Republican Iraq: A Study in Iraqi Politics Since the Revolution of 1958* (London: Oxford University Press. 1969), p. 87; Phebe Marr, *The Modern History of Iraq* (Boulder, Colorado: Westview Press, 1985), p. 159.

Arab nation-state. After all, Egypt, Syria, and Iraq were the geographic and cultural heart of the Arab world, and their unity would trigger a tidal wave that would sweep all skeptics and naysayers into historical oblivion.

The nationalist generation unquestioningly believed that they had formed a nation; the state now awaited them.

CHAPTER NINE

ARAB NATIONALISM'S DOWNWARD SLIDE, 1958–1967

The announcement broadcast on Radio Baghdad on September 11, 1958 was curt, uncharacteristically devoid of the kind of hyperbole to which Iraqi listeners had become accustomed since the outset of the revolution. It said simply: "In view of the dictates of public interest and upon the recommendation of the Minister of Defense, we decree the following: to relieve Staff Colonel 'Abd al Salam 'Aref from his post as Deputy Commander in Chief of the armed forces."[1] Three weeks or so later, in an even shorter statement, General 'Abd al-Karim Qasim relieved 'Aref of all his cabinet posts, and adding insult to injury, appointed him ambassador to Bonn.[2]

The heart of every Arab nationalist must have skipped a beat or two at the news of 'Aref's demotion. Of the two leaders of the Iraqi revolution, he was seen as the one who was committed wholly, and without any reservations, not just to Arab nationalist ideals and principles, but also to unity with the United Arab Republic (UAR).

---

[1] Benjamin Shwadran, *The Power Struggle in Iraq* (New York: Council for Middle Eastern Affairs Press, 1960), p. 35.
[2] Ibid.

It was 'Aref who, without consulting Qasim, had demanded immediate unity with the UAR in his first talks with Gamal 'Abd al-
Nasir in Damascus a few days after the military takeover in Iraq.
He is reported to have told Nasir not to bother with Qasim, por-
traying his senior partner as "Iraq's Neguib"[3] (the early figurehead
of Egypt's revolution who was later ousted by Nasir). He even went
so far as to tell Nasir that if Qasim were to object to unity with the
UAR, then he, 'Aref, would kill him with one bullet. Taken aback,
Nasir interrupted 'Aref, telling him: "No, brother 'Abd al-Salam.
Let us not have this kind of talk. He (Qasim) is your senior col-
league, and things have to be done through dialogue and persuasion."[4] Back in Iraq, 'Aref blazed his way through the length and
breadth of the land, making numerous speeches, in which he extolled the virtue of Arab unity and the leadership of Nasir. The
UAR president was undoubtedly his hero, which moved one foe to
remark that in his speeches, 'Aref "ignored the leader of the revolution (Qasim) and praised Jamal 'Abd al-Nasir. Was 'Abd al-Nasir
the leader of the revolution?"[5] Indeed, Qasim, who by then was
being called by his own supporters, *al-Za'im al-Awhad* (the sole
leader) was hardly enamored with his junior partner. He made a
point of devaluing 'Aref's role in Iraq's revolution to foreign visi-
tors.[6] More concretely, Qasim began to quietly clip 'Aref's wings
by undercutting his power base in the army, while 'Aref gallivanted
around the country making speeches.[7] By September, Qasim felt

[3] Majid Khadduri, *Republican Iraq: A Study in Iraqi Politics Since the Revolution of
1958* (London: Oxford University Press, 1969), p. 87; Phebe Marr, *The Modern History of
Iraq* (Boulder, Colorado: Westview Press, 1985), p. 159.

[4] 'Ali Karim Sa'id, *'Iraq 8 Shibat, 1963: Min Hiwar al-Mafahim ila Hiwar al-Damm,
Muraja'at fi Dhakirat Taleb al-Shabib* (Iraq of 8 February, 1963: from a dialogue over
norms to a dialogue of blood, reviews in the memory of Taleb Shabib) (Beirut: Dar al-Kunuz
al-Adabia, 1999), fn. 2, pp. 282–283.

[5] The speaker was Colonel Majid Amin, the leftist prosecutor general of *Mahkamat al-
Sha'ab* (the People's Court), which was set up immediately after the revolution to try members of the *ancien regime*, but in due course became a vehicle for settling scores as the
revolution turned in on itself. This statement was made in 'Aref's trial for allegedly at-
tempting to assassinate Qasim. See Shwadran, *The Power Struggle in Iraq*, p. 37.

[6] See, for example, Salah Nasr, *'Abd al-Nasir wa Tajribat al-Wuhda* ('Abd al-Nasir and
the unity experiment) (Beirut: al-Watan al-'Arabi, 1976), pp. 171–172, 175.

[7] Khadduri, *Republican Iraq*, pp. 92–93.

strong enough to dispatch 'Aref to Bonn. 'Aref, however, resisted his unceremonious exit, and for his pains was arrested on November 4 "on the charge of plotting against the security of the homeland."[8] This date marks the first erosion in the hitherto seemingly all-conquering Arab nationalist movement.

What was especially worrying for the Arab nationalists was that the arrest of 'Aref seemed to result not just from the personal rivalry between the two leaders of the Iraqi revolution, but from a wider political divide among and within the "progressive" forces that together had toppled the *ancien regime*. Behind 'Aref were the nationalists, those who demanded immediate unity: Ba'thists, Nasirists, and the like. Qasim, however, had created a coalition consisting of Communists, Kurds, unaffiliated leftists, and Iraqi nationalists, such as those who belonged to the National Democratic Party. As the struggle intensified, the dormant sectarian sensitivities surfaced again, depicting the efforts at Arab unity as essentially a Sunni project, designed to ensure the ultimate subjugation of the non-Sunni communal groups. The group that coalesced around Qasim adopted the slogan "Iraq first" as a counterbalance to the Arab nationalist demand of "unity now." The "Iraq first" group was not necessarily averse to some form of union, but theirs was a much looser conception than that held by the nationalists, at most a federal arrangement in which Iraq would retain considerable autonomy.

The conflict came to a head on March 9, 1959 when an attempted coup against Qasim by Arab nationalist officers failed. The rebellion, centered in the northern city of Mosul, received substantial help from the UAR. The point man was Colonel 'Abd al-Hamid Saraj, head of intelligence in the UAR's northern region (Syria). Saraj was apprised of the conspiracy from its very inception, and his men held a number of meetings with the Iraqi conspirators, who received not only arms and money, but prior to the announcement of the rebellion, also a radio transmitter to balance

---

[8] British Broadcasting Corporation, *Summary of World Broadcasts, Part IV: The Arab World, Israel, Greece, Turkey, Iran* (hereafter cited as *SWB*), November 6, 1958, p. 6.

"Radio Baghdad" which was controlled by Qasim loyalists. Indeed, Nasir, who was on a visit to Damascus, prolonged his stay in anticipation of the coup's success and Qasim's removal.[9] The break now was total, the mood never more bitter, the rhetoric malevolently shrill and personal.

The invective began in Iraq's *Mahkamat al-Sha'ab* (People's Court), which over the previous months had been holding daily public and televised trials of prominent members of the monarchy's political order. The prosecutor accused the UAR of direct involvement in, and responsibility for, the failed coup attempt, and called Nasir a pharaoh.[10] The president of the court, Colonel Fadhil al-Mahdawi, identified the pharaoh in question as none other than "Ramsis," adding an impromptu rhyme: "*Nasir ya Ramsis, ya Khadim al-Ingilis*" (Nasir, O' Ramsis, O' Servant of the English).[11] Meaningless as this rhyme might have been, it was met with ecstatic approval in the theater that was *Mahkamat al-Sha'ab*, which as a rule was filled with die-hard Qasim supporters. Nasir countered with his own battery of personal insults, labeling Qasim a Communist, an anti-Arab, and most famous of all "*Qasim al-'Iraq*" (divider of Iraq).[12] He also belittled Qasim's role in the Iraqi revolution, and insinuated that it was 'Abd al-Salam 'Aref who was the real leader of the revolution.[13] The UAR's propaganda machine continued relentlessly this character assassination, linking Qasim with every anti-Arab cause and endeavor, and pouncing on his increasing reliance on the leftists and Communists in his struggle with Iraq's pro-Nasir nationalists. Naturally, the "Voice of the Arabs" made sure to work the universally detested Israel into the mix:

[9] Sa'id, *'Iraq 8 Shibat, 1963* (Iraq of 8 February, 1963), fn. 2, pp. 282–283.

[10] *SWB*, March 11, 1959, p. 11.

[11] *SWB*, March 12, 1959, p. 10.

[12] Al-Jumhuriya al-'Arabiya al-Muttahida (UAR), *Majmu'at Khutab wa Tasrihat wa Bayanat al-Rais Gamal 'Abd al-Nasser, al-Jusi' al-Khamis* (The collection of speeches, statements and communiqués of President Gamal 'Abd al-Nasir, volume five) (hereafter cited as *Khutab*) (Cairo: Maslahat al-Isti'lamat, 1959), p. 353.

[13] United Arab Republic, *President Gamal 'Abd al-Nasser's Speeches and Press Interviews* (hereafter cited as *Speeches*) (Cairo: Information Department, 1959), p. 149. Nasir returned to the same theme a few days later. See *SWB*, March 19, 1959, p. 10.

Israel does not want Arab unity to be achieved, nor the Arab cause
to succeed and be victorious. [Qasim] and the Communists want
the same. Israel does not want the UAR to have good relations with
the Iraqi Republic or cooperation between them. The Communists
and [Qasim's] government want the same. All these aims, decisions
and accusations are in harmony in the propaganda of Baghdad, the
Communists and Israel.[14]

To be accused of doing Israel's bidding was the last straw for the
Iraqi leadership. Colonel al-Mahdawi, under the full glare of television lights, declared "openly and firmly that Syria and Egypt . . .
must be liberated from Nasserite fascist rule."[15] Qasim himself
stayed aloof from the mudslinging match, allowing Mahdawi and
others to trade below-the-belt punches, until April 1, when he contrasted his encouragement of democracy with Nasir's mistrust of it,
and then pointedly suggested that the statement was particularly
relevant to the Syrians.[16] And lest people might mistake the statement for an April Fool's stunt, he renewed his government's interest
in the "Fertile Crescent" plan originally devised by Nuri al-Sa'id.
Qasim admitted that he had considered Nuri's plan to be reactionary, but now that Iraq had been liberated, the plan would serve the
two countries and the region well.[17] By now the verbal acrimony
had reached a level of personal vindictiveness that greatly surpassed
the earlier airwave duels between Nasir and Nuri al-Sa'id.

What was especially galling to Nasir and the Arab nationalists
was Qasim's credentials. He was, after all, no easy prey to the nationalist assault. Unlike Nuri al-Sa'id of Iraq, Camille Chamoun of
Lebanon, King Husayn of Jordan, or King Sa'ud of Saudi Arabia,
he was no "reactionary," but a "revolutionary" in his own right,
who enjoyed considerable domestic support, particularly among
the poor classes—the peasants, workers, slum dwellers. He was an
enemy of "imperialism," and the friend of Nasir's mentors in the

---

[14] *SWB*, March 13, 1959, p. 8.
[15] *SWB*, March 18, 1959, p. 9.
[16] *SWB*, April 3, 1959, p. 8; see also Shwadran, *Power Struggle in Iraq*, p. 50.
[17] Qasim's interview with *al-Thawra* (Baghdad), November 16, 1959.

Kremlin. All this made him a greater threat to Nasir and Arab nationalism than Nuri ever was. After all, the nationalist contention all along had been that Arab unity would occur once the Arab states succeeded in delivering themselves from "imperialism." And here was Iraq, salvation at hand, emancipated and liberated, yet steering an independent, even contradictory, course from the Arab nationalist caravan under Nasir's stewardship.

It is thus clear that the struggle between Nasir and Qasim was more than a conflict between two leaders, or even between two states. It was a confrontation between two ideological paths: *al-qawmiya* (Arab nationalism) and *al-wataniya* (nationalism based on state sovereignty). In a sense, here was a reenactment of the nineteenth century philosophical debate between the German and the Anglo-French schools. The German school would stress *al-qawmiya*, with its emphasis on the oneness of the people (the *volk*) under a unifying language and a continuous historical experience. Political and geographic divisions that might have separated members of the nation were artificial and therefore irrelevant to the definition of *al-qawmiya*. The Anglo-French school, however, would embrace *al-wataniya*, the nationalism built (or at a minimum, nurtured) through state institutions within a geographically limited space, even if the citizens were to speak different languages and/or profess different ethnicities. In Iraq, those who espoused *al-wataniya* were the diverse groups that advocated the "Iraq first" policy. And it was these groups, the determined bearers of the *wataniya* banner, that mounted the first real challenge to the seemingly unstoppable march of Arab nationalism toward comprehensive Arab unity.

The phrase "first real challenge" is used advisedly. After all, the Nasir-led Arab nationalism had been confronted by state nationalisms before the Iraqi revolution. As we have seen, the kingdoms of Iraq, Jordan, and Saudi Arabia vigorously contested Egypt's conception of an all-engulfing, purposely irredentist Arab nationalism, advocating instead the inviolability of state sovereignty, while recognizing that they indeed were part of a larger cultural community. These sentiments had been echoed by the newly independent state of Tunisia. Gaining independence in 1956, Tunisia's Habib Bourguiba followed a pro-Western policy at the height of Nasir's "anti-Western" crusade, and for this infraction he was vilified by Egypt. Bourguiba, the tough political activist, was not going to cower to Nasir. Affirming Tunisia's sovereign right to pursue its own national interest, he went on the offensive in 1958, accusing Nasir of bullying the other members of the Arab League, and when Egyptian radio responded with the usual savage onslaught, Tunisia severed diplomatic relations with Egypt.

Vigorous as it undoubtedly was, this affirmation of *wataniya* by Tunisia and the three monarchies was not the "real challenge" to Nasir's Arab nationalism that was posed by Qasim's Iraq. The monarchies were easily dismissed by the Egyptians as puppets of Western imperialism, belittling their *wataniya* as a reactionary response undertaken by an isolated and frightened political elite that simply did the bidding of its foreign masters, and that could not and did not represent the true interests and wishes of the *Arab* people in Iraq, Jordan, and Saudi Arabia. In Tunisia, there was no question as to Bourguiba's popularity amongst the people, but Tunisian *wataniya* hardly represented a real threat to Nasir's Arab nationalism because the North African country was simply too far geographically and too peripheral perceptually from the center of the Arab world. North Africa was marginal to what had always been the core of Arab political and intellectual activity, Egypt and the Fertile Crescent.

This is precisely why Qasim's insistence on Iraq's political independence, supported by the "Iraq first" constituency, constituted the first real challenge to the nationalist (*qawmi*) hopes for Arab unity. At one time, an actual Arab unity had been but a fantasy clung to by the coffee bar set of nationalist idealists and dreamers, yet, incredulously and some thought miraculously, this fantasy became a realizable hope with the creation of the UAR, especially after the demise of the Iraqi monarchy and the staunch anti-Nasirite, Nuri al-Sa'id. And now these once euphoric *qawmiyeen* (nationalists) watched, aggrieved and dumbfounded, as the Arab nationalist march, seemingly so near to its ultimate goal of Arab unity, came against the roadblock of the "Iraq first" *wataniya*. This abrupt reversal of fortunes led to a sense of near despair that was echoed by Nasir himself when he described the developing events in Iraq as the end for Arab nationalism.[18] That, of course, was too harsh an assessment. In retrospect, it was not the end of Arab nationalism; more precisely it was the point at which, after four years of continuous and sometimes spectacular ascent, Arab nationalism began its gradual descent. But the road was still long, and other potholes were still to be encountered in the downhill slide of Arab nationalism. The next serious erosion in the fortunes of Arab nationalism occurred some three years later with the secession of Syria from the UAR.

Given the precipitance with which unity was declared, problems and difficulties were bound to plague the new state. To start with, Nasir knew little, if anything, about Syria. In 1954, before his conversion to the Arab nationalist cause, he had been attacked vehemently by the Syrian Ba'thists for having told a Syrian official that Syria was free to unite with Iraq, Jordan, or Turkey as long as such a move was approved by the Syrian people. It was galling to the Ba'thists, as well as to other Arab nationalists, that an Arab leader would commit the cardinal sin of not distinguishing between Arab and Turk.[19] And this statement was made a mere four years before he were to become the president of Syria! Indeed, Nasir's confidant, the journalist Muhamed Hasaneen Haykal, confirms that this ignorance of Syria had improved but little in the intervening four years.[20]

---

[18] Ahmad Hamroush, *Qissat Thawrat 23 Yuliyu, al-Jusi' al-Rabi': 'Abd Al-Nasir wa al-'Arab* (The story of the 23 July revolution, volume four: 'Abd al-Nasir and the Arabs) (Cairo: Dar al-Mawqif al-'Arabi, 1983), p. 156.

[19] Kamel Abu Jaber, *The Arab Ba'th Socialist Party: History, Ideology and Organization* (Syracuse, New York: Syracuse University Press, 1966), p. 35; see also John Devlin, *The Ba'th Party: A History from Its Origins to 1966* (Stanford, California: Hoover Institution, 1976), p. 80.

[20] Fuad Mattar, *Bisaraha 'an 'Abd al-Nasir: Hiwar ma'a Muhamed Hasaneen Haykal* (Frankly on 'Abd al-Nasir: a conversation with Muhamed Hasaneen Haykal) (Beirut: Dar al-Qadhaya, 1975), p. 135; also Muhamed Hasaneen Haykal, *Ma Alathi Jara fi Suriya* (What happened in Syria) (Cairo: al-Dar al-Qawmiya li al-Tiba'a wa al-Nashr, 1962), p. 66.

The Ba'th, however, became Nasir's major ally at the time of the announcement of the Syrian-Egyptain union. They accepted the dissolution of their party, but believed that Ba'thist principles would constitute the ideological foundation of the new state. As Michel Aflaq put it: "We will be officially dissolved but we will be present in the new unified party, the National Union. Born of the union of the two countries, this [unitary party] cannot be animated by principles other than those of the Ba'th."[21] The Ba'th, therefore, saw Nasir as a "splendid capture or recruit whose personal prestige would add power to the [Ba'th's] ideas."[22] In the opinion of Khalid al-'Azm, Syria's defense minister before the Union, the party's fidelity to Nasir in the initial period of the union stemmed from the many powers given to the Ba'th in Syria by Nasir, which allowed it to become the dominant political group in the country in the first year of the union.[23] On the other hand, Nasir's reliance on the Ba'th in that period could have stemmed from a belief, inflated by Ba'thist leaders, in the party's stature as the backbone of the popular forces supporting unity in Syria.[24] But bitter disappointment was soon to come to both Nasir and the Ba'th.

Ba'thist hopes of at least sharing power with Nasir had diminished considerably by mid-1959. Salah Bitar was to put the blame for those dashed hopes on Nasir for his failure "to accept a necessary association of other progressive leaders in the management of the Arab cause and its policies."[25] By the same token, the Ba'th seemed to have a somewhat elasticized notion of the meaning of

---

[21] Quoted in Malik Mufti, *Sovereign Creations: Pan-Arabism and Political Order in Syria and Iraq* (Ithaca, New York: Cornell University Press, 1996), p. 95.

[22] From an interview with Salah Bitar by the British journalist Robert Stephens. See Robert Stephens, *Nasser: A Political Biography* (London: Allen Lane / Penguin Press, 1971), p. 333.

[23] Khalid al-'Azm, *Mudhakarat Khalid al-'Azm, al-Jusi' al-Thalith* (Memoirs of Khalid al-'Azm, volume three) (Beirut: al-Dar al-Muttahida li al-Nashr, 1973), pp. 167–168.

[24] Sami Gawhar, *al-Samitun yatakalamun: 'Abd al-Nasir wa Madhbahat al-Ikhwan* (The silent speak: 'Abd al-Nasir and the massacre of the brotherhood) (Cairo: al-Maktab al-Musri al-Hadith, 1975), p. 114.

[25] Stephens, *Nasser: A Political Biography*, p. 343; On the subject of Ba'thist hopes to lead through 'Abd al-Nasir, see Mattar, *Bisaraha 'an 'Abd al-Nasir* (Frankly on 'Abd al-Nasir), pp. 137–138.

sharing. For instance, Ba'thist ministers in the northern region (Syria) embarked on appointing mostly Ba'thist personnel in their respective ministries, a practice that led to widespread dissension among the large numbers of employees not affiliated with the party. Nasir responded by insisting on a nonpartisan committee that would oversee all appointments to ensure the absence of ideological bias. This, the Ba'th took as a sign of Egyptian hostility to the party.[26] Ba'thist resentment began to seep through to the party's adherents within the Syrian army. Such murmurings were bound to reach Nasir's ear, as a result of which forty Syrian officers, twenty of whom were Ba'thists, were transferred to Egypt.[27]

On the level of the political leadership, the first ominous sign for the Ba'th appeared as early as October 1958 with Nasir's announcement of his first UAR cabinet. This included only fourteen Syrians among thirty-four members, with all the key posts going to Egyptians. During 1959, the Ba'thists frequently complained of being decreasingly consulted by the Egyptians, and that an effort was being made to cut them off from their political base in Syria.[28] In the elections of the Syrian National Union in July 1959, the Ba'th Party could only manage 5 percent of the seats, subsequently accusing the Egyptian leadership and its supporters in Syria of rigging the elections against them.[29] By December, the conflict between Nasir and the Ba'th had become irreconcilable. Without consulting their Syrian governmental colleagues, leading Ba'thist cabinet ministers resigned from the central and regional cabinets

[26] Sulayman al-Madani, *Haula' Hakamu Suriya, 1918–1970* (Those who governed Syria, 1918–1970) (Beirut: Dar al-Anwar, 1996), pp. 121–122; Nasr, *'Abd al-Nasir wa Tajribat al-Wuhda* ('Abd al-Nasir and the unity experiment), p. 149.

[27] Nasr, *'Abd al-Nasir wa Tajribat al-Wuhda* ('Abd al-Nasir and the unity experiment), p. 150; al-Madani, *Haula' Hakamu Suriya* (Those who governed Syria), p. 122.

[28] *Al-Ahram* (Cairo), November 17, 1961.

[29] A Ba'thist supporter, however, argues that the deteriorating economic conditions brought about by Egyptian bureaucratic socialism, was blamed on the Ba'th by the Syrian population which resulted in the Party's poor electoral performance. See Nagi 'Abd al-Nabi Bazi, *Suriya: Sira' al-Istiqtab: Dirasa wa Tahlil li Ahdath al-Sharq al-Awsat wa al-Tadakhulat al-Duwaliya fi al-Ahdath al-Suriya, 1917–1973* (Syria: the struggle of polarization; a study and analysis of Middle Eastern affairs and international interventions in Syrian affairs, 1917–1973) (Damascus: Dar Ibn al-'Arabi, 1996), p. 309.

of the UAR.[30] During the following two years, the Ba'th became one of the harshest critics of Nasir's rule in Syria.

The resignation of such Ba'thist luminaries as Salah Bitar and Akram Hourani was a major blow not just to the UAR, but also to the Arab nationalist movement in the region as a whole. What the UAR had succeeded in doing was to provide a unified goal for the various nationalist groups in the Arab world. The Ba'thist resignations split the movement between the Ba'thists on the one hand, and the other nationalist groups, such as the Nasirists, George Habash's group, *Harakat al-Qawmiyeen al-'Arab* (the Arab Nationalists Movement), and a host of unaffiliated nationalists. In fact, it led to some defections from within the Ba'th Party, most notably the Party's two elder statesmen in Iraq and Jordan, Fuad al-Rikabi and 'Abdullah al-Rimawi. All this resulted in weakening the Arab nationalist movement. Nasir admitted as much. Reflecting on the experience of the UAR, Nasir said in 1963: "The resignation of the Ba'thist Cabinet members was a major mistake, and I have the courage to tell you that my precipitant acceptance of these resignations also was a major mistake."[31]

Beyond the Ba'th, more groups and constituencies who had vigorously supported the Union were having second thoughts. The Syrians had imagined the UAR as a union of equals under the leadership of Nasir. The problem was that for all intents and purposes, there could be no equality between a country of twenty-six million people and another of four million people. Syria had little choice but to follow in Egypt's shadow, and to do things the way Egyptians did them. Especially distressing to the Syrians was the spectacle of their administrative, legislative, and military systems being gradually absorbed into Egypt's.

What ultimately was most destabilizing for the UAR was the growing Syrian resentment of the wholesale military changes and transfers directed at the Syrian officer corps. One of the most embittered was General 'Afif al-Bizri, who, as Syria's chief of staff, liter-

---

[30] Ahmad 'Abd al-Karim, *Hisad: Sineen Khasiba wa thimar Murra* (Harvest: fertile years and bitter fruit) (Beirut: Baysan, 1994), pp. 405–407.

[31] Sa'id, *'Iraq 8 Shibat, 1963* (Iraq of 8 February, 1963), fn. 1, pp. 214–215.

ally forced the concept of total merger between Egypt and Syria on recalcitrant politicians. Yet shortly after the announcement of the UAR, his objection to Egyptian-inspired command changes in the Syrian army allowed Nasir to remove this leftist army officer. Bizri retaliated by sending an urgent message to Iraq's General Qasim urging him not to join the UAR "in which the Syrians had lost their independence and their very being."[32] Hafiz al-Asad, later to rule Syria for thirty years until his death in 2000, related his own resentment when as a young air force officer he had just returned from a training stint in Moscow to discover that the Aleppo Air Academy, where he had won his wings, had been transferred to Egypt, together with part of the Homs Military College. Asad found that "the Syrian officer corps was buzzing with stories of sackings, transfers and slights at the hands of the overbearing Egyptians."[33]

As the early euphoria in Syria subsided and the indignation of key elements of Syrian society increased, Nasir responded by depending more on a small circle of operatives in his intelligence and security services. By the summer of 1959, Colonel 'Abd al-Hamid Saraj, the head of the universally feared and detested security apparatus, the *Duxieme Bureau*, had become Syria's most powerful political figure. Some of Nasir's most ardent and loyal supporters were warning him of Saraj's excesses and stifling authoritarianism. Riad Taha, a prominent Lebanese journalist, and sometimes a Nasir confidant, writes in his memoirs that as early as June 1959, he told Nasir that the UAR was no longer secure, since even those who had supported him were beginning to hold back. Taha pointedly told Nasir: "when the Syrians gathered around you, they thought they would no longer live in a police state, yet they are living under Hamid al-Saraj." He then reminded the president that "the Syrians had tasted democratic freedoms in the past, and grown accustomed to them."[34] But to no avail. Nasir's successes

---

[32] See Riad Taha, *Qissat al-Wuhda wa al-Infisal: Tajribat Insan 'Arabi khilal Ahdath 1955–1961* (The story of unity and secession: the experience of an Arab person during the events of 1955–1961) (Beirut: Dar al-Afaq al-Jadida, 1974), p. 141.

[33] Patrick Seale, *Asad of Syria: The Struggle for the Middle East* (Berkeley: University of California Press, 1988), p. 59.

[34] Taha, *Qissat al-Wuhda wa al-Infisal* (The story of unity and secession), pp. 145–146.

thus far had been built not on political pluralism, but on an authoritarianism centered on one man; his own proclivity then was for a strong and centralizing authoritarian rule. In a later remark to an Iraqi delegation, Nasir dismissed the notion of the "separation of powers," calling it a "major deception," and declaring that in reality it simply could not exist.[35] Added to all this was Nasir's conviction in the sheer anarchy of Syrian society and politics. Consequently, rather than heed the advise of his Syrian supporters, Nasir gave Saraj even more powers, essentially tying the future stability of Syria and the UAR to the savagery of Saraj's "iron rule." Ex-President Shukri al-Quwatly, the man who in February 1958 had stood with Nasir basking in the adulation of the Syrian masses, later would remark that "the Nasserite system relegated the majority of the (Syrian) population to the rank of traitors, governing by terror and trampling on the honor and dignity of citizens."[36] Even the Egyptian journalist, Muhamed Hasaneen Haykal, Nasir's close friend and confidant, when enumerating the reasons for the eventual failure of the UAR, pointed the finger at the excessively repressive police system created by Saraj. In Haykal's words, the coercive machinery of Nasir's protégé and right-hand man in Syria had taken "the form of a severe and destructive cancer."[37] He could have added however that it was a cancer that his president and friend seemed content to live with.

On top of all the political maladies, the economic problems were mounting too. Syria's economy had been built on private enterprise with very little intrusion by the state. Three years prior to the Egyptian-Syrian merger, a report by the International Bank for Reconstruction and Development (IBRD) concluded that one of the main features of what the Bank described as Syria's rapid economic development was that it had been "almost wholly due to private enterprise."[38] Joining with Egypt in the UAR, however, meant that

[35] Sa'id, '*Iraq 8 Shibat, 1963* (Iraq of 8 February, 1963), fn. 1, p. 213.

[36] Malcolm Kerr, *The Arab Cold War: Gamal Abd al-Nasser and his rivals, 1958–1970*, 3rd ed. (London: Oxford University Press, 1971), p. 34.

[37] *Al-Ahram* (Cairo), November 24, 1961.

[38] Mufti, *Sovereign Creations*, p. 58.

Syria would have to conform to the socialist principle of state control of the economy which was practiced by Egypt. But the Syrian business class could not accept Nasir's economic restrictions as readily as its Egyptian counterpart. Moreover, with Cairo becoming the UAR capital, Syrian businessmen had to obtain their licenses and permits in the Egyptian city. As though it was not enough to deal with an already inhospitable environment, the Syrians had to travel to the Egyptian capital, and once there, had to navigate through the maze of Egypt's bureaucratic conundrum, a far cry from the personal and direct relationship that had existed in pre-union Syria between business and government.[39] And because of the cumbersome political structure that Nasir created less for its efficiency and more to cater for the sensitivities of both parties,[40] the Syrian businessmen could not count on the Syrian ministers in the Central Cabinet in Cairo to solve their problems.[41] Very soon money began to leave Syria for European capitals, which only added to the deterioration of Syria's economic conditions.[42] The disaffection of Syria's businessmen mirrored the earlier alienation of the country's landowning class. The Agrarian Reform Law, promulgated in September 1958 to bring Syria in line with Egypt, was greeted with much resentment by Syria's powerful landowners, and the situation was not helped by a succession of bad harvests that resulted in severe shortages of basic commodities.

In the midst of these mounting problems in Syria, a regional crisis, involving Nasir's Iraqi nemesis 'Abd al-Karim Qasim, erupted suddenly. The crisis presented Nasir with some uncomfortable choices relating to the meaning and intent of Arab nationalism and Arab unity. The affair began auspiciously with the agreement in June 1961 between Britain and the ruler of Kuwait for an end to the status of the small Gulf sheikhdom as a British protectorate. Kuwaiti celebrations were cut short abruptly when a few days after

[39] 'Abd al-Karim, *Hisad (Harvest)*, pp. 397–403.
[40] Sayed Mare'i, *Awraq Siyasiya* (Political papers) (Cairo: al-Maktab al-Musri al-Hadith, 1978), pp. 400–402.
[41] 'Abd al-Karim, *Hisad (Harvest)*, p. 403.
[42] Bazi, *Suriya: Sira' al-Istiqtab* (Syria: the struggle of polarization), p. 311.

the announcement of the agreement, Qasim in a major speech not only withheld his recognition of the new state, but made it clear that he intended to return Kuwait to its former status under Ottoman rule as an integral part of Iraq.[43] Adding insult to injury, Qasim appointed the ruler of the oil-rich sheikhdom mayor of Kuwait, a position that carried a salary of about $500 a month! Disarmed by Qasim's announcement, the Kuwaiti ruler requested immediate British protection, and on July 1, British troops began to pour into Kuwait. Simultaneously, Egypt took the lead to hasten Kuwaiti entry into the Arab League, thus legitimizing Kuwaiti sovereignty. The League also sanctioned the dispatch of Arab forces made up of Egyptian, Jordanian, and Saudi troops to replace the British. By September, the crisis had fizzled.[44] Any threat of an Iraqi military operation had dissipated,[45] and the bulk of the international community had extended diplomatic recognition to Kuwait.

While Nasir could take comfort in his role in what turned out to be a thoroughly humiliating affair for his Iraqi enemy, the Kuwaiti crisis, nevertheless, did present him with some uncomfortable issues. After all, Kuwait was hardly a shining light on the Arab nationalist path. Rich, backward, and ruled by a despotic and feudalist order, Kuwait was all that the UAR president professed to detest and struggle against. And Iraq, regardless of Nasir's contempt for Qasim, was considered a "progressive" country. In his declared crusade against "Arab reaction," and in his commitment to revolutionary "Arab unity," Nasir could have been expected to support the Iraqi position. After all, Egypt's behavior in the region

[43] *SWB*, June 27, 1961, p. 9. Thirty years later after making exactly the same claim, another Iraqi dictator, Saddam Husayn, would suffer a devastating military defeat at the hand of an international coalition led by the United States.

[44] Marr, *The Modern History of Iraq*, pp. 180–181.

[45] In fact, there never was any military threat. Immediately after Qasim's announcement, the commander of the southern military air base at Shu'aiba, Air Force Colonel 'Isam Dawisha, flew to Baghdad to receive what he thought would be orders for some kind of a military operation. He was surprised however to hear the commander-in-chief of the Iraqi air force, Brigadier Jalal al-Awqati, tell him to be very careful not to allow any Iraqi plane to penetrate Kuwaiti air space. When Dawisha cited Qasim's speech, al-Awqati replied: "Don't take notice of this madman. You think the English would just let us walk into Kuwait?" Conversation with the author's father, Air Force Colonel 'Isam Dawisha.

rested on the maxim that revolutionary and progressive countries should not be impeded by "outdated" notions of boundaries and sovereignty in carrying out their revolutionary mission.[46] However, deeply hostile to Qasimite rule, the Egyptian leadership declared its support of Kuwait's right to safeguard its independence and self-determination. Later on, Egypt faced a further dilemma in its declared policy goals when the military forces of "imperialist" Britain landed in Kuwait. This meant that "while supporting the Kuwaiti people against Qasim's stupidity, [Egypt] also supported the Iraqi people against the British concentrations near them."[47] The net result was yet another affirmation that unity schemes, whether entered freely or through coercion, would succeed only with the participation, or at a minimum the blessings, of Egypt.

Nasir's victory over Qasim was dimmed by the situation in Syria, in which deteriorating economic conditions were compounding a rapidly worsening political situation and adding to mounting political tensions within the Syrian armed forces. Nasir became convinced that the merchants, landowners, and other members of the capitalist classes, abetted by the conservative and pro-West regimes of Saudi Arabia and Jordan, were behind all the trouble, purposely undermining the economy in order to weaken the UAR. He decided that efforts at compromise and coexistence were no longer tenable. Nasir thus embarked on a sweeping socialization of the economy. The whole of the cotton trade was taken over, and all import-export firms were brought under public control. All banks, insurance companies, heavy industry, and most medium-sized and light industries were nationalized. Maximum land ownership was halved to a hundred feddans (about 104 acres), and no income in any organization was allowed to exceed $14,350. These measures were the straw that broke the camel's back for these for-

[46] See for example, *al-Ahram* (Cairo), December 29, 1961; *al-Ahram* (Cairo), October 19, 1962; *al-Muharir* (Beirut), April 2, 1963. Nasir, however, was cognizant of the dilemma of on the one hand conducting normal state to state relations, and on the other hand, asserting the primacy of nationalism's right to disregard notions of political sovereignty. For this consult the United Arab Republic, *The Charter* (Cairo: Information Department, 1962), pp. 78–79.

[47] *Khutab*, volume five, p. 501.

midable economic interests. The estrangement of Syrian capitalism was now complete.[48] The financial and landowning classes began to work actively with other disgruntled elements inside Syria as well as with Egypt's adversaries abroad.[49] It is instructive that an official statement put out on Radio Damascus shortly after Syria's secession declared that a major bone of contention was "the Syrian economy [which] had developed through the efforts of individual activity."[50] On September 28, the Syrian army made its move.

Initially, the Syrian secessionist officers claimed that they demanded no more than some reforms within the Syrian armed forces.[51] They reiterated their loyalty to the UAR under Nasir's presidency, and they asked for an audience with Marshall 'Abd al-Hakim 'Amer, the Egyptian Commander-in-Chief of the UAR armed forces, who was then in Damascus. The negotiations yielded a communiqué which was broadcast on Syrian radio emphasizing that military reforms were going to be enacted as a result of the military move, and that the confidence of the Syrian army in the leadership of the UAR was unshakeable. Whether this had been a mere ploy,[52] or whether the officers began to fear an impending military response from Egypt,[53] Radio Damascus soon broadcast another communiqué negating the earlier one, and effectively declaring a military coup against those "who humiliated

[48] Muhamed Hasaneen Haykal argues that the Syrian capitalists supported the establishment of the UAR because they sought a strong government that would fight Communist influence in Syria and provide the country with much needed political stability that would be conducive for increased economic activity. Once al-Nasir introduced his socialist measures, Haykal says, the Syrian merchants and businessmen changed their tune arguing that Syria could not survive without a vibrant commercial environment, and that what worked for Egypt would not work for Syria. See Haykal, *Ma Alathi Jara fi Suriya* (What happened in Syria), pp. 65–66.

[49] Hamroush, *Qissat Thawrat 23 Yuliyu* (The story of the 23 July revolution), pp. 88–89; see also *SWB*, October 4, 1961, p. 12.

[50] *SWB*, October 3, 1961, p. 5.

[51] The following details are taken from the account by Salah Nasr, who was Nasir's intelligence chief. See Nasr, *'Abd al-Nasir wa Tajribat al-Wuhda* ('Abd al-Nasir and the unity experiment), pp. 257–268.

[52] Al-Madani, *Haula' Hakamu Suriya* (Those who governed Syria), p. 142; Nasr, *'Abd al-Nasir wa Tajribat al-Wuhda* ('Abd al-Nasir and the unity experiment), p. 260.

[53] Bazi, *Suriya: Sira' al-Istiqtab* (Syria: the struggle of polarization), p. 320.

Syria and degraded her army."[54] This theme was repeated a number of times in the days following the coup,[55] probably because the coup leaders quickly realized that support for the coup fell short of their expectations.

Even though the coup was popular among Syria's socioeconomic and political elite, it was by no stretch of the imagination a popular revolution. To begin with, a number of military units, especially those in Aleppo and Latakia, continued throughout the day of the rebellion to broadcast their loyalty to the UAR. Only after protracted negotiations with the secessionist officers and the realization that much blood would be shed did they agree to join the revolt. Then there were large and widespread demonstrations against the secession in the streets of the main Syrian cities, in which many demonstrators were killed and injured by the secessionist army units.[56] Quiet returned only after Nasir declared that he would not intervene in Syria. But it was a quiet born not of consent but of sadness and dismay. True, a number of Arab countries were very pleased with Syria's secession. Jordan could not hide its glee, and immediately recognized the new regime, to be followed by equally jubilant Saudi Arabia and Iraq. However, the satisfaction of Husayn, Sa'ud, and Qasim was not shared by the majority of Arabs. Most people in Arab cities and towns listened to the news with aggrieved silence.

Momentous as it was, the Syrian secession did not mean the end of the Arab nationalist movement. Wounded, the nationalist spirit continued to live on. So ingrained had it become, that whatever their ideological persuasion, Arab leaders as a matter of course, could not but pay lip service to the nationalist goal of uniting the

---

[54] *Times* (London), September 29, 1961. Seemingly believing that this was a winning theme, the new Syrian rulers kept going back to it in the days following the coup.

[55] See, for example, *SWB*, October 1, 1961, p. 10; *SWB*, October 4, p. 12; *SWB*, October 6, p. 9.

[56] For the widespread resistance to the Syrian coup, see Mattar, *Bisraha 'an 'Abd al-Nasir* (Frankly on 'Abd al-Nasir), pp. 142–143; Nasr, *'Abd al-Nasir wa Tajribat al-Wuhda* ('Abd al-Nasir and the unity experiment), 261–262, 271; Eberhard Kienle, "Arab Unity Schemes Revisited: Interest, Identity and Policy in Syria and Egypt," *International Journal of Middle East Studies*, vol. 27, no. 1 (February 1995): 57.

Arab people and their countries. Soon after seceding from the UAR, the new Syrian prime minister, Ma'moun al-Kuzbari, announced his government's plan to pursue an Arab union.[57] It might well have been a rhetorical flourish, but the man was responding to what he knew lay firmly in his people's hearts. Similarly, numerous Syrian politicians, including the Ba'thist leader Akram Hourani, who had lent his name to the secessionist cause, issued a communiqué advocating a comprehensive unity based on socialist and democratic principles.[58] It was an effort to publicly cleanse their reputations of past sins, and to try to reclaim their nationalist credentials by reaffirming their commitment to Arab unity.

By no means dead, Arab nationalism still did suffer a very serious setback. If Iraq's refusal to join the UAR was the first dent in Arab nationalism's seemingly impregnable armor, the dissolution of the UAR was a significant fracture. Only three years earlier in the summer and fall of 1958, people from around the Arab world had filled the streets, euphoric in the hope that the actual union of two states and the very real possibility of two, even three, more joining in would become the very foundation upon which comprehensive Arab unity would be built. Now in the fall of 1961, all they could do was to shake their heads at the debris, and dream of what might have been. Nor could they, as they had become accustomed to, turn to their hero for deliverance, for even the biggest dreamer or the most loyal supporter could not but treat the secession as a major defeat for Nasir and if not a devastating, then a significant, blow to his prestige as the unifying symbol of Arab nationalism and the acknowledged impresario of the Arab nationalist march.

Nasir himself well appreciated the extent of the setback. His eyes almost welling with tears, he described Syria's secession as more dangerous an assault on Arab nationalism than the tripartite attack on Egypt during the 1956 Suez Crisis.[59] It was not merely the loss

[57] Kienle, "Arab Unity Schemes Revisited: Interest, Identity and Policy in Syria and Egypt, p. 55.

[58] Ibid.

[59] *Speeches, 1961*, p. 243; Stephens, *Nasser*, p. 341; Anthony Nutting, *Nasser* (London: Constable, 1972), p. 267.

of Syria that weighed heavily on his heart; it was the impetus the secession gave to those who had vowed to fight the rising Arab nationalist tide and to stop it from achieving its ultimate goal of Arab unity. The "Arab reactionaries," as Nasir called them, would take heart from the secession and would now go on the offensive against Arab nationalism.[60] But he insisted that Arab nationalism would never be defeated, and that the UAR (Nasir had decided not to change the name) would continue to carry the nationalist torch, and carry it vigorously and purposefully. In May 1962, Nasir enunciated a new radical National Charter. In it, he declared angrily and, to his adversaries, ominously:

> The United Arab Republic, firmly convinced that she is an integral part of the Arab nation, must propagate her call for unity and the principles it embodies, so that it would be at the disposal of every Arab citizen, without hesitating for one moment before the outworn argument that this would be considered a interference in the affairs of others.[61]

The so-called reactionaries, buoyed by the mishaps that befell Nasir, accepted the challenge and mounted their own campaign against Nasir's nationalism, now generally equated with "communism" and "Soviet socialism."[62] The Saudis, drawing on their status as the guardians of al-Ka'ba, Islam's holiest shrine, came up with their own "Islamic Charter," which criticized "fake nationalism based on atheistic doctrine."[63] The Islamic Charter represented not just a blunt denunciation of Nasir's Arab nationalism, but also an invitation to other Arabs and Muslims to consider an alternative ideational path. The Islamic alternative also came with a seductive financial-inducement package, in which the Saudis opened their wallets, overflowing with "petro-dollars," in order to help open the eyes of the doubters to the true path. By now, the balance of

[60] See for example, *Speeches, 1961*, pp. 285–286; *SWB*, October 4, 1961, p. 12; *al-Jumhuriya* (Cairo), October 30, 1961; *Speeches, 1961*, pp. 347–361.

[61] The United Arab Republic, *The Charter*, p. 79.

[62] See *SWB*, March 20, 1962, p. 14; *SWB*, February 16, 1962, p. 8; *SWB*, July 18, 1962, p. 12.

[63] Tom Little, *Modern Egypt* (London: Ernest Benn, 1967), p. 199.

forces at the "state," if not the "popular" level, seemed to favor
the foes of the champion of Arab nationalism. This was readily
apparent in the Arab League meeting in the Lebanese resort town
of Shtoura in August 1962. Once assembled, the Syrians accused
the Egyptians of interfering in Syria's internal affairs, a claim
readily and vigorously supported by the Saudi, Jordanian, and
Iraqi delegations. Civility was thrown to the wall, and the Arab
multitude was treated to the spectacle of middle-aged men, many
balding and overweight, throwing punches and chairs at one another. The unseemly fracas necessitated the intervention of the Lebanese police. The indignant Egyptians walked out of the meeting,
alone and isolated, and the Arab nationalist march walked alongside, dispirited and in disarray.

To the nationalist generation these were indeed depressing times.
The Arab world was bitterly divided, as far from comprehensive
unity as it has ever been. The conservative Arab leaders, who had
been contemptuously dismissed by the nationalists as "reactionaries" ready to be elbowed out into historical oblivion, seemed to
be on the ascendancy in the prevailing "Arab Cold War."[64] What
was even more distressing was that this group was backed by the
"progressive" Qasim of Iraq and Bourguiba of Tunisia, who while
not perceived by the nationalists as reactionary, nevertheless were
ardent upholders of *wataniya*, of the sanctity of their states against
the *qawmi* force of Arab nationalism.

It was in this period of stagnation for Arab nationalism, with
hardly a glimmer of a light at the end of the tunnel, that on September 26, a group of army officers seized power in Yemen, one of the
most backward countries in the Arab world, shortly after the death
of the absolute ruler, Imam Ahmad, and proclaimed the birth of
the Yemeni Republic. The leader of the military putsch, Brigadier
'Abdallah al-Sallal, immediately cabled Nasir depicting the coup as
a social movement against reaction and tyranny, and as a political
movement dedicated to the Arab nationalist goal of comprehensive

[64] The term was coined by Malcolm Kerr.

Arab unity.[65] Cairo waited only a couple of days until the Egyptian leadership became convinced that "the revolution represented . . . the free Yemeni will,"[66] before recognizing the infant republic. A nationalist revolution in one of the most backward countries in the Arab world, which also happened to border on Saudi Arabia, constituted a huge shot in the arm for Nasir and radical Arab nationalism.

By the same token, however, the Yemeni revolution represented a great danger to the stability of Saudi Arabia. "Within twenty-four hours of the revolution," Nasir would later say, "it became evident that King Sa'ud would not keep quiet."[67] Saudi resolve was strengthened when after an early uncertain period, it transpired that Imam Badr, the son of Ahmad, had escaped to the mountains of Yemen, where he embarked on gathering support from the northern tribes. Saudi Arabia immediately promised money and arms. The leaders of the coup responded by requesting Egyptian help. Nasir, believing that only limited military support was required, decided on September 30 to dispatch trainers, advisers, and military equipment to San'a, Yemen's capital. What he did not know at the time was that he had taken the very first steps toward embroiling the Egyptian armed forces in a protracted conflict that would last for over five inconclusive years, and which would have a debilitating impact on Egypt's morale and economy. Before the end of the year, the number of Egyptian troops had risen from one hundred to eight thousand; and it did not take long for the Egyptian General Staff to realize that the main brunt of the war would have to be borne by the Egyptians. In 1963, the number of Egyptian troops in Yemen rose to twenty thousand, then it increased to forty thousand in 1964, and reached a staggering seventy thousand in 1965. Nasir would later admit that his Yemeni venture was "a miscalculation; we never thought that it would lead to what it did."[68]

What were the bases for this "miscalculation"? To begin with, Cairo was duped by the early signs of huge popular support for

[65] *SWB*, October 1, 1962, p. 4.
[66] *Al-Ahram* (Cairo), October 19, 1962.
[67] *Speeches, 1962*, pp. 258–259.
[68] Interview with *Look*, March 4, 1968, reported in *Times* (London), March 5, 1968.

the military move in San'a. Haykal wrote that "when it became clear that all the people were with the revolution, the UAR gave it its full support."[69] But that betrayed a total misunderstanding of Yemeni demographics and geography.[70] The support for the coup came predominantly from the populations of the cities and southern plains. But the inhabitants of the northern mountains and the western desert were fiercely loyal to the Imam whom they considered to be their potentate as well as the hallowed Commander of the Faithful. These people were tribal, less open to the world, and warlike. And the mountainous terrain they inhabited made it extraordinarily arduous for an adversary to defeat them.

And then there was the abiding and unwavering conviction among nationalists in the universal appeal of Arab nationalism. Intellectually, the Egyptian leaders, and indeed all those who believed in Arab nationalism, had always separated the people from their rulers, believing fervently that if left to their own devices, the people would indubitably join the nationalist march. The popular response to Egypt's Arab nationalist policies over the Baghdad Pact, the Suez Crisis, and the formation of the UAR, as well as the widespread and spontaneous pro-UAR demonstrations that erupted in Syria in the immediate wake of the secessionist coup, confirmed this leadership-people divide in the minds of the Egyptian leaders. Nasir and his colleagues simply refused to accept that people whom they believed had been made by their reactionary leaders to live in thirteenth-century conditions would refuse to join the nationalist march and its modernizing ways.[71] That the people of Yemen had not expressed a vociferous and public desire to do so was to the Egyptians no more than a function of the tyrannical rule under which they labored. While that view was perhaps true in the cities and among the swelling ranks of the literate middle classes, it was less true among the people of the countryside, and particularly among groups harboring strong tribal identity and liv-

---

[69] *Al-Ahram* (Cairo), October 19, 1962.

[70] It is interesting to note that the similar misreading of geography and demography led to the American and Soviet debacles in Vietnam and Afghanistan, respectively.

[71] *Al-Ahram* (Cairo), December 12, 1961.

ing in geographically isolated areas. While Arab nationalism had indeed made impressive inroads into traditional values and belief systems, it was pure wishful thinking to believe that in every corner of the Arab world, minds had been changed and centuries-old outlooks had been transformed. It was far too premature to pronounce the demise of traditional habits and ways, or to declare the victory of modernity; certainly not among the tribes in the northern mountains of Yemen. And by the time the Egyptian troops finally withdrew in December 1967, the debilitating war had alienated many Egyptians from the ideal of Arab nationalism, cementing an isolationist impulse not to get mired in the quicksand of Arab politics. To Arab nationalists generally, the disappointment at the unsuccessful prosecution of the Yemeni war tarnished further the halo of invincibility that accompanied the Arab nationalist tide during its glory days between 1955 and 1958.

But that was not yet the pervasive feeling in early 1963. On the contrary, in the few months following Egypt's decision to intervene on the side of the Yemeni Republicans, when hopes were still high that the defeat of the "reactionaries" was at hand, Nasir's prestige as the only true defender of Arab nationalist principles soared, and with that, Arab nationalism seemed to regain some of the momentum and aura it had lost with the Syrian secession. A further victory was achieved when four Saudi princes and seven air force pilots, followed by the commander-in-chief of the Jordanian air force and two of his officers, defected to Cairo.

The process was crowned in February and March of 1963, when military coups in Baghdad and Damascus eradicated two political orders most hostile to Nasir's leadership of Arab nationalism. The two coups brought in Ba'thist leaderships, who, proclaiming their fidelity to the Arab nationalist creed, took the initiative in approaching Nasir to discuss plans for a tripartite unity amongst Egypt, Syria, and Iraq. On March 14, talks on possible unity began in Cairo.

It was evident that the Ba'thist approach to Nasir was made as much for domestic legitimation and stability as for devotion to

Arab nationalism and Arab unity.[72] To the new leaders in Damascus and Baghdad, unity with Egypt would constitute "the biggest political act [they] could take back to their people."[73] A member of the Syrian delegation admitted to the overriding motivation of the new rulers in Damascus with surprising veracity: "Sir, in all frankness, we . . . wish to exploit your excellency's name. Without a doubt. That's all there is to it. We are speaking openly."[74] Neither coup was on a sure footing. Both had disaffected constituencies back home, thus each needed the endorsement of the still magical name of Nasir.

The Iraqi and Syrian Ba'thists sought Nasir's prestige, but disdained his political control. They were especially cautious about the form of the proposed unity. Learning from the experience of 1958, they rejected organic amalgamation. The Iraqis appeared burdened by their country's special condition, with its various ethnic and sectarian dislocations. Consequently, they advocated the creation of a federal arrangement that would be called the United Arab State.[75] The Syrians, cognizant of their experience in the UAR, shared this vision of loose association. After reiterating the obligatory Ba'thist cliché of "we are one people and one community from the ocean to the Gulf," Salah Bitar tempered it with the admission that the Ba'thists nevertheless did not "negate the existence of regions."[76] In Ba'thist tortuous lexicon, "regions" meant "states."

---

[72] For instance, shortly after the announcement of the Syrian military coup was made on the radio, widespread demonstrations filled the streets demanding the immediate restoration of the United Arab Republic. See Bazi, *Suriya: Sira' al-Istiqtab* (Syria: the struggle of polarization), p. 332.

[73] Al-Jumhuriya al-'Arabiya al-Muttahida, *Mahadhir Jalsat Mubahathat al-Wuhda* (Proceedings of the meetings on the discussions of unity) (Cairo: National Printing and Publishing House, 1963) (hereafter cited as *Mahadhir*), p. 574. The proceedings were published in Cairo soon after the negotiations broke down and recriminations began. Talib Shabib, a leading member of the Iraqi delegation, confirms that, notwithstanding some minor details, the Egyptian published account is generally accurate. See Sa'id, *Iraq 8 Shibat, 1963* (Iraq of 8 February, 1963), p. 220. The Syrian participants Sami al-Jundi and Jamal Attasi also vouch to the general accuracy of the published proceedings. See Bazi, *Suriya: Sira' al-Istiqtab* (Syria: the struggle of polarization).

[74] Quoted in Mufti, *Sovereign Creations*, p. 149.

[75] Sa'id, *Iraq 8 Shibat, 1963* (Iraq of 8 February, 1963), fn. 1, p. 208.

[76] Mufti, *Sovereign Creations*, pp. 151–152.

On their side, the Egyptians approached the talks with the utmost mistrust, a wariness that dated back to the collective resignation of the Ba'thist ministers from the UAR cabinet in December 1959; to the endorsement by Salah Bitar and Akram Hourani of Syria's secession; and to alleged Ba'thist activities in the Egyptian army that were aimed at creating an anti-Nasir movement. Nasir lambasted the Ba'thist negotiators for "facilitating the secession" and trying to "influence the situation in Egypt itself in the delicate period that followed the secession." He considered the behavior of the Ba'th "to be a crime."[77] So suspicious was Nasir that he continuously questioned the real motive of the two Ba'thist delegations in seeking a tripartite unity. Was it to place Egypt between the Syrian hammer and the Iraqi anvil?[78] In light of this abiding suspicion, and in order to safeguard Egypt's central position in any such union, Nasir focused consistently throughout the talks on the anticipated role of the political leadership of the projected union.[79] The Ba'thists endeavored to reassure him by proposing a leadership structure that would include one member of each country independently of Nasir who would be the chairman. In this way, as one Syrian delegate pointedly put it, "the problem of being caught between the hammer and the anvil . . . would not arise."[80] But the secessionist experience had left an indelible mark on Nasir. His seemingly endless mistrust of the Syrians became the dominant ob-

[77] *Mahadhir*, p. 7.

[78] *Mahadhir*, p. 124; see also Sa'id, *Iraq 8 Shibat, 1963* (Iraq of 8 February, 1963), p. 220. Talib Shabib, Iraq's foreign minister and a member of the Iraqi delegation, recounts that the existence of two Ba'thist votes to one Egyptian weighed heavily on Nasir's calculations throughout the duration of the talks. Nasir initially suggested that Egypt and Syria unite first and then as one entity deal with Iraq. When this was rejected, he suggested an Iraqi-Syrian merger into one entity. Throughout this, the Ba'thists persisted in demanding some form of tripartite union. See Sa'id, *Iraq 8 Shibat 1963* (Iraq of 8 February, 1963), pp. 213–214.

[79] *Mahadhir*, p. 20. It is interesting to note that this concern to be the top dog in any union seems to be the staple of authoritarian leadership. In 1979, when Iraq and Syria were discussing the possibility of some unity arrangement, Saddam Husayn, addressing a conference of Iraqi ambassadors, said he welcomed unity "if we were in control." After all, he added, "the country that is bigger and has greater resources and wealth must be in control, and Baghdad should be the capital of the union." See Sa'id, *Iraq 8 Shibat, 1963* (Iraq of 8 February, 1963), fn. 1, p. 208.

[80] *Mahadhir*, p. 217.

stacle to any constructive move toward unity. He even suspected that the Syrians would "try to turn the Iraqis against us,"[81] and he predicted in a kind of self-fulfilling prophecy, that as a result of inevitable future disagreements with the Syrian Ba'thists, "Egypt will withdraw from the unity before four months had elapsed."[82] With all this suspicion and mistrust, only the loosest of unity arrangements could be expected to emerge. Consequently on April 17, a declaration announced a transitory period of two years of close cooperation, at the end of which a federal constitution would be promulgated.

While this skeletal and rather vacuous arrangement fell far short of nationalist expectations, the announcement of the accord was met with much elation, and "crowds swarmed the streets throughout much of the Arab world, shouting, Nasser, Nasser!"[83] As with every upsurge in nationalist sentiment, the one Arab ruler who took the full brunt of the tripartite unity announcement was Jordan's Hashemite monarch, who once again had to resort to harsh methods to quell the popular fury which erupted in the streets of his capital.[84] Husayn's response was predictable, but the Arab leadership that ended up being most perturbed by the unity was paradoxically the very one that had sought it. The sight of their streets seething with resurgent adulation for Nasir made the Syrian Ba'thists reevaluate the wisdom of signing the accord. They immediately mounted a concerted media campaign in which non-Ba'thist nationalists and Nasirists were depicted as blind followers of Nasir, and described repeatedly as more royal than the king. The implication was that the pro-Nasir elements were not just doing Nasir's bidding in Syria; they were in fact constantly outbidding him.[85] Hardly two weeks had passed before those who were perceived as

[81] Ibid., p. 53.

[82] Ibid., p. 77.

[83] Michael N. Barnett, *Dialogue in Arab Politics: Negotiations in Regional Order* (New York: Columbia University Press, 1998), 142.

[84] Adeed Dawisha, "Jordan in the Middle East: The Art of Survival," in *The Shaping of an Arab Statesman: Abd al-Hamid Sharaf and the Modern Arab World*, ed. Patrick Seale. (London: Quartet Books, 1983), p. 64.

[85] Sa'id, *Iraq 8 Shibat, 1963* (Iraq of 8 February, 1963), fn. 1, p. 221.

allies of the Egyptian president were purged from the army, and soon after from the political leadership in Syria. This sparked major riots in Damascus and Aleppo by Nasir's supporters, which were brutally put down by Ba'thist-controlled security forces.[86]

Nasir could take no more. On May 17, exactly one month after the announcement of the accord, Nasir's confidant (and mouth-piece), the journalist Muhamed Hasaneen Haykal, wrote that coex-istence, let alone cooperation, with the Syrian Ba'th was no longer possible.[87] The break reached a violent climax on July 18, when the Ba'thists crushed a pro-Nasir coup in Syria, and executed twenty-seven of the plotters. Exasperated and enraged, Nasir, in a major speech on July 22, bitterly denounced Syria's Ba'thist lead-ers, declaring that no longer would he be "bound to the present fascist regime in Syria," and that the Damascus clique were fraudu-lent and treacherous, as well as being "inhuman and immoral."[88] The break now was total.

With the acrimonious conclusion of this latest chapter of Egyp-tian-Syrian relations, the prospects for comprehensive Arab unity all but disappeared. There was a half-hearted effort to establish some form of union between the two Ba'thist regimes in Syria and Iraq, but beyond the signing of a cultural agreement, the promise of future military and economic union, and much talk of fidelity to the Arab cause, nothing of any substance was achieved.[89] This was partly because by then the Iraqi Ba'thist order was beginning to unravel, and partly because the Iraqi and Syrian leaders had embarked on the venture initially for the primary purpose of seek-ing legitimation through the aura of Nasir's name. Now that Nasir had shunned the whole affair, the tangible benefits for giving up sovereignty were no longer readily discernible.

The cause of Arab nationalism was bound to suffer. To the thou-sands who had cheered and danced in the streets, the descent from

---

[86] These events are ably summarized in Seale, *Asad of Syria*, pp. 81–83.

[87] *Al-Ahram* (Cairo), May 17, 1963.

[88] The full text of this, one of Nasir's most bitter speeches, can be found in *Speeches, 1963*, pp. 118–156.

[89] Bazi, *Suriya: Sira' al-Istiqtab* (Syria: the struggle of polarization), pp. 333–334.

jubilation to despair was startlingly abrupt. To those who had celebrated the April 17 accord, Arab nationalism as an ideology and
political movement was meaningless if its ultimate goal, the organic unity of all Arabs, was unrealizable. Yet when opportunities
presented themselves, narrow political interests triumphed over the
"Arab idea." And Nasir, with all his charisma and broad political
support could not get the bickering and politically precarious
Ba'thists to surrender their state sovereignties for the good and
glory of the Arab nation. Nor was there any rush to unity after
'Abd al-Salam 'Aref ousted the Iraqi Ba'thists from power in November 1963. This was the same 'Aref, who, as one of the two
leaders of the Iraqi revolution in 1958, had gone to Damascus and
pledged to bring Iraq into the UAR regardless of Qasim's position
on the subject. Yet apart from one or two barren gestures in 1964,
this time 'Aref made little serious effort to pursue political unity
with his hero, the president of the UAR. 'Aref by now had been
bitten by the infectious bug of political power, and was in no hurry
to relinquish the presidency of Iraq. Once, in a cabinet meeting, he
dismissed the idea of unity with Egypt, quipping that amongst all
the members of the cabinet, he as the president would be the biggest
loser in any unity scheme.[90] *Wataniya*, even in its highly combustible form in Syria and Iraq, seemed to emerge victorious yet again.

What happened next was to further affirm the continuing ascent
of *wataniya* and decline of *qawmiya*, and the catalyst this time was
Israel. Paradoxically, since the Suez Crisis of 1956, the Jewish state
had not figured much in Arab nationalist discourse. The accepted
assumption throughout the Arab world was that the "illegitimate
entity" (in the Arab media, the word *laqita*, meaning illegitimate,
more often than not accompanied references to Israel) was behind
every ill that befell the Arab world. But beyond this "truth," accepted universally whenever people talked politics, it was surprising how the discourse of the "Arab Cold War" seemed to skirt over

---

[90] 'Abd al-Karim Farhan, *Hisad Thawra: Mudhakarat Tajribat al-Sulta fi al-'Iraq, 1958–
1968* (Harvest of revolution: memoirs of the experience of the political authority in Iraq,
1958–1968) (Damascus: Dar al-Buraq, 1994), p. 149. See also Sa'id, *Iraq 8 Shibat, 1963*
(Iraq of 8 February, 1963), p. 208.

Israel and Zionism. For instance, in a content analysis of Nasir's speeches between September 1961 and September 1962, "Zionism" with 67 references came a long way behind "imperialism" (281 references) and "reaction" (232 references). There were only 17 references to David Ben-Gurion, the then-prime minister of Israel, compared to 143 to King Sa'ud and 161 to King Husayn. And while Israel received a healthy dose of references, more than Jordan or Saudi Arabia, this statistical disparity was due to Nasir's tendency to treat Israel merely as a child of imperialism. Israel rarely was referred to as an autonomous category, but was generally attached almost ipso facto to "imperialism."[91] Depending on the particular period in time, the brunt of the nationalist assault was aimed at British, American, and even at times Soviet, imperialism; at the forces of "reaction" in the area, meaning the kings of Jordan and Saudi Arabia, and the Syrian secessionists; and at the Communists, obstructionists, and fascists, references that targeted Qasim, Bourguiba, and of course the post-1963 Syrian Ba'thists during times of noncooperation with Nasir. In this enumeration of the enemies of Arab nationalism, Israel was always in the nationalist consciousness, but had not been thrust forward to take pride of place as the direct target of Arab political rhetoric.

This was to change in the fall of 1963, when Israel approached the completion of its project to divert some 75 percent of the Jordan River for irrigation and industrial development inside Israel. Arab leaders had at different times in the past threatened that such a diversion would be regarded as an act of aggression by Israel, and as such would have to be met by force. However, weakened by the dislocations within their ranks, and consumed by the acrimony and recriminations that pervaded their relations, the Arabs generally could do little to follow their bold words with political or military action. The only ones who did were the Syrians. Brash

---

[91] A. I. Dawisha, "Perceptions, Decisions, and Consequences in Foreign Policy: The Egyptian Intervention in the Yemen," *Political Studies*, vol. 25, no. 2 (June 1977): 208. The Ba'th Party showed a similarly tepid concern with Israel, paying "consistently greater attention in its literature to the theme of strengthening the Arab nation through unifying it." Devlin, *The Ba'th Party*, p. 26.

and brimming with revolutionary fervor, the Ba'thist leaders, most of whom were still in their early thirties, tried their hand at the military option but were mauled badly by the Israelis, so who better to take out their frustration than on their Arab brethren, especially Nasir, who had been denouncing them bitterly since the collapse of the tripartite talks, and whom they now accused of weakness and cowardice in the face of Israel.

Nasir, however, did not take the bait. He was in no mood to be dragged into a precipitous war with the Israelis, particularly since by then the Egyptian military commitment to the Yemeni Republican cause had reached thirty-five thousand troops. And there was no end in sight. The royalist tribal forces, supported and abetted by Saudi Arabia, were if anything gaining the upper hand. It was time for a critical ideological, as well as diplomatic, reevaluation. On December 23, 1963, in a major speech, Nasir declared:

> In order to confront Israel, which challenged us last week when its Chief-of-Staff stood up and said, 'we shall divert the water against the will of the Arabs, and the Arabs can do what they want', a meeting between Arab Kings and Heads of State must take place as soon as possible, regardless of the conflicts and differences between them. Those with whom we are in conflict, we are prepared to meet; those with whom we have a quarrel, we are ready, for the sake of Palestine, to sit with.[92]

It was a foregone conclusion that the Arab leaders would respond positively to Nasir's redefinition of Egypt's ideological thrust. How could they not? In his statement, Nasir had effectively eschewed the revolutionary mission of Arab nationalism, and was in fact endorsing the long-held position of his Arab adversaries, who always had emphasized cooperation among the Arab states on the bases of sovereignty and complete equality. Consequently, a parade of Arab leaders arrived in Cairo in January 1964 to attend an Arab summit conference. The scene at the Cairo airport was one for the eye to behold. Bitter enemies only a few days earlier,

---

[92] *Speeches, 1963*, p. 311.

the Arab kings and presidents embraced and kissed one another on the cheeks as though they were long lost friends. For the next two-and-a-half years, the Arab world was to experience a period of inter-state tranquility not encountered since before the announce-ment of the Baghdad Pact in January 1955. Egyptian-Jordanian diplomatic relations were restored, and the personal relations be-tween the leaders of the two countries became openly cordial to the extent that King Husayn raised no objection to the creation of the independent Palestine Liberation Organization (PLO), or to its military wing, the Palestine Liberation Army (PLA). Egypt's rela-tions were also markedly improved with Ba'thist Syria and with the conservative Moroccan king, and in March 1964, Egyptian-Saudi diplomatic relations were resumed.

Arab nationalists must have found all this diplomatic activity disorienting and not a little disheartening. After all, for almost a decade Arab nationalism, their cherished *qawmiya*, had meant an unrelenting assault on "state sovereignty," a revolutionary cru-sade against "artificial" political boundaries, so that on some glo-rious day, which the nationalist generation had thought would not be too far off, they would witness the realization of Arab national-ism's ultimate goal of one unified Arab nation-state. And here was the high priest of this revolutionary nationalism embracing the very symbols of state sovereignty, the scorned, yet clearly resur-gent, *wataniya*.

Nasir was not insensitive to these nationalist concerns. He thus hastened to imbue the ensuing state-to-state diplomacy with ideo-logical meaning. He did this by making Israel, which had not fig-ured much in inter-Arab debates, the culprit for the shift in his policy toward the other Arabs. His argument was that by diverting the water of Jordan River, Israel was not simply confronting Syria and Jordan; it was clearly and arrogantly daring the whole Arab world to do something about it. The cause of Arab nationalism would suffer untold harm if the Arabs, consumed by strife in their midst, were not to respond vigorously. In this new and dangerous circumstance, what needed to be emphasized was not Arab organic unity, but the unity of effort and ranks among the Arab states in order to confront this sworn enemy of Arab nationalism.[93] In one sweeping statement, the goal of Arab nationalism was pared down from "Arab unity" (the fusion of all Arabs into one state) to "Arab solidarity" (the unity of effort and purpose among sovereign Arab states). And indeed, this new definition was enshrined in the resolutions of the second Arab Summit in September 1964, which convened in the Egyptian city of Alexandria. As a signatory to the resolutions, Egypt pledged to "respect the sovereignty of each of the Arab states and their existing regimes in accordance with their constitutions and laws, and to refrain from interfering in their internal affairs."[94] To the incredulous Arab nationalist, sovereignty had become the cornerstone of the new definition of Arab nationalism.

This is not to imply that this was the first time that Nasir had thought of, or talked about, the solidarity of the Arab states as not being necessarily contradictory to the intellectual tenets of Arab nationalism or to the meaning of Arab unity. For instance, in January 1958, in his effort to put the brakes on the Syrians' insistent demands for immediate unity, he explained that "solidarity is a step toward unity. It is the answer if we cannot achieve unity."[95] Again in August 1961, he argued that Arab unity "extends on an Arab front which begins with Arab solidarity and ends with constitutional unity."[96] What made his affirmation for Arab solidarity in 1964 different and more worrisome to nationalists was the way the concept was publicly institutionalized in the resolutions of the September 1964 summit, and in the wide-ranging diplomatic strategies and policies that constituted its political acceptance, indeed its approbation. And even though Egypt's leaders and nationalist narrators continued to affirm their belief in Arab unity, the resolutions of the 1964 summit bode ill for the cause of Arab nationalism's ultimate goal.

[93] *Khutab, volume four*, p. 447.
[94] Quoted in Barnett, *Dialogues in Arab Politics*, p. 152.
[95] *Egyptian Gazette* (Cairo), January 29, 1958.
[96] *SWB*, August 15, 1961, p. 9.

Nationalist thought and action from Sati' al-Husri to Nasir had predicated on the essentialist idea that Arabs constituted a cultural unity which had undergone forcible political dislocation, and that the Arab situation with its many states was an unnatural thing. Arab nationalism was obliged by definition, imperatively even deterministically, to right the wrongs of Arab division, to unify the segmented entity, and to bring it back to its natural condition. To the committed Arab nationalist, accepting the sovereignty of the Arab states negated the very essence of this axiomatic belief. The necessity of confronting Israel's "mortal" threat might have been a legitimate rationalization for eschewing Arab unity in favor of the solidarity of Arab states, but deep in their hearts the Arab nationalists saw it as yet another setback for *qawmiya*, accelerating its descent from the dizzying heights it had reached in the summer of 1958. Even if one were to accept the tenet that Arab unity was a dialectical process, and that its ultimate goal had not been discarded but temporarily shelved, there can be little doubt that *wataniya* received a major and indisputable boost, for "Arab solidarity" implied an admission that the sovereign Arab states, not the larger nation, bore the main responsibility for the defense of nationalist causes.

The period of inter-state political tranquility came to an end in 1966, when a combination of events ushered in what turned out to be a short-lived radical period. To begin with, King Faysal of Saudi Arabia (who, in a palace coup, had succeeded his brother Sa'ud to the throne) had made highly publicized visits to Iran and Jordan in which he had called for an Islamic summit that would unite the Muslims against ideas alien to Islam.[97] The Egyptians took that to be a pointed reference to Egypt's espousal of nationalist and socialist doctrines. Particularly worrying to Nasir was the role of Iran, since its shah was a pivotal member of the Western alliance, the Central Treaty Organization, a major supplier of oil to Israel, and an active supporter of the Yemeni royalists. Nasir's response was swift and categorical. "We are against the Islamic

---

[97] Peter Mansfield, *Nasser's Egypt* (London: Penguin Books, 1969), p. 76; *Times* (London), December 22, 1965.

Conference," he declared in a major speech in February 1966, "just like we were against the Baghdad Pact . . . and all other imperialist and reactionary movements."[98] Nasir seemed to think that the two-year respite had given the conservatives added strength and resolve to mount a new drive against Egypt and the progressive forces in the Arab world. His alarm, which at the beginning of 1966 centered on political moves in the Middle East region, was elevated to the level of an international conspiracy in the early summer of 1966. In quick succession, the International Monetary Fund refused to grant Egypt a loan of $70 million and the United States deferred negotiations on an Egyptian request for $150 million worth of surplus food.[99] In both cases, Egypt's costly military involvement in Yemen was cited as the reason.[100] Meanwhile, the ouster of two of the original founders of the nonaligned movement, presidents Sukarno of Indonesia and Nkrumah of Ghana, by pro-Western forces only served to reinforce the Egyptian perception of a worldwide anti-progressive offensive. It was therefore in such a setting that this era of solidarity and cooperation among the Arab states, regardless of their ideological orientation, came to an end. On July 22, 1966, Nasir virulently denounced the "pro-West Arab 'reactionaries' ,'" declaring that cooperation with these "elements" had become impossible.[101]

In his assault on the "reactionaries, " Nasir could not but draw near to the existing "progressive" forces in the Arab world, even, in some cases, against his better judgment. Such was the case of his accelerating entanglement with Syria. In February 1966, an aggres-

---

[98] *Khutab, volume five*, p. 501; *SWB*, February 25, 1966, p. 7. The shah became the target of a particularly vicious tongue-lashing by Nasir and his media spokesmen. See *Khutab, volume five*, p. 488; *al-Ahram* (Cairo), April 13, 1966.

[99] *New York Times*, May 5, 1966.

[100] The Egyptians, however, believed that such a reason was nothing but a smokescreen meant to obscure the innate hostility of the American administration. Nasir had felt that a certain rapport had developed between him and President Kennedy. And indeed Egyptian-American relations were comparatively cordial during the Kennedy era. That, however, was to dramatically change when Lyndon Johnson became president. The Egyptians believed that the new president and some of his key advisors, particularly the Rustow brothers, were incurably pro-Israeli, and consequently vehemently anti-Nasir.

[101] *SWB*, July 25, 1966, p. 15.

sive Marxist-oriented, neo-Ba'thist leadership had come to power in a bloody coup intent on carrying out a "revolutionary struggle" against Israel and the "Arab reactionaries." The new Syrian leaders, with their Marxism wrapped around Arab nationalism, advocated the "liberation of Palestine" not necessarily as an ultimate goal, but as a step in the process of forging a new unified and progressive Arab social and political order. Given their ideological orientation, they talked incessantly about the need for mass struggle on the Vietnam model, which in the late 1960s was all the rage among the angry, idealistic, and disenfranchised groups worldwide. Syria's soul mates were naturally the infant Palestinian guerrilla groups, who were mounting their own people's struggle, in the sense that at least then they took orders from no Arab government. The Syrians thus were bound to actively support the guerrillas, as a result of which, the level of violence on the borders with Israel steadily rose throughout 1966. While Nasir was wary of Syria's provocative ways, lest he might be embroiled in a premature war with Israel, he also felt he needed to support the radical Syrians against the Jewish state and the Arab "reactionaries," whom he believed, yet again, to be actively working against all "radical" and "progressive" elements in the Arab world. As rumors intensified about impending plots against Syria, Egypt responded emphatically that "Damascus does not stand alone against imperialist plots."[102] Egypt then added an incendiary gesture (how incendiary, it did not appreciate at the time) when it signed a defense alliance with Syria which asserted that aggression against either state would be considered an attack on the other.

The symbolism of this act was not lost on the Arab world. Nasir, after the inactive years of Arab solidarity, rose again to the forefront of people's consciousness as the defender of Arab rights and the only viable leader of Arab nationalism. Nasir's prestige undoubtedly gained an immense boost, but alas it would be short-lived. The defense pact, the very act that brought Nasir back into the very center of Arab politics, also paved the way for the chain

---

[102] *Al-Ahram* (Cairo), August 26, 1966.

of events destined to lead to the disastrous war that in retrospect became Arab nationalism's Waterloo.

In April 1967, in an air battle between Israeli and Syrian jet fighters over the Golan Heights, the Israelis shot down six Syrian planes, and Damascus was subjected to the indignity of an impromptu air display by the brash Israelis. Incensed by this public humiliation, yet cognizant of Israel's glaring superiority, the Syrians requested Egypt's military assistance, and lest the Egyptians vacillated, Cairo was reminded of its obligations to Syria under the terms of the recent defense pact. In this highly charged milieu, hemmed in by a military alliance that he signed more for its symbolic value than for its strategic utility, and limited by an increasingly frenzied public opinion demanding no less than the restoration of Arab rights in Palestine, Nasir made the fatal move in the middle of May of sending his army into the Sinai and closing the Straits of Tiran to Israeli shipping. The Arabs went wild at this first real challenge to Israeli power and arrogance since 1948. The pressure on other Arab leaders to fall in line was immense. At the end of May, King Husayn arrived in Cairo to sign a defense pact with Egypt and place his forces under Egyptian command. The Iraqis joined the pact soon after, and dispatched an armored division to help on the Syrian front. Caught in the ensuing frenzy, the Saudis sent a brigade to join their Arab brethren at the front as well. It seemed that almost everyone believed in the inevitability of war and the certainty of defeating the "illegitimate entity." At times it was almost surrealistic. For instance, in his farewell address to the mechanized division dispatched to the Syrian front, Iraqi President 'Abd al-Rahman 'Aref asked his troops to behave properly and with decorum in their forthcoming occupation of Israel![103] Nasir, however, was far more of a realist. He did not share in the universal hysteria, and he was not one to underestimate the military prowess of Israel. Once his forces moved into Sinai, Nasir tried to de-escalate the conflict, sending repeated signals to Tel Aviv and

---

[103] Ahmad Hamroush, *Qissat Thawrat 23 Yuliyu: Kharif 'Abd al-Nasir, al-Jusi' al-Khamis* (The story of the July 23 revolution: the autumn of 'Abd al-Nasir, volume 5) (Cairo: Maktabat Madbuli, 1984), p. 236.

Washington of his preference for a political solution to the crisis. He hoped for an Israeli acquiescence, which would give him a political victory without the risk of war. But if war was to come he thought he was ready for it.[104]

Swept by the emotions of those days, the nationalists, not unlike the bulk of the Arab populations, believed that victory was right around the corner, and once achieved, it would infuse new life into Arab nationalism and endow it with new vigor and potency. But it was not to be. What awaited them round the corner was not the anticipated victory but a devastating military and political calamity. In six days in early June 1967, Israel defeated all the Arab armies that were ranged against it,[105] occupying in the process large chunks of land belonging to the three countries that bordered on it. From the Egyptians, the Israelis seized the Sinai Peninsula, including the Gaza Strip; from the Syrians, they wrested the Golan Heights, and from the Jordanians they took the entire West Bank of the Jordan River. Most heartbreaking was the loss of East Jerusalem. By the end of the sixth day, June 11, 1967, the Israelis, had they so wished, could have marched almost unhindered into Damascus, Cairo, and Amman. Such was the extent of Israel's military victory.

As the Arabs lay in emotional tatters, stunned by the overwhelming reversal of fortunes, for which they had not been psychologically prepared, Arab nationalism, even if people were not fully aware of it then, was reaching the end of its extraordinary journey. Like an old pugilist, whose days of glory were now a thing of the past, Arab nationalism lay on the floor battered and benumbed waiting for the count to ten to begin. The sun, which had shown so brightly on Arab nationalism, had finally set.

[104] See Efraim and Irani Karsh, "Reflections on Arab Nationalism," in *Middle Eastern Studies*, vol. 32 no. 4 (October 1996): 383–386.

[105] For a concise analysis of Israel's decision to go to war, especially the division of opinion between the civilians and the military, see Avi Shlaim, *The Iron Wall: Israel and the Arab World* (New York: W.W. Norton & Company, 2000), pp. 236–241.

CHAPTER TEN

1967 AND AFTER: THE TWILIGHT
OF ARAB NATIONALISM

The Six Day War of June 1967 is generally accepted as a seminal event in Arab contemporary history, but some analysts disagree with the contention that it also was Arab nationalism's last stand. They argue that even after June 1967, "Arabism still shaped how Arab states were expected to present themselves, represented a source of symbolic capital, subjected them to Arab public opinion, and held them accountable to each other."[1] This is of course correct. Arabism was not lost as an identity; it continued to set general parameters Arab regimes would be loath to transgress. And Arab leaders knew that the policies they devised for their states would be scrutinized and judged beyond the confines of their territorial boundaries by a wider "Arab public." But what continued to live on was Arabism *not* Arab nationalism.[2] Arabism was merely the remnant of Arab nationalism, what the Arabs were left with after

---

[1] Michael N. Barnett, *Dialogues in Arab Politics: Negotiations in Regional Order* (New York: Columbia University Press, 1998), p.164. In the longer passage from which this quote is drawn, Barnett employs the term "Arabism" in a sense indistinguishable from that of "Arab nationalism."

[2] Chapter 1 of this book endeavored to draw conceptual distinctions among the terms Arabism, Arab nationalism, and pan-Arabism.

Arab nationalism hit the deck in June 1967. What the Six Day War did was to irretrievably rob Arab nationalism of the crucial element of unification. While Arabs, in whatever state they lived, continued to recognize their membership in the cultural space called "the Arab world," a recognition shared by rulers and subjects alike, they no longer truly believed in the viability of organic political unity. During the years of the nationalist era, the decade prior to the 1967 War, people felt that it was not inconceivable that some form of political unity would occur during their lifetime. Even as the prospect grew more remote with every setback that befell the Arab nationalist cause from late 1958 onward, it continued to live in the aspirations of the people, particularly among the ranks of the nationalist generation. Bernard Lewis, writing in 1963, observed:

> The rulers . . . appear to be guided, in their policies, by the interests of their states and countries rather than those of the pan-Arab cause. But such loyalties and allegiances do not yet correspond to the deeper feelings of the people. [State] patriotism has its claims, but the older rallying cries of faith and kin, now uttered in the new language of Arab nationalism, are infinitely more potent.[3]

Arab nationalism and its radical goal of comprehensive Arab unity lived on as long as Gamal 'Abd al-Nasir and Egypt dominated Arab politics. Iraq's unwillingness to join the United Arab Republic (UAR), Syria's secession from the union, the wasteful and inconclusive military operation in Yemen, the collapse of the 1963 unity talks, had bruised Nasir, leading to questions about his ability to unite the Arabs. But such was the seduction of the dream, the longing of people for it, and their belief in the powers of Nasir's charisma to bring it to fruition that it continued to live on. Indeed, hopes were revived by the events immediately preceding the 1967 War, and who could tell what might have happened had Egypt and the Arabs, not Israel, won a famous victory. But Nasir lost, and lost infamously. And unlike the other "setbacks," the scope of this

---

[3] Bernard Lewis, *The Middle East and the West* (Bloomington: Indiana University Press, 1964), p. 94.

defeat was such that even the most ardent utopian now discerned the permanent eclipse of Nasir's charisma. What was left was no more than a sense of cultural proximity, an intellectual recognition of common habits and custom, a belief that something called "Arabism" does indeed exist. Yes, they were Arabs, those people who lived in the various Arabic-speaking countries. Most of them agreed on that. But after 1967, hardly any of them believed in their eventual political unity. It was *Arab statism* not *Arab nationalism* that defined the post-1967 era, *wataniya* not *qawmiya* that determined political relations among the Arab states. And the change began with Nasir himself.

The Six Day War had cost Egypt dearly in life and material. Egypt's human losses were detailed by Nasir himself in a melancholy speech he delivered a few months after the debacle of the war. Ten thousand soldiers and fifteen hundred officers had been killed, and the Israelis captured five thousand men and five hundred officers.[4] In terms of equipment, Egyptian losses were estimated at six hundred tanks and three hundred and forty combat aircraft.[5] Beyond these horrendous losses, the war was responsible for many domestic and economic maladies. A huge migration to an already overpopulated Cairo from the canal cities of Isma'iliya, Suez, Port Sa'id, and others was underway, and Egypt's authorities, still in shock over the lightening disaster that had befallen them, had no way to deal with this new and potentially incendiary predicament. The postwar state of Egypt's structurally fragile economy was not short of desperate. The Suez Canal, Egypt's major export earner, was now closed to international shipping, and the oil fields of Sinai were under Israeli control. And, of course, on top of all this adversity there was the humiliating and potentially destabilizing presence of Israeli troops on Egyptian soil. Not surprisingly, Nasir possessed neither the capabilities nor the compulsion to pursue the radical goals of Arab nationalism. By necessity his sights were

[4] American University of Beirut, *al-Watha'iq al-'Arabiya al-Siyasiya, 1967* (Arab political documents, 1967) (Beirut: AUB Press, n.d.), p. 718. (Hereafter cited as *Watha'iq*).

[5] Institute for Strategic Studies, *The Military Balance, 1967–1968* (London: ISS, 1967), p. 50.

turned inward to Egypt's plight, to its monstrous postwar problems, many of which verged on the unsolvable.

Egypt's primary objective now became "the eradication of the consequences of the defeat,"[6] and all the country's activities, including its involvement in inter-Arab affairs, were made totally dependent on the consummation of this overriding objective. Egypt's policy rationale became exclusively statist. "Our attitude toward any Arab state," explained Nasir, "depends on that state's attitude toward the battle."[7] In fact, Nasir could have used more appropriately the plural form of the word, for Egypt had more than one herculean battle on its hands: the battle to rescue the country from the shambles that was its economy; the battle to tackle the immense problems of the mass human exodus from the war zone; the battle to overcome the ensuing alienation of society and to restore to it a sense of self-worth, a semblance of dignity; and, of course, the battle to regain occupied Egyptian land. The focus had to be on Egypt; *wataniya* was now the name of the game.

This statist proclivity was cemented at the Summit of Arab Heads of State, which convened in the Sudanese capital, Khartoum, in August 1967. It was clear even before the convening of the Summit that the meeting would endorse "an interpretation of Arabism that was consistent with sovereignty."[8] Egypt's acceptance of this principle was made easier when Saudi Arabia, Kuwait, and monarchical Libya extended an annual grant of $280 million to Egypt to compensate it for the loss of land and revenue. Nasir now became economically beholden to the oil-rich, conservative, and pro-Western states, the very states against which his Arab nationalist onslaught was aimed. The prophet of Arab nationalism now seemed ready to abandon any hope for Arab unity, and it was only natural that the flock would follow the lead and begin to see the state in a more traditional sense, devoid of its "revolutionary" trappings.

---

[6] *Al-Ahram* (Cairo), August 30, 1967.

[7] *Watha'iq*, 1968, p. 378.

[8] Barnett, *Dialogues in Arab Politics*, p. 167.

Attitudes would change so quickly that within a few years the discourse of revolutionary nationalism, au courant in the 1950s and 1960s, would begin to sound peculiarly out of place in the pragmatic and businesslike atmosphere of the 1970s.[9] Even the journalist Muhamed Hasaneen Haykal who, as we have seen, had famously characterized Egypt not just as a state, but also as a revolution, carrying its mission for a unitary Arab future across state boundaries,[10] now conceded the passing of his theory. In the post-1967 era, Haykal observed, the rise of the statist, oil-rich countries and the growing respect for the political power of "money" all but made the pre-1967 focus on "revolutionary struggle" a thing of the past. He encapsulated this dramatic and consequential transformation in his celebrated phrase that *tharwa* (wealth) had taken over from *thawra* (revolution).[11] The Khartoum Summit and the institutionalization of the power of petro-dollars put the seal of legitimacy on *wataniya* as the basis of inter-Arab politics.

The ascendancy of particularistic, subnational identity was, paradoxically enough, underscored by a nonstate, "revolutionary" movement. The Palestine Liberation Organization (PLO) did not emerge as an independent movement until 1967, not least because Palestinian nationalism did not emerge from under the all-encompassing shadow of Arab nationalism until the War of June 1967. In the pre-1967 period, educated and politically aware Palestinians tended to be ardent supporters of Arab nationalism, and much like other Arabs they defined the struggle with the Jewish state not as the Palestinian-Israeli conflict, but as the Arab-Israeli conflict. And why ever not? Their Arab brethren had resources the Palestinians did not possess: large armies, wealth, and perhaps most crucially, sovereign territories from which they could wage the inevitable war of liberation. When the time came for the torch of the struggle to be lit, the Palestinians would undoubtedly participate in the deliv-

---

[9] Adeed Dawisha, "Jordan in the Middle East: The Art of Survival," in *The Shaping of an Arab Statesman: 'Abd al-Hamid Sharif and the Modern Arab World*, ed. Patrick Seale (New York: Quartet Books, 1983), p. 69.

[10] *Al-Ahram* (Cairo), December 29. 1961.

[11] Mohamed Heikal, *Sphinx and Commissar: The Rise and Fall of Soviet Influence in the Arab World* (London: Collins, 1978), p. 262.

erance of their homeland, *but* only as a part of the combined Arab effort. After all, even the PLO was established by the Arab states in 1964, and given an army, the Palestine Liberation Army (PLA), which was supposed, when the call came, to partake alongside other Arab armies in the liberation of "Arab Palestine."

True, challenges to this vision and the organizational schema that accompanied it began before 1967, when some younger Palestinians, dazzled by the heroic triumph of the Algerian war of independence, began to form "Resistance" groups that charted a "revolutionary" course of liberation independent of the Arab states.[12] By 1967, a few of these groups had mounted what essentially were hit-and-run operations which, if nothing else, proved to be annoyances and irritants to Israel. One of the better known of these groups was al-Fatah, formed by a young, Cairo-educated engineer, Yasir Arafat.[13] But until the June 1967 War, the Arabs continued to be the primary custodians of Palestinian aspirations, and the PLO of traditionalists and notables continued to receive the patronage of the Arab system and whatever legitimacy it bestowed. Even an eloquent and committed advocate of Palestinian nationalism such as the historian Rashid Khalidi, who maintains that a Palestinian identity began to emerge as early as the late Ottoman era, accepts that in the 1955–1967 period, it was submerged by the pervasive force of Arab nationalism. Khalidi concedes that for many Palestinians during this period, Arab nationalism "retained its appeal both as an idea that had long been popular among Palestinians . . . as well as what appeared to be a practical means to the achievement of their shared goal of the liberation of their country."[14]

[12] The best work on the origins, organization, and development of the "Palestinian Resistance" is Helena Cobban, *The Palestinian Liberation Organization: People, Power and Politics* (London: Cambridge University Press, 1984).

[13] According to the biographer of Arafat, the origin of al-Fatah dates all the way back to the mid-1950s. Ironically, the first underground cell of the organization was formed by its two founders, Arafat and Khalil al-Wazir in Kuwait. Nasir's Egypt had obliged the two Palestinian radicals to seek refuge in the then-British protectorate! See Alan Hart, *Arafat: A Political Biography* (Bloomington: Indiana University Press, 1984), p. 121.

[14] Rashid Khalidi, *Palestinian Identity: The Construction of Modern National Consciousness* (New York: Columbia University Press, 1997), p. 183. On the same subject, see also

The Arabs' spectacular *hazima* (rout) in the Six Day War changed all that. To the Palestinians, it signaled the impotence of Arab nationalism to help their cause, drawing a lesson of self-reliance from the whole ignominious affair. From now on, the struggle against the Israelis would be carried out under the banner of Palestinian nationalism. The Palestinians would eschew the tired and discredited old way of classic warfare, employing instead guerrilla tactics made famous by the extraordinary successes of the Algerians and Vietnamese. The Palestinian scenario was simple: the guerrillas would set up traps and ambush patrols, they would move by night and disappear by day, lightly armed phantoms, hitting the enemy where it least expected it, wreaking havoc and consternation among the people who usurped their land and who basked in the arrogance of their swift and effortless 1967 victory.

If the Palestinians needed a psychological boost, it was to come in the spring of 1968 at the town of Karameh in Jordan. A rather large Israeli force sent to destroy the guerrilla base inside the town was ambushed by Palestinian commandos and Jordanian army units. The Israelis suffered substantial losses. In military terms, however, the Israeli operation achieved its goal in that it did succeed in destroying the base. But the fact that the Palestinian fighters stood their ground, fought valiantly, and, along with the Jordanians, ended up inflicting casualties on the "invincible" Israelis, was hailed by Palestinians and Arabs alike as a remarkable victory. Whether by accident or design, the Palestinians chose the right town to flex their muscles. In Arabic, the town's name, Karameh, meant dignity, and the engagement with the Israelis became rooted in Palestinian and Arab psyche as "the battle for dignity,"[15] a dignity that had been lost, some believed irretrievably, in June 1967.

Karameh had an electrifying impact on the guerrillas' recruitment efforts. Long lines of young men in various Arab cities waited to be enlisted by guerrilla representatives. Spontaneous fund-rais-

---

John W. Amos II, *Palestinian Resistance: Organization of a Nationalist Movement* (New York: Pergamon Press, 1980), pp. 18–19.

[15] See W. Andrew Terrill, "The Political Mythology of the Battle of Karameh," in *The Middle East Journal*, vol. 55, no. 1 (Winter 2001).

ing activities took place throughout the Arab world. Pro-guerrilla demonstrations filled Arab streets, and the valor of the guerrillas was extolled in mosques, schools, and other public meetings places. The degradation of the *Arab* effort in the War of June 1967[16] and the glorification of the *Palestinian* performance in Karameh in March 1968 accelerated the symbolic shift in Arab consciousness from the national (Arab) to the subnational.

This symbolic shift was to gather momentum a couple of years later in yet another military confrontation that involved the Palestinian guerrillas. Except this time the Palestinians ended up on the losing side. The spectacular growth in the numbers and the power of the Palestinian guerrilla movement sooner or later was bound to come against "state interests," particularly those countries adjacent to the Jewish state, notably Jordan, within whose borders most of the guerrillas resided and from whose land they struck at Israel. Through an elaborate network of military, social, economic, and administrative institutions, the Palestinian presence in the Hashemite Kingdom became almost a state within a state. By 1970, two military and political structures existed in Jordan, largely independent of each other and increasingly wary of the other's intentions and motives: the Hashemite monarchy and the PLO. King Husayn's resentment of this state of affairs and his efforts to confine the power and activities of the guerrillas led to mounting domestic tension. In the summer of 1970, it had become clear that a military confrontation between the two antagonistic sides could be averted only through the authoritative intervention of President Nasir. The wounded leader of Arab nationalism still had enough prestige, and his country still commanded center stage in Arab geostrategic politics, and because of this, King Husayn and Yasir Ara-

---

[16] Derogatory comments not only about the Arab states and their armies, but also about Arabs generally, were common. The author, who resided in London at the time, remembers an interviewer from BBC Television being told by one young man waiting in a long line to be enlisted that various disasters of the past had almost convinced him that *al-'Arab jarab*, meaning that the Arabs were useless lepers. However, Karameh had restored his faith "in at least some of the Arabs." He then went on to describe the "Palestinian Resistance" in glowing, adoring terms. When asked about the country of his origin, he replied that it was no longer of any consequence, because he was now a "Palestinian."

fat (by now the leader of the PLO), would go to Nasir and Cairo seeking support for their respective causes.

Nasir was torn. He did sympathize with Husayn against the "anarchic" behavior of the Palestinian guerrillas inside his country. After all, Husayn's complaint was based on the concept of sovereignty, a concept that, since the Khartoum Summit, had constituted the fundamental ideological basis of the post-1967 political order. Furthermore, Nasir was not convinced that Palestinian guerrilla tactics would defeat Israel. The essence of this argument was elucidated, prophetically as it turned out, by Haykal in an article that went against the prevalent euphoria in the wake of Karameh. Haykal maintained that guerrilla tactics could not be decisive in Israel where the terrain was open, where the "oppressors" outnumbered the "oppressed," and where in contrast to Vietnam or Algeria, the guerrillas could not seek immunity from enemy retaliation and attack because Israel possessed the capability to strike anywhere in the Arab world. This made the idea that defeating Israel through guerrilla warfare no more than a myth propagated by ill-informed romantics. The task of defeating Israel, concluded Haykal, could only be accomplished by the entire forces of the Arab world, of which the Palestinian Resistance would constitute an integral part.[17] Even so, given his own emotional proclivities and the acknowledged popularity of the Palestinian Resistance in Egypt as well as in the rest of the Arab world, Nasir could hardly appear to be abandoning the Palestinian cause. He had, after all, earlier conceded that the emergence of the Palestinian Resistance was playing an important role in reviving the Arab situation after the lows of his own defeat in June 1967.[18]

Not only Nasir but other "radical" leaders suffered the same inner dilemma. Take the case of the Algerian Houari Boumedienne. As the president of a state, he could not but sympathize with Jordan's determination to safeguard its sovereignty. But as a prominent figure in Algeria's long and bloody war of liberation, he de-

[17] *Al-Ahram* (Cairo), August 16, 1968.
[18] *Watha'iq*, 1967, p. 718.

clared himself unable to "remain indifferent to any action whose aim is to put an end to the Palestinian Resistance."[19] It is worth repeating here that this dual concern for Jordan and the Palestinians remained at the ruling elite level. At the popular level, the overwhelming support of the Arab public was given unreservedly to the Palestinian Resistance.

Nasir, avoiding the attendant emotionalism of the situation, urged both Husayn and Arafat to exercise caution and patience in dealing with each other. The Palestinians, who were becoming wary of Nasir's revolutionary commitment, did not heed his advice. After all, the professed leader of radical Arab nationalism had just agreed to an American initiative sponsored by the United States secretary of state, William Rogers, which included not just a ceasefire on the Egyptian-Israeli front, but also an Egyptian agreement for peace talks with the Israelis through United Nations representatives.[20] Arafat and the Palestinian Resistance had opposed the Rogers plan bitterly and had taken heart from Egypt's initial dismissal of the plan and the American secretary of state, who was vilified for "wanting to buy Arab destiny with empty words"[21] and for possessing an "enormous talent for evading the truth."[22] Not surprisingly, the Palestinians saw in Nasir's later acceptance of the plan an abandonment of the struggle and an affirmation of the primacy of Egypt's "statist" interests. To the Palestinians, Nasir's counseling of caution was the advice not of an Arab nationalist leader, but of the president of a state, articulating concerns that were not at all different from those of the Jordanian monarch.[23]

Had Arafat and his chief lieutenants accepted Nasir's counsel, they might have saved their organization and people much suffer-

[19] Barnett, *Dialogues in Arab Politics*, p. 179.

[20] See A. I. Dawisha, *Egypt in the Arab World: The Elements of Foreign Policy* (London: Macmillan, 1976), p. 58. For an Egyptian perspective on the reasons for Egypt's acceptance see Muhamed Hasaneen Haykal's detailed explanation in *al-Abram* (Cairo), July 31, 1970.

[21] *Al-Ahram* (Cairo), March 13, 1970.

[22] *Al-Ahram* (Cairo), March 20, 1970.

[23] Indeed, at times during the meeting, Arafat was taken aback by the stridency of Nasir's criticism of PLO activity in Jordan. It seems that Nasir even hinted that the Palestinian organization was hurting the interests of Arab nationalism. See Barnett, *Dialogues in Arab Politics*, p. 179.

ing and humiliation. But they were riding a tidal wave of popular support so intoxicating that it blinded them to the reality of the balance of forces in Jordan. The Royal Jordanian Army, made up primarily of fiercely loyal bedouin units, was itching for a show-down, which it knew it would decisively win. But rather than tem-pering their activities, the Palestinians increased their challenge to the domestic authority and internal stability of the Jordanian state. By the end of the summer, the situation had become untenable and hopelessly polarized. Anarchy reigned, and it was clear that some-thing had to give. Here is how the king described what was happen-ing in Jordan:

> We were in the fight which I believe was a turning point in the life of Jordan. We didn't want it. We tried our very best to avert the deterioration [of the situation]. But the Palestinian resistance gained strength. They had moved from the Jordan valley to the towns. . . . We had thousands of incidents of Palestinians breaking the law, of attacking people. It was a very unruly state of affairs in the country, and I continued to try to restore order . . . Toward the end I felt I was losing control. The army began to rebel. I had to spend most of my time running from one unit to another.[24]

By September 1970, clashes between the Jordanian army and the Palestinian guerrillas had escalated in frequency and intensity. After a multiple airplane hijacking operation by the Palestinians, the military skirmishes developed into a bloody, full scale civil war on September 16.

Six days later, as the Palestinians were losing the war badly with horrifying loss of life, an emergency summit of the Arab Heads of State convened in Cairo. Husayn was unrepentant, vigorously defending Jordan's statist interests: "The state will exercise its full sovereignty over everyone present on its territory. All shall respect that sovereignty."[25] When, finally, Husayn was persuaded to sign an agreement to end the war eleven days after it had started, some

---

[24] This extract is from an interview with King Husayn conducted by Avi Shlaim. See *New York Review of Books*, July 15, 1999, pp. 16–17.

[25] Barnett, *Dialogues in Arab Politics*, p. 180.

three thousand Palestinian guerrillas and civilians had perished, and the bulk of the Palestinian guerrillas had been expelled from Jordan. By the end of the following year, when the Jordanian army ruthlessly eliminated a few remaining PLO pockets in northeast Jordan, the complex institutional structure, the state-within-a-state that the Palestinians had proudly and defiantly built lay in shambles, decimated not by Israel but by an Arab army intent on defending the sovereignty of its state. The Palestinians' first excursion into Arab politics, their first challenge to the state-based Arab political order, which had been enshrined in the Khartoum Summit, proved to be a costly and dismal failure. With a zeal that occasionally bordered on downright savagery, Jordan had successfully defended its state sovereignty.

The next assertion of the primacy of statist *wataniya* came from Egypt, the very country which had, during the 1950s and 1960s, presented itself and had been seen by others as the heart of *qawmiya*, the very core of Arab nationalism. Nasir died suddenly right after the conclusion of the Cairo Summit in September 1970. His vice president, Anwar al-Sadat, succeeded him. Cavalierly dismissed as *Bikbashi aywah* (Colonel Yes-man), and with no political base, Sadat could do little but promise to follow faithfully on the values and policies of his towering predecessor. In his efforts to legitimize his rule against potential rivals during the first year of his presidency, Sadat would often invoke the legacy of Nasir, proclaiming his undying allegiance to that sacred memory and its principles.[26] Indeed, at times he seemed to be more stridently Nasirist than Nasir had been. In a major speech to the Arab Socialist Union (ASU), the Nasir-created sole political organization in Egypt, Sadat not only reminded his audience that Egyptians belonged to "the Arab nation both historically and by common destiny," but also promised that Egypt under his leadership would "serve as the van-

---

[26] Typical of Sadat's proclamations of loyalty was the following statement: "We find ourselves without [Nasir's] presence among us, without his mind, organization and leadership, although his thoughts, principles and attitudes remain as an inexhaustible treasure for us forever." British Broadcasting Corporation, *Summary of World Broadcasts, Part IV: The Arab World, Israel, Greece, Turkey, Iran* (hereafter cited as *SWB*), November 16, 1970, p. 3.

guard of the Arab revolutionary march."[27] These were words that Nasir himself had abandoned after the Khartoum Summit of 1967. And later events, as we shall see, hardly suggest a commitment by Sadat to these revolutionary and Arab nationalist ideals. Rather, such utterances were simply the manifestations of his own political weakness in the initial phase of his presidency.

Thanks to Nasir, this would not last long. Sadat had inherited an organizational structure that Nasir had built specifically to maintain the primacy of the presidency over all walks of life in Egypt. Once Sadat was able to root out potential rivals,[28] he used the Nasirist political and administrative system to cement his own authority and political control. By 1972, Sadat had fully emerged from the overbearing shadow of his predecessor, and with that, Egypt's ideological orientation became progressively more inward-looking, boasting an almost uncontested "Egypt first" orientation. Sadat's earlier adherence to "Arab unity" became fully subordinated to the value of "Egyptian patriotism," a concept which even though acted upon in the last years of Nasir's rule was, in fact, hardly publicized or publicly celebrated as an autonomous ideological category. As early as July 1972, less than two years after the death of Nasir, Sadat would make the "forthcoming battle with Israel" a function first and foremost not of Arab nationalism and unity, but of Egyptian patriotism and domestic unity.[29] The eminent Egyptian political scientist, Ali Hillal Dessouki, in a study of Egypt's foreign policy confirms the clearly "Egyptian" *watani* orientation in Sadat's foreign policy objectives in the 1970s. According to Dessouki, these objectives were: the restoration, preferably through negotiation, of Egyptian territories occupied by Israel since 1967; the termination of the war with Israel, as the economic cost had become unbearable; the improvement of relations with Washington, as the United States was the only country capable of

[27] *SWB*, November 16, 1970, pp. 3–4.

[28] An informative and interesting, although clearly self-serving, account of the process by which Sadat's potential rivals were neutralized can be found in Anwar el-Sadat, *In Search of Identity: An Autobiography* (New York: Harper and Row, Publishers, 1977), pp. 204–225.

[29] *SWB*, July 26, 1972, p. 17.

influencing Israel; the rejuvenation and modernization of Egypt's economy through the import of modern Western technology and private capital; and the modification of Egypt's global and regional policies in order to better pursue these objectives.[30] Stunningly absent from these objectives, which were articulated and acted upon by Sadat until his assassination in 1981, was any reference to "Arab nationalism," "Arab unity," or "Arab revolution," terms that were almost the staple diet of Nasirist speeches. "Egypt" became Sadat's single-minded concern, constituting the primary motivation for his two momentous decisions: the October 1973 War, and his trip to Jerusalem and the consequent peace treaty with Israel.

Even though references to "Arab" occupied land were initially made, the 1973 War was fought to achieve first and foremost specifically Egyptian goals. From the very beginning, Sadat's target was the Sinai Peninsula, where a successful challenge to the status quo would force the Israelis to rethink their occupation of the region. True, the surprise attack on Israel on October 6, 1973 came simultaneously from the Egyptian and Syrian fronts after months of planning by the military commands of the two Arab countries,[31] and the coordinated offensive might have seemed to the Syrians and other Arabs as a concerted "Arab" action designed to achieve "Arab" goals, but to the Egyptians, it was undertaken merely to weaken Israel's military response by forcing it to fight on two fronts.

Details of the planning for the attack reveal as much deception as coordination. Patrick Seale, relying on the memoirs of General Sa'ad al-Shazly, commander of the Egyptian armed forces at the time, concludes that President Asad of Syria was "hoodwinked" by Sadat.[32] Asad was made to believe that the war would be prose-

[30] Ali E. Hillal Dessouki, "The Primacy of Economics: The Foreign Policy of Egypt," in *The Foreign Policies of Arab States*, eds., Bahgat Korany and Ali E. Hillal Dessouki. (Boulder, Colorado: Westview Press, 1988), p. 128.

[31] For the details of the preparations for the October War, see Saad Shazly, *The Crossing of the Suez* (San Francisco: American Mideast Research, 1980).

[32] Patrick Seale, *Asad: The Struggle for the Middle East* (Berkeley: University of California Press, 1989), p. 199, see also Shazly, *The Crossing of the Suez*, p. 37.

cuted until both the Sinai and Golan Heights were liberated, but that was never Sadat's intent. The Sinai was the only concern of the Egyptian president. Sadat treated coordination with Syria as completely dependent on his conception of Egyptian interests, and indeed no sooner had coordination begun with the two countries launching their simultaneous offensive, than it ended. Ten days into the war, Egypt's conditions for the cessation of the fighting were outlined by Sadat in a speech to the Egyptian National Assembly without prior consultation with Asad. The Syrian president was naturally piqued, reminding his comrade-in-arms that he had the right to know Sadat's proposals before hearing them on the radio.[33] Then on October 22, Sadat accepted a cease-fire unilaterally in the face of fierce Syrian protestations. Two days earlier, Asad had sent a letter urging Sadat to stay the course. Sadat did not even bother to reply.[34] Consequently, the first time the Syrians heard about Egypt's decision was at the Security Council when the Egyptian representative announced his government's acceptance of the cease-fire.[35]

If the Syrians or anyone else had any doubt about Sadat's determination to chart a separate course for himself and his country, these doubts were to be dispelled in 1975 when Sadat signed on to a plan presented by the American secretary of state, Henry Kissinger, in which the Israelis would pull back from their positions on the Suez Canal in return for an Egyptian renunciation of the use of force against Israel. The arrangement undoubtedly served Egypt's interests, for it allowed Egypt to reopen the Canal, and to regain the oil fields in Abu Rudeis. But it could not have escaped Sadat's notice that the plan was not short of a disaster for the "Arab cause" because it took Egypt out of the Arab-Israeli conflict, thus not only neutralizing the most powerful Arab country, but also closing the book forever on Israel's geostrategic nightmare of fighting on two fronts. The incensed Syrians berated Sadat, accus-

---

[33] Mohamed Heikal, *The Road to Ramadan* (London: Collins, 1975), p. 231; see also Seale, *Asad: The Struggle for the Middle East*, pp. 219–220.

[34] Seale, *Asad: The Struggle for the Middle East*, p. 221.

[35] Heikal, *The Road to Ramadan*, pp. 238–240.

ing him of abandoning the Arab cause. With not so much as batting an eyelid, Sadat unequivocally asserted that his responsibility was to Egypt.[36] By now it had become "painfully obvious," writes Patrick Seale, "that Egypt's pan-Arab phase, which had begun twenty years earlier, was over . . . Sadat's ideological somersault was so complete that it seemed a sort of 'anti-Suez,' setting in reverse everything Nasser had stood for."[37] Sadat's agreement to Kissinger's plan manifestly illustrated his espousal of Egyptian *wataniya* at the expense of Arab *qawmiya*.

Sadat was on a roll, a *wataniya* roll, so to speak. He now thought simply and almost exclusively of Egypt's interests, especially of alleviating the considerable social and economic problems that had beset the country through many years of economic stagnation, which he fervently believed were brought about by costly forays into Arab politics and debilitating wars with Israel. Since the October War, he had gradually and successfully reoriented Egypt's policies and concerns away from the Arab world. He now had to deal with the perennial problem of Israel. He needed to move Egyptian-Israeli relations to a point where peace was realizable, regardless of developments on the wider Arab arena. To do this, he had to break what he called "the psychological barrier," the wall of fear and mistrust built on thirty years of wars and conflicts between Arab and Jew. He needed a gesture of peace that would be grand in its scope and climactic in its impact. He thus resolved to take his plea for peace into the very heart of Israel, to Jerusalem no less. If his move were to eventually bring peace to the other Arabs, then that would be a welcome bonus, the icing on the cake. But it was mainly to serve Egypt's interests that he undertook his electrifyingly dramatic trip to Israel in December 1977. As much as that trip delighted Israelis and Westerners, it stunned Arabs into doleful disbelief. And the Arabs' general disposition did not improve when the Jerusalem trip was followed by the Camp David Accord in the fall of 1978, and finally with the Israeli-Egyptian Peace Treaty in

---

[36] *Times* (London), September 10, 1975.
[37] Seale, *Asad of Syria*, p. 261.

the spring of 1979.[38] This triggered an immediate diplomatic break with the rest of the Arab countries. And Egypt, once the heart and center of Arab politics now resided at its extreme periphery.

Arab condemnation of Egypt's action was universal, both at the popular and elite levels. Almost everyone in the Arab world, it seems, saw the peace treaty as a betrayal of fundamental Palestinian and Arab rights, and Sadat's assurance that he had not signed a separate peace treaty, but one that also catered to Palestinian interests, was met with universal Arab derision. In a sense, Arab fury reflected the growing awareness that what drove Arab political issues were "state interests," and broader Arab concerns transcending state boundaries took a backseat, or worse were left behind somewhere on the road. What Sadat was able to accomplish, no other Arab leader would have dared to even contemplate a decade earlier.[39] His action might have been the work of an authoritarian leader, but there can be little doubt that, in spite of some opposition, there was general support in Egypt for ending the state of belligerency with Israel and redirecting the government's energies to the immense challenges on the home front. "He (Sadat) was particularly thick skinned when it came to Arab nationalist causes," writes Michael Barnett in explaining the peace treaty with Israel, "and Egyptian society was drifting toward a more Egypt-centered view of Arab politics and thus was more receptive to his

---

[38] By far the most authoritative account of the political journey that eventually led to the Egyptian-Israeli peace treaty is William B. Quandt, *Camp David: Peacemaking and Politics* (Washington, D.C.: The Brookings Institution, 1986).

[39] The exception of course was al-Habib Bourguiba, the popular and populist leader of Tunisia, who suggested in 1965 that Arabs would do well to think about the possibility of negotiations with Israel with a view to concluding a lasting peace. Even though Tunisia was geographically and politically peripheral to central Arab concerns, Bourguiba's statements elicited a venomous tirade from Egypt's propaganda organs, and Nasir called the Tunisian leader an "Arab setback" and an "agent for imperialism and Zionism." See al-Jumhuriya al-'Arabiya al-Muttahida, *Majmou'at Khutab wa Tasrihat wa Bayanat al-Rayis Gamal 'Abd al-Nasir* (The collection of the speeches, statements and communiqués of President Gamal 'Abd al-Nasir) (Cairo: Maslahat al-Isti'lamat, n.d.), p. 368. The result was that Bourguiba was virtually ostracized from Arab politics until the Six Day War, when Tunisia dispatched a small fighting force to Egypt. Bourguiba obviously had learned his lesson because in the Khartoum Summit, he was a signatory to a resolution that bound all Arab states to a policy of no recognition of Israel.

policies."[40] And even though the other Arab states condemned Egypt's "statist" policies, arguing for all Arab foreign policies to remain within the general parameters of "Arab consensus," the heated debate itself suggested a sensitivity to the concept of *wataniya* among Arab countries. It was not Egypt's decision to pursue its national interest that they were angry about, it was Sadat's penchant to go it alone, not to consult with them, to treat them with an indifference bordering on contempt. Even an "understanding" Arab leader such as King Husayn would recount the whole episode with more than a passing annoyance:

> I was very angry. I really was upset about it. . . . Before [Sadat] went on this venture, we had been working with President Carter on the idea of a summit meeting in Geneva with all the countries concerned together with the Americans and Soviets. . . . Sadat's move shocked me, especially against a background of Nasser's [promise not to] move on his own with Israel until he could make up for the damage he caused Jordan in that unrealistic and terrible 1967 War. Sadat was the exact opposite. . . . Yet I went and saw him. I said fine. And he went to Washington and I called him there. . . . And then I was on my way back and as we passed through Spain, the Camp David Accords were signed. So we were never a part of it in Jordan, and the Camp David Accords imposed on us in Jordan a role that we had not been consulted about, of essentially providing security in the West Bank, with joint patrols and this and that and the other but without even having a say in it. And that is where we couldn't take it.[41]

So the displeasure of Arab rulers and governments was aimed more at Sadat's methods and less at Egypt's pursuit of its national interests. After all, some of the most ardent of Sadat's critics had themselves pursued, or shortly were about to pursue, policies that smacked more of *wataniya* than *qawmiya*.

---

[40] Barnett, *Dialogues in Arab Politics*, pp. 197–198.
[41] King Husayn's interview with Avi Shlaim in *New York Review of Books*, July 15, 1999, pp. 17–18.

Syria's military intervention in Lebanon in 1976 was a case in point. The essence of Lebanon's political system was derived from an understanding reached in 1943 among the country's various religious sects in which political and administrative posts were distributed in proportion to their numbers in the population.[42] This potentially volatile confessional system worked as long as Lebanon was not subject to outside intrusions. But, the growing potency of Nasirist Arab nationalism began to strain the fragile communal ties inside Lebanon, which reached a breaking point with the radicalization of the Palestinian Resistance after June 1967. Palestinian military operations were launched from bases in the south of Lebanon, and after the guerrillas' expulsion from Jordan in 1970–1971, the south of Lebanon became their only military / strategic haven. The majority of Lebanese Muslims felt that Lebanon was duty-bound to extend all possible support to the Palestinians, whereas most Christians resented what they perceived to be an inexcusable infringement of Lebanese sovereignty by the Palestinians. This attitudinal divide was reinforced by Israel's announced policy of instant and punitive retaliation against countries harboring Palestinian guerrillas. Israel's shelling of border villages and incursions into Lebanese territory became a regular occurrence, so that over the next few years, many villages in South Lebanon were gradually deserted by their inhabitants, most of whom took up residence on the outskirts of Lebanon's capital, Beirut, in ghetto-type shantytowns. By 1975, the combination of Israeli attacks on Lebanon, the Palestinian-induced anarchy, and the extensive widespread demographic dislocations left Lebanon sitting on a powder keg waiting to explode. It came as no surprise therefore that a bloody and debilitating civil war would erupt and last for the next decade and a half.

When Syria sent its military forces across the border into Lebanon in 1976, the political leadership in Damascus insisted that the action was motivated by "Arab nationalist" considerations. The

[42] For excellent analyses of the structure of Lebanon's political system, see Michael Hudson, *The Precarious Republic: Modernization in Lebanon* (New York: Random House, 1968) and Leonard Binder, ed., *Politics in Lebanon* (New York: John Wiley, 1966).

confessional conflict in Lebanon between Christians and Muslims in which the Palestinians participated was seen in Syria as "dividing the Arab nation [and] undermining the principles of Arab nationalism."[43] Every effort had to be made to put an end to the sectarian killings "for the sake of the Arab cause and the Arab nation."[44] And these sentiments were in fact to be expected from a country that characterized itself as "the beating heart of Arabism," and that was ruled by the virulently Arab nationalist Ba'th Party. These themes were touched on by the Syrian president, Hafiz al-Asad, in a major speech delivered after Syrian armor moved into Lebanon. Enumerating the reasons for Syria's military intervention, Asad was unequivocal: "The problem in Lebanon concerns the Arab nation, so it is in consequence an internal Arab problem." He added that it was on behalf of the "Arab nation" that Syria had intervened, for if the bloodshed among Arabs was to be allowed then it would "have led to many negative repercussions within the Arab homeland, repercussions that could affect the Arab national consciousness."[45] Yet outside of Syria, few took Asad's reasoning at its face value, inclined to believe instead that the reason for the military intervention had more to do with Syria's national interest and its hegemonic attitude toward Lebanon.

And Syria indeed had a problem explaining away the target of its initial military thrust. It was not the supposed "anti-Arab nationalist" Lebanese Christians, who had persistently and vigorously defended Lebanese sovereignty against what they perceived as a "Muslim-dominated" Arab unity; rather, Syrian military might was directed against the Muslim nationalists and their allies the Palestinians. Arab nationalists would understandably wonder aloud how it was that Syria, the "beating heart of Arabism," could have joined forces with "the Christian isolationists against its Arab

---

[43] Al-Ba'th (Damascus), April 1, 1976.

[44] Al-Ba'th (Damascus), September 23, 1975.

[45] President Hafiz al-Asad, Speech Delivered Before a General Plenum of Local Government, July 20, 1976 (Damascus: Baath Arab Socialist Party, 1976), pp. 45–48, pp. 75–76; see also Adeed I. Dawisha, Syria and the Lebanese Crisis (London: Macmillan, 1980), pp. 104–105.

nationalist tradition."[46] Others were less nuanced. Asad's main backers, the Soviet leaders "insisted" that he end his assault on the Palestinians and the Lebanese Muslims, otherwise "the imperialists and their collaborators will be able to bring the Arab people and the area's progressive movements under their control."[47] At the opposite spectrum, the Israeli prime minister, Yitzhaq Rabin, not known for his avid support of Arab nationalism, gleefully gave the Syrians Israel's full blessing for killing Palestinian "terrorists."[48] The Arabs were uniformly dismissive of Syria's claims to have acted on behalf of the Arab nation, demanding the complete withdrawal of Syria's invading forces. Anti-Syrian demonstrations occurred in front of Syrian embassies in Arab and other foreign capitals. The rival Ba'thist regime in Baghdad bitterly attacked "the fascist ruling clique in Damascus for this hideous crime against the Arab people of Palestine,"[49] and in a blaze of publicity dispatched troops to the Syrian-Iraqi border "to execute their historic duty."[50] By nature less shrill than their colleagues north of the border, members of the Saudi media reflected their king's displeasure with what was happening in Lebanon.[51] Egypt promptly withdrew its diplomatic mission from Damascus and asked the Syrians to close their embassy in Cairo. To cap it all, the PLO leader, Yasir Arafat, bitterly denounced Asad, and called for an all-out war against Damascus. And generally Arabs agreed, for after all, here was Hafiz al-Asad, the self-proclaimed "lion of Arabism . . . slaughtering Arabism's sacred cow."[52] In short, most Arabs believed that far from serving the interests of the "Arab nation," the Syrian operation was undertaken at best to achieve Syria's national security inter-

---

[46] This was how Salah Bitar, one of the founders of the Ba'th Party who lived in exile in Paris, framed the question in a *Le Monde* article, quoted in Seale, *Asad of Syria*, pp. 285–286.

[47] *Guardian* (London), October 3, 1976.

[48] Quoted in Seale, *Asad of Syria*, p. 285.

[49] *Al-Thawra* (Baghdad), June 2, 1976; the same venomous tone was reproduced in all Iraqi newspapers, radio, and television, all of which, of course, were government controlled.

[50] *Al-Thawra* (Baghdad), June 9, 1976.

[51] *SWB*, June 4, 1976, pp. 8–9.

[52] Seale, *Asad of Syria*, p. 285.

ests, and at worst to realize its irredentist proclivities and hegemonic attitudes.

If Syria's intervention in Lebanon reflected the country's particularistic state interests, then perhaps the military operation could best be explained not so much in terms of Syria's "imperialist" attitudes,[53] but by the way the leadership defined the country's security interests and its demographic structure. Asad and the Syrian leadership believed that the Lebanese civil war would provide Israel with the excuse to intervene in Lebanon allegedly to save the Christians from the "Muslim" Arabs. Asad further suspected that once in Lebanon, the Israelis would turn their attention to the real target of their ambition, Syria. It was for this reason that Damascus reiterated repeatedly that the security of Syria was inseparable from that of Lebanon.[54] And this fear of Israeli perfidy certainly would explain why Syria sent its armed forces to the rescue of Lebanon's Christians against its natural allies, the Muslim-Palestinian alliance.

The other likely reason for Syria's haste to intervene in Lebanon was the sectarian structure of its own demographic makeup. Although Sunni Muslims formed about 65 percent of the population, the bulk of the ruling elite, including Asad, belonged to the 'Alawite sect, an esoteric offshoot of Shi'ism. Representing little more than 11 percent of the population, the 'Alawites were bound to engender deep Sunni resentment of their political dominance. Beyond this primary fissure, other smaller, yet politically and economically significant, communities, such as the Druze, Christians, and Kurds, added to the country's societal heterogeneity.[55] Given Lebanon's geographic, historic, and cultural proximity to Syria,[56] it was

---

[53] In reviewing the maladies suffered by Syria as a result of its Lebanese operation, Asad bitterly remarked: "we did not go into Lebanon to achieve any regional ambitions, nor for any selfish or opportunistic motives. On the contrary, it was at the expense of our economy and our daily bread." *Events* (London), October 1, 1976, p. 20.

[54] For example, *SWB*, June 28, 1975, p. 7; *al-Ba'th* (Damascus), September 23, 1975; Asad, *Speech Delivered Before a General Plenum of Local Government*, pp. 14–16.

[55] See Dawisha, *Syria and the Lebanese Crisis*, p. 59.

[56] Most Syrians believed that Lebanon was part of the historic notion of "Greater Syria," and that the political division of the two countries was artificially created by the French to serve their own colonial interests. Regardless of the historic validity of this claim, Syrians fervently believe it to be true.

in Syria's interests to put the lid on any confessional eruption in Lebanon, lest it spill over into Syria's own fragile demographic structure. In any case, whether motivated by hegemonic ambitions, or whether induced by fears over security and / or demographic vulnerabilities, the intervention of Syria, the "beating heart of Arabism," in Lebanon was undertaken to achieve primarily Syrian national interests against the protestations of literally the whole of the Arab world.

And so by the 1980s, the idea of the sovereignty of the Arab state had become institutionalized not just in the rules of the game that governed political relations within the Arab world, but also, and more crucially, in the very consciousness of the Arab public, rulers and subjects alike. Few Arabs in the 1980s and 1990s thought about Arab nationalism in the same way an earlier generation had done in the pre-1967 period. Whereas in those days Arab nationalism was synonymous with Arab political unity, now it had turned into a kind of universalist concept, a cultural Arabism with certain political overtones in the sense that it provided an umbrella under which sovereign territorial states were expected to conduct their business. In the 1980s and 1990s even this modest expectation proved too difficult to realize. One reason for this was the lack of popular pressure on leaders to conform to the strict norms of Arab nationalism. People had accepted the resilience of their states, had been co-opted into the body politics, and had become first and foremost citizens of their respective states, even if they happened to harbor little love for the regime. While, as a cultural group, the Arabic-speaking people were aware of the many bonds that brought them together, they now also accepted the segmentations within the Arab world,[57] demarcations that predicated on notions of citizenship, economic interest, territoriality, and increasingly, identity.

It was not that most people no longer considered themselves to be Arab, it was simply that the bonds of Arab nationalism no longer exercised the same hold on the Arab psyche that they did

[57] See Ghassan Salame's excellent analysis in "Inter-Arab Politics: The Return of Geography," in *The Middle East: Ten Years After Camp David*, ed. William B. Quandt (Washington, D.C.: The Brookings Institution, 1988), pp. 319–353.

two or three decades earlier. When Israel invaded Lebanon in the summer of 1982, there certainly was great concern in the Arab world, but there was also a stunning paucity of popular eruptions in Arab cities. Compare this with the pervasive demonstrations, riots, and mini-rebellions in various Arab states that accompanied the tripartite attack on Egypt in 1956. Between 1980 and 1988, Arab Iraq fought a debilitating war against Persian Iran, yet few Arabs cared, and some were in fact hostile. Syria's Asad passionately detested Iraq's leader Saddam Husayn, and as such supported Iran unreservedly. This was bound to raise eyebrows, as Syria took great pride in projecting itself as the "heart of Arabism."

But people did not dwell on Syria's support for Iran too long. After all, Syria was a sovereign state with a right to pursue its interests and define its international relations. "Nationalist" Libya, too, was hardly a paragon of support for the Iraqis. Depending on the mood of its mercurial leader, Mu'amer al-Qadhafi, Libya's political bearing continued to oscillate wildly between the two warring parties. From others there were words of support, but precious little else. Iraq did receive money from the oil-rich Gulf states, but that was more to bolster Iraq as a security shield for themselves against the messianic vagaries of the Iranian ayatollahs than to any attachment to Arab nationalism. On the popular level, Iraq trumpeted the inflow of "Arab volunteers" into its armed forces to fight the Persian common enemy. Most of these "volunteers," however, were Egyptians and Sudanese who had arrived in Iraq in large numbers in the 1970s seeking employment, and were drafted in the army by the Iraqi authorities. In reality, there were probably less "real volunteers" from Arab countries helping "Arab" Iraq in its war effort (which at times, particularly 1982–1983 and 1986–1987, was pretty desperate) than those who participated in non-Arab Afghanistan's war against the Soviet Union. Naturally Islam had something to do with this, but that was precisely the measure of the decline of Arab nationalism against other competitive identities. Indeed, the only genuine popular eruption in the Arab world after the 1970s occurred in Palestinian occupied territories in the late 1980s, and it had very little, if anything, to do with Arab nationalism. It was wholly Palestinian inspired, built on purely Palestinian concerns, and carrying exclusively Palestinian aspirations.

Of course, the status-quo Arab kings and presidents had been leading the charge away from revolutionary Arab nationalism. But even those Arab leaders who had been the most ardent Arab nationalists, believing in the inseparability of the "Arab homeland," were themselves undergoing an attitudinal transformation. Hafiz al-Asad, the committed Ba'thist since his teenage years, was now talking about state sovereignty and independence. Referring to Lebanon, the one country that Syrians perceived as the most natural candidate for unity with Syria, Asad confided as a matter-of-fact that Syrians and Lebanese may be one people, "but we are two states."[58] Even a more startling transformation occurred to that other erstwhile Ba'thist, Iraq's Saddam Husayn.

In the late 1970s and early 1980s Iraq, under brisk presidential prompting, began to actively tap into its long history, exploring the rich heritage that predated the country's Arab / Islamic identity. This found vigorous expression in literature, arts, and architecture, and had the effect of fostering national pride in the country's long and distinguished history.[59] These conveyors of popular culture would refer to the inhabitants of such ancient civilizations as Babylonia, Akkadia, Assyria, and Sumeria as "Iraqi" men and women, as "our grandfathers," and "great ancestors."[60] The message that was conveyed, with the undoubted blessings, even instigation, of Saddam was this: while partaking in the encompassing Arab culture and political arrangements, Iraq still boasted a unique identity which emerged from an illustrious, multi-civilization history, and which consequently gave the country a sense of distinctiveness from, even superiority over, the other Arabs. The conclusion is obvious. The Iraqi state is a legitimate entity, and is simply a manifestation of the people's uniqueness.

[58] Quoted in Seale, *Asad of Syria*, p. 350.

[59] See Amatzia Baram, "Mesopotamian Identity in Ba'thi Iraq," *Middle Eastern Studies*, vol. 19, (October 1983).

[60] Ibid., p. 436.

The case for the legitimacy of the Iraqi state did not rest solely on the country's "Mesopotamian" heritage. To Saddam Husayn, the long-standing Ba'thist and Arab unity buff, it was also a function of critical psychological transformations which had occurred among the Arabs as a whole. By the 1980s, Saddam was arguing that comprehensive and organic Arab unity was no longer possible, or indeed even desirable to the new pragmatic Arabs. This new formulation is encapsulated in the following statement which he made in September 1982, and which clearly conceives of Arab unity as a political solidarity among independent and separate Arab states:

> Arab unity can only take place after a clear demarcation of borders between all countries. [It] must not take place through the elimination of the local and national characteristics of any Arab country. . . . The question of linking unity to the removal of boundaries is no longer acceptable to present Arab mentality. It could have been acceptable ten or twenty years ago. We have to take into consideration the change which the Arab mind and psyche have undergone. We must see the world as it is. Any Arab would have wished to see the Arab nation as one state. . . . But these are sheer dreams. The Arab reality is that the Arabs are now twenty-two states, and we have to behave accordingly. . . . Unity must give strength to its partners, not cancel their national identity.[61]

And these twenty-two states were going their own separate ways, each concerned with its own national interest and with formulating policies designed to strengthen its sovereign status and enhance its internal security. If the thought of Arab political arrangements came to mind, it was only as a way of fortifying the states' security against the rising challenge of a new revolutionary movement that had stepped into the void left by the demise of Arab nationalism. In the 1980s and 1990s, radical Islam had become for the Arab regimes what Arab nationalism was in the 1950s and 1960s.

---

[61] These are excerpts from an interview given by Saddam Husayn to chief editors of Kuwaiti newspapers and broadcast on Iraqi radio. This particular quote comes from Christine Moss Helms, *Iraq: Eastern Flank of the Arab World* (Washington, D.C.: The Brookings Institution, 1984), pp. 114–115.

When Arab nationalism reigned supreme, it was able to relegate other ideas and ideologies to peripheral, even inconsequential, status. However, unlike liberal constitutionalism or Marxism, Islam could never be eradicated from people's inner concerns; it was embedded in the very fabric of Arab Muslim society. On a personal level, Islam continued to constitute a crucial element of identity, but that was where it stayed; overwhelmed by Arab nationalism, it was unable to manifest itself politically. On the few occasions when it did, the custodians of the nationalist narrative marshaled the brutal and unforgiving power of the state to keep it at bay.

With the catastrophic defeat of Arab nationalism in June 1967, radical Islamic groups became more active, more adventurous, and consequently more prominent. Their search for recruits grew easier, as people, in their search for an alternative to the increasingly discredited secular nationalism, reoriented their vision to the past, to Muslim esprit de corps, to an authenticity untouched by corrupting foreign values. If a spur was needed to finally shift radical Islam from the wings to the center stage of political activity, it was provided by the Iranian revolution of 1978–1979. Here was the irrefutable proof of what Muslims, guided by their faith, could achieve. Here was a live demonstration of the power of Islam to put Islam in power.

The Iranian revolution and the establishment of the Islamic Republic of Iran gave heart to Muslim radicalism in the Arab world. In the 1980s, significant challenges to the Arab states from Islamic fundamentalist movements occurred in Egypt, Syria, Iraq, Lebanon, Algeria, Tunisia, Bahrain, and, to a lesser extent, Saudi Arabia, Jordan, and Morocco. These groups mounted their challenge to the established Arab political order in the name of social justice and Muslim unity.[62] Carrying their Islamic identity on their sleeves, they were contemptuously dismissive of modernity with its alien ideas of "sovereignty" and "nationalism." They publicly condemned these notions as *hulul mustawrada*, imported ideas from the anti-Islamic

---

[62] For a thorough exposition of the ideas of the Islamic radicals, see Emmanuel Sivan, *Radical Islam* (New Haven, Connecticut: Yale University Press, 1991).

West, that should be unceremoniously discarded.[63] To the Muslim radicals, *al-Islam huwa al-hal,* "the only solution was Islam," and they could have added, the only permissible identity was Islamic. Arab nationalism was simply a by-product of the new *jahiliya,* the contemporary "age of ignorance" resembling that of the pre-Islamic era. The Islamist assault not only undermined further the Arab nationalist cause, but it also impelled the Arab state to strengthen its institutions in order to ensure its stability. The net result was an even greater emphasis on state sovereignty.

The primacy of the interests of the "state" produced a new form of regional political arrangements. Concerned about the regional repercussions of the Iranian Islamic revolution and the Iran-Iraq War, and fearing the radicalizing impact of Iran's Islamic model on their populations, the Gulf states of Kuwait, Bahrain, Saudi Arabia, Qatar, the Sultanate of Oman, and the United Arab Emirates joined together to form the Gulf Cooperation Council (GCC) in September 1981. Even though at first sight the GCC seemed to represent an intermediate step toward comprehensive Arab unity, it was in fact nothing of the sort. To begin with, it was geography, not national identity, that constituted the real foundation of this political arrangement. Secondly, the members of the GCC publicly spurned ideology, emphasizing instead economic and security cooperation among sovereign states. When asked why only the six Gulf states and not others, GCC representatives responded, with not so much as a hint of discomfort or incertitude, that the six GCC states shared certain historical and cultural traits that set them apart from the other Arabs.[64] In a similar move, three North African states, Morocco, Algeria, and Tunisia, geographically proximate and seeking economic cooperation formed the Arab Maghrebi Union.

---

[63] Yusuf al-Qardawi, *al-Hulul al-Mustawrada wa Kaifa Janat 'ala Ummatina* (The imported solutions and how they harmed our nation) (Cairo: Maktabat Wahbeh, 1977); see also Shukri B. Abed, "Islam and Democracy," in *Democracy, War and Peace in the Middle East,* eds. David Grantham and Mark Tessler (Bloomington: Indiana University Press, 1995), pp. 124–126.

[64] See Barnett, *Dialogues in Arab Politics,* p. 201. To the question why Iraq was not invited to join, one GCC member allegedly replied: "Do you see Iraqis wearing *i'gal wa chafiya,*" (the headdress usually worn by Gulf men).

As the century drew to a close, it also closed the book on Arab nationalism. Those few old souls who continued to cling obstinately to its revolutionary message seemed strangely out of place in the 1990s. An observer at a conference on Arab nationalism and unity which convened in Beirut in 1994, wrote:

> [T]he conferees appeared to represent an extinct tribe using strange words—indeed, a language incomprehensible in our time. Most of them had grey hair and stooping backs. Some needed canes to help them walk. Some had hearing aids and shaking hands that made it difficult for them to write, and others had difficulty getting the words out.[65]

What was left of Arab nationalism by the end of the twentieth century from what it was in its heyday four decades earlier was a modified version that the political scientist Shibley Telhami calls the "New Arabism." Telhami argues that two trends distinguished this new Arabism from the Arab nationalism of old. First, the direction of the new Arabism was bottom-up; it was not inspired by state institutions or by charismatic leadership, but by disaffected intellectual elites trying to chart a political course independently from the state. Second, the new Arabism was nourished by a new regionally based media, which, because it was driven by profit, had to appeal to themes that were unifying in nature.[66] Telhami sees this "New Arabism" as "an independent transnational movement in the Arab world."[67] But one is hard put to consider this "new version" of Arabist sentiment as analogous to the Arab nationalism of the 1950s and 1960s, moved as it was by the almost obsessive drive to organic Arab unity. To begin with, the disaffected Arab

---

[65] The words are those of Fahmi Huwaydi, a well-known Egyptian journalist, who holds moderate Islamist views. His impressions of the conference appeared in *al-Ahram (Cairo)*, May 17, 1994. This particular quote from the article is taken from Martin Kramer, *Arab Awakening and Islamic Revival: The Politics of Ideas in the Middle East* (London: Transaction Press, 1996) p. 3.

[66] Shibley Telhami, "Power, Legitimacy, and Peace-Making in Arab Coalitions: The New Arabism," in *Ethnic Conflict and International Politics in the Middle East*, ed. Leonard Binder (Gainesville: University Press of Florida, 1999), pp. 56–57.

[67] Ibid., p. 56.

elites of the 1990s might have had differences with their governments over a whole spectrum of issues, but not over the sovereignty
of their respective states. And this was reflected as well in the re-
porting of the new media. Apart from the Palestinian cause, which
by the way was supported not only by Arabs, but also by non-Arab
Muslims and still many others, this media was as sensitive to state-
centered concerns as to regionally based issues. Whatever this
"Arab transnational movement" was supposed to do, it certainly
could not challenge or even question the legitimacy and sovereignty
of the Arab state.[68]

So at the *qawmiya* level, what Arabs were left with at the dawn
of the twenty-first century was merely a recognition of a cultural
proximity that at best set vague general parameters for political
action. And the efficacy of even this meager role is questionable.
Where were these parameters when Arab Syria sided with Persian
Iran against Arab Iraq, or when Jordan signed a peace treaty with
Israel? In the latter instance, some displeasure was voiced by a few
Arab governments (including, hypocritically, that of Egypt), but it
amounted to very little, and it soon fizzled out.

It is probably the case that the "disaffected intellectual elite"
of this new "Arabism" would have disapproved strongly of these
policies and considered them a disgrace to Arab principles. But
sulking away at the tables of sidewalk cafés does not measure up
to the tumultuous passions engendered by the popular eruptions
of the nationalist generation two or three decades earlier. It is not
that the Arab states and their citizens no longer considered themselves to be Arab, or that they did not feel strongly about certain
"Arabist" issues; it was simply that sublimating state interests to
such considerations was now a thing of the past, as arcane and
archaic as Arab nationalism itself.

---

[68] In a subsequent article, Telhami expounds on the limitations of this new Arabism, one
of which is the absence of the goal of Arab unity. See Shibley Telhami and Michael Barnett,
eds., *Identity and Foreign Policy in the Middle East* (Ithaca, New York: Cornell University
Press, 2002).

CHAPTER ELEVEN

THE DEMISE OF ARAB NATIONALISM:
A POSTMORTEM

It took some time for the light to finally go out on Arab nationalism, but the power generating it was turned off in June 1967.
After the Six Day War, Arab nationalism's slide toward political marginality became irreversible. And what stamped on it
this sense of fatality was the fact that it was Egypt under Gamal
'Abd al-Nasir that lost. Egypt's devastating defeat was Arab nationalism's mortal loss, for, as this book has made abundantly
clear, the fate of Arab nationalism during the struggles, triumphs,
and reversals of the 1950s and 1960s was inexorably linked to
Egypt and its charismatic president. Had it just been Syria or Jordan, or even both, who lost the war, it would not have been the
unmitigated disaster for Arab nationalism that the June war
turned out to be. But Arab nationalism could not survive the ab-
ject humiliation inflicted on its acknowledged prophet, who,
through his shrill and overzealous propaganda machine, had
promised a fabled triumph in this *al-Ma'raka al-Masiriya*, the battle of destiny. Indeed, "The Voice of the Arabs," in a baffling act
of self-deception, continued to proclaim victory after victory on

the Sinai battleground long after the Egyptian army had been summarily defeated.[1]

Intrinsically linked to Egypt's defeat was the consequential loss of charisma by Nasir. Max Weber defined charisma as "a certain quality of an individual personality by virtue of which he is set apart from ordinary men and treated as though endowed with supernatural, superhuman or, at least, specifically exceptional qualities."[2] It was these perceived qualities that allowed Nasir to assume the uncontested leadership of the Arab nationalist march, and that made him the only person capable of uniting the Arabs and defeating their enemies. The charismatic halo began to fade after the collapse of the United Arab Republic (UAR),[3] but it essentially evaporated with the June 1967 rout. "The charismatic relationship between [Nasir] and the masses formed during the bright youthful days of Bandung and Suez," Fouad Ajami writes, "was shattered with the defeat; another variant born out of despair and a sense of loss, sustained him until his death. He would stay in power not as a confident, vibrant hero, but as a tragic figure, a symbol of better days, an indication of the will to resist."[4] Ajami overstates Nasir's weakness, for the Egyptian president was still the most influential Arab leader. After all, at the height of the Jordanian civil war in September 1970, where did King Husayn, Arafat, and the other Arab leaders go but to Cairo and to Nasir to resolve the crisis?[5] Yet, influential as he might have been, this Nasir was not the charismatic leader that he was a decade earlier. To the flock, he seemed

[1] See Douglas A. Boyd, *Broadcasting in the Arab World: A Survey of the Electronic Media in the Middle East*, 2nd ed. (Ames: Iowa State University Press, 1993), p. 323.

[2] Max Weber, *The Theory of Social and Economic Organization*, translated by A. M. Henderson and Talcott Parsons (London: Oxford University Press, 1947), p. 358.

[3] 'Ali Karim Sa'id, *'Iraq 8 Shibat 1963: Min Hiwar al-Mafahim ila Hiwar al-Damm, Muraja'at fi Dhakirat Taleb Shabib* (Iraq of 8 February, 1963: from a dialogue over norms to a dialogue of blood, reviews of the memory of Taleb Shabib) (Beirut: Dar al-Kunuz al-Adabiya, 1999), p. 217.

[4] Fouad Ajami, *The Arab Predicament: Arab Political Thought and Practice Since 1967* (London: Cambridge University Press,1981), p. 85.

[5] See Mohamed Heikal, *Nasser: The Cairo Documents* (London: New English Library, 1972), pp. 15–18.

no longer possessed of the superhuman qualities of old, and among the other Arab leaders, he was now at most first among equals. Even his most loyal followers and disciples, now freed from his charismatic hold, began to jump ship. Such was the course of action taken by the Arab Nationalist Movement (ANM), which, since the mid-1950s, had unquestioningly tied its fate to Nasir. After the 1967 debacle, the ANM publicly abandoned "Nasirism" which they now branded as a "bourgeois movement which had been destined to fail" and espoused instead Marxist-Leninist principles.[6] The Six Day War was the culmination of a string of setbacks and reversals suffered by Nasir since Iraq's refusal to join the UAR. Defeat was no longer a word; it had become a culture, chipping away at the charisma of Nasir and the mystique of Arab nationalism.

One reason for these setbacks was the gradual loss of "imperialism" as the target of Egypt's Arab nationalist mission. At the time of the Egyptian revolution, there were very few "truly" independent Arab countries. Even those who were allegedly sovereign states with memberships in the United Nations, such as Egypt and Iraq, still had British bases and personnel on their soil. So imperialism, which for the Arabs subsumed colonialism under its definitional umbrella, became the much needed "other" for Arab nationalism.[7] The anti-imperialist crusade began with Egypt's assault on the Baghdad Pact, and from there moved on to all imperialist interests, projects, and alleged agents in the area. Imperialism was a convenient "other." The "imperialist forces" were outsiders, alien to the area, had committed many injustices against the Arab people, and therefore were "deserving" of the abuse heaped upon them. And that in a nutshell defined much of the fight against impe-

---

[6] 'Abdallah Saloom al-Samara'i, "Harakat al-Qawmiyeen al-'Arab wa Dawruha fi al-Wa'i al-Qawmi" (The Arab nationalist movement and its role in nationalist awareness), *al-Mustaqbal al-'Arabi*, no. 84 (February 1986): 86.

[7] For the importance of the "other" to the formation of national identity, see Edward Said, *Orientalism*, 2nd ed. (New York: Vintage Books, 1994), pp. 331–332. For the primacy of the anti-imperialist struggle in Nasir's perceptions, see A. I. Dawisha, "Perceptions, Decisions and Consequences in Foreign Policy: The Egyptian Intervention in the Yemen," *Political Studies*, vol. 25, no. 2 (June 1977). The struggle against colonialism also constitutes the third "fundamental" principle of the constitution of the Ba'th Party. See Sylvia Haim, ed., *Arab Nationalism: An Anthology* (Berkeley: University of California Press, 1962), p. 234.

rialism. It was as much language as it was concrete policies. Hurl-
ing insults at the once invincible outsiders was as good as defeating
them militarily.[8] And Arab nationalism prospered as long as it
could ride the verbal anti-imperialist bandwagon.

By the 1960s, however, imperialism had become less relevant:
British presence in Egypt and Iraq was eliminated; the Baghdad
Pact was defeated; Jordan's British chief of staff, Sir John Glubb,
was dismissed; Lebanon's pro-Western Camille Chamoun was replaced by the independent Fuad Shihab; and the Algerians, sacri-
ficing a million dead in a heroic struggle, had triumphed over
French colonial power. As the custodian of the Arab nationalist
narrative, Nasir had to find new targets, new "others." So Arab
nationalist fury was turned against Arab countries that Nasir
deemed to be "reactionary." But in such a milieu, with Arab pitted
against Arab, there were no easy victories to be had. No word or
term could match the symbolic power and emotional resonance of
"anti-imperialism," with its conceptual separation of Arab from
non-Arab, of "us" from "them." Iraq's Qasim, Saudi Arabia's Faysal, or the monarchists in Yemen could not be defeated on symbolism alone. By 1967, the loss of the "imperialist other" had done
considerable harm to Nasir's charisma, to his perceived ability to
bring the other parts of the Arab world into his Arab nationalist
caravan. And there could be little doubt that this symbolic diminution of Nasir's aura was as devastating for Arab nationalism as the
June 1967 military defeat of Egypt and the other Arabs.

In any case, in the aftermath of June 1967, Nasir faced horrendous domestic problems that effectively claimed every iota of his
energies, and relegated Arab nationalist issues to the outer periphery of his concerns. To begin with, there were the hordes of Israeli
soldiers camped on the eastern bank of the Suez Canal, a mere
three hours away from Cairo, and if their commanders had felt like
making the three-hour trek, Nasir knew that he did not have an

---

[8] See Adeed Dawisha, "Anti-Americanism in the Arab World: Memories of the Past in
the Attitudes of the Present," in *Anti-Americanism in the Third World*, eds. Alvin Z. Rubinstein and Donald E. Smith (New York: Praeger, 1985), pp. 67–83.

army to stop them. Then there was the abysmal condition of the structurally fragile economy, made even weaker by the financial strains of war and its attendant demographic dislocations. The task of domestic reconstruction was herculean, robbing Nasir of any inclination to look beyond Egypt's now contested frontiers.

Moving away from revolutionary Arab nationalism and its essential ingredient of comprehensive and organic Arab unity, Nasir was at least partly to blame for the growing prominence of other competing identities and ideologies. Nor did his mounting dependence on the financial support of status-quo, conservative Arab states, that had vigorously fought Nasir's Arab nationalism bode well for the continued health and vibrancy of the Arab nationalist creed. Pragmatic considerations outweighed ideological fidelity in Nasir's decision to seek détente with the status-quo forces in the area. He signaled this change of attitude by closing down the "Voice of the Arabs" radio station, which for so long had been the voice of radical Arab nationalism. By the end of the Khartoum Summit meeting, *wataniya* had been consecrated as the dominant ideology, regulating inter-Arab relations on the principle of state sovereignty.

Of course, as we have seen, this was no sudden revelation. The *qawmiya-wataniya* debate had been an ongoing battle for some time. Even in its heyday, Arab nationalism had to contend with statist sentiments. Sati' al-Husri voiced the frustrations of Arab nationalists in an introduction to a book published in the 1950s. Written in the form of an elegy, the introduction was entitled, *How Strange*:

> We rebelled against the English; we rebelled against the French . . .
> We rebelled against those who colonized our land and tried to enslave us . . .
> We repeated the red revolutions many times, and we continued with our white revolutions over a number of years . . .
> And for this we endured so much suffering, sustained so many losses, and sacrificed so many lives . . .

But:

> When we finally gained our liberty, we began to sanctify the borders
> that they had instituted after they had divided our land. . .
> And we forgot that these borders were but the boundaries of the
> "solitary confinement" and the "house arrest" which they had
> imposed on us![9]

Part of the reason for this lament was that the interests of Arab
political and economic elites in most cases had become contingent
on the survival of their particular state. It was hardly surprising
that these elites were loath to put their interests at risk for the sake
of Arab unity.[10] Consequently, those who espoused *wataniya* argued that Arab nationalism was used as a license to threaten and
coerce recalcitrant domestic elites, thus making irredentism the
order of the day.[11] Beyond economic interests, the *wataniya* advocates relied on geopolitical and cultural arguments in making their
case. They insisted that Arab nationalists had to understand that
while various Arab states might accept an overarching Arab identity, geographic and even cultural separation were real and potent
enough to preclude an organic unity. And indeed, the decline of
Arab nationalism from 1958 onward testifies to the potency of this
argument.

Iraq was a case in point. Many Iraqi nationalists who had supported Nasir in his feud with the pro-British Nuri al-Sa'id were
nevertheless wary about such phrases as "the Arab people of
Iraq,"[12] that were used incessantly by Nasirists and Ba'thists, and
which did not acknowledge the existence of a non-Arab Kurdish

---

[9] Abu Khaldun Sati' al-Husri, *al-'Uruba Awalan* (Arabism first) (Beirut: Dar al-'Ilm li al-
Malayeen, 1955), p. 7.

[10] Walid Kazziha, "al-Qawmiya al-'Arabiya fi Marhalat ma bein al-Harbayn al-'Alamiyatayn," (Arab nationalism in the period between the two World Wars) in *al-Mustaqbal al-
'Arabi*, no. 5 (January 1979): 61.

[11] See Abbas Kelidar, "A Quest for Identity," *Middle Eastern Studies*, vol. 33, no. 2 (April
1997): 411. See also Selim Matar, *al-Dhat al-Jariha: Ishkalat al-Hawiya fi al-'Iraq wa al-
'Alam al-'Arabi "al-Shirqani"* (Wounded essence: problems of identity in Iraq and the Arab
"Eastern" world) (Beirut: al-Mu'asasa al-'Arabiya li al-Dirasat wa al-Nashr, 1997), pp.
196–197.

[12] Riad Taha, *Qissat al-Wuhda wa al-Infisal: Tajribat Insan 'Arabi Khilal Ahdath 1955–
1961* (The story of unity and secession: the experience of an Arab person during the events
of 1955–1961) (Beirut: Dar al-Afaq al-Jadida, 1974), p. 96.

community that represented around 20 percent of the Iraqi population. Nor were many Arab Shiites sold on Arab unity, which they perceived as a primarily Sunni project. It was this communal mosaic which was Iraq that afforded Qasim the opportunity to fend off efforts to join Iraq into the UAR at a time when Arab nationalism seemed triumphantly unstoppable. Qasim promoted an "Iraq First" identity, emphasizing the country's historical status as the cradle of great pre-Arab civilizations. He pointedly added the Akkadian eight-point star of Ishtar to the national flag, as well as incorporating the insignia of the sun god Shamash to Iraq's national emblem.[13] The prestige of Arab nationalism suffered much, as Iraq, throughout the five years of Qasim's rule, pursued policies that were vehemently anti-unionist, promoting vigorously Iraq's sovereignty and its own national (*watani*) interests.

Indeed, even when the Ba'thists took over at the helm of power in 1968, their enthusiasm for Arab nationalist projects was tempered by a recognition of the limited capacities of their fervently unionist Party, as well as of their country's own needs. A Party resolution admitted that

> . . . there were deficiencies and mistakes in the understanding and definition of the dialectical connection between the local (watani) tasks with which the party [was] confronted . . . and [the Arab nationalist] tasks. . . . The party was pushed into the [Arab nationalist] arena. . .in a way that largely exceeded its capability [before] many tasks were accomplished on the local Iraqi level . . . such as stabilizing the regime . . . and [fully] solving the Kurdish problem.[14]

It was not that the Iraqi Ba'thist regime had abandoned its commitment to *qawmiya*, rather they felt that focusing on the country—achieving some form of political harmony, reviving its economy, building its infrastructure, and especially solving its ethnic and sectarian problems—was a more pressing need than a full-fledged

[13] Amatzia Baram, "Mesopotamian Identity in Ba'thi Iraq," *Middle Eastern Studies*, vol. 19, (October 1983): 427.

[14] Quoted in Amatzia Baram, "Qawmiyya and Wataniyya in Ba'thi Iraq: The Search for a New Balance," *Middle Eastern Studies*, vol. 19 (April 1983): 193.

charge toward Arab unity. In instructing an educational committee, Saddam Husayn said: "When we talk of the [Arab] nation we
should not forget to talk about the Iraqi people. . . . When we talk
about the Arab homeland we should not neglect to educate the
Iraqi to take pride in the piece of land in which he lives . . . [Iraqis]
consist of Arabs and non-Arabs, [so] when we talk of the great
[Arab] homeland, we must not push the non-Arabs to look for a
country outside Iraq."[15] Could there be a clearer expression of the
effort to reorient the ideological compass of party loyalists, indeed
to subvert their lifelong Ba'thist beliefs? *Qawmiya* was certainly
not discarded, but it was *wataniya*, which was the immediate focus
of concern. Saddam was essentially preaching political realities, for,
aspirations aside, it was the internal condition of Iraq that was the
stuff of politics.

The Syrian Ba'thists were no less centered on Syria. When they
scrambled to Cairo after the Ba'thist coup of March 1963 to talk
unity with Nasir, their motives were more local than regional. Arab
nationalism was the publicly articulated goal, but the more pressing motive was their own legitimation inside Syria. "We need to
exploit your excellency's name," a member of the Syrian delegation
told Nasir, "that's all there is to it."[16] And in the talks the Syrian
Ba'thists, the stalwart propagators of comprehensive Arab unity,
insisted on such measures of autonomy that would render any
union a loose, almost inconsequential, federal arrangement. And
in any case, the talks simply afforded the Syrian Ba'thists the
breathing space they needed to neutralize all opposition to their
rule in Syria, including pro-Nasir unionist elements.

Cynical as their maneuvering might have been, the Syrian Ba'thists were in fact reflecting an ideological duality that was ingrained
in Syria's sociopolitical fabric between *qawmiya* and *wataniya*, between perceiving itself as "the beating heart of Arabism" on the
one hand, and the center of *bilad al-Sham* (Greater Syria) on the
other hand. The latter concept was given intellectual coherence by

[15] Ibid., p. 196.
[16] Quoted in Malik Mufti, *Sovereign Creations: Pan-Arabism and Political Order in Syria and Iraq* (Ithaca, New York: Cornell University Press, 1996), p. 150.

Antun Sa'ada as early as the 1930s,[17] and even though Sa'ada was executed in 1949, his party outlawed shortly thereafter, and his program swept aside in the 1950s by a triumphant Arab nationalism, his ideas of a certain Syrian uniqueness and excellence would still find an echo in Syrian sensibility. If this sense of separateness was dormant during the 1950s, the Arab nationalist decade, then Syria's experience under the UAR might have moved it to the forefront of Syrian consciousness.[18] Regardless of the grandiose rhetoric about Arab unity, successive Syrian leaders have always catered first and foremost to Syria's interests. And President Hafiz al-Asad, who ruled Syria from 1970 to 2000, was no exception. While beating the drums of Arab nationalism at every opportunity, Asad was a pragmatic, even Machiavellian, politician whose regional and international policies were made with Syria's and his own interests in mind.[19]

And then in Egypt, in Nasir's own backyard, with all the means utilized by the authoritarian state to implant *qawmiya* into the Egyptian psyche, Egyptian *wataniya* could not be elbowed out. As late as 1963, after almost a decade of concerted Arab nationalist campaign, Nasir would voice his misgivings about the depth of the Arab orientations of his countrymen.[20] Given the inherent strength of this feeling of "Egyptianism," it was hardly surprising that Nasir's successor, Anwar al-Sadat, would use it in order to get out from under the overbearing memory of his towering predecessor.

Sadat began by changing the name of the state from the United Arab Republic to the Arab Republic of Egypt, "where 'Arab' is

[17] For a concise exposition of Sa'ada's ideas, see Majid Khadduri, *Political Trends in the Arab World: The Role of Ideas and Ideals in Politics* (Baltimore: Johns Hopkins University Press, 1970), pp. 186–194.

[18] Itamar Rabinovich, *Syria Under the Ba'th, 1963–1966: The Army Party Symbiosis* (Jerusalem: Israel Universities Press, 1972), p. 20.

[19] See R. Stephen Humphreys, *Between Memory and Desire: The Middle East in a Troubled Age* (Berkeley: University of California Press, 1999), pp. 73–74.

[20] Al-Jumhuriya al-'Arabiya al-Muttahida, *Mahadhir Jalsat Mubahathat al-Wuhda* (The proceedings of the meetings on unity discussions) (Cairo: National Printing and Publishing House, 1963), p. 94. "The centuries of Ottoman tyranny," writes Muhamed Hasaneen Haykal, "isolated [Egypt] from the [rest of the Arabs]. Egypt . . . was unable to shift its attention from its own soil so that it can look across the Sinai and discover its Arab position." *Al-Ahram* (Cairo), November 3, 1961.

only the adjective and 'Egypt' is the noun."[21] And as we have seen, Sadat's policies, especially after the October 1973 war, which culminated in the 1979 Egyptian-Israeli peace treaty, were motivated solely by considerations of Egypt's interests. These policies were undertaken without regard to the rest of the Arabs; indeed, they were perceived universally in the Arab world to be *against* the Arab will. Simultaneously, Sadat embarked on a policy of cultural reorientation toward Egypt. This was evident in subtle changes in school curricula, highlighting Egypt's long history, cultural prominence, and unique personality,[22] and in the emphasis in the government-controlled media on Egyptian domestic affairs and on foreign policy items that spotlighted Egypt's prestige and status in international affairs. By the end of the 1970s, *wataniya* had won the day in Egypt.

It was not only the state, but also sub-state identities that competed with Arab nationalism for people's allegiance. In a number of Arab states, tribe, religion, and sect continued to be major, even primordial, foci of citizens' loyalties. This was, as we have seen, a considerable obstacle to the growth of Arab nationalism before World War II. In the Arab nationalist lexicon, terms such as *shu'ubiya* (loosely depicting ethnic and sectarian particularism) or *al-'asabiya al-qabaliya* (tribal solidarity) were steeped in disparaging and derisive undertone. So with the spectacular rise of Arab nationalism in the 1950s, it became decidedly unfashionable to profess a tribal or sectarian identity. But that did not mean that these identities were expelled from people's consciousness; rather, they were just not readily or vociferously advertised.

In some states of course, tribal affiliations were the backbone of popular support that shielded local leaderships from the advancing tide of revolutionary Arab nationalism. That was certainly the case with Saudi Arabia, where the tribally based demographic structure contributed significantly to the stability of the political order. In the process of transferring the loyalty of the bedouin from tribe to

[21] Eberhard Kienle, "Arab Unity Schemes Revisited: Interest, Identity, and Policy in Syria and Egypt," *International Journal of Middle East Studies*, vol. 27 (February 1995): 66.
[22] Ibid.

state, successive Saudi monarchs made sure to act, and be perceived, simply as tribal overlords. An example of this endeavor was the *Majlis*, which was institutionalized in 1952 by a royal decree, granting every subject, in true tribal fashion, the right of access to the royal family. In these gatherings, the ruler was expected to settle disputes, take note of complaints, acknowledge proclamations of loyalty, listen to poetic renderings, or simply take part in general conversation. Such efforts to continue and maintain tribal identity allowed the Saudi rulers to withstand Nasir's Arab nationalist onslaught for over a decade between 1957 and 1967. But the Saudis did not stop there. They also created a military force, the National Guard, which was independent of the regular armed forces, and which was entrusted with safeguarding the monarchy even if Nasirist elements succeeded in infiltrating the regular armed forces. The novelty about the National Guard was that it was composed almost exclusively of bedouins from tribes inhabiting the Nejd province of Saudi Arabia, from which the House of Saud originated.

Bedouin military personnel were also singularly responsible for the survival of King Husayn of Jordan, at times in the face of seemingly impossible odds. Jordan's "Arab Legion" was initially formed to combat bedouin anarchy in the newly created country. In a stroke of genius, the Legion's founder, the British officer John Glubb, decided to harness the warlike quality of the bedouins by recruiting them into the army. Very quickly, the Arab Legion became the Arab world's most disciplined fighting force. But one thing that Glubb did not change was tribal solidarity, which was nurtured every step of the way to make the Legion "the bedouin prop of the Hashemite polity."[23] This certainly saved Husayn's throne during an attempted coup by Nasirist officers in 1957. The following description of events gives a flavor of the tribal connection:

> In the evening of 13 April, Hussein received a visit from his uncle
> ... accompanied by beduin officers who had just arrived from
> Zerqa. They brought sensational reports. At that very moment, *ha-*

---

[23] Uriel Dann, *Studies in the History of Transjordan, 1920–1949: The Making of a State* (Boulder, Colorado: Westview Press, 1984), p. 11.

dari (non-beduin)[24] officers were inciting certain regiments to march
on Amman and "save the country" by arresting or even assassinat-
ing the king. [Hussein] confronted Abu Nawar (the suspected leader
of the coup) who professed amazement. Hussein then took Abu
Nawar with him to Zerqa. . . to investigate. In the meantime, excitement in Zerqa had risen to fever pitch. Bloody brawls broke out
between beduin and *hadari* units. In some cases, beduin soldiers
assaulted and locked up [Anti-King] officers. Other beduin soldiers
poured out onto the Amman road, cheering [the King] and vowing
death to Abu-Nawar. Hussein addressed them, embraced them, and
swore brotherhood.[25]

In contrast to Husayn's conscious solicitation of the tribal connection, successive Iraqi governments endeavored through education and the coercive powers of the state to quell the tribal spirit
and submerge tribal identity into that of the Iraqi state. And then
in the 1950s came the Arab nationalist offensive and its contemptuous belittling of tribalism as "reactionary," unable to address the
Arabs' contemporary concerns. The nationalists employed a powerful argument in Iraq: The Arabs were once a great people, but
then they embarked on a seemingly endless journey into oblivion,
and when they finally stirred from their deep slumber around the
turn of the twentieth century, they arose into a world that was no
longer theirs; a Western world; a world of technology, science, and
cultural advancements associated with modern ways. To catch up
with the West, the Arabs had to absorb Western ideas, to leave
behind the old ways, turn the corner and take the route of modernity. And tribalism was decidedly not the stuff of modernity. Given
the dominance and political power of this argument in the ideological and political discourse of the 1950s and 1960s, one would think
that tribalism and tribal values would recede into downright irrele-

---

[24] *Hadar* had historically denoted settled communities, and in Jordan it symbolically separated the cities, especially the capital Amman, from the rest of the country. The implication
here was that the urbanites were particularly susceptible to Arab nationalism, especially as
the Palestinian community was almost entirely urban.
[25] Uriel Dann, *King Hussein and the Challenge of Arab Radicalism: Jordan, 1955–1967*
(London: Oxford University Press, 1989), p. 59.

vance. Yet the eminent Iraqi sociologist 'Ali al-Wardi, writing about Iraq in the late 1960s, tells us that even in the cities modernization was superficial, that in their essence many of the city folk were bedouin, and that the trappings of modernity, such as Western clothing, simply camouflaged deeply ingrained tribal values.[26] As late as 1982, a leading member of Iraq's Ba'th Party would lament that, along with sectarianism, tribalism was "tearing the unity of society to pieces."[27] And indeed, in the wake of the Gulf War, in a concerted effort to shore up his waning support in Iraq, that erstwhile Arab nationalist and lifelong member of the Ba'th Party, Saddam Husayn, would draw on this enduring reservoir of tribal values, and elevate tribalism to the forefront of Iraq's political and ideological concerns.[28]

Iraq's sectarian divisions were another hurdle in the Arab nationalist march. The country's Shiite majority never overcame its suspicion of Arab nationalism as an essentially Sunni project. Shiite grievances against the Sunnis were primarily political, pertaining to Sunni dominance over Iraq's political order. The Shiites would point to the paucity of their numbers among the decision-making elite and in the ranks of the administrative and military institutions.[29] Iraqi leaders, such as 'Abd al-Salam 'Aref, who carried Arab nationalism on his sleeves, but was well known for his anti-Shiite prejudices, only added to this sectarian tension.[30] Conse-

---

[26] 'Ali al-Wardi, *Lamahat Ijtima'iya min Tarikh al-'Iraq al-Hadith, al-Jusi' al-Rabi', min 'Am 1914 ila 'Am 1918* (Sociological aspects of modern Iraqi history, volume four, 1914–1918) (London: Dar Kufan li al-Nashr, 1992), pp. 402–403

[27] Amatzia Baram, "Neo-Tribalism in Iraq: Saddam Hussein's Tribal Policies, 1991–96," *International Journal of Middle East Studies*, vol. 29 (February 1997): 2–3.

[28] See Adeed Dawisha, " 'Identity' and Political Survival in Saddam's Iraq," *Middle East Journal*, vol. 53, no. 4 (Autumn 1999): 562–567; see also Baram, "Neo-Tribalism in Iraq: Saddam Hussein's Tribal Policies, 1991–96."

[29] 'Abd al-Karim al-Uzri, *Tarikh fi Dhikrayat al-'Iraq, 1930–1958* (History in the memoirs of Iraq, 1930–1958) (Beirut: Markaz al-Abjadiya li al-Saf al-Taswiri, 1982), pp. 242–243.

[30] 'Aref was inclined to think of Iraqi Shiites as Persians, and indeed was not averse to let slip such thoughts even to Shiite members of the Ba'th Party. See Selim Matar, *al-Dhat al-Jariha* (Wounded essence), p. 172. Moreover, It was not only Shiites who were the target of 'Aref's Sunni prejudices but Christians too. He once told a Syrian minister that he could not understand how the Arab Nationalists Movement (ANM) could allow a Christian (George

quently, Shiite enthusiasm for Arab unity projects were tempered
by the fear that they would render the Shiites a minority in an Arab
Sunni world.[31]

It is not that the Shiites did not believe in Arab nationalism, or
that they did not consider themselves to be Arabs. Some of the
marvels of Arabic writings were penned by Shiite men of learning.[32]
And as we have seen, Iraqis of all religions and denominations
flocked to the Arab nationalist cause under Nasir's leadership in
the 1950s and 1960s. But that did not mean that tribalism or sectarianism were wiped out, for they were too deeply ingrained to
disappear; they simply retreated into the recesses of people's consciousness. So, once Arab nationalism began to suffer reverses and
setbacks, and Nasir's ability to work his magic came to be questioned, all the particularistic, anti-national, tendencies were to re-
emerge and come to the forefront again.

Another competitor with Arab nationalism for people's loyalty
was radical Islam. In one sense, this competition is surprising because there are elements of each in both. The vast majority of Arabs
are Muslims, and the most glorious periods of Arab history occurred during the dazzling medieval Islamic empires. Similarly, all
Muslims, moderate or radicals, could not but admit to the central
role of the Arabs in their religion. After all, Islam was born in the
Arabian Peninsula, the Prophet Muhamed was Arab, and God's
message was revealed in Arabic. One would think that the
two social movements would share a cooperative relationship. Instead, it was downright hostile. Arab nationalists, from Husri to
Nasir and Aflaq, accepted the special place that Islam occupied

---

Habash) to lead "the youth of Muhamed." See Sa'id, 'Iraq 8 Shibat, 1963 (Iraq of 8 February, 1963), p. 308.

[31] Hanna Batatu, The Old Social Classes and the Revolutionary Movements of Iraq: A
Study of Iraq's Old Landed and Commercial Classes and of its Communists, Ba'thists
and Free Officers (Princeton, New Jersey: Princeton University Press, 1978), p. 818; also
Yitzhak Nakash, The Shi'is of Iraq (Princeton, New Jersey: Princeton University Press,
1994), p. 134.

[32] See Mir Basri, A'lam al-Adab fi al-'Iraq al-Hadith (Eminent men of letters in modern
Iraq), two volumes, (London: Dar al-Hikma, 1994). It is instructive to see how many Shiites
figure in Basri's comprehensive list of Iraqi men of letters.

within the Arab nationalist movement,[33] but stressed only those aspects of Islam that were moral and spiritual in nature. They resolutely rejected Islam's political and constitutional implications, and insisted on its complete subordination to Arab nationalism. The nationalists vehemently argued that it was not religious, but linguistic and historical, ties that would knit the Arab nation into a cohesive whole.

This of course was sheer blasphemy to the radical Muslim groups, and nationalists became the target of these groups' *jihad*. The concept of jihad, holy struggle, was central to the lexicon of Islamic militancy. Jihad was to be waged against the perceived enemies of Islam, those who would try to infuse Muslim society with alien and blasphemous ideas, imported primarily from the West. And to the Muslim radicals, the secular nationalists, who propagated ethnicity at the expense of religion and advocated the separation of Islam from politics, were perhaps the greatest offenders.

Islamic militancy made little headway among an Arab population fired by the premises and promises of secular Arab nationalism, but as the sun set on nationalism, it rose on Islamic militancy. This does not mean that there had been no manifest Islamic opposition in the 1950s and 1960s. Indeed there was. But its potency, both objectively and in the eyes of those whom it challenged, took a mammoth qualitative leap as nationalism nursed its fatal wounds after 1967. In the last three decades of the twentieth century, radical Islam became the main opposition force to Arab leaders, many of whom professed nationalist credentials. The *Islamiyoun* (as the Islamic radicals called themselves) mounted challenges to Arab governments throughout the Middle East, the most notable of which were against the Ba'thist government in Iraq in the late 1970s, the other Ba'thists in Syria in the 1980s, Algerian secular leaderships in the 1990s, and successive Egyptian governments during all of the three decades. The rejuvenation of Islam as a radical political alternative robbed nationalism of whatever

---

[33] See Walid Khadduri, "al-Qawmiya al-'Arabiya wa al-Dimuqratiya: Muraja'a Naqdiya," (Arab nationalism and democracy: a critical review) *al-Mustaqbal al-'Arabi*, no. 228 (February 1998): 45.

chance of recovery it might have entertained after 1967. Arab nationalism found itself squeezed out from the political arena by the dominance of *wataniya* at the official state level and radical Islam at the popular level.

But why did Arab nationalism fall prey so easily to these other emerging political forces? How could an ideology, once so mighty, collapse and disintegrate because of a few setbacks? Did Arab nationalism, while projecting an image of invincibility, actually lack inner strength and vitality? These questions were asked many times, and many answers were given. R. Stephen Humphreys hints at perhaps the most compelling answer:

> Arab nationalist thinkers . . . had looked at the crucial problem confronting them and their people as one of identity rather than as one of institutions. The question was, who is an Arab, not how can the Arabs build a common political life and effective institutions of government? . . . Very few writers asked seriously how [the projected Arab] state would be constituted, how the relationships among its many disparate regions were to be defined, and how different social groups would be represented within the political system.[34]

Although Humphreys does not spell it out, what is implied here is that the inability of Arab nationalism to survive political setbacks was at least partly due to the disinterest of its custodians in creating workable democratic institutions.[35] In a democracy, chief executives derive their authority from the constitutional legitimacy of the political system, yet authoritarian systems elevate their political leaders to positions of dominance over the legal-institutional structure, thus making the legitimacy of the political system and its values dependent solely on the leader's credibility. In other words, when an authoritarian leader falls, the system's ideology and values become singularly vulnerable, since they are not underpinned by

---

[34] Humphreys, *Between Memory and Desire*, pp. 66–67.

[35] Sa'ad al-Din Ibrahim, "Thawrat Yuliyu wa I'adat Tafsir al-Tarikh" (The July revolution and the reassessment of history), in *Misr wa al-'Uruba wa Thawrat Yuliyu* (Egypt, Arabism and the July revolution), eds. Sa'ad al-Din Ibrahim, et al. (Beirut, Lebanon: Markaz Dirasat al-Wuhda al-'Arabiya, 1983), p. 13.

constitutional arrangements independent of the leader. On the other hand, democratic systems and their values transcend the personality, policies, and / or survival of their political leaders. The old European dictum "the King is dead, long live the King" denoted if not necessarily constitutional, then at least procedural, legitimacy. Later with the spread of popular democracy, the dictum would acquire constitutional substance by signifying the continued legitimacy of the political institutions regardless of its leader.

Nationalism operated throughout its glory days in a sea of authoritarianism, and this happened not because of some unfortunate circumstance. Indeed, it was the way Arab nationalism was defined and developed which was to blame, if not wholly then at least partially, for the absence of democracy. And when nationalism was to finally collapse, there were precious few institutions to come to its rescue.

We have seen that the tenets of Arab nationalism, as formulated by Sati' al-Husri, reflected the ideas of nineteenth- century German cultural nationalism. To German nationalist thinkers, unifying the nation was the supreme goal and a sacred act, which necessitated subsuming individual will into the national will.[36] Notions of liberty or freedom were distractions, and when they contradicted the national will, they had to be repressed. How else would the eminent German historian, Heinrich von Trietschke justify the annexation in 1871 of the German-speaking population of Alsace, the majority of whom wanted to remain politically within France. "We desire," Trietschke says in a chilling tone, "even against their will, to restore them to themselves."[37]

This authoritarian and coercive streak in the tenets of German cultural nationalism was reinforced in the wake of the Prussian defeat at the hands of Napoleon at Jenna in 1806. The word liberty was indeed resurrected, but it was endowed with a meaning quite different from the one used by the English and French. English and French nationalisms were the ideological responses to indigenous

[36] Elie Kedourie, *Nationalism* (London: Hutchinson University Library, 1960), p. 47.
[37] Hans Kohn, *The Ideas of Nationalism: A Study in its Origins and Background* (New York: Macmillan, 1944), p. 582.

efforts to liberalize the absolutist state and create a liberal and virtuous society. German nationalism, on the other hand, peaked in
the aftermath of the war with France. Its goals were not to

> ... secure better government, individual liberty, and due process
> of law, but ... to drive out a foreign ruler and to secure national
> independence. The word liberty did not mean primarily, as it did for
> the western peoples the assertion of the rights of the individual
> against his government, but of the independence of the nation
> against foreign rule. ... When the western peoples strove for regen-
> eration, they were primarily concerned with individual liberty; in
> central and eastern Europe the demand for regeneration often cen-
> tered on the unity and power of the group.[38]

This was the intellectual legacy upon which Husri was to build
his theory of the Arab nation. Arab nationalism, until its final decline late in the twentieth century, continued to reflect the tenets of
German cultural nationalism. Arab nationalists would advocate
the rejuvenation of the Arab nation, its political unity, its secularism, and its sovereignty. Yet, reflecting the illiberal connotations of
cultural nationalism, Arab nationalists would have little to say
about personal liberty and freedom. Husri once said that "the form
of government was of no great interest to him ... public attention
should focus on the problem of unity: it [was] the national duty of
every Arab to support the leader who is capable of achieving Arab
unity."[39] On the rare occasions when advocates of Arab nationalism spoke of personal liberty, they were quick to emphasize that the
priority of the committed Arab nationalist cannot be his personal
liberty, but his nation's well being. In the words of Husri himself:
"patriotism and nationalism before and above all ... even above
and before freedom."[40] As we have seen, this illiberal streak in
Husri's political ideas were aimed especially at those Arabic-speak-

---

[38] Hans Kohn, *Prelude to Nation-States: The French and German Experience, 1789–
1815* (London, 1967), p. 254.

[39] Majid Khadduri, *Political Trends in the Arab World: The Role of Ideas and Ideals in
Politics* (Baltimore: Johns Hopkins Press, 1970), p. 201.

[40] Abu Khaldun Sati' al-Husri, *Safahat min al-Madhi al-Qarib* (Pages from recent history)
(Beirut: Markaz Dirasat al-Wuhda al-'Arabiya, 1984), p. 42.

ing people who did not share his views, and who might have been less than ablaze with exuberance at the prospect of being called Arabs. Husri's response is uncompromising: "under no circumstances should we say: 'as long as [an Arab] does not wish to be an Arab, and as long as he is disdainful of his Arabism, then he is not an Arab.' He is an Arab whether he wishes to be one or not. Whether ignorant, indifferent, undutiful, or disloyal, he is an Arab, but an Arab without feelings or consciousness, and perhaps even without conscience."[41]

Husri did not offer remedies, specific methods by which "Arabs without conscience" would be, in Trietschke's words, "restored to themselves." Michel Aflaq was not so coy. Aflaq, founder and philosopher of the Ba'th Party, whose writings bear the unmistakable influence of Husri's ideas, candidly identified "cruelty" as the most reliable instrument to affect the desired transformation: "When we are cruel to others, we know that our cruelty is in order to bring them back to their true selves, of which they are ignorant."[42] Indeed, Aflaq defined cruelty in this context as prescribed by the nationalist's love for his people.

Husri's nationalist beliefs were of course carried into the 1950s and 1960s, becoming the clarion call for the nationalist avalanche of those two decades. By then, Arab cultural nationalism had emerged triumphant over other competing ideologies and identities, capturing the hearts and minds of that quintessentially nationalist generation, a generation that fervently believed in Arab nationalism as the vehicle by which a glittering past would be transformed into a distinguished future. But that was easier said than done. The task ahead was fraught with untold difficulties and obstacles: there were the foreign powers still in control of much Arab land; there was the Arabs' own lethargy and lack of purpose; there were the political divisions, artificially created, so nationalists

---

[41] Abu Khaldun Sati' al-Husri, *Abhath Mukhtara fi al-Qawmiya al-'Arabiya* (Selected studies on Arab nationalism) (Beirut: Markaz Dirasat al-Wuhda al-'Arabiya, 1985), p. 80.

[42] Michel Aflaq, *Fi Sabil al Ba'th* (For the sake of resurrection) (Beirut: Dar al-Tali'ah, 1963), pp. 161–162; also Kanan Makiya, *Republic of Fear: The Politics of Modern Iraq* (Berkeley: University of California Press, 1998), p. 206.

believed, but clearly gaining acceptance and legitimacy with the passage of time; and there were all those regional, sectarian and tribal identities, which to the Arab nationalists were products of "false consciousness" encouraged and perpetuated by the colonialists and imperialists. This was to be a titanic struggle, and as the nationalists embarked upon it, they naturally had little patience for words such as liberty, freedom, and democracy.[43] What need was there to listen to another point of view, to argue a contrary perspective? Would it not be a distraction, a diversion from the course of the struggle? Were all Arabs not united in their one sacred endeavor to effect an organic unity of their lands and their peoples, and to free them of Western domination? How could there be a contrary position to that?

Not only had Husri's intellectual tradition sunk well into the nationalist psyche, but it was affirmed and accentuated by the political circumstances of the era. The nationalist generation of the 1950s and 1960s came to believe fervently that the West would purposely and effectively block the goals of Arab nationalism, that it would see the nationalist vision of an independent and assertive Arab nation as a perilous move against Western economic and political interests in the area. The nationalist struggle, therefore, became essentially a struggle against the West.

In the midst of this nationalist ferment emerged the charismatic Nasir. And he would vilify the West as the uncommonly perfidious "other," the undying nemesis of the Arabs, the determined obstacle to their progress. In fiery speeches, Nasir would remind Arabs continuously of their glorious history and of their military and intellectual superiority over the West. All the catch phrases of Husri's cultural nationalism were there: The glory of the Arabs' heritage, the excellence and originality of their forefathers, the overwhelming power of the Arabs when they were united, their ensuing weakness as they quarreled and dissolved into many small entities, and the necessity to unite now in order to be free and strong again.

---

[43] Khadduri, "al-Qawmiya al-'Arabiya wa al-Dimuqratiya" (Arab nationalism and democracy), p. 42.

In promising the Arabs freedom, Nasir echoed Husri's conception; it was not personal freedom and liberty, rather, it was freedom from Western domination. Liberal democracy had no place in this new order.[44] Nasir did not offer it; he disdained it. "The separation of powers," he once said, "is nothing but a big deception, because there really is no such thing as the separation of powers."[45] But neither did the nationalist multitude in those heady days ask for democracy, let alone demand it. The illiberal intellectual tradition of cultural nationalism, combined with the anti-Western struggle, which had reached a crescendo in the 1950s and 1960s, necessitating in the minds of most Arabs the centralization of power, contributed to the emergence of Nasir's popular and populist, yet singularly authoritarian, rule.

The Ba'th Party, the other leader of the Arab nationalist march, followed a parallel route. The custodians of Ba'thist ideology focused their intellectual energies on "Arab unity" and the "anti-imperialist struggle," but said little about democratic institutions. While the constitution of the Ba'th Party did assert the principle of the people's sovereignty and Ba'thist support for a constitutional elective system, it also gave the Party and the ensuing Ba'thist state the central role in determining the scope and extent of political freedoms. From the very beginning, Aflaq's ideas were endowed with a "strong statist strain [in which] individual self-realization [would] derive from participation in the general will of the community."[46] From then on, "freedom" on the whole would be associated with the struggle against imperialism rather than with individ-

---

[44] Ahmad Hamroush, *Qissat Thawrat 23 Yuliyu: Kharif 'Abd al-Nasir, al-Jusi' al Khamis* (The story of the 23 July revolution: the autumn of 'Abd al-Nasir, fifth volume) (Cairo: Maktabat Madbouli, 1983), pp. 386–387. See also Sami Gawhar, *al-Samitun Yatakalamun: 'Abd al-Nasir wa Madhbahat al-Ikhwan* (The silent speak: 'Abd al-Nasir and the slaughter of the [Muslim] brothers) (Cairo: al-Maktab al-Misri al-Hadith, 1975), pp. 89–92.

[45] Quoted in Sa'id, *'Iraq 8 Shibat 1963* (Iraq of 8 February, 1963), p. 213. It was not enough for Nasir that people should share his ideological proclivities and political vision. They had to be part of, and committed to, the system that he built. See Mustafa 'Abd al-Ghani, " 'Abd al-Nasir wa al-Muthaqafun" ('Abd al-Nasir and the intellectuals), *al-Mustaqbal al-'Arabi*, no. 262 (December 2000): 110.

[46] Raymond A. Hinnebusch, *Authoritarian Power and State Formation in Ba'thist Syria: Army, Party, and Peasant* (Boulder, Colorado: Westview Press, 1990), p. 89; on the inherent

ual liberty.[47] This illiberal orientation would be reinforced during the Party's flirtation with political power in the 1950s and early 1960s, so that in the Party's Sixth National Congress held in 1963, the Ba'th would reject unequivocally the notion of liberal parliamentarianism, espousing instead the Soviet concept of democratic centralism linked to the Party's role as the "vanguard" political institution in the state.

The misfortunes of liberal democracy in the Arab world were compounded by its association with the pro-Western forces in the area. To the nationalist, it was not only Israel which was the "puppet" of the West, but also, and perhaps more galling to the nationalist cause, the status-quo, traditional Arab elites. The nationalists charged that these elites, in Saudi Arabia, Lebanon, Jordan, and in pre-republican Egypt and Iraq, were totally dependent on the Western powers for their survival. And in return for Western patronage and protection, the traditional elites were doing the West's bidding in the area. The central and most repeated element of Nasir's assault against the "enemies of Arab nationalism" was this perceived association with Western imperialism. And his extensive and ever-hungry propaganda machine quickly took the hint. They mounted a relentless and on the whole vicious campaign against the Arab friends of the West, labeling them all as the "lackeys of imperialism." The leaders of monarchical Iraq had no right to speak on the affairs of their own country, because they spoke "on behalf of Western imperialism."[48] The Christian president of Lebanon had no right to speak on behalf of Arab Christians because he was "an underling of the West."[49] As for King Husayn of Jordan, a favorite target of Egyptian propaganda, he was reminded of the assassination of his grandfather by a Palestinian, then allowed omi-

---

contradiction between "democracy" and "revolution" in Ba'thist doctrine, see Elie Kedourie, *Democracy and Arab Political Culture* (Washington, D.C.: The Washington Institute, 1992), p. 90.

[47] John F. Devlin, *The Ba'th Party: A History from its Origins to 1966* (Stanford, California: Hoover Institution Press, 1976), p. 31.

[48] British Broadcasting Corporation, *Summary of World Broadcasts, Part IV, the Arab World, Israel, Greece, Turkey, Iran* (hereafter cited as *SWB*), May 13, 1958, pp. 2–3.

[49] *SWB*, June 2, 1958, p. 1.

nously to ponder a rhetorical question: "Did imperialism save [your] grandfather from his end at the hands of the people?"[50] During this era, the highest negative value in the minds of the nationalist generation was attached to "Western imperialism."

The problem for democracy was that this antipathy to Western imperialism translated into a hostility not only to the policies of the West, but also to its institutions. A number of pro-Western Arab countries had adopted parliamentary systems which were modeled on the British or French political systems. Egypt, Iraq, and Jordan had parliaments and legislative councils since the 1920s, and Syria and Lebanon immediately after they gained their independence in the wake of World War II. By the second half of the 1940s and early 1950s, all of these countries had experimented with various forms of multiparty politics. Admittedly, theirs were by no means true liberal democracies when judged by Western standards. There were, of course, cases of rigged elections, harassment of opposition parties, institution of emergency laws, and the like. But, when all was said and done, these systems still were far more open and far more civil than those subsequently instituted by the nationalist generation. Take the case of the press in Egypt and in Iraq. In prerevolutionary Egypt, Cairo boasted fourteen dailies and twenty-three weeklies, and Alexandria, Egypt's second largest city, had fourteen dailies and seven weeklies. All were either privately owned or belonged to political parties, which made for a vibrant and free-wheeling press. In monarchical Iraq, one year before the 1958 military coup which toppled the monarchy and created a nationalist government, fourteen nongovernment newspapers were published in Baghdad, five in Mosul, and four in Basrah. While the government would occasionally ban a newspaper for a particularly virulent attack, the ban typically would last for a short period and the paper would duly reappear. After the Egyptian and Iraqi nationalist revolutions, the press came under strict government control, and in both countries a handful of state-owned dailies were published, distinguished from each other only by the title on the front page.

[50] SWB, October 8, 1966, p. 5.

Similarly, while in the pre-Nasirist era, the concept of competitive political parties was admittedly neither universally nor uniformly applicable, the nationalist generation in the 1950s and 1960s endeavored to de-legitimize the very concept itself. For instance, one of the favorite slogans shouted by rioters and demonstrators in celebration of the demise of Iraq's monarchy in July 1958 was *al-Qawmiya al-'Arabiya tufny al-Ahzab al Gharbiya* (Arab nationalism exterminates the Western political parties). It was not just that there was no need for different parties with different visions, since all Arabs supposedly adhered to one unifying vision, namely, the nationalist creed. It was more pernicious: political parties would undermine the nationalist march; they would sow divisions in Arab ranks; they would become fifth columns for greedy outside powers. Nasir argued that these parties would not subordinate their own interests to the general good,[51] particularly in the underdeveloped world, still suffering from social cleavages and foreign domination.[52] Hence, if political parties were allowed in Egypt, Nasir charged, they would act merely as agents for the intelligence services of the various imperialist powers.[53] Ba'thist writers and activists echoed this sentiment in their development of the Party's ideology and political orientations, both of which exhibited mounting disdain for a Western-inspired multiparty system. In a sense, the position of Nasir and the Ba'th was essentially a fusion of the existential element of anti-Westernism with the intellectual legacy of cultural nationalism. The result was the elimination of multiparty systems, and their replacement with unitary political institutions, whose function was purely to mobilize.

As long as Arab nationalism dominated the political and psychological landscape, it suffered little from its authoritarian proclivities. But as the reverses set in, climaxing in the fiasco of the 1967 Six Day War, Arab nationalism was stripped of much that had for-

---

[51] Nasir's interview with the *Sunday Times* (London), June 24, 1962.

[52] *Al-Ahram* (Cairo), July 2, 1959.

[53] *Egyptian Gazette* (Cairo), May 9, 1966. See also United Arab Republic, *President Gamal Abdel Nasser's Speeches and Press-Interviews* (Cairo: Information Department, 1959), p. 547.

tified it. Most damaging was the loss of Nasir's charisma, which not only had cemented Arab nationalism, but also contributed to the legitimation of its authoritarian character and institutions. After 1967, Arab nationalism needed more than the practices and policies of old to sustain it. Political representation and participation, freedom of expression and the rule of law, all of them woefully absent, could have provided the essential and much needed nourishment to resuscitate the ailing ideology. But the post-1967 Arab leaders, most of whom had come to prominence armed with the premises of Arab nationalism, shared Nasir's hunger for absolute power, but lacked his charismatic hold on the people. Under them, authoritarianism became ever harsher and more brutal. The unforgiving totalitarianism of these "nationalist" leaders would further alienate the people from Arab nationalism.

Spurning the democratic route, some of the authoritarian Arab rulers did indeed endeavor, rather inadvertently, to help the cause of Arab nationalism. They did this through the threat and use of physical violence, something that came naturally to them. At various times during the second half of the twentieth century, a number of Arab countries either threatened, or embarked on, military operations against other Arab countries. Invariably, these ventures were undertaken for reasons that had little to do with Arab nationalism, but they might have led to the emergence of a dominant power that could forcibly unite the Arab world. The intervention of regional and international forces doomed these ventures to certain failure. Had they been successful, however, they could have become the stepping stones for the achievement of Arab unity, the ultimate goal of Arab nationalism.

This is the essence of an intriguingly original argument advanced by Ian Lustick[54] that rests on a simple question: what explains the absence of an Arab great power? The answer, Lustick maintains, lies in a comparison of the Arab situation with that of Europe be-

[54] Ian S. Lustick, "The Absence of Middle Eastern Great Powers: Political 'Backwardness' in Historical Perspective," *International Organization*, vol. 51, no. 4 (Autumn 1997): 653–683.

tween the thirteenth and nineteenth centuries. That period of European history saw the consolidation of states at the expense of smaller entities, so that between 1500 and 1900, the number of independent polities had shrunk by a factor of twenty! And this came about not because of natural atrophy or people's desire for amalgamation, but as a result of war. Losers disappeared; winners became larger and stronger, and sought further conquests.[55] Lustick describes this violence-based integrative process as it occurred in a few of the more obvious cases:

> In Britain the wars of Alfred the Great and of the Plantagenet and Tudor monarchs [created] the United Kingdom. In France, wars conducted by Capetian and Valois kings from the Ile de France produced, over centuries, the great state we know as France. In Russia the czars fought wars of expansion and repression to join Slavic territories west of the Urals and vast expanses of Asia east of the Urals to the domain ruled from Muscovy. Using Prussia as a base, Bismarckian diplomacy and a series of wars against Austria, France and others produced Germany. In Italy, Piedmont fought wars against Austria, sponsored Garibaldi's landing in Sicily, and marched its army down the Italian peninsula to destroy the old Bourbon monarchy, thereby eliminating the jealous rivalries among separate principalities and city-states that had for so long divided Italians.[56]

What made these forcible absorptions possible, Lustick contends, was the absence of actual or potential interference by outside powers.[57] By way of contrast, in the Middle East, "the effect of great power intervention and enforcement of international norms has been . . . to prevent potential regional hegemons from exercising their relative capacities by conquering or otherwise coercively integrating their neighbors."[58]

How accurate is Lustick's contention! A case in point can be surmised from the events that occurred in the aftermath of the July

[55] Ibid., p. 656.
[56] Ibid., p. 658.
[57] Ibid., pp. 656–657.
[58] Ibid., pp. 661–662

1958 Iraqi revolution. Iraq had rid itself of the anti-Nasir, Hashemite mantle and was expected to immediately join Nasir's United
Arab Republic (UAR). In those heady days of nationalist frenzy, the
pro-Western, "reactionary" governments of Jordan and Lebanon
were considered doomed by nationalists and others. No one
doubted the imminent absorption of these two weak states into the
UAR.[59] Indeed, such was their predicament, that Nasir would not
have needed to use military force. But those who waited for the
inevitable to occur had not reckoned on the West's determination
to come up with a "vigorous response" to avert "the complete elimination of Western influence in the Middle East."[60] The day after
the Iraqi revolution, American troops landed in Lebanon, to be
followed two days later by British troops arriving in Jordan. And
indeed, it is very difficult to see how these two regimes would have
survived absorption into the UAR had it not been for the military
intervention of the two outside powers.

Another relevant example was Egypt's intervention in Yemen,
which began in 1962. A successful intervention would not have
amalgamated Yemen into Egypt; that never was Egypt's goal. But
it would have confirmed Egypt's role as the hegemon of the area;
and by so doing, would have rekindled the nationalist spirit,
allowing it to challenge Western interests more vigorously. And it
could have been done on the cheap, or so Nasir thought at the
beginning of the affair. Initially, the news could not have been more
encouraging. A group of nationalist officers executed a military
coup against an archaic and absolutist monarchy. The monarch
had been killed and the officers seemed in control of the country.
They asked Egypt for a symbolic military contribution, which they
felt would deliver the coup de grace to any remaining monarchist

---

[59] See for example the assessment of two distinguished British journalists, Peter Snow in
his *Hussein: A Biography* (New York: Robert B. Luce, Inc., 1972), pp. 128–129, and Robert
Stephens, *Nasser: A Political Biography* (London: Allen Lane / Penguin Press, 1971), pp.
287–288. Even American intelligence gave the Hashemite king little chance of survival, see
Uriel Dann, *King Hussein and the Challenge of Arab Radicalism* (London: Oxford University Press, 1989), p. 93.

[60] Dwight D. Eisenhower, *The White House Years, vol. II: Waging Peace* (New York:
Doubleday, 1965), p. 270.

sentiment. It would also demonstrate to one and all Egypt's centrality and unrivaled prestige in the Arab world, and could undermine the stability of Saudi Arabia and the other pro-Western regimes of the Arabian Peninsula.[61] Nasir dispatched a battalion, which was expected to make no more than a courtesy call. He then sat back awaiting the glory that came with his painless gesture. Five years later he would withdraw a huge Egyptian army from Yemen, which at its peak had amounted to almost half of Egypt's armed forces. Nasir would later lament: "I sent a battalion, but I had to support it with seventy thousand soldiers!"[62] The symbolic gesture turned out to be "Nasir's Vietnam."

How did that happen? Admittedly, there were purely local reasons that had little to do with outside interference: the support accorded to the coup in the cities was not reciprocated among the warlike northern tribes, and contrary to Republican claims, Imam Badr, Yemen's monarch had not been killed. The Imam was able to escape and made his way to the fiercely loyal tribes. But crucially, the monarchist forces were able to receive, throughout the five years of Egyptian involvement, consistent and substantial logistical, military, and material support from Saudi Arabia and its Western backers. Huge arms deals with Britain and the United States bolstered Saudi Arabia's army and air force,[63] and as a signal to the Egyptians, British pilots even flew the newly acquired combat aircrafts for a while.[64] All this allowed the Saudis to dispatch planeloads of arms to the monarchists, and as a result the Egyptian army became bogged down in an unwinnable war that cost Egypt "thousands of lives and millions of dollars."[65] There can be little doubt that the failure of Egypt's venture in Yemen was due in no small measure to the commitment of outside powers not to afford Nasir the oppor-

---

[61] Lustick, "The Absence of Middle Eastern Great Powers," p. 670.

[62] Ahmad Hamroush, *Qissat Thawrat 23 Yuliyu, al-Jusi' al-Rabi': 'Abd al-Nasir wa al-'Arab* (The story of the 23 July revolution: 'Abd al-Nasir and the Arabs, volume four) (Cairo: Dar al-Mawqif al-'Arabi, 1983), p. 123.

[63] *Observer* (London), February 28, 1965; *Times* (London), May 2, 1966.

[64] *Daily Telegraph* (London), May 30, 1966.

[65] Gawhar, *al-Samitun Yatakalamun* (The silent speak), p. 123.

tunity to expand his power, and possibly his domain, at the expense of such local actors as Yemen and Saudi Arabia.

This Western commitment was not aimed at Nasir alone. Other irredentist Arab leaders received the same treatment. In 1961, when Kuwait gained its independence from the British, Iraq's leader 'Abd al-Karim Qasim laid claim to it, asserting that Kuwait had always been a part of Iraq. And for good measure, he put the Iraqi army on alert. Whatever Qasim's true intentions were, for he indeed was a most mercurial man, any opportunity for action disappeared when five days after his announcement, British troops entered Kuwait, remaining there until a joint Arab force replaced them. Almost thirty years later, another Iraqi leader was able to go a step further, occupy Kuwait, and amalgamate it into Iraq. Saddam Husayn's victory, however, was short-lived, and he and his long-suffering people were soon to experience the full and ferocious force of Western displeasure.

One more example might suffice. In the bloody September 1970 civil war in Jordan, the king had to contend not only with the Palestinian guerrillas, but also with the machinations of his northern neighbor, the fiercely nationalist Ba'thist regime in Syria. Damascus was intensifying its saber rattling, vilifying the pro-Western king and swearing its undying commitment to the Arab Palestinian cause. As the Palestinian military situation worsened, the Syrians decided to take on the Jordanians. On September 18, Syrian troops crossed into Jordan, taking the town of Irbid the following day. It was not clear what Syria's objectives were. Later on, President Asad would tell Patrick Seale that he did not intend to overthrow the king, but simply wanted to protect the Palestinians from a sure massacre.[66] On the other hand, King Husayn and the United States were convinced that the Syrians sought the overthrow of Jordan's government, thereby making Jordan a client of Syria, very much in the same vein as Lebanon. Whatever Syria's true intentions were, the Americans decided to act quickly to save the king and preserve

---

[66] Patrick Seale, *Asad: The Struggle for the Middle East* (Berkeley: University of California Press, 1988), p. 158.

the status quo. But this time, and with Husayn's approval, they solicited the help of Israel. The rapidly unfolding situation is vividly described by Patrick Seale:

> On 21 September, on the morrow of Husayn's cry for help, Henry Kissinger and Yitzhak Rabin, Israel's ambassador in Washington agreed a plan for Israel to launch air and armoured strikes against Syrian forces the next day. The plan was then approved by Nixon and Husayn. And in preparation for the strikes Israel made much publicized military deployments in the direction of Jordan. Washington also put airborne troops on the alert and an American armada headed for the Eastern Mediterranean. Emboldened by these preparations, Husayn's own armour and air force then engaged the Syrians on 22 September. . . . Asad took the heavy hint. He had no intention of committing himself to unequal combat with Israel, let alone with the United States. . . . So on 22 September, before Israel attacked, he withdrew to his side of the border.[67]

These are some of the instances in which the West, by exercising its imperious and overwhelming power, prevented local states from effecting "substantial change in the number, size, or internal regimes of states."[68] Consequently, unlike pre-twentieth century Europe in which local rulers expanded their domain, then consolidated the realm through war and coercion, no Arab state was allowed to accumulate power and territory, and by so doing create the possibility for one unified Arab state, the ultimate goal of Arab nationalism. Western powers were not about to allow the emergence in the Arab world of a Prussia, a Piedmont, or an Ile de France. And certainly they did not.

"Political ideas," Fouad Ajami notes, "make their own realities. Often in defiance of logic, they hold men and are in turn held by them, creating a world in their own image, only to play themselves out in the end, shackled by routine problems not foreseen by those who spun the myth, or living past their prime and ceasing to move

---

[67] *Ibid.*, p. 160.
[68] Lustick, "The Absence of Middle Eastern Great Powers," p. 657.

people sufficiently."[69] And so it was with Arab nationalism. Many factors mitigated against its continued success. Some of these were internal to the region, others were external to it. Some were inherent in the very ideology of nationalism, others emerged as unforeseen consequences of historical development. In the end, as an idea and an ideology, Arab nationalism ran its course, eventually failing because it could not deliver on its promise to bring about the unity of the Arab people.

By the end of the twentieth century, when Arab nationalism had lost its vibrancy and political direction, when people no longer believed in the viability, even in a remotely aspirational form, of a politically comprehensive Arab unity, and when as a result Arab nationalism had been overtaken by other forces and ideologies, such as state *wataniya* and radical Islam, people tended to forget the majesty that Arab nationalism once was. "Of all the ideologies," writes R. Stephen Humphreys, "that have played on the Middle Eastern stage in this century—bourgeois liberalism, Marxism, Islamism—none has had a greater impact both within the region and throughout the world, none excited more hope and anxiety, than Arab nationalism."[70]

The English explorer, Freya Stark, traveling in Iraq in the 1930s, recalls one semi-literate Arab telling her: "What do we live for, if not the words that are spoken of us when we die?"[71] Not unlike all people, ideas, whether dead or still alive, should be judged not by their prevailing status or health, but by what they accomplished in their days of vibrancy. Arab nationalism, in its heyday, bestowed many gifts on its children: independence from the outsider; purposeful strides onto the road to social and economic modernity; a sense of dignity after the long years of colonization; a set of words and phrases that allowed the Arabs to narrate their own history; an abiding belief in their own ability to sweep aside all doubters

---

[69] Fouad Ajami, "The End of Pan-Arabism," *Foreign Affairs*, vol. 57, no. 2 (Winter 1978 / 79): 355.

[70] Humphreys, *Between Memory and Desire*, p. 61.

[71] Freya Stark, *Baghdad Sketches* (Evanston, Illinois: Northwestern University Press, 1996), p. 165.

and naysayers who blocked the way to progress. For too long, the Arabs had languished under foreign control, suffering the sense of unremitting inferiority so typical of people who were not the masters of their own house. And naturally, they looked for remedies to even the odds. Not until the Arab nationalist tide of the 1950s and 1960s would the Arabs acquire the confidence in their own prowess to believe that they could stand up to the mighty colonizers. The Arabs had become accustomed to turning the other cheek, not out of generosity but out of submission and inferiority; now, during the nationalist decades, they could stand up, be counted, and slap back. In a sense it was this regeneration of Arab self-confidence, this revitalization of the Arab spirit that was Arab nationalism's greatest gift and most enduring accomplishment.

But like a great dynasty that falls on hard times, bringing ruin onto its realm, and is eventually remembered more for its shortcomings than its achievements, Arab nationalism, by the end of the century, was remembered mostly for the debacle of the 1967 war, for Arab divisions that led to weakness, for its inability to come to the aid of its Palestinian children, for its big, resonant, and meaningless words, and for actions that were distinguished only by their meagerness. By the end of the twentieth century, many Arabs saw Arab nationalism not as the mirror that had allowed them to delve into their glorious past and glean from it future possibilities, but as the mirror that their political leaders had turned on their own people, blinding them with empty rhetoric and preventing them from seeing the true, mostly abysmal, state of affairs.

And much of this is indeed justified, for in a sense, the nationalist assurance of Arab salvation, of international power and dominance, predicated on the realization of what the nationalists believed to be the inevitable consecration of the unified state. But that did not come to pass. The inability of the Arabs to achieve Arab unity signaled the demise of Arab nationalism, and with that sank the hopes and the expectations of the nationalist generation. And by the end of the twentieth century, there was little that was left of nationalism's goal of Arab unity but the debris of broken promises and shattered hopes.

Bibliography

Books and Articles

al-Abaydah, Anis, *Rashid Rida: Tarikh wa Sira* (Rashid Rida: history and biography) (Tripoli: Jarrus Press, 1993).

'Abd Mustafa, 'Abd al-Jabbar, *Tajribat al-'Amal al-Jabhawi fi al-'Iraq Beina 1921–1958* (The experiment of oppositional work in Iraq between 1921–1958) (Baghdad: Manshurat Wizarat al-Thaqafa wa al-Funoon, 1978).

Abed, Shukri B., "Islam and Democracy," in *Democracy, War and Peace in the Middle East*. Edited by David Grantham and Mark Tessler (Bloomington: Indiana University Press, 1995).

Abu Diab, Fawzi, *Lubnan wa al-Ummam al-Muttahida* (Lebanon and the United Nations) (Beirut: Dar al-Nahdha al-'Arabiya, 1971).

Abu Jaber, Kamel, *The Arab Ba'th Socialist Party: History, Ideology and Organization* (Syracuse, New York: Syracuse University Press, 1966).

Adams, Charles C., *Islam and Modernism in Egypt: A Study of the Modern Reform Movement Inaugurated by Muhammad 'Abduh* (London: Oxford University Press, 1933).

Addi, Lahouari, "The Failure of Third World Nationalism," in *Journal of Democracy*, vol. 8 (October 1997).

Adonis and Khalida Sa'id, *al-Kawakibi* (Beirut: Dar al-'Ilm li al-Malayeen, 1982).

Aflaq, Michel, *Fi Sabil al-Ba'th* (For the sake of resurrection) (Beirut: Dar al-Tali'ah, 1963).

Ajami, Fouad, *The Arab Predicament: Arab Political Thought and Practice Since 1967* (London: Cambridge University Press, 1981).

———, "The End of Pan-Arabism," *Foreign Affairs*, vol. 57, no. 2 (Winter 1978 / 79).

Algosaibi, Ghazi A., *The 1962 Revolution in Yemen and its Impact on the Foreign Policy of the UAR and Saudi Arabia* (Unpublished University of London Ph.D. Thesis, 1970).

'Allush, Naji, *al-Thawra wa al-Jamahir: Marahil al-Nidhal al-'Arabi wa Dawr al-Haraka al-Thawriya, 1948–1961* (The revolution and the masses: the stages of the Arab struggle and the role of the revolutionary movement, 1948–1961) (Beirut: Dar al-Tali'a li al-Tiba'a wa al-Nashr, 1973).

'Ammara, Muhamed, *al-A'mal al-Kamila li 'Abd al-Rahman al-Kawkibi* (The complete works of 'Abd al-Rahman al-Kawkibi) (Beirut: al-Mu'asasa al-'Arabiya li al-Dirasat wa al Nashr, 1975).

Amos II, John W., *Palestinian Resistance: Organization of a Nationalist Movement* (New York: Pergamon Press, 1980).

Anderson, Benedict, *Imagined Communities: Reflections on the Origin and Spread of Nationalism* (New York: Verso, 1990).

Antonius, George, *The Arab Awakening: The Story of the Arab National Movement* (Beirut: Khayat's, 1938).

al-'Aqqad, 'Abbas Mahmoud, *al-Fusul: Majmou'at Maqallat Adabiya wa Ijtima'iya* (Chapters: a collection of literary and social writings) (Beirut: Dar al-Kitab al-'Arabi, 1967).

———, "Misr wa al-Misriyun" (Egypt and the Egyptians) in *Sawt Misr* (The voice of Egypt). Edited by 'Abbas Mahmoud al-'Aqqad, et al. (Cairo: al-Hay'a al-Misriya al-'Amma li al-Kitab, 1975).

al-'Azm, Khalid, *Mudhakirat Khalid al-'Azm, al-Mujalad al-Thani* (The memoirs of Khali al-Azm, second volume) (Beirut: al-Dar al-Muttahida li al-Nashr, 1972).

al-Azmeh, Aziz, "Nationalism and the Arabs," in *Arab Nation, Arab Nationalism*. Edited by Derek Hopwood (New York: St. Martin's Press, Inc., 2000).

al-Baghdadi, 'Abd al-Latif, *Mudhakarat 'Abd al-Latif al-Baghdadi, al-Jusi' al-Awal* (Memoirs of 'Abd al-Latif al-Baghdadi, volume one) (Cairo: Al-Maktab al-Musri al-Hadith, 1977).

al-Barak, Fadhil, *Dawr al-Jaysh al-'Iraqi fi Hukumat al-Difa' al-Watani wa al-Harb ma'a Britania sanat 1941* (The role of the Iraqi army in the national defense government and the war with Britain in 1941) (Baghdad: al-Dar al-'Arabiya li al-Tiba'a, 1979).

Baram, Amatzia, "Mesopotamian Identity in Ba'thi Iraq," *Middle Eastern Studies*, vol. 19 (October 1983).

———, "Neo-Tribalism in Iraq: Saddam Hussein's Tribal Policies, 1991–96," *International Journal of Middle East Studies*, vol. 29 (February 1997).

———, "Qawmiyya and Wataniyya in Ba'thi Iraq: The Search for a New Balance," *Middle Eastern Studies*, vol. 19 (April 1983).

Barnett, Michael N., *Dialogues in Arab Politics: Negotiations in Regional Order* (New York: Columbia University Press, 1998).

Basri, Mir, *A'lam al-Adab fi al-'Iraq al-Hadith* (Eminent men of letters in modern Iraq), two volumes (London: Dar al-Hikma, 1994).

Batatu, Hanna, *The Old Social Classes and the Revolutionary Movements of Iraq: A Study of Iraq's Old Landed and Commercial Classes and of Its Communists, Ba'thists, and Free Officers* (Princeton, New Jersey: Princeton University Press, 1978).

Bazzi, Naji Abd al-Nabi, *Suriya: Sira' al-Istiqtab; Dirasa wa Tahlil li Ahdath al-Sharq al-Awsat wa al-tadakhulat al-Duwaliya fi al-Ahdath al-Suriya, 1917–1973* (Syria: the struggle of polarization; a study and analysis of Middle Eastern affairs and international interventions in Syrian affairs, 1917–1973) (Damascus: Dar Ibn al-'Arabi, 1996).

Berque, Jacques, *Egypt: Imperialism and Revolution* (New York: Praeger, 1972).

Binder, Leonard, ed., *Politics in Lebanon* (New York: John Wiley, 1966).

———, *The Ideological Revolution in the Middle East* (New York: John Wiley, 1964).

Birdwood, Lord, *Nuri As-Said: A Study in Arab Leadership* (London: Cassell, 1959).

Boyd, Douglas A., *Broadcasting in the Arab World: A Survey of the Electronic Media in the Middle East*, 2nd ed. (Ames: Iowa State University Press, 1993).

Brubaker, Rogers, *Citizenship and Nationhood in France and Germany* (Cambridge, Massachusetts: Harvard University Press, 1992).

Burke, Edmund, *Reflections on the Revolution in France*. Edited with an introduction and notes by J. G. A. Pocock (Indianapolis: Hackett Publishing Co., 1987).

Bush, M. L., *Renaissance, Reformation and the Outer World* (New York: Humanities Press, 1967).

Chalala, Elie, "Arab Nationalism: A Bibliographical Essay," in Pan *Arabism and Arab Nationalism: The Continuing Debate*. Edited by Tawfic E. Farah (Boulder, Colorado: Westview Press, 1987).

Chejne, Anwar G., "Egyptian Attitudes Toward Pan-Arabism," *Middle East Journal*, vol. 11, no. 3 (Summer 1957).

Childers, Erskine B., *The Road to Suez* (London: Macgibbon and Kee, 1962).

Choueiri, Youssef M., *Arab Nationalism: A History* (Oxford: Blackwell Publishers, 2000).

Cleveland, William L., *A History of the Modern Middle East*, 2nd ed. (Boulder, Colorado: Westview Press, 2000).

———, *The Making of an Arab Nationalist: Ottomanism and Arabism in the Life and Thought of Sati' al-Husri* (Princeton, New Jersey: Princeton University Press, 1971).

Cobban, Helena, *The Palestinian Liberation Organization: People, Power and Politics* (London: Cambridge University Press, 1984).

Coury, Ralph M., "Who 'Invented' Egyptian Arab Nationalism? Part 1," *International Journal of Middle East Studies*, vol. 14 no. 3 (August 1982).

———, "Who Invented Egyptian Arab Nationalism?, Part 2," *International Journal of Middle East Studies*, vol. 14, no. 4 (November 1982).

Dahbour, Omar and Micheline R. Ishay, eds., *The Nationalism Reader* (Atlantic Heights, New Jersey: Humanities Press, 1995).

Danielson, Virginia, "Performance, Political Identity and Memory: Umm Kulthum and Gamal 'Abd al-Nasir," in *Images of Enchantment: Visual and Performing Arts of the Middle East. Edited by* Sherifa Zuhur (Cairo: The American University in Cairo Press, 1998).

Danielson, Virginia, *The Voice of Egypt: Umm Kulthum, Arabic Song and Egyptian Society in the Twentieth Century* (Chicago: University of Chicago Press, 1997).

Dann, Uriel, *King Hussein and the Challenge of Arab Radicalism: Jordan, 1955–1967* (New York: Oxford University Press, 1989).

———, *Studies in the History of Transjordan, 1920–1949: The Making of a State* (Boulder, Colorado: Westview Press, 1984).

al-Darraji, 'Abd al-Razzak 'Abd, *Ja'far Abu al-Timman wa Dawrahu fi al-Haraka al-Wataniya fi al-'Iraq* (Ja'far Abu al-Timman and his role in the Iraqi national movement) (Baghdad: Wizarat al-Thaqafa wa al-Funoon, 1978).

Dawisha, Adeed, "Anti-Americanism in the Arab World: Memories of the Past in the Attitudes of the Present," in *Anti-Americanism in the Third World.* Edited by Alvin Z. Rubinstein and Donald E. Smith (New York: Praeger, 1985).

———, *Egypt in the Arab World: The Elements of Foreign Policy* (London: Macmillan, 1976).

———, " 'Identity' and Political Survival in Saddam's Iraq," *Middle East Journal*, vol. 53, no. 4 (Autumn 1999).

———, "Jordan in the Middle East: The Art of Survival," in *The Shaping of an Arab Statesman: Abd al-Hamid Sharaf and the Modern Arab World.* Edited by Patrick Seale (London: Quartet Books, 1983).

———, "Nation and Nationalism: Historical Antecedents to Contemporary Debates," *International Studies Review*, vol. 4, no. 1 (Spring 2002).

———, "Perceptions, Decisions, and Consequences in Foreign Policy: The Egyptian Intervention in the Yemen," *Political Studies*, vol. 25 no. 2 (June 1977).

———, *Syria and the Lebanese Crisis* (London: Macmillan, 1980).

———, "The Assembled State: Communal Conflicts and Governmental Control in Iraq," in *Ethnic Conflict and International Politics in the Middle East.* Edited by Leonard Binder (Gainesville: University Press of Florida, 1999).

Dawisha, Karen, *Soviet Foreign Policy Towards Egypt* (London: Macmillan, 1979).

Dawn, C. Ernest, *From Ottomanism to Arabism: Essays on the Origins of Arab Nationalism* (Urbana: University of Illinois Press, 1973).

———, "The Origins of Arab Nationalism," in *The Origins of Arab Nationalism.* Edited by Rashid Khalidi, Lisa Anderson, Muhamed Muslih, and Reeva S. Simon (New York: Columbia University Press, 1991).

Dessouki, 'Ali E. Hillal, *al-Siyasa wa al-Hukum fi Misr: al-'Ahd al Birlimani, 1923–1952* (Politics and rule in Egypt: the parliamentary era, 1923–1945) (Cairo: Maktabat Nahdhat al-Sharq, 1977).

——— , "The New Arab Political Order: Implications for the 1980s," in *Rich and Poor States in the Middle East: Egypt and the New Arab Order.* Edited by Malcolm H. Kerr and El-Sayed Yassin (Boulder, Colorado: Westview Press, 1982).

————, "The Primacy of Economics: The Foreign Policy of Egypt," in *The Foreign Policies of Arab States*. Edited by Bahgat Korany and Ali E. Hillal Dessouki (Boulder, Colorado: Westview Press, 1988).

Deutsch, Karl W., *Nationalism and Social Communication*, 2nd ed. (Cambridge, Massachusetts: MIT Press, 1966).

Devlin, John, "The Baath Party: Rise and Metamorphosis," *The American Historical Review*, vol. 96, no. 5 (December 1991).

————, *The Ba'th Party: A History from its Origins to 1966* (Stanford, California: Hoover Institution Press, 1976).

Dimashqiya, Nadim, *Mahattat fi Hayati al-Diblomasiya: Dhikrayat fi al-Siyasa wa al-'Ilaqat al-Duwaliya* (Stations in my diplomatic life: memoirs of politics and international relations) (Beirut: Dar al-Nahar li al-Nashr, 1995).

Eden, Anthony, *Full Circle* (London: Cassell, 1960).

Eisenhower, Dwight D., *The White House Years, vol. 2: Waging Peace* (New York: Doubleday, 1965).

Eppel, Michael, *The Palestine Conflict in the History of Modern Iraq: The Dynamics of Involvement, 1928–1948* (London: Frank Cass, 1994).

Farag, E. S., *Nasser Speaks: Basic Documents* (London: The Morssett Press, 1972).

al-Fatah, Fikrat 'Abd, *Siyasat al-'Iraq al-Kharijiya fi al-Mintaqa al-'Arabiya, 1953–1958* (Iraq's foreign policy in the Arab region, 1953–1958) (Baghdad: Wizarat al-Thaqafa wa al-I'lam, 1981).

Frankland, N. and V. King, eds., *Documents on International Affairs, 1956* (London: Oxford University Press, 1959).

Gallman, Waldeman J., *Iraq Under General Nuri: My Recollections of Nuri al-Sa'id, 1954–1958* (Baltimore: Johns Hopkins University Press, 1964).

Gawhar, Samir, *al-Samitun Yatakalamun: 'Abd al-Nasir wa Madhbahat al-Ikhwan* (The silent speak: Abd al-Nasir and the massacre of the [Muslim] brothers) (Cairo: al-Maktab al-Misri al-Hadith, 1975).

Gellner, Ernest, *Nations and Nationalism* (Ithaca, New York: Cornell University Press, 1983).

Gershoni, Israel and James P. Jankowski, *Egypt, Islam and the Arabs: The Search for Egyptian Nationhood, 1900–1930* (New York: Oxford University Press, 1986).

————, "Print Culture, Social Change and the Process of Redefining Imagined Communities in Egypt," *International Journal of Middle East Studies*, vol. 31, no. 1 (February 1999): 82.

————, *Redefining the Egyptian Nation, 1930–1945* (London: Cambridge University Press, 1995).

Gerth, H. H. and Mills, C. Wright, eds., *From Max Weber: Essays in Sociology* (London: Routledge & Kegan Paul, 1948).

al-Ghani, Mustafa 'Abd, " 'Abd al-Nasir wa al-Muthaqafun" ('Abd al-Nasir and the intellectuals), *al-Mustaqbal al-'Arabi*, no. 262 (December 2000).

Gibb, H.A.R., *Islamic Society and the West: A Study of the Impact of Western Civilization on Moslem Culture* (London: Oxford University Press, 1950).

Greenfeld, Liah, *Nationalism: Five Roads to Modernity* (Cambridge, Massachusetts: Harvard University Press, 1992).

Gubser, Peter, *Politics and Change in al-Karak, Jordan: A Study of a Small Arab Town and Its District* (London: Oxford University Press, 1973).

Haim, Sylvia, ed., *Arab Nationalism: An Anthology* (Berkeley: University of California Press, 1962).

al-Hakim, Tawfiq, *'Awdat al-Ruh* (The return of the soul) (Beirut: Dar al-Kitab al-Lubnani, 1974).

Hamroush, Ahmad, "Fikrat al-Qawmiya al-'Arabiya fi Thawrat Yuliyu," (Arab nationalist thought in the July revolution) in *Misr wa al-'Uruba wa Thwrat Yuliyu* (Egypt, Arabism and the July revolution). Edited by Sa'ad al-Din Ibrahim (Beirut: Markaz Dirasat al-Wuhda al-'Arabiya, 1983).

——, *Qissat Thawrat 23 Yuliyu: 'Abd al-Nasir wa al-'Arab, al-Jusi' al-Rabi'* (The story of the July 23 revolution: 'Abd al-Nasir and the Arabs, volume 4) (Cairo: Dar al-Mawqif al-'Arabi, 1983).

——, *Qissat Thawrat 23 Yuliyu: Kharif 'Abd al-Nasir, al-Jusi' al-Khamis* (The story of the July 23 revolution: the autumn of 'Abd al-Nasir, volume 5) (Cairo: Maktabat Madbuli, 1984).

al-Hasani, Abd al-Razzak, *Tarikh al-Wizarat al-'Iraqiya, al-Jusi' al-Thalith, 1930–1933* (The history of Iraqi cabinets, vol. 3, 1930–1933) (Baghdad: Dar al-Shu'un al-Thaqafiya al-'Amma, 1988).

Hastings, Adrian, *The Construction of Nationhood: Ethnicity, Religion, and Nationalism* (Cambridge, England: Cambridge University Press, 1997).

Hart, Alan, *Arafat: A Political Biography* (Bloomington: Indiana University Press, 1984).

Heikal, Muhamed Hasaneen, *Ma Alathi Jara fi Suriya* (What happened in Syria) (Cairo, Egypt: al-Dar al-Qawmiya li al-Tiba'a wa al-Nashr, 1962).

——, *Nasser: The Cairo Documents* (London: New English Library, 1972).

——, *The Road to Ramadan* (London: Collins, 1975).

——, *Sphinx and Commissar: The Rise and Fall of Soviet Influence in the Arab World* (London: Collins, 1978).

Helms, Christine Moss, *Iraq: Eastern Flank of the Arab World* (Washington, D.C.: The Brookings Institution, 1984).

Hinnebusch, Raymond A., *Authoritarian Power and State Formation in Ba'thist Syria: Army, Party, and Peasant* (Boulder, Colorado: Westview Press, 1990).

Holborn, Hajo, *A History of Modern Germany, 1648–1840* (New York: Alfred A. Knopf, 1966).

Hourani, Albert, *A History of the Arab Peoples* (New York: Warner Books, 1991).

——, *Arabic Thought in the Liberal Age. 1798–1939* (London: Oxford University Press, 1970).

——, "The Arab Awakening Forty Years After," in Albert Hourani, *The Emergence of the Modern Middle East* (London: Macmillan, 1981).

Hourani, Cecil A., "The Arab League in Perspective," *Middle East Journal*, vol. 1, no. 2, (April 1947).

Howard, Michael, *The Lessons of History* (New Haven, Connecticut: Yale University Press, 1991).

Hudson, Michael C., *Arab Politics: The Search for Legitimacy* (New Haven, Connecticut: Yale University Press, 1977).

———, *The Precarious Republic: Modernization in Lebanon* (New York: Random House, 1968).

Humphreys, R. Stephen, *Between Memory and Desire: The Middle East in a Troubled Age* (Berkeley: University of California Press, 1999).

Husayn, Taha, *Mustaqbal al-Thaqafa fi Misr* (The future of culture in Egypt) (Cairo: al-Hay'a al- 'Amma li al-Kutab, 1993).

Hussein I, His Majesty King, *Uneasy Lies the Head* (New York: Bernard Geis Associates, 1962).

al-Husri, K., "The Iraqi Revolution of July 14, 1958," *Middle East Forum*, vol. 41 (1965).

al-Husri, Abu Khaldun Sati', *Abhath Mukhtara fi al-Qawmiya al-'Arabiya* (Selected studies on Arab nationalism) (Beirut: Markaz Dirasat al-Wuhda al-'Arabiya, 1985).

———, *Ara' wa Ahadith fi al-Qawmiya al-'Arabiya* (Views and discussions on Arab nationalism) (Beirut: Dar al-'Ilm li al-Malayeen, 1964).

———, *Ara'a wa Ahadith fi al-Wataniya wa al-Qawmiya* (Views and discussions on patriotism and nationalism) (Beirut: Markaz Dirasat al-Wuhda al-'Arabiya, 1984).

———, *Ma Hiya al-Qawmiya: Abhath wa Dirasat 'ala Dhaw'i al-Ahdath wa al-Nadhariyat* (What is nationalism?: enquiries and studies in light of events and theories) (Beirut: Dar al-'Ilm li al-Malayeen, 1963).

———, *Muhadharat fi Nushu' al-Fikra al-Qawmiya* (Lectures on the emergence of the national idea) (Beirut: Markaz Dirasat al-Wuhda Al-'Arabiya, 1985).

———, *Safahat min al-Madhi al-Qarib* (Pages from recent history) (Beirut: Markaz Dirasat al-Wuhda al-'Arabiya, 1984).

———, *al-'Uruba Awalan* (Arabism first) (Beirut: Dar al-'Ilm li al-Malayeen, 1965).

Hutchinson, John, *Dynamics of Cultural Nationalism: The Gaelic Revival and the Creation of the Irish Nation-State* (London: Allen and Unwin, 1989).

Ibrahim, Sa'ad al-Din, "Thawrat Yuliyu wa I'adat Tafsir al-Tarikh" (The July revolution and the reassessment of history), in *Misr wa al-'Uruba wa Thawrat Yuliyu* (Egypt, Arabism and the July revolution). Edited by Sa'ad al-Din Ibrahim, et al. (Beirut: Markaz Dirasat al-Wuhda al-'Arabiya, 1983), p.13.

al-Jamali, Muhamed Fadhil, *Safahat min Tarikhina al-Mu'asir* (Pages from our contemporary history) (Cairo: Dar Su'ad al-Sabah, 1993).

Jankowski, James, "The Government of Egypt and the Palestine Question, 1936–1939," *Middle Eastern Studies*, vol. 17, no. 4 (October 1981).

———, and Israel Gershoni, *Rethinking Nationalism in the Middle East* (New York: Columbia University Press, 1997).

Jawahiri, Muhamed Mahdi al-, *Dhikrayati* (My memoirs) (Damascus: Dar al-Rafidayn, 1988).

Joesten, Joachim, *Nasser: The Rise to Power* (Westport, Connecticut: Greenwood Press Publishers, 1974).

Kader, Haytham A., *The Syrian Social Nationalist Party: Its Ideology and Early History* (Beirut: n.p., 1990).

al-Karim, Ahmad 'Abd, *Hisad: Sineen Khasba wa Thimar Mura* (Harvest: fertile years and bitter fruit) (Beirut: Bisan li al-Nashr wa al-Tawzi', 1994).

Karsh, Efraim and Irani, *Empires of the Sand: The Struggle for Mastery in the Middle East, 1789–1923* (Cambridge, Massachusetts: Harvard University Press, 1999).

———, "Myth in the Desert, or Not the Great Arab Revolt," *Middle Eastern Studies*, vol. 33, no. 3 (July 1997).

———, "Reflections on Arab Nationalism," *Middle Eastern Studies*, vol. 32, no. 4, (October 1996).

Kayali, Hasan, *Arabs and Young Turks: Ottomanism, Arabism and Islamism in the Ottoman Empire, 1908–1918* (Berkeley: University of California Press, 1997).

Kazziha, Walid, "al-Qawmiya al-'Arabiya fi Marhalat ma bayn al-Harbayn al-'Alamiyatayn," (Arab nationalism in the period between the two World Wars) *al-Mustaqbal al-'Arabi*, no. 5 (January 1979).

Kedourie, Elie, *Arabic Political Memoirs and Other Studies* (London: Frank Cass, 1974).

———, *Democracy and Arab Political Culture* (Washington, D.C.: The Washington Institute, 1992).

———, *Nationalism* (London: Hutchinson University Library, 1961).

———, "The Bludan Congress on Palestine, 1937," *Middle Eastern Studies*, vol. 17, no. 1, (January 1981).

Kelidar, Abbas, "A Quest for Identity," *Middle Eastern Studies*, vol. 33, no. 2 (April 1997).

Kerr, Malcolm H., *Islamic Reform: The Political and Legal Theories of Muhammad 'Abduh and Rashid Rida* (Berkeley: University of California Press, 1966).

———, *The Arab Cold War, 1958–1970* (London: Oxford University Press, 1971).

Kessler, Martha Neff, *Syria: Fragile Mosaic of Power* (Washington D.C.: National Defense University Press, 1987).

Khadduri, Majid, *Political Trends in the Arab World: The Role of Ideas and Ideals in Politics* (Baltimore: Johns Hopkins Press, 1970).

———, *Republican Iraq: A Study in Iraqi Politics Since the Revolution of 1958* (London: Oxford University Press, 1969).

———, "The Scheme of Fertile Crescent Unity: A Study in Inter-Arab Relations," in *The Near East and the Great Powers*. Edited by Richard N. Frye (Cambridge, Massachusetts: Harvard University Press, 1951).

Khadduri, Walid, "Al-Qawmiya al-'Arabiya wa al-Dimuqratiya: Muraja'a Naq-diya" (Arab nationalism and democracy: a critical review), *Al-Mustaq-bal al-'Arabi*, no. 228, (February 1998).

Khalidi, Rashid, "Arab Nationalism: Historical Problems in the Literature," *American Historical Review*, vol. 96, no. 5 (December 1991).

———, *Palestinian Identity: The Construction of Modern National Conscious-ness* (New York: Columbia University Press, 1997).

———, Lisa Anderson, Muhammad Muslih, and Reeva S. Simon, eds. *The Ori-gins of Arab Nationalism* (New York: Columbia University Press, 1991).

Khalidi, Walid, "Thinking the Unthinkable: A Sovereign Palestinian State," *For-eign Affairs*, vol. 56, no. 4 (July 1978).

Khoury, Philip S., "Continuity and Change in Syrian Political Life: The Nineteenth and Twentieth Centuries," *The American Historical Review*, vol. 96, no. 5 (December 1991).

———, *Syria and the French Mandate: The Politics of Arab Nationalism, 1920–1945* (Princeton, New Jersey: Princeton University Press, 1987).

———, *Urban Notables and Arab Nationalism: The Politics of Damascus, 1860–1920* (London: Cambridge University Press, 1983).

Kienle, Eberhard, "Arab Unity Schemes Revisited: Interest, Identity, and Policy in Syria and Egypt," *International Journal of Middle East Studies*, vol. 27, no. 1 (February 1997).

Kirk, George, "The Arab Awakening Reconsidered," *Middle Eastern Affairs*, vol. 13, no. 6, (June–July 1962).

Kohn, Hans, "Arendt and the Character of German Nationalism," *The American Historical Review*, vol. LIV, no. 4 (July 1949).

———, *Nationalism: Its Meaning and History* (Princeton, New Jersey: D. Van Nostrand Company, Inc., 1955).

———, *Prelude to Nation-States: The French and German Experience, 1789–1815* (London: D. Van Nostrand Company, Inc., 1967).

———, *The Ideas of Nationalism: A Study in Its Origins and Background* (New York: Macmillan, 1944).

Kramer, Martin, *Arab Awakening and Islamic Revival: The Politics of Ideas in the Middle East* (New Brunswick, New Jersey: Transaction Publishers, 1996).

———, *Islam Assembled: The Advent of the Muslim Congresses* (New York: Co-lumbia University Press, 1986).

Lacouture, Jean, *Nasser: A Biography* (New York: Alfred A. Knopf, 1973).

Landau, Jacob M., *The Politics of Pan-Islam: Ideology and Organization* (Ox-ford: Clarendon Press, 1990).

Landis, Joshua, "Syria and the Palestine War: Fighting King 'Abdullah's 'Greater Syria Plan'," in *The War for Palestine: Rewriting the History of 1948*. *Edited by* Eugene L. Rogan and Avi Shlaim (Cambridge, England: Cam-bridge University Press, 2001).

Lesch, Ann Mosely, *Arab Politics in Palestine, 1917–1939: The Frustration of a National Movement* (Ithaca, New York: Cornell University Press, 1979).

Lewis, Bernard, *The Middle East and the West* (Bloomington: Indiana University Press, 1964).

———, *The Multiple Identities of the Middle East* (New York: Schocken Books, 1998).

Lipsky, G. A., et al., *Saudi Arabia* (New Haven, Connecticut: Hraf Press, 1959).

Little, Tom, *Modern Egypt* (New York: Praeger, 1967).

Longrigg, Stephen Hemsley, *Syria and Lebanon Under French Mandate* (London: Oxford University Press, 1958).

Love, Kennet, *Suez: The Twice Fought War* (New York: McGraw Hill, 1969).

Lustick, Ian S., "The Absence of Middle Eastern Great Powers: Political 'Backwardness' in Historical Perspective," *International Organization*, vol. 51, no. 4 (Autumn 1997).

Lukitz, Liona, *Iraq: The Search for National Identity* (London: Frank Cass, 1995).

———, "The Antonius Papers and *The Arab Awakening* Fifty Years On," *Middle Eastern Studies*, vol. 30, no 4, (October 1994).

Madani, Suleiman al-, *Ha'ula' . . . Hakamu Suriya, 1918–1970* (Those who ruled Syria, 1918–1970) (Damascus: Dar al Anwar, 1996).

Makiya, Kanan, *Republic of Fear: The Politics of Modern Iraq*, updated ed. (Berkeley: University of California Press, 1998).

Mansfield, Peter, *Nasser's Egypt* (Harmondsworth, Surrey: Penguin Books, 1965).

Ma'oz, Moshe, "Attempts to Create a Political Community in Modern Syria," in *Middle Eastern Politics and Ideas: A History from Within*. Edited by Ilan Pappe and Moshe Ma'oz (London: Tauris Academic Studies, 1997).

Mare'i, Sayed, *Awraq Siyasiya* (Political papers) (Cairo: al-Maktab al-Misri al-Hadith, 1978).

Marr, Phebe, "The Development of a Nationalist Ideology in Iraq, 1920–1941," *The Muslim World*, vol. 75, no. 2 (April 1985).

———, *The Modern History of Iraq* (Boulder, Colorado: Westview Press, 1985).

Matar, Fuad, *Bisaraha 'An 'Abd al-Nasir: Hiwar ma'a Muhamed Hasaneen Haykal* (Candidly about 'Abd al-Nasir: a conversation with Muhamed Hasaneen Haykal) (Beirut: Dar al-Qadhaya, 1975).

Matar, Jamil, and 'Ali al-Din Hillal, *Al-Nidham al-Iqlimi al-'Arabi: Dirasa fi al-'Ilaqat al-Siyasia al-'Arabiya* (The Arab regional system: a study in Arab political relations) (Beirut: Markaz Dirasat al-Wuhda al-'Arabiya, 1980).

Matar, Selim, *al-Dhat al-Jariha: Ishkalat al-Hawiya fi al-'Iraq wa al-'Alam al-'Aabi "al-Shirqani,"* (Wounded essence: problems of identity in Iraq and the "Eastern" Arab world) (Beirut: al-Mu'asasa al-'Arabiya li al-Dirasat wa al-Nashr, 1997).

Mill, John Stuart, "Considerations on Representative Government," in *Nationalism. Edited by* Omar Dahbour and K. R. Minogue (New York: Basic Books, 1967).

Mufti, Malik, *Sovereign Creations: Pan Arabism and Political Order in Syria and Iraq* (Ithaca, New York: Cornell University Press, 1996).

Muhamed, Su'ad Rauf, *Nuri al-Sa'id wa Dawrahu fi al-Siyasa al-'Iraqiya, 1932–1945* (Nuri al-Sa'id and his role in Iraqi politics, 1932–1945) (Baghdad: Maktabat al-Yaqdha al-'Arabiya, 1988).

Musa, Salame, *al-Mu'alafat al-Kamila, al-Mujaled al-Awal: Sanawat al-Takween* (Complete works, volume one: years of formation) (Cairo: Salame Musa li al-Nashr wa al-Tawzi', 1998).

———, *al-Yawm wa al-Ghad* (Today and tomorrow) (Cairo: Elias An tun Elias, 1928).

Mushtaq, Taleb, *Awraq Ayami,1900–1956, al-Jusi' al-Awal* (Papers of my days, volume one) (Beirut: Dar al-Tali'a li al-Tiba'a wa al-Nashr, 1968).

Muslih, Muhammad, "The Rise of Local Nationalisms in the Arab East," in *The Origins of Arab Nationalism*. Edited by Rashid Khalidi, et al. (New York: Columbia University Press, 1991).

Nadhmi, Wamidh Jamal 'Umar, "Fikr Sati' al-Husri al-Qawmi" (The nationalist thought of Sati' al-Husri), *al-Mustaqbal al-'Arabi*, no. 81 (November 1985).

al-Nahlawi, Hanafi, *'Abd al-Nasir wa Umm Kulthum: 'Ilaqa Khassa Jiddan* ('Abd al-Nasir and Umm Kulthum: a very special relationship) (Cairo: Markaz al-Qada li al-Kitab wa al-Nashr, 1992).

Nakash, Yitzhak, *The Shi'is of Iraq* (Princeton, New Jersey: Princeton University Press, 1994).

Nasr, Nasim and Sami Mufrij, *Multaqa al-Shu'ub: aw Mujaz Tarikh Syriya wa Lubnan* (The meeting of peoples: an abridged history of Syria and Lebanon) (Damascus: Matba'at al-Jami'a, n.d.).

Nasr, Salah, *'Abd al-Nasir wa Tajribat al-Wuhda* (Abd al-Nasir and the experience of unity) (Beirut: al-Watan al-'Arabi, 1976).

Nasser, Premier Gamal Abdul, *Egypt's Liberation: The Philosophy of the Revolution* (Washington, D.C.: Public Affairs Press, 1955).

Nuseibeh, Hazem Zaki, *The Ideas of Arab Nationalism* (London: Kennikat Press, 1972).

Nutting, Anthony, *Nasser* (London: Constable, 1972).

———, *The Arabs: A Narrative History from Muhammed to the Present* (New York: The New American Library, 1964).

Olson, Robert W., *The Ba'th and Syria, 1947–1982: The Evolution of Ideology, Party and State* (Princeton, New Jersey: The Kingston Press, Inc.,1982).

Oren, Michael B., "A Winter of Discontent: Britain's Crisis in Jordan, December 1955–March 1956," *International Journal of Middle East Studies*, vol. 22 no. 2 (May 1990).

Petran, Tabitha, *Syria* (New York: Praeger, 1972).

Podeh, Elie, *The Quest for Hegemony in the Arab World: The Struggle Over the Baghdad Pact* (Leiden: E. J. Brill, 1995).

Porath, Yehoshua, *In Search of Arab Unity: 1930–1945* (London: Frank Cass, 1986).

———, *The Palestinian Arab National Movement: From Riots to Rebellion* (London: Frank Cass, 1977).

Prizel, Ilya, *National Identity and Foreign Policy: Nationalism and Leadership in Poland, Russia, and Ukraine* (Cambridge, England: Cambridge University Press, 1998).

al-Qardawi, Yusuf, *al-Hulul al-Mustawrada wa Kaifa Janat 'ala Ummatina* (The imported solutions and how they harmed our nation) (Cairo: Maktabat Wahbeh, 1977).

Qasmiyya, Khayriya, *Al-Hukuma al-'Arabiya fi Dimashq, 1918–1920* (The Arab government in Damascus, 1918–1920) (Cairo: Dar al-Ma'arif bi Misr, 1971).

Qubain, Fahim I., *Crisis in Lebanon* (Washington, D.C.: The Middle East Institute, 1961).

———, *Education and Science in the Arab World* (Baltimore: Johns Hopkins University Press, 1966).

Rabinovich, Itamar, *Syria Under the Ba'th, 1963–1966: The Army Party Symbiosis* (Jerusalem: Israel Universities Press, 1972).

Radwan, Fathi, *72 Shahran Ma'a 'Abd al-Nasir* (72 months with 'Abd al-Nasir) (Cairo: Dar al-Huriya, 1986).

Ramm, Agatha, *Germany 1789–1919: A Political History* (London: Methuen, 1967).

Renan, Ernest, "What is a Nation?" in *Nation and Narration*. Edited by Homi K. Bhabha (London: Routledge, 1990).

Riad, Mahmud, *Mudhakirat Mahmud Riad, 1948–1978, al-Jusi' al-Thani* (The memoirs of Mahmud Riad, 1948–1978, volume two) (Cairo: Dar al-Mustaqbal al-'Arabi, 1986).

Russell, Malcolm B., *The First Modern Arab State: Syria under Faysal, 1918–1920* (Minneapolis: Bibliotheca Islamica, 1985).

Rustow, Dankwart A., *A World of Nations* (Washington D.C., The Brookings Institution, 1967).

Ryan, Alan, *J. S. Mill* (London: Routledge and Kegan Paul, 1974).

Sadat, Anwar, *In Search of Identity: An Autobiography* (New York: Harper and Row, 1977), p.152.

Safran, Nadav, *Egypt in Search of Political Community: An Analysis of the Intellectual and Political Evolution of Egypt, 1804–1952* (Cambridge, Massachusetts: Harvard University Press, 1961).

Safwat, Najdat Fathi, *Al-'Iraq fi Mudhakirat al-Diblumasiyeen al-Ajanib* (Iraq in the memoirs of foreign diplomats) (Baghdad: Maktabat Dar al-Tarbiya, 1984).

Sahab, Ilyas, "Sati' al-Husri: al-Mufakir wa al-Da'iya wa al-Numudhaj," (Sati' al-Husri: the thinker, the advocate and the role model), *al-Mustaqbal al-'Arabi*, no. 1 (May 1978).

Sa'id, 'Ali Karim, *Iraq 8 Shibat 1963: Min Hiwar al-Mafahim ila Hiwar al-Dam; Muraja'at fi Dhakirat Taleb Shabib* (Iraq 8 February 1963: from a dialogue over norms to a dialogue of blood; reviews in the memory of Taleb Shabib) (Beirut: Dar al-Kunuz al-Adabiya, 1999).

Said, Edward, *Orientalism*, 2nd ed. (New York: Vintage Books, 1994).

Salame, Ghassan, *al-Siyasa al-Sa'udia al-Kharijia Mundhu 'Am 1930* (Saudi foreign policy since 1930) (Beirut: Ma'had al-Inma'i al-'Arabi, 1980).

———, "Inter-Arab Politics: The Return of Geography," in *The Middle East: Ten Years After Camp David*. Edited by William B. Quandt (Washington, D.C.: The Brookings Institution, 1988).

Salem, Paul, *Bitter Legacy: Ideology and Politics in the Arab World* (Syracuse, New York: Syracuse University Press, 1994).

al-Samarai', Abdallah Saloom, "Harakat al-Qawmiyeen al-'Arab wa Dawruha fi al-Wa'i al-Qawmi," (The Arab nationalist movement and its role in the national consciousness), *al-Mustaqbal al-'Arabi*, no. 84 (February 1986).

Satlof, Robert, *From Abdullah to Hussein: Jordan in Transition* (New York: Oxford University Press, 1994).

Seale, Patrick, *Asad: The Struggle for the Middle East* (Berkeley: University of California Press, 1988).

———, *The Struggle for Syria: A Study of Post-War Arab Politics, 1945–1958* (New Haven, Connecticut: Yale University Press, 1986).

Shawkat, Naji, *Sira wa Dhikrayat thamaneena 'Aman, 1894–1974* (Biography and memoirs of eighty years, 1894–1974) (Baghdad: Maktabat al-Yaqdha al-'Arabiya, 1990).

Shazly, Saad, *The Crossing of the Suez* (San Francisco: American Mideast Research, 1980).

Sheikho, Muhamed Ismat, *Suriya wa Qadhiyat Falasteen, 1920–1949* (Syria and the issue of Palestine, 1920–1949) (Damascus: Dar Qutayba, 1982).

Shlaim, Avi, *Collusion Across the Jordan: King Abdullah, the Zionist Movement, and the Partition of Palestine* (Oxford, England: Clarendon Press, 1988).

———, "Israel, the Great Powers, and the Middle East Crisis of 1958," *Journal of Imperial and Commonwealth History*, vol. 27, no. 2 (May 1999).

———, *The Iron Wall: Israel and the Arab World* (New York: W. W. Norton and Company, 2000).

Shwadran, Benjamin, *The Power Struggle in Iraq* (New York: Council for Middle Eastern Affairs Press, 1960).

Simon, Reeva S., *Iraq Between the Two World Wars: The Creation and Implementation of a Nationalist Ideology* (New York: Columbia University Press, 1986).

———, "The Teaching of History in Iraq Before the Rashid Ali Coup of 1941," *Middle Eastern Studies*, vol. 22, no. 1 (January 1986).

Sivan, Emmanuel, *Radical Islam* (New Haven, Connecticut: Yale University Press, 1991).

Smith, Anthony D., "The Nation: Invented, Imagined, Reconstructed," in *Reimagining the Nation*. Edited by Marjorie Ringrose and Adam J. Lerner (Buckingham, England: Open University Press, 1993).

Smith, Charles D., " 'Cultural Constructs' and other Fantasies: Imagined Narratives in *Imagined Communities*; Surrejoinder to Gershoni and Jankowski's 'Print Culture, Social Change, and the Process of Redefining

Imagined Communities in Egypt,' " *International Journal of Middle East Studies*, vol. 31, no. 1 (February 1999).

————, "Imagined Identities, Imagined Nationalisms: Print Culture and Egyptian Nationalism in Light of Recent Scholarship," *International Journal of Middle East Studies*, vol. 29, no. 4 (November 1997).

Snow, Peter, *Hussein: A Biography* (New York: Robert B. Luce, Inc., 1972).

Stark, Freya, *Baghdad Sketches* (Evanston, Illinois: Northwestern University Press, 1996).

Stephens, Robert, *Nasser: A Political Biography* (New York: Simon and Schuster, 1971).

al-Suwaydi, Tawfiq, *Mudhakirati: Nisf Qarn min Tarikh al-'Iraq wa al-Qadhiya al-'Arabiya* (My memoirs: half a century of the history of Iraq and the Arab undertaking) (Beirut: Dar al-Kitab al-'Arabi, 1969).

Szyliowicz, Joseph S., *Education and Modernization in the Middle East* (Ithaca, New York: Cornell University Press, 1973).

Taha, Riad, *Qissat al-Wuhda wa al-Infisal: Tajribat Insan 'Arabi Khilal Ahdath 1955–1961* (The story of unity and secession: the experience of an Arab person during the events of 1955–1961) (Beirut: Dar al-Afaq al-Jadida, 1974).

Tahan, Muhamed Jamal, *al-A'mal al-Kamila li al-Kawakibi* (The complete works of al-Kawakibi) (Beirut: Markaz Dirasat al-Wuhda al-'Arabiya, 1995).

Tauber, Eliezer, *The Emergence of the Arab Movements* (London: Frank Cass, 1993).

————, *The Formation of Modern Syria and Iraq* (London: Frank Cass, 1995).

Telhami, Ghada, *Palestine and Egyptian National Identity* (New York: Praeger, 1992).

Telhami, Shibley, "Power, Legitimacy, and Peace-Making in Arab Countries: The New Arabism," in *Ethnic Conflicts and International Politics in the Middle East*. Edited by Leonard Binder (Gainesville: University Press of Florida, 1999).

————, and Michael Barnett, eds., *Identity and Foreign Policy in the Middle East* (Ithaca, New York: Cornell University Press, 2002).

Terrill, W. Andrew, "The Political Mythology of the Battle of Karameh," *Middle East Journal*, vol. 55, no. 1 (Winter 2001).

Tibi, Bassam, *Arab Nationalism: A Critical Enquiry* (New York: St. Martin's Press, 1981).

————, "The Simultaneity of the Unsimultaneous: Old Tribes and Imposed Nation-States in the Modern Middle East," in *Tribes and State Formation in the Middle East*. Edited by Philip S. Khoury and Joseph Kostiner (Berkeley: University of California Press, 1980).

Trevelyan, Humphrey, *The Middle East in Revolution* (London: Macmillan, 1970).

al-Uzri, 'Abd al-Karim, *Tarikh fi Dhikrayat al-'Iraq, 1930–1958* (History in memoirs of Iraq, 1930–1958) (Beirut: Markaz al-Abjadiya li al-Saf al-Taswiri, 1982).

Vatikiotis, P. J., "Dilemmas of Political Leadership in the Arab Middle East: The Case of the UAR," *American Political Science Review*, vol. 55 no. 1 (March 1961).

————, *The History of Modern Egypt: From Muhammed Ali to Mubarak*, 4th ed., (Baltimore: Johns Hopkins University Press, 1991).

Wallach, Janet, *Desert Queen: The Extraordinary Life of Gertrude Bell* (New York: Doubleday, 1996).

al-Wardi, 'Ali, *Lamahat Ijtima'iya min Tarikh al-'Iraq al-Hadith, al-Jusi' al-Rabi', min 'Am 1914 ila 'Am 1918* (Sociological aspects of modern Iraqi history, part four, 1914–1918) (London: Dar Kufan li al-Nashr, 1992).

————, *Lamahat Ijtima'iya min Tarikh al-'Iraq al-Hadith, al Jusi' al-Sadis, min'Am 1920 ila 'Am 1924* (Sociological aspects of modern Iraqi history, part six, 1920–1924) (London: Dar Kofan li al-Nashr, 1992).

Weber, Eugene, *Peasants into Frenchmen: The Modernization of Rural France, 1870–1914* (London: Chatto and Windus, 1979).

Weber, Max, *The Theory of Social and Economic Organization*. Translated by A. M. Henderson and Talcott Parsons (London: Oxford University Press, 1947).

Westerfield, H. B., *The Instruments of American Foreign Policy* (New York: Thomas Y. Crowell Company, 1963).

Williams, Lynn, "National Identity and the Nation State: Construction, Reconstruction and Contradiction," in *National Identity*. Edited by Keith Cameron (Exeter, England: Intellect, 1999).

Woolbert, Robert Gale, "Pan-Arabism and the Palestine Problem," *Foreign Affairs*, vol. 16, no. 2 (January 1938).

Yaghi, Ismail Ahmad, *Al-'Ilaqat al-'Iraqiya al-Urdiniya, 1941–1958* (Iraqi-Jordanian relations, 1941–1958) (Cairo: Dar al-Sahwa, 1988).

Yapp, M. E., *The Near East since the First World War: A History to 1995*, 2nd ed. (London: Longman, 1996).

Ziadeh, Nicola, *Shamiyat: Dirasat fi al-Hadhara wa al-Tarikh* (Shamiyat: studies in culture and history) (London: Riad El-Rayyes Books, 1989).

Zeine, Zeine Nur al-Din, *Al-Sira' al-Duwaly fi al-Sharq al-Awsat wa Wiladat Dawlatai Suriya wa Lubnan* (The international struggle in the Middle East and the birth of the two states of Syria and Lebanon) (Beirut: Dar al-Nahar li al-Nashr, 1977).

————, *Nushu' al-Qawmiya al-'Arabiya ma'a Dirasa Tarikhiya fi al-'Ilaqat al-'Arabiya al-Turkiya* (The emergence of Arab nationalism with a historical study of Arab-Turkish relations) (Beirut: Dar al-Nahar li al-Nashr, 1979).

Zinner, P. E., ed., *Documents on American Foreign Relations, 1957* (New York: Harper and Brothers, 1958).

Newspapers and Other Documents

Al-Ahram (Cairo)
Al-Ba'th (Damascus)

Al-Hayat (Beirut, London)
Al-Muharir (Beirut)
Al-Quds al-'Arabi (London)
Al-Sharq al-Awsat (London)
Al-Thawra (Baghdad)
Daily Telegraph (London)
Egyptian Gazette (Cairo)
Events (London)
Guardian (London)
New York Review of Books
Observer (London)
Sunday Telegraph (London)
Sunday Times (London)
Times (London)
American University of Beirut, *al- Watha'iq al-'Arabiya al-Siyasiya, 1967* (Arab
    political documents, 1967) (Beirut: AUB Press, n.d.).
British Broadcasting Corporation, *Summary of World Broadcasts: Part IV, The
    Arab World, Israel, Greece, Turkey, Iran* (London, various years).
International Institute for Strategic Studies, *The Military Balance* (London: IISS,
    various years).
al-Jumhuriya al-'Arabiya al-Muttahida, *Mahadhir Jalsat Mubahathat al-Wuhda*
    (Proceedings of the meetings on unity discussions) (Cairo: National
    Printing and Publishing House, 1963).
———, *Majmou'at Khutab wa Tasrihat wa Bayant al-Rai's 'Gamal Abd al-Nasir*
    (The collection of the speeches, statements and communiqués of Presi-
    dent Gamal 'Abd al-Nasir), various volumes (Cairo: UAR, various
    years).
President Hafiz al-Asad, *Speech Delivered Before a General Plenum of Local Gov-
    ernment, July 20, 1976* (Damascus: Baath Arab Socialist Party, 1976).
United Arab Republic, *The Charter* (Cairo: Information Department, 1962).
United Arab Republic, *President Gamal Abd al-Nasser's Speeches and Press Inter-
    views, 1958* (Cairo: Information Department, n.d.).
United Nations, Department of Economic and Social Affairs, *Statistical Yearbook*
    (various years).

Index